★ ★ ★

BATTLE FOR BATANGAS

GLENN ANTHONY MAY

Battle for Batangas

A Philippine Province at War

YALE UNIVERSITY PRESS   NEW HAVEN & LONDON

Designed by James J. Johnson.
Set in Century Schoolbook type by
Keystone Typesetting, Inc., Orwigsburg,
Pennsylvania. Printed in the United
States of America by Edwards Brothers
Inc., Ann Arbor, Michigan.

The paper in this book meets the
guidelines for permanence and
durability of the Committee on
Production Guidelines for Book
Longevity of the Council on Library
Resources.

10   9   8   7   6   5   4   3   2   1

*Library of Congress Cataloging-in-
Publication Data*

May, Glenn Anthony.
  Battle for Batangas : a Philippine
province at war / Glenn Anthony May.
    p.   cm.
  Includes bibliographical references
(p.   ) and index.
  ISBN 0–300–04850–5 (cloth)
  1. Batangas (Philippines : Province)—
History.   2. Philippines—History—
Insurrection, 1899–1901.   I. Title.
DS688.B3M39   1991
959.9′1—dc20   90–45074
                                    CIP

TO THE MEMORY OF
Harry J. Benda

Contents

Illustrations

Acknowledgments

During the decade or so that I have worked on this book, I have received help from scores of people on both sides of the Pacific. Archivists have assisted me in locating documents; fellow academics have given me leads about source materials and provided feedback about earlier formulations of my ideas; research assistants have helped me to struggle through difficult Tagalog texts; strangers in Manila and the province of Batangas have told me what they know about the Philippine past; relatives, friends, and professional colleagues have boosted my spirits. Belatedly, let me express my gratitude to the following individuals: the late Domingo Abella, Juana Abello, Carolina Afan, Natividad Aguila, Ellen Alfonso, Reynaldo Atienza, Rico Azicate, Robert H. Black, Kathleen Bowman, Mariano Cabrera, Pacita Calupaz, Jose Caubalejo, Corazon Apacible Cañisa, Nayan Chanda, Bernadita Reyes Churchill, Antonio Claudio, John Cluff, Lina Concepcion, Romeo Cruz, Crisostomo Cuasay, Michael Cullinane, Lincoln Day, Damian Decipeda, Ken

De Bevoise, Don Denoon, Paz Luz Dimayuga, Constantino Diokno, Felisa Diokno, Christine Dobbin, John Dwyer, Joseph Esherick, Pearl Evans, Edward Ezell, Doreen Fernandez, Fr. Pablo Fernandez, O.P., Juan R. Francisco, Lewis Gleeck, Chuck Grench, Mila Guerrero, Mudjahirin Hamja, Catherine Heising, Michael Hunt, Atanacio Ilagan, Reynaldo Ileto, Ed de Jesus, Melinda Quintos de Jesus, Nick Joaquin, Charles Keyes, Don Kloster, Jess Lacdao, Dionisio Laygo, Brian Linn, Helen Liu, Bill Loy, Ruth Mabanglo, Meloy Mabunay, Severino Magsombol, Maria Cleofe Z. Marpa, Oda Martin, Virginia Matheson, Elizabeth May, Ron May, Rose Marie Mendoza, Stuart Miller, Allan Millett, Maria Luisa Moral, Hank Nelson, Francisco Nemenzo, Ambeth Ocampo, Esteban de Ocampo, Bill O'Malley, John Orton, Norman Owen, Patricia Paez, Akil Pawaki, Serafin Quiason, Msgr. Salvador Quizon, Vince Rafael, Gloria Rodriguez, Jim Rush, Arcadia Saballones, Bonifacio Salamanca, Zeus Salazar, Bayani Sarmiento, Fr. John Schumacher, S.J., Enid Scofield, William H. Scott, Calixto Silva, Eliseo Silva, Richard Sommers, Oskar Spate, Ramon Tarnate, Tina Torres, Emilio Vergara, Ed Villegas, Isabel Malvar Villegas, Jose Villegas, and Peter Xenos. Special thanks are reserved for Caitriona Bolster, Brian Fegan, Akira Iriye, Alfred McCoy, David Marr, Tony Reid, and Peter Stanley, all of whom read and provided critical comments on portions of this book; Lawrence Kenney of Yale University Press, who tightened and otherwise improved the text; and Greg Koester, who prepared the maps.

Research on this project was made possible by financial support from a number of institutions. I wish to express my appreciation to the Henry Luce Foundation, the National Endowment for the Humanities, the Philippine-American Educational Foundation, the Research School of Pacific Studies of the Australian National University, the University of Oregon, and the University of Texas at Arlington.

I would also like to thank the journals, publishing agencies, and organizations listed below for giving me permission to use material from previously published articles: *Annales de Démographie Historique* (la Société de Démographie Historique); *Bulletin of the American Historical Collection;* Council on East Asian Studies, Harvard University; *Hemisphere; Journal of Southeast Asian Studies; Pacific Historical Review; Philippine Studies;* and Yale University Southeast Asia Studies.

I owe my greatest debt, and I dedicate this book, to a man who died in 1971, long before I began research on this project. Charming, charismatic, demanding, and brilliant, Harry Benda was the most remarkable person I have ever met. Harry showed me that the study of the past could be exciting, and, more important, he offered me encouragement at a time in my life when I badly needed it. Harry's premature death was a body blow to the historical profession, to the field of Southeast Asian studies, and to hundreds of students like me who lost a mentor and a friend. I miss you, Harry.

Introduction

On one level, this book simply tells a story: it examines the course of the Philippine-American War in the Tagalog-speaking province of Batangas, south of Manila. For readers who like to pigeonhole the books they read, this one might be considered either local history or the history of warfare. I have attempted to view a brief period of Philippine history through a provincial prism. In addition, although I have not written military history of the traditional kind, I have tried to convey a sense of what life was like for the soldiers and civilians who participated in a long-ago war.

In the process of telling that story, I have raised a number of questions about existing scholarship on the war. For approximately three decades, the standard account of the Filipino side of the conflict has been Teodoro Agoncillo's *Malolos: The Crisis of the Republic*. Agoncillo's book is, by his own admission, a celebration of the role of the Filipino "masses" in the anticolonial struggle. "If I appear inclined to sympathize with the masses," he writes, "it is because their faith in the cause of the Republic was unshaken and their patriotism and self-sacrifice unsullied by selfish motives." The villains of his story are the "Haves" (Agoncillo also refers to them as the plutocrats and the middle class), who, in his view, betrayed their countrymen by collaborating with the Americans and undermining the war effort. He directs his harshest criticism at Trinidad H. Pardo de Tavera, Benito Legarda, Cayetano Arellano, and other Manila-based men of means, all of whom quickly cast their lot with the Americans.[1] Agoncillo's interpretation of the war has been adopted by many historians, perhaps most notably Renato Constantino, who restated and elaborated on it in his popular college-level survey of Philippine history *The Philippines: A Past Revisited.*[2]

My own research on Batangas casts doubt on Agoncillo's analysis of resistance and collaboration in the Philippine-American War. As I demonstrate in this volume, the economic and political elites of Batangas constituted the backbone of the local resistance. Some elite Batangueños led the military units that fought against the U.S. Army; others provided money, food, and general support to the resistance forces. Also, while a case can be made that humble barrio-dwellers in Batangas rallied to the cause during the final stages of the conflict, for much of the war lower-class support for the resistance appears to have been less dogged than Agoncillo and his followers have claimed.[3]

Such findings do not, by themselves, revise completely our picture of the Philippine-American War. My inquiry has, after all, been largely restricted to a single province, and it is not impossible that different patterns of behavior prevailed in other parts of the Philippines. (Indeed, a recent book-length study of the war—William H. Scott's *Ilocano Responses to American Aggression, 1900–1901*—suggests that lower-class commitment to the Filipino cause may have been stronger in northwestern Luzon than in Batangas; but, significantly, it *does* confirm my findings about the role of the local political and economic elites in the anti-American struggle.)[4] Still, I believe I have issued a strong challenge to the traditional view of the Philippine-American War. The role of local elites cannot simply be discounted, and the attitude of poor peasants cannot simply be assumed.

My challenge to existing scholarship has not been confined to the chronological limits of the Philippine-American War. In order to understand what happened in Batangas during the war against the Americans, I have found it necessary to probe the decades immediately preceding that struggle, and, as might be expected, I have looked closely at the revolution against Spain that engulfed the Tagalog-speaking provinces of Luzon between 1896 and 1898.

Again I was struck by a discrepancy between the documentary record and certain basic points of interpretation in the scholarly literature. Although most students of the period have tended to view the Philippine Revolution as, to use the words of Agoncillo (who borrowed them from Ortega y Gasset), a "revolt of the masses," the historical evidence shows that, in Batangas, it might be as accurate to see it as the continuation of a decade-long struggle between local influentials and agents of the Spanish Crown.[5] What is more, while lower-class Batangueños no doubt participated in the events of 1896–1898—they fought in the revolutionary armies, supplied the troops, and otherwise contributed to the cause—a considerable number of them did so less out of a sense of commitment than out of a sense of obligation to their upper-class patrons.

Less overtly revisionist—but in my view equally noteworthy—are other aspects of my story. Although the period described in these pages was obviously one of trauma, I have found that it brought to the fore some important everyday (that is to say, nontraumatic) characteristics of turn-of-the-century Filipino society. Traumas do that, of course, for while they sometimes provide the occasion for aberrant behavior, they more often allow us to see, more distinctly than in less traumatic times, certain fundamental realities of life in any society. So, for example, the process of creating an officer corps in Batangas during the Philippine-American War underscored the key role of various types of personal relationships in Batangueño society (in particular, relationships formed by young males from elite families at local secondary schools), and the task of recruitment of common soldiers pointed up the strength of patron-client bonds in the province. Also, the patterns of support and nonsupport for the local resistance can largely be explained by other realities of provincial life: the nature of the social structure, the character of municipal politics, family connections, religious beliefs. My point is not simply that there were certain observable continuities in attitude, behavior, and personal interactions in Batangas. It is rather that, in this period of trauma, a few realities appeared to be more compelling than others.

In addition to exploring the nature of turn-of-the-century Philippine society, I examine the relationship between the human and nonhuman actors in the battle for Batangas. One incontrovertible fact about the period 1896–1902 is that a massive population loss took place in Batangas—one generally attributed to the policies of the U.S. army of occupation. But my own research reveals a much more complex epidemiological dynamic: that the demographic catastrophe may have been triggered not only by human agents—American, Spanish, and Filipino—but also by ecological factors and by the peculiar relationship between mosquitoes and carabaos (water buffalo) in the provincial landscape.

★ ★ ★

When I began work on this project, I intended to write a genuinely bifocal study: to devote as much attention to the American side of the battle for Batangas as to the Filipino. I soon discovered, however, that the problems that intrigued me most related to the Filipino participants, and so the Americans were slowly but surely relegated to the role of supporting actors. Still, I think I have made a few contributions of consequence to our understanding of the American side of the conflict, and above all I have tried to provide a corrective to the somewhat monochromatic pictures of the U.S. Army in the Philippines that appear in much of the literature. In my view—a view limited, admittedly, to the geographical boundaries of a single province—the Americans were neither as uniformly nasty nor as praiseworthy as they have been portrayed.[6] That they were guilty of atrocities and lesser abuses cannot be denied, but much of the time the overwhelming majority of them maintained relatively civil relations with the noncombatants they encountered. That they established schools and municipal governments also cannot be denied, but it must be recognized that these actions had a minimal impact on the war effort.

My effort to add shades of gray to the black and white pictures thus far produced will, I suspect, displease not a few readers. For reasons I do not fully understand, scholars on both sides of the Pacific appear to approach the question of American behavior in the Philippine-American War with remarkably fixed opinions about how things must have been. I can imagine, for example, that there will be a strong resistance to my argument—I prefer to call it my demonstration—that American policies in the final stages of the Batangas campaign were not alone (or even primarily) responsible for the mortality crisis that transpired. So be it. But if I am to be criticized, I hope that my critics will base their critiques on the historical evidence and not on their prejudgments of it.

★ ★ ★

In recent years much has been written about the general subject of popular uprisings and popular movements in the Third World, and I would be remiss were I to ignore the relation between my own study and that body of literature. Perhaps the most influential theoretical studies of the subject have been written by scholars of Southeast Asia—most notably, James Scott, a spokesman for the "moral economy" approach, and Samuel Popkin, a proponent of "political economy." At bottom, Scott, Popkin, and their followers have been engaged in a debate on two related issues: the nature of the peasant weltanschauung and the causes of popular uprisings and movements in Southeast Asia. Scott, Benedict Kerkvliet, and other moral economists have argued that peasants are essentially risk-averse (that is, they are inclined to accept a life of bare subsistence rather than gamble on making a profit and risk falling below the subsistence threshold); typically protected from economic disaster by a kind of traditional insurance system (a system of rural relationships that guarantees peasants a bare minimum in hard times through assistance provided by the village and by local patrons); and inclined to view these subsistence guarantees as a moral right. They suggest, further, that popular rebellions in rural Southeast Asia often issue from a breakdown of the traditional insurance system, creating a situation in which peasants experience severe hardships and come to believe that their right to subsistence is being violated. Popkin, by contrast, views peasants as rational economic actors, interested far more in profit maximization than risk-aversion. Arguing that traditional insurance systems do not provide effective guarantees of peasant welfare and that peasants consequently place little faith in them, he asserts that peasant movements should be seen as efforts to overthrow the traditional order rather than to defend traditional rights and relationships.[7]

What is striking about the situation described in this book is that, while the successive struggles in Batangas (the revolution against Spain, the resistance against Americans) may properly be described as popular movements, since they involved the participation of tens of thousands of common men and women, the principal cause of people's involvement may have been neither their perception that a traditional ethic had been violated nor their desire to destroy an oppressive rural order. Rather, they participated—at least many of them did—because in a real sense the traditional order was still largely intact and functioning, and under those circumstances the province's patrons, the elites who had both a stake and an interest in the anticolonial struggles, were able to enlist the support or the compliance or both of their lower-class clients. To be sure, as time passed it became apparent that the bonds linking patrons and clients in turn-of-the-century Batangas were not uniformly strong, and, in the long run, the character of the resistance underwent a transformation. But at its core and for much of its duration, the popular struggles in Batangas were essentially elite-fueled.

Again, I am not claiming that the pattern of behavior I describe in

Batangas necessarily prevailed throughout the Philippines during the period 1896–1902. In other provinces the anti-Spanish and anti-American struggles may have more closely resembled the kinds of popular movements depicted by Scott and Popkin. But having conceded that much, I hasten to point out that the struggles in Batangas were anything but atypical in the Southeast Asian past. The uprisings in late nineteenth-century Vietnam against French rule and most of the anticolonial revolutions of the twentieth century strongly resemble that in Batangas. Indeed, throughout the Third World, elite-fueled popular movements have always been as common as the types of popular struggles that have attracted the attention of the moral and political economists.

Two obvious conclusions follow from the above observations. First, one should treat with a healthy skepticism existing models of peasant mentality and popular uprisings. Popular movements, like peasant minds, have taken many forms in Southeast Asia, and perhaps the majority of them were organized and directed by local elites. They were no less popular, in the literal sense, for being so, although there can be no doubt that they were different from the uprisings described by Scott and Popkin. Second, one should be alert to the possibility that a movement may have had something other than a single, unitary character. As I have already pointed out, most of those who have written about the Philippine Revolution of 1896 and the Philippine-American War have not entertained that possibility, and their accounts may be seriously flawed. Regional variations in the Philippines have always been conspicuous, and they likely produced marked differences in Filipino behavior during the period 1896–1902. Before any effort is made to provide a comprehensive explanation of popular participation in the Philippine Revolution and the Philippine-American War, we might be wise to find out more about the events themselves.

Such conclusions may sound like the sort of cautionary advice that historians, who tend to be less theoretically daring than political scientists and anthropologists, are inclined to give: more archives need to be explored; more questions need to be asked; better distinctions need to be made. But possibly a small dose of caution is overdue. Although no sane historian believes in such a thing as objective truth, few would question the notion that historical argument must rest on a firm foundation of evidence. In the case of the turn-of-the-century popular struggles in the Philippines, some of the most oft-repeated arguments can be shown to rest on a very meager evidential basis indeed. Before we can effectively generalize, we must, I believe, dig more deeply.

A Note about Spelling and Terminology

A few words of explanation are in order about my spelling of Spanish and Filipino names, places, and terms. As a general rule, I have spelled the names of all Spaniards, all institutions introduced by the Spaniards, and all official positions during the Spanish regime according to accepted Iberian usage, including the use of accents: thus, Manuel Sastrón, *principalía, capitán municipal,* and so forth. Two exceptions, both of them educational institutions that outlived Spanish rule, are the Colegio de San Juan de Letran and the University of Santo Tomas.

Names of Filipino people and places have, in accordance with local usage, been rendered without accents—hence, Jose Rizal, Mariano Trias. In addition, a few turn-of-the-century orthographic peculiarities have been preserved—for example, the use of *c* or *qu,* rather than *k,* in most cases (Maquiling rather than Makiling; Mataasnacahoy rather than Mataasnakahoy); *ao* rather than *aw* (Banajao rather than Banahaw). Most Filipino actors in the battle for Batangas spelled things this way, and I thought it appropriate to retain their spelling whenever possible. (Two Filipino actors, however, Vicente Lukban and Macario Sakay, spelled their family names with the letter *k,* and in my references to them I elected to use the *k.*)

One orthographic question has proved troublesome—the rendering of three place-names that *at the time* were spelled in two different ways: Muntinlupa (sometimes rendered as Muntinglupa); Biñan (Biñang); and Bauan (Bauang). In all three cases I have decided, arbitrarily, to adopt the first-mentioned spelling.

Throughout this book, I use two terms to refer to the region in which the province of Batangas is located: *southwestern Luzon* and *the southern Tagalog region.* The first is self-explanatory. The second is generally used to refer to the Tagalog-speaking provinces south of Manila—Cavite, Batangas, Laguna, Tayabas (now Quezon), and part of Morong (Rizal).

Prologue: December 1899

The Filipino war against the United States was in its eleventh month, and it was going badly. From the beginning the Americans had concentrated their operations in the area north of Manila, although they had made forays into the provinces of Cavite and Laguna. In battle after battle in the northern theater, the enemy had beaten the elite troops of the Filipino Army led by Gen. Emilio Aguinaldo, the former municipal official from Cavite who had risen to prominence during the revolution of 1896–98 against Spain. Belatedly, Aguinaldo had acknowledged the Americans' superiority in conventional warfare, and in mid-November 1899 he had ordered the remaining troops under his immediate command to begin using guerrilla tactics.[1] So it happened that the Americans were on the point of shifting their attention to the southern half of Luzon.

For some time rumors had circulated throughout the province of Batangas that an invasion was imminent, and the frequent appearance of U.S.

ships in Batangas and Balayan bays in recent weeks seemed to confirm the reports.[2] Aware of the danger, Miguel Malvar, the Filipino commander in Batangas, issued an alert. In Batangas City,* the provincial capital, where Lt. Col. Mariano Cabrera directed defensive preparations, there was a flurry of activity as regular troops, local militia units, and the police force, all suffering from an acute shortage of weapons and ammunition, were deployed to meet the anticipated seaborne attack. One detachment was stationed in the seaside barrio of Tabangao, and three others occupied positions along the coast. A larger force, led by veterans of the earlier fighting in Laguna, was positioned in the town center.[3]

This was the situation on the eve of the invasion of Batangas. The Americans, aggressive and confident, were clearly coming; the local defenders, undermanned and underequipped, were clearly bracing. Who among them could have suspected that more than two years would pass before the battle for Batangas was resolved?

*In this book, I refer to the capital of the province as Batangas City, its current name. At the turn of the century, it was known simply as Batangas. I use the current name to avoid confusion between the name of the town and that of the province.

★ ★ ★ ★ ★ ★ ★ ★ ★ ★

PART ONE

Before the Battle

1

Late Nineteenth-Century Batangas: Geography, Society, Politics, & Fundamental Realities

T O UNDERSTAND the events that were to engulf Miguel Malvar and his fellow Batangueños, we must know more about the province in which they lived. The Philippine-American War may have been a contest between two nation-states, one in its infancy and the other in its late adolescence, but it was also, for much of its duration, a collection of local struggles. The nature of the struggle about to occur in Batangas would be determined in large measure by certain preexisting realities of provincial life—geography, the social order, the disease regime, education, and politics—and at the outset we must focus our attention on them.[1]

★ The Setting

To approach the province of Batangas from Manila, most travelers today take the South Super Highway to the town of Santo Tomas, a journey of about forty miles along a southeasterly arc through a region that has become increasingly industrialized, urbanized, and integrated into the metropolitan economy. But to gain another, perhaps more revealing visual perspective on Batangas, one should go almost directly south, rather than southeast, to a place called Tagaytay City, located in a mountainous section of southern Cavite.

There, at an elevation of about two thousand feet, one can glimpse Batangas's spectacular terrain. Directly ahead lies Lake Taal, one of the natural wonders of the Philippine archipelago, seventeen miles from north to south and thirteen from east to west, with a large volcanic island in the middle. The island's terrain is rugged, and the crater of the active volcano near its center rises more than a thousand feet. Just west of the lake is a vast expanse of rolling countryside. Lush vegetation predominates, but one can also see hundreds of plots devoted to the cultivation of rice, sugar cane, and other crops. Also visible is an intricate web of rivers and streams that cut across and irrigate the land and then flow to the distant South China Sea. Farther to the west is Mount Batulao, a splendid, stately peak measuring close to twenty-five hundred feet, and weather permitting, one can see the scores of lesser mountains and hills that line the western coast of the province.

On the other side of Lake Taal is terrain of equal beauty and even greater irregularity. Slightly to the northeast of the lake is Mount Maquiling, sprawling and majestic, more than three thousand feet in height; directly east of the volcano lie two mountains, Mount Dalaga and Mount Malepunyo, guarding the approach to the province of Quezon (formerly, Tayabas); and overlooking the southeastern corner of the lake is Mount Macolod. Farther to the southeast, near the town of Lobo, at least half a dozen peaks rise more than two thousand feet.

The view from Tagaytay City offers a valuable insight into the battle for Batangas. Of course, much has changed since the days of Miguel Malvar. Several new crops are now cultivated in the fields of Batangas; some families who owned large plots of land at the turn of the century have sold their holdings to others; new roads and houses have been built. But the big picture, the awe-inspiring terrain, is little different today from what it was in December 1899.[2]

Here, topographically speaking, was an almost ideal setting for the waging of unconventional warfare. The rugged countryside—the mountains and hills that command the provincial landscape, the omnipresent canyons and ravines, the rivers and streams—offered countless opportunities that could be exploited by a determined guerrilla force: hundreds of hiding places where the troops could rest, regroup, and plan their operations and thousands of

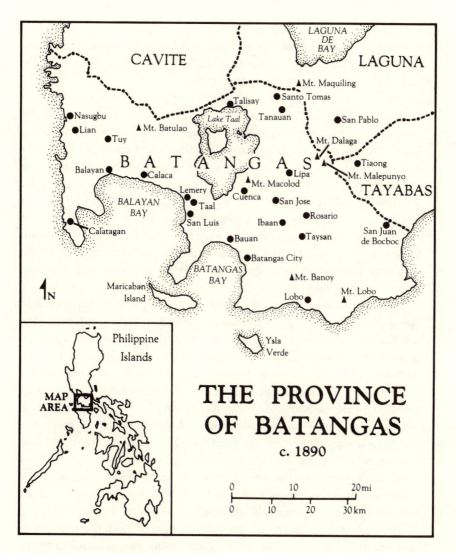

THE PROVINCE
OF BATANGAS
c. 1890

0   10   20mi

0   10   20   30km

1. The Province of Batangas, c. 1890

natural obstacles that could work to their advantage when they were being pursued by an enemy force. The land itself would play a prominent role in the unfolding provincial drama. Had it been less formidable, the battle for Batangas might have ended sooner than it did.

At the turn of the century about 300,000 people lived on this land, spread out over an area of slightly more than one thousand square miles. They resided in twenty-two separate *pueblos* (towns), the largest of which was Lipa, with a population of close to 40,000. Only slightly less populous were Batangas City, the provincial capital, and Bauan, both with more than 30,000 inhabitants. All three towns were located just to the east of the geographical center of the province, and, as it happened, about two-thirds of the province's population lived in that same general area. The western part of Batangas boasted four towns—Nasugbu, Lian, Tuy, and Balayan—but, according to the Spanish census of 1887, only the last had more than 15,000 residents. The mountainous southeastern corner of the province was even less densely inhabited.[3]

Although census figures convey a rough idea of population distribution in the province, they do not, by themselves, provide a sense of what Filipino communities were really like. In fact, a town in the Philippines bore a much closer resemblance to an American county than to a municipality. In Lipa, only about 4,000 of the 40,000 inhabitants lived in the *población,* or town center, where the church, public buildings, and principal market were located. The vast majority lived in the more than forty barrios that radiated out in all directions, and for many miles, from the población. Not infrequently, a few of the barrios of one town were actually closer to the población of another, and it was not uncommon for the residents of such outlying communities to petition the central authorities for a redrawing of the administrative boundaries whenever they felt they were not receiving fair treatment from their own municipal officials.[4]

Batangas was primarily an agricultural province, but the sea figured prominently in people's lives. Many of the towns were situated near the coast, and a sizable percentage of the population depended on the sea for its livelihood. Batangueños also derived sustenance and income from the province's rivers and streams and from the waters of Lake Taal.

★ The Social Order: The Upper Rungs

Late nineteenth-century Batangas was known throughout the archipelago for its wealth. Indeed, with the exception of the western Visayas, Manila, and perhaps Pampanga, no part of the Philippines had a more powerful economic elite. Most of the wealthy families owed their good fortune to the world market's seemingly insatiable demand for sugar and coffee, both of which Batangas produced in abundance for much of the century. Men like Lorenzo Lopez, a resident of Balayan, acquired large tracts of land, planted them to cane, made huge profits, diversified, and along the way built sturdy, splendid, stone-walled mansions with galvanized iron roofs. Lopez's residence, located on Calle San Jose in Balayan's población, was valued in 1890 at 4,000 pesos, a substantial amount in an era when an agricultural worker earned no more than a peso or two a week. In addition, he owned warehouses, sailing vessels, sugar mills, and vast estates on the island of Mindoro. Francisco Martinez, his main rival in the sugar industry, had holdings estimated at half a million pesos.[5]

The wealth was not confined to Balayan. In Batangas City, another center of sugar production, no fewer than thirty individuals owned houses valued at more than 2,000 pesos. Additional evidence of economic success could be found within these dwellings. An inventory of one house on Calle Madrid in the población listed, among other things, three sofas, six "Vienna" chairs, sixteen "European" chairs, twenty other chairs, two writing desks, one round marble table, one game table, three sideboards, several beds and wardrobes, and an assortment of statues, pedestals, jars, lamps, mirrors, tablecloths, and curtains.[6] Such possessions were only a part—in some cases, a small part—of the holdings of Batangas City's wealthy families, since most also owned agricultural land, draft animals, farm implements, sugar and rice mills, carriages, and much more.

In Lipa, consumption was more conspicuous still, fifty-four of the townspeople owning residences valued at over 2,000 pesos. At the top of the list was Gregorio Aguilera Solis, a man of letters as well as means, whose five houses and one warehouse were appraised at 56,500 pesos. Not far behind were various members of the Catigbac, Luz, and Africa clans.[7] In Lipa, fortunes were made in coffee production, which began in earnest in the 1860s. In 1887, the town produced 4.4 million kilograms of coffee, which brought its cultivators an income of more than 2 million pesos. "These were the days of prosperity for Lipa," recalled Teodoro Kalaw, a famous scholar and politician raised in the town, "when people everywhere talked of its very rich aristocracy, its handsome carriages drawn by huge horses, its almost fabulous wealth." To a large extent, this high society was Hispanized:

> Its language was Spanish; Spanish were its customs, manners, and social forms; Spanish were its dances, its music. The social atmosphere

was an importation from Spain and included its peculiar faults and vices. Money was splurged on clothes, interior decoration, and pictures; on rare crystals and china ordered from Europe; on curtains of the finest silk, on stuffed chairs from Vienna, on exquisite table wines and foods. Lipa society sought to equal the halls and banquets of Spain herself, the Metropolis, the Guiding Star, the Ideal.[8]

Paz Luz Dimayuga, daughter of Manuel Luz, one of Lipa's richest men, told me in 1976 about life under her father's roof. The furniture, she remembered, was mainly in the style of Louis XV, although the piano was Spanish-made; there were a number of Venetian mirrors, and the chandeliers were in a different style as well. The house had thirteen servants—a cook, a coachman, several *yayas* (female caretakers of children), a few youths to serve food and run errands; members of the family were hardly ever obliged to concern themselves with household chores. Manuel Luz spent most of his days in the barrio of Balete, close to the shores of Lake Taal, where he oversaw the activities of the tenants who worked his large estates. Evenings, however, he spent in the *sala,* enjoying a pastime that to him was a passion: music. Luz himself played the piano and the violin, and all of his twelve children learned at least one instrument. At nightly family gatherings, every child was expected to play a piece or two, recite a poem, or sing a song. Occasionally, friends or neighbors were invited for informal recitals. And then, of course, there were the balls, not so splendid as the extravaganzas presided over by the Solis family, but impressive all the same, where diamond-bedecked ladies in fancy dress danced the *valse* and *rigadon* into the wee hours with handsome, elegantly attired, fortune-seeking Spaniards.[9]

As the century drew to a close, balls were held less frequently in Lipa. Beginning in 1889, a combination of insect pests and parasitic fungi attacked the coffee plants, with dire consequences. Export statistics tell much of the story. Between 1883 and 1888, the Philippines exported an average of 6.5 million kilograms of coffee yearly, most of it produced in Batangas. By 1890, coffee exports had fallen to 4.5 million; by 1891, to 2.8 million; and by 1892, to 1.4 million. In Lipa, almost all the coffee plants were destroyed and so too, in a sense, were many of the aspirations of the town's economic elite. The province's coffee industry was not eliminated: in time, new plants appeared, and even today Lipa produces a modicum of coffee for the Manila market. But after 1889, coffee became a minor crop in Batangas, and the majority of estates formerly planted to coffee—most of Manuel Luz's land in Balete, for example—soon converted to other crops. Although Lipa's leading families

1. Lipa, Batangas, 1900

remained well-off by the colony's and the province's standards, the boom days were over.[10]

As cash-cropping took hold in late nineteenth-century Batangas, there were ever-increasing opportunities to earn money in nonagricultural pursuits. Lawyers and physicians made sizable incomes; a doctor in Lipa once boasted that at the height of the coffee boom he collected more than 70,000 pesos in fees during a three-month period. Merchants also proliferated, and towns like Balayan, Batangas City, Taal, and Lipa had hundreds of small shopkeepers, owners of stalls in the public market, and itinerant tradespeople, who engaged in the sale of rice, dried and fresh fish, eggs, cigarettes and cigars, *tuba* and *basi* (the locally produced alcoholic beverages), cotton thread and buttons, woven fabrics, hats, and other items. Many of these retailers were *chinos,* except in Taal, where the Chinese had long been excluded, and so were many owners of the larger scale commercial concerns in the province—*sari-sari* (variety) and hardware stores, retail and wholesale shops specializing in sugar and coffee, other stores engaged in the sale of "comestibles y bebidos de Europa y China." There were speculators, too, who sold rice in quantity, carabaos, and cattle and bought horses, sugar, coffee, and other locally produced items which they transported to Manila and other places in search of a profit. Only a handful of these merchants and speculators had incomes comparable to those of the large landholders of the province, but the commercial sector offered a reasonable prospect of upward mobility.[11]

In retrospect, when one considers the sophistication of late nineteenth-century Batangas high society and the growth of the province's economy, it seems almost unbelievable that a few years later, during the Philippine-American War, a large segment of the American press would portray Filipinos as uniformly backward and benighted and the Philippine economy as uniformly stagnant and underdeveloped. Actually, the economy of Batangas was highly dynamic, as a few of the business dealings of a leading merchant and speculator, Manuel Arguelles of Batangas City, reveal. The owner of a residence in the población valued at 2,000 pesos, a shipping line, many cattle, sugar mills in Bauan and Ibaan, a rice store and liquor business in Bauan, a cloth store in Batangas City, and other concerns, Arguelles was constantly in motion. Between January 1896 and March 1897, he recorded nine transactions in the notarial offices of the provincial capital, probably only a fraction of the business dealings he engaged in during the period but enough to give a sense of his entrepreneurship. Two of the recorded transactions were contracts commonly known as *pactos de retro.* In the typical

2. Taal, Batangas, c. 1900

13

3. *Taal Church, c. 1900*

14

4. *Balayan, Batangas, c. 1900*

15

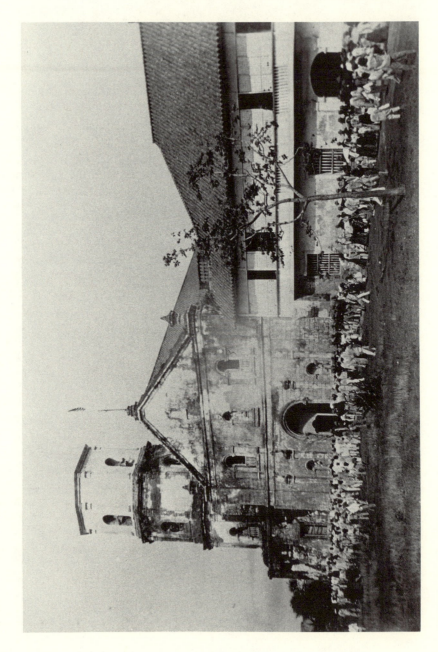

5. Balayan Church, c. 1900

16

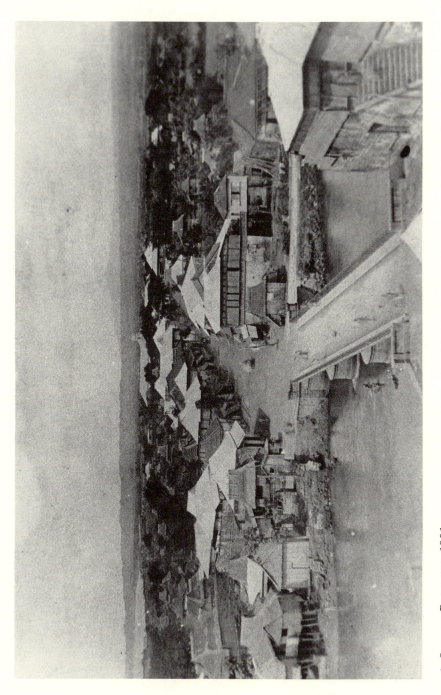

6. *Lemery, Batangas, 1901*

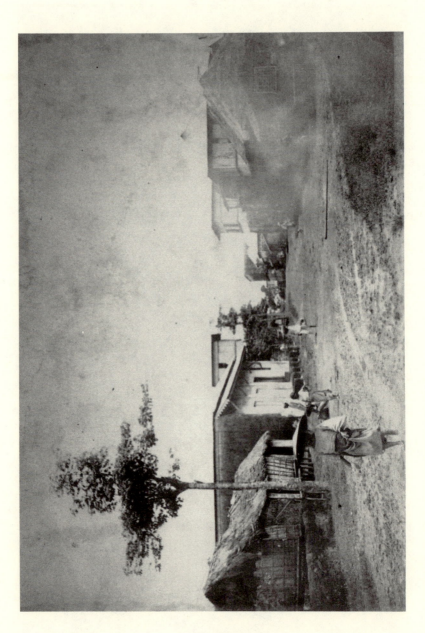

7. *Calle Real, San Jose, Batangas, 1900*

18

pacto de retro, a property-owner conveyed title to one or more parcels of land to a moneylender (in these cases, Arguelles) with the option to regain the title if he or she repaid the loan within a designated period of time. The pacto de retro was a popular business arrangement in the Philippines of the nineteenth century, and Arguelles concluded many. He acquired property outright as well, purchasing two parcels of land in Rosario in April 1896, another in the same town in February 1897, and still another in the provincial capital a week later. Finally, Arguelles made two simple loans, both guaranteed by mortgages, in September 1896 and sold one of his sugar mills in January 1897. By any standard, Manuel Arguelles was financially ambitious.[12]

The occupants of the upper rungs of the provincial socioeconomic ladder constituted a small, albeit important, segment of the population. But how small? That seemingly straightforward question is far from simple, since it involves, among other things, a number of testing definitional and methodological problems. Readers who enjoy wrestling with such matters are encouraged to turn to Appendix A for an extended discussion, but for the others, suffice it to say that, if we define the economic elite of Batangas as *the members of the immediate families of Batangueños who owned residences valued at 240 pesos or more,* that group appeared to number between forty-five hundred and six thousand in the early 1890s, or approximately 1.5 to 2 percent of the population. In fact, however we define *economic elite,* one thing seems clear: the number of rich people in the province of Batangas was very, very small.

★ The Social Order: The Lower Rungs

Even more challenging than estimating the size of the economic elite of Batangas is providing a clear picture of the remaining 98–98.5 percent of the population, who occupied the lower rungs on the provincial socioeconomic ladder. Most historians of the Philippines hardly make the effort. It has become accepted practice to describe indigenous society as essentially two-tiered, with the elite ("Haves") at the top and the rest of the population ("the masses" or "the people," typically portrayed as an undifferentiated lumpen peasantry) at the bottom. As it happens, such a picture corresponds fairly closely to descriptions of indigenous society that appeared in many nineteenth- and early twentieth-century travelers' accounts—but it is a gross distortion of Philippine social realities.

Common sense alone suggests that the provincial socioeconomic ladder had more than two rungs. Between the extremes of great wealth and grinding poverty were individuals of middling means—schoolteachers, small shopkeepers, artisans (carpenters, tailors, blacksmiths), owner-cultivators of plots of several hectares, and others. Moreover, even among the badly off, income and living conditions varied considerably. Hence, if it is useful to "disaggregate" the economic elite—to show that the group consisted not only of landed proprietors but also of merchants and speculators, physicians and lawyers—it is just as useful to disaggregate the masses, to point out the heterogeneity behind the label.

Looking first at adult males, one sees thousands of independent farmers struggling to make a living on small parcels of land and thousands of tenants toiling for a percentage of the harvest on the estates of landlords; large numbers of day laborers working at minimal wages for landlords and tenants alike; domestic servants doing the lifting and other heavy work in the houses of the better-off; fishermen, especially in seaside towns like Nasugbu and Batangas City; owners of stalls in the town markets; itinerant hawkers; and a number of others involved in various types of menial labor.[13] As for adult females, in addition to supervising the households, they participated in the backbreaking agricultural tasks of transplanting and harvesting palay, picked coffee berries, worked as servants in the homes of the wealthy, and supplemented the family income by spinning, weaving, and embroidering. But occupational categories such as those enumerated above were anything but rigid, a point driven home to the American census authorities in 1903, when they attempted to conduct an occupational census of the archipelago: "Among the Filipinos there is little specialization. Few among them, either men or women, devote themselves exclusively to one occupation. A man works part of the day at farming and devotes part of the night to fishing, and whether he has reported himself to the census as a farmer or a fisherman was very much of an accident. The same thing holds throughout quite a range of [vocations], especially those of the lower classes."[14]

Furthermore, differentiation existed *within* these fluid occupational subgroups. Not all tenant farmers were poor. Although most held parcels of two hectares or less and struggled to get by, hundreds occupied larger plots and were able to make more substantial incomes.[15] In addition, relations between tenant and landlord varied a great deal and were typically most favorable to the tenants on small estates, where frequent contact was possible, and least favorable on the largest ones, where the establishment of personal relationships between the two was unlikely. Jose Caubalejo, a native of Calatagan, and Atanacio Ilagan, from the town of Nasugbu, lived and worked on properties owned by Pedro Roxas, a Spaniard whose vast holdings encompassed much of western Batangas. Neither one ever met Roxas, both dealt exclusively with his agents, and both complained about Roxas's failings as a landlord, citing the high rates of interest he charged on loans, his unwillingness to help his tenants during hard times, and so on. Emilio Vergara, by contrast, was a tenant on a smaller estate in Mataasnacahoy, a barrio of Lipa. Vergara's landlord, Claro Recinto, was a wealthy man by provincial standards, with landholdings in excess of fifty hectares, but he had no more than a few dozen tenants. According to Vergara, all the tenants knew Recinto well, felt that he treated them fairly, and respected him, although he also made clear that the respect was mixed with a measure of fear, since they depended on Recinto's goodwill for their economic well-being.[16]

Such obvious disparities in the conditions of tenure in rural Southeast Asia have occasionally been ignored in the historical literature. Over the years, much has been written about patron-client ties in the region—the dyadic, presumably reciprocal relationship between superordinate and subordinate in which each provides services for the other—and, typically, scholars point to the landlord-tenant relationship as an example of such ties. We are told that a landlord customarily provided loans and seed for tenants and paid for the weddings of a tenant's children, and that the tenant, in exchange, was expected to furnish labor services and gifts of food for the landlord.[17] There is truth in this paradigm; indeed, landlord-tenant relations in turn-of-the-century Batangas often conformed to it, as they did in the case of the Vergara family and Claro Recinto. But often the relationship was distinctly asymmetrical and to a certain extent exploitative. Wenceslao Retana's brief ethnographic study of Batangas, published in 1888, gives testimony on this last point. "The life of the *indio* tenants who reside in the countryside is laborious, destitute, and full of privations," Retana wrote.

> Rare, very rare is the tenant who is not in debt to his landlord, a debt that brings into being a type of slavery to which he is subjected. As a general rule, the *indios* who are engaged in agricultural labor enter into service by taking out a loan that increases little by little as time passes. The harvest arrives, and out of the few pesos that the landlord should hand over to the tenant, he gives only a trifle, because the remainder is deducted to cover the debt. . . . The debt, therefore, never disappears; the debt holds [the tenant] down.[18]

In summary, landlord-tenant relations in nineteenth-century Batangas were not uniform: some tenants lived comfortably, but most did not; some were treated well, others were exploited; some felt a measure of loyalty and respect toward their landlords, others felt resentment. The closer one looks at the so-called masses of Batangas, the more differences are evident among them.

That last, simple point has suggestive comparative implications. In light of the manifest variety of vocations as well as variations in crop specialization, land tenure, and wealth from town to town, it would have been remarkable—indeed, miraculous—if the heterogeneous majority that historians often call the masses had responded as one to any appeal either from indigenous leaders or American invaders. Unlike the residents of Vietnamese hamlets of the 1960s, to whom historians have often compared them, Filipino barrio-dwellers of the late nineteenth century had no sense of loyalty to an indigenous nation-state. And they had been neither politicized, propagandized, or otherwise instructed by trained cadres, nor hardened by a generation of fighting against a colonial power. Under these very different circumstances, their response to American occupation, though it showed superficial similarities, was vastly unlike that of Vietnamese hamlets of the 1960s. And whatever else the response was, it was not—nor could one expect it to be— unified and uniform.[19] The behavior of lower-class Batangueños in a period of crisis would reflect attitudes and relationships formed during the generations of relative normality that preceded the crisis: in a real sense, the trauma of warfare would merely bring into sharper focus the fundamental realities of peacetime Batangas.

In spite of the diversity among Batangas's masses, certain generalities can be made about the poor residents of the province. Let us begin with the home—one that bore little resemblance to the homes of the wealthy, Hispanized residents of the province. As I noted above, most occupants of the lower rungs lived not in the poblaciones but in the barrios, several miles from the public buildings and splendid mansions. Their dwellings, simple structures with bamboo walls and floors and thatched roofs made from the leaves of the nipa palm, contained a modicum of furniture, some sleeping mats, a few crudely made garments for each member of the household, various other possessions, and, in most cases, an *altarcito* (small altar) before which the family would say prayers in the evening. On average, each house contained six occupants.[20]

Most of the work in the home was done by women. They cooked the food and did the washing (usually at a nearby stream, since the houses had no running water), tended to the children, made the clothes, went to market, and did a hundred other chores.[21] The family's diet varied little from day to day, its principal components being rice, fruit (especially *lanzones* and *chicos*), vegetables, and a bit of fish or meat; on special occasions, the provincial delicacy, goat, was served.[22] The women of the house indulged in tobacco, betel, and *panguingui,* a game of cards; the men, in tuba, basi, *monte,* another card game, and the cockpit. And even when the men were away from the cockpits, they were often in the company of their cocks, which they caressed and groomed for hours at a time and treated as affectionately as any human member of the household. The children played, did their chores, and worked in the paddy from time to time.[23]

The field of vision of most barrio-dwellers was restricted to their barrios and their towns. They had occasional contact with the authority of the state—when, for example, the *cabeza de barangay,* the local headman, exacted taxes or obliged the men to provide labor services. Some traveled to other towns, even to other provinces, and a number migrated, usually in times of hardship. But most had little contact with the outside world, spending much of their lives within a five-to-ten-mile radius of their birthplace. In 1896, of the 288 marriages recorded in Batangas City, 264 (92 percent) were unions of individuals who were natives of the town. And according to official records, only 38 of the 1,119 people who died in Batangas City in 1896 had been born elsewhere.[24]

For the men of the house, the rhythms of work differed from those of Manuel Luz, Manuel Arguelles, and others of the economic elite. Although there was, as I noted, a great variety of vocations among Batangas's poor and although Batangas was best known for its production of sugar and coffee, most adult males in Batangas—like those throughout the Philippines— worked in the paddy, engaged in the cultivation of wet rice. The work was hard, enervating, and financially unrewarding. "The peasant, with his bare back and chest, works . . . almost every day," wrote Retana, "and he consequently is forced to endure the great heat of a burning sun, the discomforts of the rain showers, the rigors of the storms, to say nothing of the dangers posed by the excrescences from the slime in the paddy."[25]

Lowland rice was grown in two stages. First, in May, as the rainy season made its appearance, seed was broadcast in a prepared seedbed, usually a sideplot, where the young plants would be allowed to grow to a height of about twelve inches. As the plants progressed, the farmer turned to the chore of preparing the main rice field for transplanting. He flooded the field with water, and then he, his carabao, and perhaps some other men (neighbors, adult male family members, or hired laborers) would pulverize the soil with a harrow, transforming it into a muddy mass. After that, they would pass over the field several times more, working the soil in the narrow furrows with colters and finally leveling the mud. The second stage began with the transplanting. During the transplanting, men and women worked side by side, singing rhythmically as they transferred the rice plants to the main rice field. In the following weeks, the rice field would be flooded periodically until the plants started to bloom and the fruit appeared. The fruit would be allowed to ripen—which occurred about 120 days after the initial sowing of the seeds—and finally harvesting would begin. The spikes would be cut, tied in bundles, allowed to dry in the field, and gathered; and once gathered, the rice would be cleaned, either at a rice mill or by hand. Then it was time to start over again—the sowing, the plowing, the transplanting, and all the rest—since rice cultivators always tried to get two crops a year from their paddies.[26]

A final, noteworthy characteristic of the masses of Batangas was their religion, Catholicism. Late every afternoon, when the church bells sounded, many Batangueños turned in the direction of the church, bowed their heads, and softly said a prayer; in the morning, at noon, and at bedtime, too, prayers were said. Most people attended church on Sundays, holy days, and ceremonial occasions (baptisms, confirmations, marriages, funerals), and a number went to mass every day. Just as virtually every house had its altarcito, so virtually every Batangueña had a rosary hanging around her neck. Each town had a patron saint, and each celebrated a festival in the saint's honor.[27]

The observance of rituals and attendance at church did not, of course, guarantee that Batangueños would follow all the Lord's commandments to the letter. The ecclesiastical and civil records show that sexual indiscretions were not uncommon in the population at large. Of the 13,339 births recorded in the province in 1893, fully 702 (5.26 percent) were illegitimate.[28] Since not all intercourse leads to conception and not all legitimate offspring are conceived after the parents' nuptials, it seems reasonable to assume that at least several thousand Batangueño adults were having sex with someone other than their legal mate over the course of each year. Adherence to the Catholic faith did not ensure either that the faithful would revere the appointed human agents of God's will. As any reader of the novels of Jose Rizal is aware, there was more than a little tension in the late nineteenth-century Philippines between elite Filipinos and the Spanish-born members of the regular clergy who served as priests in many parishes. In Batangas, where in the early 1890s sixteen of the twenty parishes were staffed with members of the Augustinian and Augustinian Recollect orders, resentment against the regulars on the part of local influentials was particularly acute, and it frequently came to the surface in municipal elections.[29]

In spite of the transgressions and the tensions, everyone who commented on religious practices in Batangas in the late nineteenth century recognized that most of the populace took religion seriously. In the eyes of outsiders, the faith of the Batangueños was, if anything, too fervent, bordering on superstition. Books by travelers invariably referred to the Shrine of the Miraculous Virgin, a revered image located in Caysasay, a barrio of Taal. Each year, large numbers of people came to the shrine from Taal and other towns, usually to pray for the recovery of a family member from serious illness, since it was widely believed that the Virgin had curative powers. According to popular accounts, the Virgin had once belonged to the Spanish adventurer Juan de Salcedo, who dropped it accidentally in the Pansipit River in 1573, where it had remained for thirty years until recovered by a humble fisherman.[30] Western skeptics might be inclined to dismiss such a story as legend, a tall tale that only a backward people steeped in superstition could believe, but to the poor residents of Batangas, it was a fundamental reality—one of many that constituted a basis for action in the battle for Batangas.

★ Morbidity and Mortality

Another reality that confronted the inhabitants of Batangas was the high rate of morbidity in the province. Year after year, a wide range of maladies afflicted the people: malaria, smallpox, tuberculosis, dysentery, measles, beriberi, typhoid fever, influenza, and a host of other disorders. From time to time, cholera also made an appearance, striking quickly and taking many lives.[31] Some insight into health conditions in Batangas is provided by demographic data. According to parochial records (which probably understate the level of mortality), in the eleven-year period immediately preceding the Philippine Revolution, the annual crude death rate in Batangas averaged 37.2 per thousand—more than twice the figure for the United States, close to twice that for Europe and higher than that for any place on the planet for which we have trustworthy data save India, Singapore, and the rest of the Philippine archipelago.[32] In epidemic years, moreover, the level of mortality was appalling. In 1883, a brief episode of cholera raised the crude death rate in many towns of Batangas to more than 75 per thousand, and in 1889, outbreaks of both malaria and cholera were responsible for a provincewide crude death rate of slightly more than 80 per thousand.[33]

A number of factors combined to produce morbidity and mortality on such a scale. One was deficient sanitary practices, among them the tendency of most Filipinos to dispose of human waste near their houses or in nearby streams which might serve as the local water supply. As a result, most communities lacked a secure, potable, unpolluted water supply, and the polluted water contributed to the spread of cholera, dysentery, typhoid fever, and other enteric disorders. A second factor was nutritional deficiency, which was most prevalent among the poor but existed in all social classes for the simple reason that Batangas, like most provinces in the Philippines, had become dependent on imported polished rice, which was lacking in thiamine. Consumers of thiamine-deficient rice were far more likely to develop beri-beri, an illness which could kill by itself and which, even when it did not, debilitated its victims, compromised their immune systems, and made them easy targets for the local or imported microparasites.[34]

The high incidence of smallpox and malaria—two of the most efficient killers in late nineteenth-century Batangas—was due to other causes. Theoretically, smallpox was preventable, since a vaccine had been developed almost a century earlier by Edward Jenner, and a vaccination program had been in existence in the Philippines for much of the nineteenth century. But for various reasons the program had been ineffective: Filipinos avoided the vaccinators, vaccinators lied about the number of people whom they had vaccinated, and the vaccine used in the Philippines during the Spanish period was almost certainly inert, given that it was transported to the colony and stored there in unrefrigerated containers. Outbreaks of smallpox were thus frequent in Batangas and in other parts of the Philippines. In the town of Cuenca, for instance, 15 of the 198 people interred in 1894 evidently succumbed to smallpox, and in some communities, dozens of smallpox deaths were recorded in a single month.[35]

If human failings were to blame for the prevalence of smallpox, the astonishingly high incidence of malaria in the late nineteenth-century Philippines was not. Malaria in the Philippines is transmitted primarily by the *Anopheles minimus var. flavirostris,* an insect that lives in the foothills of the archipelago, at elevations of eight hundred to two thousand feet. The mosquito has a number of peculiar traits, not least of which is its preference for bovines, rather than human beings, as the source of its blood meals. Beginning in the 1880s, however, the anophelines of the archipelago were obliged to alter their biting patterns because rinderpest (or cattle plague) had killed most of the carabaos and cattle. Deprived of the bovine meals they favored, the mosquitoes shifted their attention increasingly to people, and as a direct consequence malaria became a far more serious health problem in the archipelago. Although reliable statistics on mortality from malaria do not exist, there is little doubt that, for the period 1889–96, malaria was by far the single largest cause of death in Batangas and in every other province of the Philippines.[36]

The epidemiological environment that prevailed in late nineteenth-century Batangas was anything but healthy. Malevolent microparasites abounded, taking advantage of human failings and environmental factors to spread ill health among the human population. This epidemiological context should be kept in mind as the battle for Batangas unfolds. For, to a large extent, the demographic catastrophes that occurred in Batangas during the successive struggles against Spain and the United States were set in train long before the outbreak of those conflicts. Warfare certainly made things worse, adding new elements of epidemiological instability to an already unstable epidemiological environment, but it was not alone responsible for the massive population losses that took place.

★ Education

Like planting cycles, religion, and disease, education was a crucial part of Batangueño life. Having compiled a dreary record in the area of education for almost three hundred years, the Spanish government made a concerted effort in the last few decades of the nineteenth century to improve primary schooling in the archipelago. A royal decree of 1863 ordered that there be at least one public primary school for each sex in every Philippine town; established a normal school in Manila to train teachers; and prescribed a primary course of study consisting of Spanish, arithmetic, geography, Christian doctrine, and several other subjects.[37] Like most decrees issued by the Crown, this one was not executed with uniform exactitude in all parts of the Philippines, and in Batangas itself compliance varied from one town to the next. An educational survey conducted in the province in 1886 revealed that nine communities out of twenty-two had failed to provide a school for girls and that language instruction was far from successful. Of the 1,509 boys then enrolled in Batangas's public primary schools, only 401 could understand Spanish, 167 could speak the language, and 123 could both speak and write it.[38] Manuel Sastrón, who published a lengthy volume on Batangas nine years later, pointed to similar defects as well as to the poor physical condition of most school buildings and the irregularity of attendance.[39]

During the same period, even more progress was made in private secondary instruction.[40] In a decree issued in 1867, the Crown had placed secondary education for boys under the general supervision of the rector of the University of Santo Tomas, who was empowered to confer all decrees and to ensure that the schools complied with a long list of standards. The Crown also adopted a new five-year secondary curriculum, which included language instruction (Spanish, Latin, Greek, and a choice of either English or French), religion, geography, philosophy, history, and science. These secondary schools were of two types. Schools of the first class, such as the Colegio de San Juan de Letran and the Ateneo Municipal, offered the full five-year course of study. In addition, dozens of schools of the second class offered part of the prescribed curriculum.

Between 1866 and 1891, the annual enrollment of boys from Batangas in secondary schools jumped from 100 to 453 (see Appendix B). A convergence of developments was responsible for the increase. One was the impetus the Crown's decrees had provided to public primary education. Spanish policy had raised both the educational consciousness and the educational expectations of many Batangueño families, and those who could shoulder the expense wanted their children to pursue their studies beyond the primary grades. At the same time, the growth of sugar and coffee cultivation in the province had increased the number of families that could afford to finance their children's schooling. A final factor was accessibility. To meet the growing demand for secondary instruction, a number of secondary schools of the second class were opened in the province. Hence, by 1891, there were seven schools of that type in Batangas, and of the 453 enrollees, 264 (58 percent) were attending the local institutions, with the remaining 189 receiving their instruction outside the province.

Secondary education for girls expanded at a more moderate pace. Only a handful of girls' secondary schools existed in the late nineteenth-century Philippines, and apparently no more than a few dozen Batangueñas were receiving such instruction in the 1890s. The principal obstacle to the growth of female education was cultural. The notion of male intellectual superiority was well entrenched in most Filipino households at the turn of the century, and it was a rare family that seriously considered the idea of providing a genuine education to young women. Thus, at a time when secondary schools of the second class were proliferating in the provinces, no comparable institutions for girls appeared in Batangas.[41]

Of the hundreds of Batangueños, most of them male, who received secondary schooling every year, a number went on to attend university. In the school year 1889–90, there were 57 young men from the province enrolled in the University of Santo Tomas in Manila; by 1895–96 the number had climbed to 92. As a survey of the enrollment lists reveals, most of the college students were, like a large proportion of the secondary students, the offspring of affluent parents. One finds, for example, the names of Jose Luz, Sixto Roxas, Cipriano Calao, and Gregorio Catigbac, all from elite families of Lipa, and also the names of Vicente Olmos and Pablo Borbon, both sons of wealthy residents of Batangas City. Furthermore, a few Batangueños—including Galicano Apacible from Balayan, Gregorio Aguilera Solis, Lauro Dimayuga, and Baldomero Roxas from Lipa—even went to Spain to continue their studies.

These educational advances would turn out to be consequential on several counts. First of all, while only a small percentage of the children in Batangas were receiving instruction during the final years of Spanish rule, a substantial percentage of the sons of well-off families were doing so. In effect, over the course of the late nineteenth century, the young male members of Batangas's economic elite families were becoming the principal members of a small but growing provincial intellectual elite.[42]

As Batangueños became better educated, they increasingly became exposed to new ideas. This was especially true of the small minority who were educated in Spain, for, in the more open political climate of the mother country and in the company of other young Filipinos who were receiving their tertiary education in Spanish institutions, they had an opportunity to read and digest books that were largely unavailable to them in the Philippines—among them, the works of Locke, Rousseau, and other liberal thinkers. The ideas espoused by these writers—notions like the sovereignty of the people—had contributed to the development of a radical consciousness in a number of Western nation-states in the past, and they would prove to be no less appealing to late nineteenth-century Filipinos.

The students' exposure to such ideas, combined with their awareness of the deficiencies of Spanish colonialism, eventually spawned the Propaganda Movement, a lobbying and educational campaign launched by members of the Filipino community in the mother country that aimed to bring about changes in Spanish government of the Philippines. Throughout the late 1880s and early 1890s, the Propagandists, who were led by Jose Rizal and Marcelo H. del Pilar and who included a number of young Batangueños (Gregorio Aguilera Solis and Lauro Dimayuga, for example) in their ranks, agitated for reforms: the end to censorship and the abuses of the Guardia Civil; the improvement of public instruction; representation of the Philippines in the Spanish Cortes; and, above all, the expulsion of the Spanish religious orders, who had come to be seen as the chief agents of Iberian colonialism and the chief obstacles to the political aspirations of Filipino elites. The Propagandists did not succeed in inducing the Spanish rulers to change their policies, but their lobbying efforts and their published writings helped raise the political consciousness of a large number of their countrymen.[43]

That last point suggests another consequence of the development of postprimary education in late nineteenth-century Batangas. Because of the rapid expansion of the provincial educational infrastructure, the Batangueños educated in Spain were not the only young men from the province who were exposed to new ideas. Books and pamphlets written in Spanish, which would have found only a minuscule number of readers in Batangas at midcentury, had a potential audience of several thousand by the 1880s. As a result, the writings produced by the Propagandists could be, and were, transmitted to the intellectual elite back home. Unwittingly, by promoting educational development, the Spaniards were helping to pave the way for the revolution against Spanish rule that would occur at the end of the century.

And they were helping to do so in another way. In the history of modern colonialism, the leaders of revolutions within the colonies invariably come from the ranks of the intellectual elite. Exposure to imported ideas often plays a part in radicalizing them, but occasionally the new ideas may matter less than the empowerment that comes with the acquisition of knowledge. Educated people, especially ones who are convinced of their capacity to rule, are far more likely to resist alien overlordship than the uneducated, downtrodden masses. Whether they realized it or not, simply by sending their sons to secondary schools and to university, the wealthy families of Batangas were sowing revolutionary seeds.

In addition to exposing a large number of young, affluent Batangueños to new ideas, Batangas's educational expansion exposed them, for extended periods, to each other. Teenage boys from all parts of the province were brought together at the local secondary schools, and over the course of a few years of instruction and shared experiences, they had a unique opportunity to form close relationships that transcended family ties and geographical boundaries. Connective links formed among the elite families of different towns, and these links—another fundamental reality—would play a crucial role in the battle for Batangas.

★ Politics

The battle for Batangas would also be affected by the nature of local politics in the late Spanish period. Political life in the nineteenth-century Philippines revolved around municipal elections, hotly contested affairs that were the first step in the complicated process by which the principal local officials were chosen.[44] Electoral procedures were spelled out in a series of laws, decrees, and circulars. For most of the last half of the nineteenth century, the right to participate in elections—but not necessarily the right to vote—was limited to four categories of adult males, who together constituted the so-called *principalía:* the incumbent *gobernadorcillo* (otherwise known as the *capitán municipal,* the ranking municipal official); the incumbent cabezas de barangay (heads of *barangays,* administrative subdivisions of the town, consisting of a designated number of families); the *cabezas reformados* (former cabezas de barangay who had held the post for a minimum of ten consecutive years); and the *capitanes pasados* (former gobernadorcillos and a few other former officeholders).

The principalía never amounted to more than a tiny fraction of the inhabitants of any town. In Santo Tomas, with a population of approximately 11,000, there were only eighty-five *principales* in 1892, and of that number fifty-eight were current cabezas and the rest former officeholders. Yet if the right to participate in elections was restricted in the nineteenth-century Philippines—and it *was* restricted—contrary to what most of the historical literature might suggest, it was not restricted to men of wealth. Of Santo Tomas's eighty-five principales, only seven (one cabeza and six former officeholders) appeared on the property assessment lists as the owners of domiciles valued at more than 240 pesos. In San Juan, four cabezas de barangay out of a total of seventy-four qualified as members of the economic elite, and in San Jose, three out of sixty-three. By and large, then, there was little correlation between membership in the principalía and membership in the provincial economic elite.

Of this small group of potential voters, only thirteen principales would be able to vote in any municipal election: the incumbent gobernadorcillo and twelve others, who would be chosen by lot, six from the ranks of the current cabezas and six from the ranks of the former officeholders. The first vote taken on election day, the only one requiring written ballots, was for the post of gobernadorcillo. The thirteen voters would be asked to write the names of their first and second choices for the office on their ballots, and once these votes were tallied, the *terna,* a list of three names to be passed on to higher authorities, could be drawn up. The first name on the terna would be that of the top vote-getter; the second, that of the runner-up; and the third, that of the incumbent gobernadorcillo.[45] The assembled thirteen would next vote for the four other members of the municipal tribunal, who would assist the gobernadorcillo in administering the town. For all these posts, only the names of the top vote-getters were recorded, and these names were also forwarded to higher authorities for approval.

The voting that took place in the municipality merely initiated the procedure by which a town's officials were chosen. The final decision about who would serve rested with the Spanish governor-general, and several months would usually pass—while a thorough investigation of the candidates favored by the voters was conducted—before he announced his choices. As a general rule, the higher authorities preferred to confer office on the men who appeared to have the support of the electorate. But they would reject the voters' choice if they believed the candidate was unqualified. In roughly a third of the gobernadorcillo elections in Batangas between 1887 and 1894, the top vote-getters were not confirmed by the governor-general.

In the Spanish scheme of things, municipal electoral contests served a vital function. Lacking a sufficiently large colonial bureaucracy, the rulers had to rely heavily on the elected Filipino officials in order to administer their archipelagic empire. Among other things, gobernadorcillos were obligated by law to collect a wide range of taxes, try minor civil and criminal cases, initiate proceedings and assemble evidence in more serious criminal cases, supervise road and bridge repairs, and carry out a score of other vital tasks. Yet for the ruled as well—or at least for an influential segment of the population—the elections had just as much meaning. At stake for them was not the opportunity to serve and please the Crown but rather access to the powers attendant to municipal office. Since the gobernadorcillo was responsible for repairing roads and bridges, he was in a position to decide which roads and bridges were to receive first priority, and that decision was of no little interest to the owners of large coffee and sugar estates in Batangas, whose economic fortunes depended in part on their ability to transport their cash crops to market. Also, because he initiated most serious legal cases and was responsible for marshaling the evidence for the courts, he could, if so inclined, quash judicial actions against parties he favored. At the same time, his judicial powers enabled him to make life difficult for anyone in his jurisdiction by embroiling that person in a string of legal proceedings. Finally, in assessing taxes and collecting fees, the gobernadorcillo could be expected to be lenient on—even bend the law for—his favorites and less accommodating to those he disliked. Gaining control over municipal government was desirable, therefore, not only because certain benefits could be derived but also because failure to do so meant that certain disadvantages might have to be endured.

To gain control of municipal office, Batangueños banded together in factions—or parties, as they were referred to. In almost every town in Batangas, two or more factions could be found, often headed by members of the local economic elite. Sometimes these local factional leaders stood for office themselves, but just as often they preferred to remain behind the scenes and promote the candidacy of someone they could control—a poor relative, an employee, even a tenant. In forty-two municipal elections in Batangas between 1887 and 1894, fewer than a third of the leading candidates for gobernadorcillo were, based on the 240-peso yardstick, members of the province's economic elite; and a large number of the others were described by contemporaries as the "creatures" of factional leaders.

Several distinct types of factions existed in late nineteenth-century Batangas, although there was some overlap among them. Some factions represented powerful economic interests, typically wealthy families engaged in sugar or coffee production. These tended to be most prevalent in towns where cash-cropping was most profitable and where, therefore, the economic stakes were high. In Balayan, a center of sugar production, the two major factions were dominated by Francisco Martinez and Lorenzo Lopez, the town's sugar barons, both of whom viewed the control of municipal office as a key to promoting their economic interests. An economic faction operated in Nasugbu, led by the administrators of the vast hacienda of the Spaniard Pedro Roxas, and another in San Jose, where the Aguila clan, owners of large coffee estates, traditionally aspired to dominate local government.

A second type of faction was led by the local parish priest. A frequent observation about the Philippines during the Spanish period is that municipal affairs were dominated by the parish priest, and indeed that was often so. In at least half a dozen towns in the province of Batangas, the cleric and his supporters drafted a slate of candidates before each municipal election, and the priest then exerted his considerable influence to get those men elected. Still another type may be characterized as the anticlerical or anti-Spanish faction. Usually led by socially prominent, economically comfortable, well-educated men, such factions echoed the anti-Spanish and antifriar feelings increasingly manifest throughout the Philippines in the late 1880s and early 1890s. These factions were powerful in Santo Tomas, Tanauan, and Taal (see chapter 2).

Because the stakes of municipal elections were perceived to be so high, electoral contests in late nineteenth-century Batangas tended to be hard-fought. Indeed, as the surviving records of those contests reveal, the contending parties were prepared to go far beyond the limits of the law to achieve victory. The factions in Batangas generally began their preparations for an election several months before it was scheduled to occur. First, a meeting or series of meetings was held by the faction leaders to decide on a slate of candidates. Next, they and the approved candidates scheduled more meetings, this time with the town's principales, at which the hosts attempted to persuade the guests how to cast their votes on election day. Such get-togethers with potential voters were technically illegal, since electoral ordinances strictly prohibited members of the principalía from meeting privately before the election to discuss their choices for the municipal posts; but ordinances notwithstanding, meetings of this sort were held in every town in the province.

To win the support of the principales, the factions employed a number of persuasive techniques. One was bribery. Usually, a small advance would be given to the principales, with the understanding that if any of them were chosen as electors, larger payments would be forthcoming so long as they voted as they were asked to vote. Wealthy factions might spend more sizable sums. In the election of 1892 in Balayan, the Martinez family, aware that many cabezas de barangay were being prosecuted for delinquency in tax collection, offered to pay the outstanding debts of any cabeza who agreed to pledge his vote. Another common technique was the use of pressure. In Talisay, Tiburcio Burgos, a faction leader and sometime gobernadorcillo, had a reputation for being vengeful. After one election, he allegedly punished those who had not voted for him by requiring them to perform labor services on festival days, and during the campaign preceding another, he threatened to imprison any principales who refused to pledge themselves to his slate of candidates. In Nasugbu, the administrators of the Roxas estate, who were the leaders of the town's largest faction, often used their economic muscle to intimidate potential voters and political opponents alike. When Pedro Ruffy, a tenant on the Roxas estate and also the town's gobernadorcillo, refused to carry out their wishes, they dispossessed him of his lands; and when some principales, who were also tenants, refused to commit themselves to the candidates favored by the administrators, they subjected them to corporal punishment.

Local politics was, in short, a serious business in late nineteenth-century Batangas, and because it was so serious it offers a glimpse of another fundamental reality of provincial life. These periodic contests for municipal office brought to the surface many of the deep-seated jealousies, antagonisms, and rivalries that divided the leading families of each town, and to a certain extent they made matters worse. The divisive tendencies visible in the local elections were not unique to Batangas or to the Philippines for that matter;

most societies suffer from them in some measure. But they were definitely pronounced in late nineteenth-century Batangas, and in the turn-of-the-century conflicts that lay ahead, they would surface again from time to time, invariably with unfortunate consequences.

★ ★ ★

Here, then, was the province of Batangas, a curious blend of heterogeneity and commonalities. The nineteenth century had brought profound changes thus far—the increase of cash-cropping, the gaining of great fortunes, educational expansion—and others were not far off. Although the Spanish rulers did not realize it at the time, the economic and educational developments that had occurred in Batangas had brought with them potentially destabilizing political consequences. As Batangas entered the 1890s, signs of instability frequently began to appear, and Batangas moved ever closer to revolution.

2

Revolution

NO EVENT in the Philippine past, excluding perhaps the overthrow of Ferdinand Marcos, has been written about as much as
the revolution of 1896, the uprising against Spanish rule that
occurred in the Tagalog-speaking provinces of Luzon. The textbooks used in
Philippine universities often devote a quarter of their length to a discussion
of the events of 1896–97, and virtually every text used in Southeast Asian
history courses in the United States deals with the revolution in considerable detail, typically depicting it as an example of an early "nationalist"
struggle in the region against colonial rule. The subject has attracted the
attention of some of the leading historians of the Philippines, and it has been
the focus of continuing, sometimes acrimonious scholarly debate.[1]

Yet, curiously, in spite of the quantity and manifest quality of the literature that has been produced, our understanding of the revolution may be
flawed in at least one respect. While the scholars who have written about the

events of 1896–97 disagree about many things, one key point of interpretation most seem to agree on is that the Philippine Revolution was, at its core, a mass-based movement. Such a view was stated most baldly and eloquently by the late Teodoro Agoncillo in his celebrated book *The Revolt of the Masses,* published in 1956. According to Agoncillo, the principal impetus behind the revolution of 1896 was the Katipunan, a presumably lower-class secret society led by Andres Bonifacio, and the heroes of that struggle—and, incidentally, of the subsequent one against the United States—were the Filipino masses, who fought bravely and enthusiastically in the face of overwhelming odds. Agoncillo also argued that the Filipino cause was undermined in both conflicts by indigenous elites, who promoted their own self-interest whenever possible and ultimately collaborated with the enemy.[2]

The following chapter calls into question the validity of such a view of the revolution, particularly as it applies to events in Batangas. It suggests, first, that the sources do not prove either that the Katipunan was a genuinely lower-class organization or that it had even spread to Batangas before the outbreak of the rebellion. Second, it demonstrates that, in the years leading up to the revolution, members of Batangas's political elite agitated doggedly against Spanish rule, and that many of the same individuals played leading roles in the actual revolutionary struggle in Batangas. Although large numbers of lower-class Filipinos undeniably participated in the events of 1896–97, it seems fair to say that, in the province of Batangas, the Philippine Revolution was as much a revolt of the elites as of the masses.

★ The Question of the Katipunan

Surviving documentation about the Katipunan, the secret organization that launched the uprising against Spain in the Tagalog provinces in August 1896, is fairly meager—several memoirs by prominent revolutionaries (Pio Valenzuela, Emilio Aguinaldo, Artemio Ricarte, Santiago Alvarez, Carlos Ronquillo, and a few others), a handful of Spanish accounts, various writings by Bonifacio and Emilio Jacinto, and relatively little else. What is more, the small number of sources that have been uncovered are, even on a superficial reading, far from unimpeachably reliable. For example, the memoirs of Aguinaldo, Ricarte, Alvarez, and Ronquillo must be used with caution on matters relating to Bonifacio, since all four memoirists were leading players in the controversial intramural squabbles that culminated in the *supremo*'s execution; and at least one source that Agoncillo relied on in his classic study—the so-called minutes of the Katipunan—has been dismissed by subsequent writers as a forgery.[3] Hence, the evidential foundation upon which scholarship about the Katipunan has rested is, at best, somewhat shaky.

Indeed, a number of the most widely accepted generalizations about the secret society do not stand up to close inspection. Secondary accounts tell us that, at the outbreak of the revolution, the Katipunan had thirty thousand members, most of whom were lower-class Filipinos. Most base their assertions on a single primary source—the memoir of Pio Valenzuela, probably written in 1914.[4] But a scrutiny of the evidence suggests that Valenzuela may not be trustworthy on this point. For one, the estimate of thirty thousand is at variance with another estimate (twenty thousand) Valenzuela made in September 1896.[5] For another, a reading of Valenzuela's discussion of the Katipunan raises further doubts about his credibility. Valenzuela informs us in his memoir that (1) according to Bonifacio, the Katipunan had no more than three hundred members as of January 1, 1896; (2) the membership of the secret society began to increase markedly in mid-March 1896 after the appearance of *Kalayaan,* an eight-page, Tagalog-language periodical edited by Emilio Jacinto; (3) a total of two thousand copies of the first and only issue of *Kalayaan* were printed; (4) toward the end of March 1896, "hundreds of people nightly joined the Katipunan in San Juan del Monte, San Felipe Neri, Pasig, Pateros, Marikina, Caloocan, Malabon, and other places"; and (5) by August 1896, the Katipunan's membership had grown to thirty thousand, with *katipuneros* "distributed among the provinces of Manila, now Rizal province, Cavite, Bulacan, Nueva Ecija, Pampanga, Batangas, and Laguna, and in the city of Manila itself."[6] Does it make sense to accept all the above at face value? How could a single issue of a periodical with such a limited print run convert so many people so quickly? And how could the rapid growth of this secret society—and, above all, the nightly meetings in the suburbs of Manila, where hundreds of new katipuneros were inducted—have taken place without the Spanish authorities immediately becoming aware of the existence of the organization?

In fact, we do not have a reliable estimate of the size of the Katipunan. Valenzuela's figure of thirty thousand is almost certainly inflated. A few other figures exist, but they too are problematical. According to Baldomero Aguinaldo, the Katipunan had fewer than three hundred members in the entire province of Cavite when the Philippine Revolution began.[7] Yet, even if we assume that his statement is dependable, we cannot project an estimate of the entire organization's membership from the data of a single province.

The evidence does not enable us to reach any firm conclusions about the social composition of the Katipunan either. In spite of the repeated claim in the secondary literature that the secret society had a largely lower-class membership, the sources are far from convincing on that point, since they allow us to identify no more than a hundred or so members of the Katipunan, and also since a number of those who can be identified—for example, Emilio Aguinaldo, Mariano Alvarez, and at least a dozen other katipuneros from the province of Cavite—were clearly not representatives of the lower classes.[8] If the documentation about the Katipunan in Cavite tells us anything at all, it is that, on the provincial level, the uprising of 1896 against Spain was largely an elite-generated phenomenon.

The points made thus far about the Philippine Revolution in general apply in equal measure to the Philippine Revolution in Batangas. As sparse as the evidence is concerning occurrences at the revolutionary center, it is plentiful in comparison to the surviving evidence about the revolutionary periphery. Even the most basic questions cannot be answered. Although secondary accounts tell us that Miguel Malvar, the famous Batangueño general, joined the Katipunan before the outbreak of the revolution, not a single primary source confirms that purported fact.[9] Nor do the sources provide us with trustworthy information about the status of the Katipunan in Batangas before August 1896. Both Agoncillo and Gregorio Zaide claim that the society had spread to the province prior to the uprising against Spain, but both base their claims on the memoir of Pio Valenzuela, citing precisely the passages I have questioned.[10] Juanito Marquez, a local historian, relying on information derived from interviews, maintains that a Katipunan chapter was founded in the town of Lipa as early as December 1894. Unfortunately, though, Marquez's interviewees were neither former katipuneros nor even contemporaries or relatives of alleged katipuneros, but rather other local historians, and one may justifiably wonder whether their statements can be credited.[11] All in all, therefore, there is insufficient evidence to substantiate the assertion that the Katipunan had penetrated into Batangas before August 1896.

The lack of knowledge about the Katipunan in Batangas is a serious deficiency. Not only does it create an unsightly gap in the narrative; it also raises a troubling question or two about the thesis of this chapter—namely, that the individuals responsible for creating a revolutionary climate in Batangas were local influentials, rather than members of the lower classes. True, there is no firm proof that the Katipunan had spread to the province before August 1896, but, by the same token, it also cannot be proved that it had not. If the Katipunan did contribute to the ferment taking place in

Batangas on the eve of the revolution, the nature and extent of that contribution simply cannot be determined from the sources.[12]

★ The Revolution in Batangas: The Historical Context

Despite the paucity and occasional unreliability of the sources, it is possible to discern the broad outlines of the revolution's course in Batangas. There are gaps in the chronology, and from time to time, important questions must remain unanswered, but in light of the evidential problems, such inadequacies cannot be avoided.

Whether or not a chapter of the Katipunan existed in Batangas before August 1896, there was a good deal of political agitation in the province, especially by members of the local political elite. In the town of Taal, for instance, a faction led by Felipe Agoncillo, Nicolas Encarnacion, Martin Cabrera, Ramon and Teofilo Atienza, Ananias Diocno, and several other men had, since the early 1880s, repeatedly challenged the decision making and authority of the Spanish rulers. The first recorded manifestation of these disputatious tendencies occurred in 1882, at a time when cholera was racing through the Philippines. In an effort to control the spread of the disease, the Spanish priest and the government physician in Taal had ordered that all the ailing inhabitants of the town be concentrated in the barrio of Caysasay. That order appeared to anger a number of local influentials, among them Encarnacion and Flaviano Agoncillo, who claimed that the facilities in Caysasay were inadequate to accommodate so many and then proceeded to resist the order. Several of these men were arrested for their actions but soon were set free, thanks to the legal skills of Flaviano's younger brother Felipe.[13]

Other incidents followed, all of them placing one or more of Taal's leading families at odds with agents of Spanish rule. As the challenges became more frequent, it began to dawn on the Spaniards residing in the province and their Filipino allies that a political faction led by Felipe Agoncillo and his friends was organizing and coordinating them. These men met secretly, sponsored candidates for municipal office in local elections, and directed a campaign designed to undermine the position of the Spanish friars in the Philippines. The anti-Spanish faction in Taal grew steadily in size and influence; in election after election, its candidates outpolled the candidates favored by the Spanish priest.[14]

Similar developments were occurring in Tanauan, where a powerful anti-Spanish faction was led by Ruperto Laurel, the town's gobernadorcillo from 1887 to 1889, Eusebio Gonzales, who held the same office immediately before

8. *Nicolas Gonzales, c. 1901*

Laurel, and Eusebio's son, Nicolas, the gobernadorcillo from 1890 to 1892. The younger Gonzales, a recent graduate of the University of Santo Tomas, was, according to the local priest, "an intimate friend of men who hold seditious and separatist ideas." Laurel, on his part, staunchly opposed the Catholic religious orders and used his public forum to broadcast his beliefs.[15]

The principal display of discontent in Tanauan took place in 1888. In March of that year, an antifriar demonstration was held in Manila, during which a delegation of gobernadorcillos marched solemnly through the streets to the office of the governor-general and presented a petition calling for the removal of the religious orders. The petitioners, echoing statements that Marcelo H. del Pilar had made earlier in the decade in a campaign against the friars in Bulacan, asserted that the regulars were "ambitious, despotic and ungrateful men" who "only inspire aversion in the sons of the Philippines" and warned that, if the government did not remove them, the people were likely to do so.[16] The town's political elite was enthusiastic about such arguments. Anastasio Castillo, a leading figure in the Laurel-Gonzales faction, drew up a petition manifesting Tanauan's support for the demonstration in Manila, and Laurel, the gobernadorcillo at the time, circulated it and convinced a large number of people to sign it. In the eyes of both the local priest and an officer of the Guardia Civil, the antireligious and separatist tendencies of these men posed a real danger to Spanish rule. Laurel, the priest asserted, was "one of the worst enemies of Spain in these islands."[17]

Perhaps the most openly defiant political faction in the province was in Santo Tomas, just north of Tanauan, where the leading figure was Miguel Malvar. The son of Maximo Malvar and Tiburcia Carpio, Miguel Malvar was born in Santo Tomas in 1865. The elder Malvar had made his money in logging operations on Mount Maquiling, the peak that straddles the border between southern Laguna and northeastern Batangas, and had invested wisely, acquiring tracts of rice and sugar land. Maximo Malvar's improving fortunes enabled him to provide his offspring with a proper education. His two oldest boys, Miguel and Potenciano, both attended the Malabanan school in Tanauan,* reputedly the best secondary institution in Batangas, and Potenciano, who was the better student, went on to San Juan de Letran, the University of Santo Tomas, and finally to a Spanish university, where he earned a medical degree. Miguel spent two years at the Malabanan school, one more at another local educational institution, and then matriculated to the world of work. He married well, engaged in commerce for a while, and

*The Malabanan school moved to the town of Bauan in the 1882–83 school year.

with his earnings purchased land on the slopes of Mount Maquiling, where he planted oranges. The orange business prospered, he grew richer, and, like many other well-to-do men in the province, he began to take an interest in local politics.[18]

Miguel Malvar first ran for the office of gobernadorcillo in 1889, heading the slate of the town's antifriar faction, which at the time was led by his father, Maximo, and his father-in-law, Ambrosio Maloles, who was also the incumbent gobernadorcillo. The balloting was close, Malvar winning second place with eight votes, two fewer than Mariano Hernandez, the candidate of the local priest and the man who was eventually appointed to the post. Shortly after the election, the priest, an Augustinian Recollect named Fr. Félix Garcés, had occasion to write to the provincial governor about the young Malvar, and the tenor of his comments made it clear that he considered the man a threat. "Miguel Malvar," he opined, "has manifested unhealthy ambitions [for political office] and . . . is intimately acquainted with people who have little affection for Spain and are subversive." The priest's reservations notwithstanding, Malvar won the election for gobernadorcillo in 1890.[19]

The rivalry between Miguel Malvar and Fr. Garcés became intense and downright nasty in the next municipal contest, which was held in April 1892. The principal contenders for the post of gobernadorcillo—and, as it would turn out, the two top vote-getters on election day—were Julio Meer, the priest's designated candidate, and Leodegario Meer, no relation to Julio, who was sponsored by Malvar. Neither candidate had strong qualifications for office. Though moderately wealthy, Julio Meer was poorly educated, and, according to various townspeople, Fr. Garcés's sponsorship of the man had its origins in the simple fact that Julio Meer's daughter was his mistress. The priest, they claimed, was attempting to win the favor of his sweetheart's father by promoting Don Julio's candidacy in the municipal election. Leodegario Meer, on his part, was completely unqualified—unemployed, uneducated, addicted to gambling, lacking in prestige. In the aftermath of the election, the priest charged that Don Leodegario was nothing more than a "creature" of Miguel Malvar, and that Malvar had publicly boasted of that fact.[20]

Almost a hundred years after the events, it is difficult, if not impossible, to determine how many illegalities were committed by the contending factions in the Santo Tomas elections of 1892, but certainly there were many. Malvar and his supporters alleged that the priest and Julio Meer had bribed the provincial governor with five hundred pesos to influence the result of the

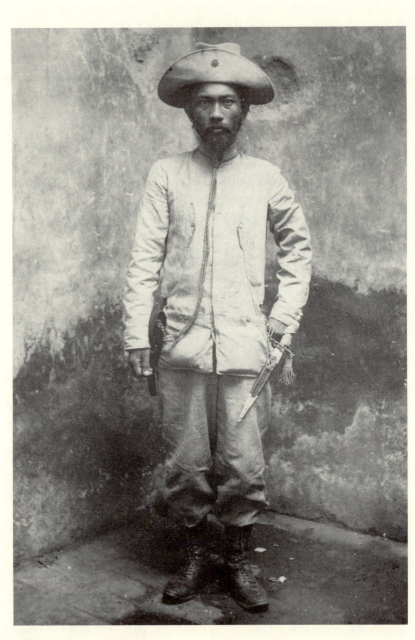

9. Miguel Malvar, c. 1902

voting; that on the day before the election Julio Meer had held a banquet, attended by the priest and the town's principales, at which both Don Julio and Fr. Garcés had appealed to the potential voters for their support; that on election day, the *sorteo*—the selection by lot of the twelve principales who would be permitted to vote—was rigged, with the result that three of the electors were close relatives of Julio Meer, one was a distant cousin, and two were friends; and finally, that when the ballots were totaled, Julio Meer was credited with one more vote than had actually been cast for him. The priest and his followers made allegations of their own. The charges and counter-charges came to the attention of the central authorities, who conducted an investigation and concluded that, all in all, the proceedings had been irregular indeed. Their solution was to annul the results and call for new elections.[21]

But the conflict between Malvar and the priest did not end there. In June 1892 new elections were held in Santo Tomas, and, if the letters of protest, petitions, and counterpetitions signed in their aftermath are to be believed, these were marked by as many illegalities as the first. Ultimately, in spite of the central authorities' belief that the candidates in the second terna were even less qualified than those in the first and the demand by a number of principales that the second elections be annulled as well, the governor-general decided to appoint as gobernadorcillo the man who had received the highest number of votes in the balloting. The winner was Maximo Malvar, the father of Miguel.[22]

The struggles in Santo Tomas, Tanauan, Taal, and several other towns in the province were signs of an emerging trend. About the same time, in various places, a number of Filipinos, most of them members of the indigenous economic and political elites, were airing their dissatisfaction with Spanish rule. This dissatisfaction was stated most directly, articulately, and insistently by Jose Rizal and other members of the Propaganda Movement, who lobbied in the mother country for reforms. But the Propagandists were only one component of a much larger, uncoordinated, and programmatically diverse upsurge of protest against Spanish rule, and the major centers of dissatisfaction were not in the Spanish cities where the Propagandists temporarily resided but in the provincial Philippines.

Compared to the activities of the Propagandists, who operated in the more open political atmosphere of the mother country, the protests in the provincial Philippines were muted and indirect. Rarely did the dissenters openly demand reform, since they knew that overt challenges to the rulers might result in their imprisonment. More often, they stated their objections in secret gatherings or, if they went public, gave their protests a symbolic form.

The principal forum of symbolic protest was the municipal election. Malvar and his faction in Santo Tomas wanted to defeat Fr. Garcés and his followers not only because electoral success would bring concrete economic benefits, and not only because it would enable them to harm their opponents and restrict their opponents' ability to harass them. They also wanted to win because, in a real sense, the municipal election was a test of power. It was an opportunity for men like Miguel Malvar—men from families that had prospered in the favorable economic climate of the nineteenth-century Philippines; men who had been sent by their families to secondary school and even to university; and men who, thanks to their economic success, the level of education they had achieved, the ideas they had been exposed to, and their experience with local administration, were convinced of their capacity to govern and deeply resented not being free to direct municipal affairs without clerical interference—to demonstrate publicly and graphically that they, not the Spanish friars, were in charge. In other words, the growing economic power and concomitant educational attainments of a privileged segment of provincial society had created political expectations that could not be realized within the context of Spanish colonialism, and the frustration of those expectations had resulted in ferment. For men like Miguel Malvar, victory in the municipal election represented at once a validation of their claim to govern and a symbolic demonstration of their discontent.

The long-term political objectives of the antifriar factions in Batangas may even have gone a step beyond the reformism espoused by the Propaganda Movement. Recall that in 1889 Fr. Garcés had described his rival, Miguel Malvar, as "intimately acquainted with people who have little affection for Spain and are subversive," and that similar charges were made about other political influentials in Batangas.[23] The accusers seemed to be suggesting that, as early as the late 1880s, members of Batangas's political elite may have been infected with the virus of separatism.

Can such accusations be believed or were they the biased judgments of interested parties? The priests and other individuals who made the charges *were* biased; they were the political enemies of the men they accused, and they were aware that their charges would have a potentially damaging effect on their opponents' political fortunes. In addition, there is little hard-and-fast evidence from other sources to confirm their accusations, for in the repressive political climate of the late nineteenth-century Philippines, individuals who held separatist notions were hardly disposed to broadcast their beliefs. Hence, we should be skeptical of the statements of Fr. Garcés and the others—fully as skeptical as we might be about Pio Valenzuela's claims concerning the Katipunan. On the other hand, the questionable nature of the accusations and the lack of independent corroborating evidence should not automatically lead us to dismiss the charges as unfounded; however biased an accuser may be, he or she may be telling the truth. The only conclusion we can reasonably draw from the surviving documentation is that there is a possibility—perhaps only a remote one—that the agenda of some of Batangas's political activists of the 1880s and early 1890s may have been separatist and even protorevolutionary, and not merely reformist.

Regardless of the truth of the charges, by the early 1890s relations between the Spanish rulers and Batangas's political influentials had become strained. In 1894, when handbills accusing a parish priest of immorality were discovered in Lipa, the provincial governor ordered the detention of two of that town's intellectuals, Gregorio Catigbac and Cipriano Calao, both graduates of the University of Santo Tomas. Catigbac managed to avoid detention; Calao was arrested and roughed up by the Guardia Civil before being released. About a year later, the long-standing conflict between the anticlerical/anti-Spanish faction in Taal and the local representatives of the Church and Crown came to a head. In July and August 1895, several residents of Taal and San Luis, all of whom were intimately associated with the parish priest of Taal, charged that Felipe Agoncillo and about a dozen other active politicos were spreading anti-Spanish and antireligious propaganda, publicly insulting members of the church hierarchy, and secretly sponsoring a subscription for the purpose of liberating Jose Rizal, who had been deported to Dapitan on Mindanao several years earlier. The accusers contended that these activists intended to set Rizal up as the leader of a movement to expel the Spaniards from the Philippines. The accusations led to an inquiry, which brought forth even more accusations; and finally, in February 1896, the governor-general reached his verdict. On the recommendation of the provincial authorities, he ordered the deportation to Mindanao of six key figures in Taal's anticlerical faction and the replacement of all of Taal's municipal officials by "loyal" residents of the town.[24] On the eve of the Philippine Revolution, then, the Spanish rulers had concluded that repressive measures were necessary to cope with Batangas's refractory political elite. Batangas may have lacked a chapter of the Katipunan, but not a climate of revolution.

★ The Revolution Comes to Batangas:
First and Second Phases

On August 19, 1896, the Spanish government in Manila learned of the existence of the Katipunan and immediately ordered the arrest of suspected dissidents. Aware of these developments, Bonifacio and his followers fled to a suburb of Manila, where they decided to launch a full-scale rebellion. Fighting erupted on August 30 at San Juan del Monte, just outside the capital, and from the outset Bonifacio's troops were mauled. In nearby Cavite province, revolutionary forces under Emilio Aguinaldo and several other leading katipuneros inflicted serious losses on the Spaniards and managed by mid-September to gain control of most towns in Cavite.[25]

Toward the end of September 1896, two armed groups of revolutionaries from Cavite—a force of several hundred men from western Cavite and a much larger aggregation from eastern Cavite led by Emilio Aguinaldo—invaded Batangas with the objective of spreading the revolution to the neighboring province. In effect, they were attempting to export their revolution. An effort by the first group to take Tuy and Lian was unsuccessful, but a few days later the units under Aguinaldo occupied the town of Talisay on the northern shore of Lake Taal.[26] So began the first phase of the revolution in Batangas—a seven-week period of intense military activity concentrated in the northern and western parts of the province. It included six more battles of consequence (two near Lemery and the others in Balayan, Nasugbu, Lian, and once again, Talisay) and brought about heavy Filipino casualties, extensive destruction of property, and a major atrocity on the part of the Spanish troops at Nasugbu, where hundreds of noncombatants were killed.[27]

The fighting between late September and mid-November caused not only considerable loss of life but also massive migration. As town after town in western and northern Batangas suffered major destruction, people abandoned them in search of safety, shelter, and sustenance. By late November 1896, Talisay, Lian, and several other communities had only a small fraction of their normal populations. Many of the missing fled to Cavite; others, to outlying areas within the province of Batangas itself.[28] In time, the population movement set in train by these battles would have devastating consequences.

From the outset of the fighting, the beleaguered populace of Batangas rallied to the revolutionary cause. Midway through the first battle at Talisay, a thousand Batangueños presented themselves to offer assistance to Aguinaldo; and after the massacre at Nasugbu, many of the town's residents

10. Emilio Aguinaldo, 1901

volunteered to serve with another group of Caviteños. In mid-October 1896, at Lian, as a force from western Cavite commanded by Santiago Alvarez besieged a Spanish detachment, many of the town's prominent men marched out to Alvarez's headquarters in the field to pay their respects. Later in the month, moreover, sizable military units composed entirely of Batangueños began to conduct operations in the vicinity of Lemery and Taal.[29]

The Batangueños who took the lead in supporting the revolution were members of the province's political elite. One of the first was Miguel Malvar, the leader of Santo Tomas's antifriar faction, who took part in the fighting in Talisay. According to Malvar's own account of his activities, he decided to join the struggle because of his earlier conflicts with the parish priest of Santo Tomas and the Spanish authorities.[30] Others who played prominent roles in the initial phases of the revolution were Arcadio Laurel, a member of Talisay's political elite, Pedro Ruffy, the onetime gobernadorcillo of Nasugbu, Santiago Rillo de Leon, formerly the gobernadorcillo and currently the justice of the peace of Tuy, and Ananias Diocno, an important figure in the antifriar faction of Taal.[31] The activity in Batangas mirrored that in Cavite in earlier years: the traditional political influentials—the elite *provincianos* who normally dominated political life in their communities—were among the first to commit themselves to the cause.

And they were not only committing themselves to the revolution, but also taking command of the armies being formed in Batangas. Their emergence as the province's military leaders can be readily understood. Men of social standing, they already commanded respect; men of landed wealth, most of them had tenants and retainers whom they could mobilize to serve in the ranks. Miguel Malvar, for example, claimed that in late 1896 he organized a force of seventy-five men, equipped with twenty-three firearms, to fight against the Spaniards, and other commanders were able to do the same.[32] Furthermore, the former gobernadorcillos who joined the revolution—men like Malvar and Santiago Rillo—had a modicum of experience in leading men in combat, a rare attribute in Philippine society. As heads of their municipalities, they supervised the *cuadrilleros,* the rural guards who were charged with keeping the peace and conducting operations against the many bandits who roamed the countryside. Gobernadorcillos were expected to, and frequently did, lead the cuadrilleros in expeditions against the bandits, although, as we shall see, their efforts were sometimes halfhearted.[33] Obviously, forays in the hills against bandits were not the same thing as battles against trained armies, and in time the deficiencies of these men as military commanders would become manifest, but, at the beginning of the conflict, these town leaders must have seemed uniquely well qualified for their military positions.

Lower-class Batangueños took part in the revolution as well. Thousands of them served as foot soldiers in the military units led by the province's political elite, and many more supplied rice and other edibles to the troops, dug trenches, ran errands, and assisted in other ways. They participated for a variety of reasons. Some *veteranos*—Jose Caubalejo of Calatagan, for example—claimed that they joined the revolutionary ranks primarily because of their dissatisfaction with Spanish rule, citing the abuses of the parish priests and unfair treatment they had received from Spanish officials. Others enlisted because they believed—naively, as it turned out—that military life would be glamorous.[34]

Some may have been drawn into the ranks for quite different reasons. In his influential book *Pasyon and Revolution,* Reynaldo Ileto has demonstrated, through an analysis of manifestoes, poems, and other texts of the revolutionary period, that Andres Bonifacio and other leaders of the anti-Spanish struggle employed language and symbols that had distinctive and extremely evocative shades of meaning to the Tagalog lower classes. A case in point is the word *kalayaan,* which is generally translated in English as "independence." Yet, as Ileto points out, such a translation, which evokes the notion of political autonomy, hardly does justice to the word. To a late nineteenth-century Tagalog audience, kalayaan meant a condition of bliss, equality, brotherhood, and justice. Thus, when Bonifacio and other leaders of the revolution appealed to the Filipino people to join their ranks and to fight for kalayaan, the Tagalog peasantry might have interpreted that appeal as a call for a veritable social as well as a political revolution. If Ileto is correct, the participation of lower-class Batangueños in the revolution was due, at least in part, to their perception that they were struggling for a change in the nature of society.[35]

But, not all Batangueños who fought in the revolution necessarily did so willingly; many were induced or compelled to do so, usually by upper-class patrons. Emilio Vergara, a poor teenager from a barrio of Lipa, entered the revolutionary army by this route. Shortly after the fighting had begun in Batangas, Julian Recinto—an officer in the Filipino Army and the eldest son of Claro Recinto, the landlord of Vergara's father—summoned young Emilio and ordered him to enlist. "I was drafted," Vergara told me. "They lacked soldiers, so they made me go with them."[36] Here, then, patron-client ties were being invoked in order to fill the ranks of the local forces. Vergara made clear that he was a most reluctant soldier: he fought not because he wanted to free the Philippines from alien rule but because his *"pangulo"* (leader) obliged him to fight. Vergara's route to military service was not uncommon. Calixto Silva, another peasant from a barrio of Lipa, was drafted, and tenants in Calatagan were induced to serve by a local influential. Some of the seventy-five men whom Malvar mobilized in late 1896 to fight for the revolution may also have been pressured into service.[37]

This conflicting evidence on motives underlines a basic truth. In spite of what Agoncillo and other scholars tell us, the Filipino lower classes, as heterogeneous as they were, were not uniformly enthusiastic supporters of the struggle against Spain. Filipino behavior varied from town to town, barrio to barrio, and house to house; and, what is more, Filipinos had a variety of reasons for behaving as they did. For every Jose Caubalejo who was a strong supporter of the revolution, there may well have been one Emilio Vergara who was not.

Some Batangueños, lower and upper class alike, did not support the revolution at all. By late October 1896, the Spanish authorities had managed to recruit hundreds of *voluntarios* from various towns in Batangas who would subsequently assist them with their pacification efforts.[38] There were reports that certain unnamed "traitors" from the towns of Lian and Balayan had attempted to sabotage the revolutionaries' military operations in Batangas.[39] Finally, throughout the period October 1896–December 1897, a number of local officials continued to cooperate with the Spanish authorities. One who did so was Nicolas Gonzales, the capitán municipal of Tanauan, who might have been expected to act otherwise in light of his long involvement with the antifriar faction of his native town. Another was Florentino de Jesus, the capitán municipal of Batangas City, who kept the Spanish troops well supplied with carabaos, horses, chickens, rice, eggs, and just about everything else they requested.[40] Why these individuals acted as they did is unknown: possibly some of them were subjected to pressure. In any case, however popular the revolution was in the province of Batangas, it did not enjoy universal support.

In this first phase of the revolution the battlefield performance of the Filipino forces in Batangas was anything but impressive. Except for the first encounter at Talisay, they lost every major battle. The relative inexperience of the troops contributed to that result, as did the fact that they suffered from a severe shortage of weapons, since they were forced to rely largely on the arms that they managed to capture from the Spaniards.[41] And so did the deficiencies of the Filipino commanders. As it happened, a large number of them—not only Batangueños like Malvar and Rillo, but also Emilio Aguinaldo and other military leaders from Cavite—were former gobernadorcillos, whose principal military experience before the revolution was in leading expeditions against bandits in the hills. True, Aguinaldo and other leaders from Cavite had scored some victories against Spanish arms in their native province, but almost all these successes were achieved in small-scale operations against seriously undermanned Spanish garrisons. Only Aguinaldo had performed creditably against large enemy forces, and even he was not always successful.[42]

In the early battles that occurred in Batangas, several of the Filipino commanders made catastrophic blunders. At Lian, the Filipino forces under Santiago Alvarez were mauled primarily because Col. Juan Cailles, assigned the task of guarding a road leading to the town, failed to do his job, enabling the Spanish troops to enter Lian unmolested and to attack Alvarez's men from the rear. At Nasugbu, another colonel, Luciano San Miguel, led his men into a trap and only a handful escaped. In the second battle at Talisay, which took place on November 12, 1896, the Batangueño commander, Arcadio Laurel, was surprised by an envelopment executed by the Spanish forces and his troops suffered heavy casualties as a result.[43] Performances like these suggested that a background in bandit-chasing was not sufficient preparation for the command of large armies.

The surge of military activity that characterized the first phase of the Philippine Revolution in Batangas was followed by three months of comparative inactivity. By mid-November 1896, it was obvious that, for the moment, the Spanish Army in the Philippines was not up to the job of regaining control of the southern Tagalog region. In the next month, the government in Madrid appointed a new governor for the Philippines, Camilo Polavieja, who soon announced that he would concentrate initially on subduing the revolutionaries in the provinces north of Manila, leaving for last the pacification of Cavite and Batangas to the south.[44] Meanwhile, the Filipino forces in Batangas were in no position to mount a major offensive. Miguel Malvar, for one, had gone into hiding on the slopes of Mount Maquiling and was attempting to reorganize his troops. Other commands were short of men because soldiers had to return to their communities to harvest the rice.[45]

This is not to say that peace prevailed in Batangas during the second phase of the revolution. On December 12, Filipino troops launched one attack near Calatagan and a second near Lemery; and, later in the month, there were encounters in the vicinity of Nasugbu, San Juan, Balayan, and once again, Calatagan. But, compared with the battles of the September–November period, these were small-scale actions, and, with the exception of the fight at Nasugbu, the casualties were minimal.[46]

★ The Third Phase

The lull ended, and the Philippine Revolution entered a new phase, in February 1897. This third phase, lasting until the end of May, was marked by two turning points: on the military front, the virtual destruction of the Filipino Army as a conventional fighting force in both Cavite and Batangas; and the resolution of a power struggle within the revolutionary ranks that saw the elevation of Aguinaldo to the presidency of the revolutionary government and the execution of the onetime supremo of the Katipunan, Andres Bonifacio.

On February 8, 1897, having pacified the provinces north of Manila to his satisfaction, Governor Polavieja informed the Ministry of War that he would shortly turn his attention to Cavite and the rest of the southern Tagalog region. His plan for the new campaign called for a multipronged attack on Cavite. One brigade under Brig. Gen. Francisco Galbis was to operate in northern Cavite, engaging the Filipinos first at the Zapote Bridge and then moving on to Bacoor. Meanwhile, the main attack force, consisting of three brigades under Maj. Gen. José Lachambre, was to converge on Cavite from the east and the south; two of them would enter Cavite from Laguna and attempt to retake the town of Silang, and the third, under Brig. Gen. Nicolás Jaramillo, was initially to patrol the northern shore of Lake Taal in order to impede the revolutionaries in northern Batangas from coming to the assistance of the Caviteños.[47]

On February 15, Galbis and Lachambre began to advance, and within a few days, their advance had turned into a rout. Unprepared for a Spanish thrust at Silang and hampered by a lack of cooperation between the Magdiwang council of the Katipunan led by Mariano Alvarez and the Magdalo council led by Emilio and Baldomero Aguinaldo, the Filipino forces in Cavite, which included a sizable contingent of Batangueños, were battered time and again. By early May, every town in the province had fallen into Spanish hands, and most of Cavite's surviving military leaders had fled.[48] Within the borders of Batangas itself, the revolutionaries suffered equally devastating reverses, culminating, at the end of May, in Jaramillo's defeat of a large Batangueño force under Miguel Malvar at Talisay. Thereafter, the Filipino military units in Batangas, like those in Cavite, would no longer have the

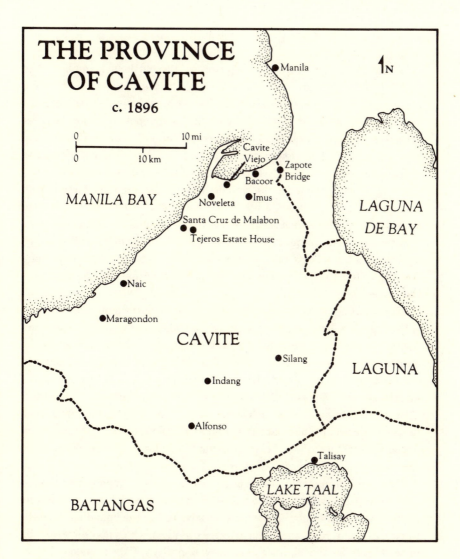

MANILA BAY

THE PROVINCE
OF CAVITE
c. 1896

0 ——— 10 mi
0 ——— 10 km

●Manila

↑N

Cavite
Viejo
Zapote
Bridge
Bacoor
●Imus
Noveleta
Santa Cruz de Malabon
Tejeros Estate House

LAGUNA
DE BAY

●Naic

●Maragondon

CAVITE

●Silang

LAGUNA

●Indang

●Alfonso

●Talisay

LAKE TAAL

BATANGAS

2. *The Province of Cavite, c. 1896*

capability of conducting a conventional military campaign against the Spaniards.[49]

While these events were transpiring on the battlefield, conflict arose within the revolutionary leadership. Historians have, of course, written and argued a good deal about these events. Some see the emerging struggle as a manifestation of class conflict, pitting Bonifacio, the spokesman for the lower classes, against upper-class Caviteños led by Emilio Aguinaldo. Others suggest that it should be viewed primarily as a factional rivalry between two branches of the Katipunan. Still others tell us that Andres Bonifacio himself was largely responsible for the trouble, having alienated his onetime supporters by making a series of unpopular decisions.[50] Although it is beyond the scope of this book to attempt to resolve the ongoing debate about events that took place in the province of Cavite, I do want to underline a simple, important point: however one interprets the conflict between Aguinaldo and Bonifacio, its outcome was determined in no small part by the actions of Batangueños.

The prominent role Batangueños played is not surprising, given the size of Batangas's military columns. Throughout Polavieja's advance, large numbers of troops from the populous province to the south took part in the military operations in Cavite. Miguel Malvar led a force of Batangueños in the fighting near the Zapote Bridge in February 1897, and by the end of March, several thousand Batangueño soldiers were present in Cavite.[51] Clearly, the commanders of such forces were bound to be men of influence in the revolutionary councils, and the groups vying for control of the revolutionary government were bound to realize that their chances of success depended on gaining the adherence of those men.

The two Batangueños who commanded the largest number of troops—and who consequently mattered most—were Malvar and Santiago Rillo, and of the two, the latter played the more decisive role in the unfolding events in Cavite. Actually, Rillo was a transplanted Caviteño, which may have contributed to his influence. Both his parents were natives of Maragondon, Cavite, and he had spent his childhood and part of his adult life in that town. Rillo then had married into a wealthy family from Batangas, and in 1884, at the age of twenty-six, he had relocated to the town of Tuy. Urbane, well educated, fluent in Spanish, and financially successful, Rillo soon entered local politics and in 1890 was elected gobernadorcillo of Tuy. At the outbreak of the Philippine Revolution, Rillo was serving as Tuy's justice of the peace, and in the subsequent period of warfare, he emerged as the leader of a sizable armed force, possibly numbering in the thousands. So here was an individual to be taken seriously—a seasoned politician, the leader of an army, and a man with strong Cavite connections.[52]

In late March 1897, revolutionary leaders convened at Tejeros, a friar estate house near the town of Santa Cruz de Malabon, to discuss how to cope with the rapidly deteriorating military situation.[53] Representatives of both the Magdiwang and Magdalo factions attended, as did a delegation from Batangas led by Rillo. Various accounts of the meeting have survived, and they disagree about many points of detail. Even so, one matter that most of them agree on is that Rillo and his delegation from Batangas had a decisive impact on the course of the Tejeros assembly.

For one, there is evidence that it was Rillo—not, as much of the secondary literature asserts, the Caviteño Severino de las Alas—who broached the idea of using the occasion to reorganize the revolutionary government. Rillo's stated motive for suggesting the reorganization was to unify the feuding regional factions "so that . . . they may become one in operations, in administration, and in any actions and decisions concerning our defense." Through unification, Rillo hoped, the Filipinos' performance on the battlefield might improve.[54] The sources also indicate that, once the assembly decided to adopt that course, over the strong objections of Mariano Alvarez and other followers of Andres Bonifacio, the delegates from Batangas supported the decision. When Bonifacio subsequently attempted to nullify the elections, which had resulted in Aguinaldo's elevation to the presidency of the revolutionary government, the Batangueño delegation adamantly insisted that the results be upheld. "Everyone knows," they declared, "our loyalty to the founder of the Katipunan and Magdiwang; but if, against all reason, the result of an election so thoroughly agreed upon among all is to be invalidated, we, the Batangueños, will impose it by force, and we will do it alone if the sons of Cavite will not respect it."[55] To underline the point, when Aguinaldo arrived at the meeting to take his oath of office, Rillo greeted him warmly and pledged his support.[56]

The clear implication of all this evidence is that the outcome of the Tejeros assembly, one of the most written-about events in Philippine history, was largely decided by the actions of Santiago Rillo and his fellow Batangueños. Rillo had thrown his influence behind the idea of unification and by doing so had helped bring about the election of Emilio Aguinaldo to the presidency. And having produced that result, he and the other Batangueño delegates were determined to stand behind it. At Tejeros, Santiago Rillo had, for all intents and purposes, committed himself to Aguinaldo and against Bonifacio.

Malvar, however, had not. Miguel Malvar had actually begun his career as a revolutionary under the command of Emilio Aguinaldo. He first joined the fighting at Talisay, the town in northern Batangas that had been briefly liberated by Aguinaldo's men in October 1896, and he had served under Aguinaldo again during the battle for Zapote Bridge in February 1897. After the last battle, he and his men had withdrawn to Indang, in the southern part of Cavite, and he was still encamped there at the time of the Tejeros meeting.[57]

In the weeks following the Tejeros assembly, Malvar tried to remain on good terms with both Bonifacio and Aguinaldo. While we cannot be certain about why he adopted that course, the sources provide a few suggestive clues. On March 24, 1897, only two days after Aguinaldo had been chosen as president of the revolutionary government, a correspondent identified only as Pepe reported to Aguinaldo that Bonifacio had arrived at Limbon, a barrio of Indang.[58] Pepe did not know why the former supremo had come to Indang or how long he planned to remain, but it seems likely that his major reason for being there was to win the adherence of Miguel Malvar, who had not yet committed himself to honoring the results of the Tejeros meeting. Having been rejected and deposed at Tejeros, Bonifacio was searching desperately for support.

But what did Malvar have to gain from supporting Bonifacio? A possible answer may be found in one of Bonifacio's letters. On April 16, Bonifacio informed Emilio Jacinto that Batangas had recently established a provincial government which recognized his authority, and that the Batangueños, under their military leader Miguel Malvar, were planning a simultaneous attack on eight towns. The supremo also reported that, in order to assist the Batangueños in their undertaking, he had given them twenty riflemen and twenty bolomen under the command of Artemio Ricarte.[59] Apparently, Bonifacio and Malvar had worked out an arrangement: Malvar had consented to acknowledge Bonifacio's authority, and, in exchange, Bonifacio had agreed to provide military assistance to Malvar, who was short of weapons and ammunition.[60]

At the same time, though, Malvar wanted to avoid alienating Aguinaldo. If Bonifacio could provide him with weapons, Aguinaldo had access to something just as valuable—rice, which was badly needed to feed the troops in the projected operations in Batangas. Thus, while he pledged his loyalty to Bonifacio, Malvar continued to report and direct requests to Aguinaldo. On April 13, he appealed to Aguinaldo and other leaders in Cavite for rice; four days later, he informed Aguinaldo of his plan to lead two thousand men in operations in western Batangas; and, three days after that, he renewed his appeals to Aguinaldo for rice. Intent on fighting the Spaniards, Malvar was forging alliances with anyone who was in a position to provide him with the supplies and equipment he required.[61]

As it turned out, Malvar's flirtation with Bonifacio did not last long. The reinforcements that Bonifacio had pledged never materialized. Ricarte and his troops left Bonifacio's headquarters on April 19 or thereabouts, ostensibly to link up with Malvar's forces, but, inexplicably, Ricarte went into hiding in southern Cavite.[62] Deprived of the promised help, Malvar launched his offensive anyway, but now he found himself fully dependent on Aguinaldo for assistance. Throughout late April and early May 1897, as he fought a series of battles against the Spaniards in Batangas, he and his subordinates communicated with growing frequency with Aguinaldo, requesting rice and other supplies and receiving much of what they asked for. Such assistance notwithstanding, the campaign ended badly, with Malvar being thrashed by Jaramillo at Talisay at the end of May 1897.[63]

The failure of Bonifacio's troops to aid Malvar was not the only reason for the end of the Malvar-Bonifacio liaison. Aguinaldo also contributed to that result. Determined to retain control over the revolutionary government, Aguinaldo decided to isolate his rival. On April 24, he warned the regional government of Batangas that the results of the Tejeros meeting were to be respected:

> I wish to impress upon your minds the fact that the Government . . . must be supported by everyone, and that if you give it your assistance you will deserve not only the thanks of the whole country but mine as well; but, on the other hand, if you should fail to give me the assistance which I request of you my regret will be great, for I shall consider your indifference to matters affecting our country as a sign of a lack of patriotism, which the Nation should punish with utmost severity and without delay.[64]

Two days later, he ordered Bonifacio's arrest and set in motion the legal proceedings that led to the supremo's execution. Now aware of Aguinaldo's determination to prevail, Malvar made no effort to intervene in Bonifacio's behalf.[65]

By the end of May 1897, as the third phase of the revolution came to a close, several matters had been resolved. The Bonifacio-Aguinaldo conflict was now over, and Aguinaldo was in undisputed control of the revolutionary government. Aguinaldo's triumph was significant on at least two counts. First, it reflected a recognition by many leaders that, because of the ongoing military crisis, more effective leadership was needed. At the same time, it removed from the scene a man, Bonifacio, whose revolutionary message appealed to the Filipino lower classes. Under the leadership of Aguinaldo, the upper-class Caviteño, the anticolonial struggle was to become one for political autonomy, but not for kalayaan. To the occupants of the lower rungs, a war under Aguinaldo's banner might, understandably, seem less attractive.

Yet, if Aguinaldo had prevailed in the councils of the state, he had not on the battlefield. The Filipino Army in Cavite and Batangas had been shattered. Aguinaldo himself was on the run, making his way by slow stages to his eventual refuge in Biak-na-bato, Bulacan. Malvar and other commanders remained in the southern Tagalog region, but after the resounding defeat they suffered at Talisay on May 31, they had retired to the hills.

★ Morbidity, Mortality, and Malnutrition

The losses that Batangas's military units were absorbing in the field were only a tiny fraction of the price that the province was paying for its support of the revolution. By June 1897, due in some measure to the military developments discussed above, certain towns in Batangas were experiencing a severe mortality crisis—the first of a series of such crises that the province would be subjected to over the next half-decade.

The high mortality levels were initially limited to the western part of Batangas, the scene of the heaviest fighting and the most extensive physical destruction. Parish records tell the story. In the town of Lian, the number of recorded burials jumped from 174 in 1896 to 515 in 1897; in the parish of Balayan, the increase was from 848 to 1,848; in Calaca, from 324 to 1,145; and in Lemery, from 471 to 814.[66] (See Appendix C.) Most striking about the sudden increase in mortality in those towns is that it occurred at a time when, because of the extensive migration caused by the fighting, all of them had perhaps half their normal populations. Astonishingly, about four times as many burials as baptisms were recorded in western Batangas in 1897.[67]

How can such a mortality crisis be explained? One contributing factor was a shortage of food. The withdrawal of people from western Batangas during the heavy fighting of late 1896 had severely disrupted harvesting activities.[68] The agricultural situation was further disrupted by a shortage of draft animals. In previous years, rinderpest had already sharply reduced the carabao population of western Batangas. The revolution made things worse in at least three ways: first, because the peasants took their work animals with them when they fled from the towns; second, because many beasts were requisitioned by the Spanish troops; and finally, because many more were killed to feed the revolutionary forces.[69] Lacking the labor of both man and beast, the towns of western Batangas were simply unable to plant or harvest enough rice to feed the people who remained. By April 1897, there were reports of a severe rice shortage in the region, and the situation would only grow worse in the next year and a half.[70] The agricultural collapse led ineluctably to widespread malnutrition, and malnutrition, in turn, contributed to the declining health of the populace.

But the food shortage was only part of the problem. Malnutrition may have weakened the people, making them easier targets for disease, but it was disease that ultimately killed them. One of the major killers was smallpox. As I noted above, outbreaks of smallpox were not uncommon in the late nineteenth-century Philippines because of the deficiencies of the government's vaccination program and the unwillingness of most Filipinos to be vaccinated, and in most towns in Batangas at least a dozen smallpox deaths were likely to occur each year. What may have made smallpox a more effective killer in 1897 was the fact that the virus was attacking people who were already suffering from severe dietary deficiencies.[71]

The other major killer was malaria, another persistent cause of ill health, and mortality as well, but not often mortality on such a scale. Again, malnutrition, by compromising the immune systems of the people, likely increased the killing power of the disease. But another factor was also at work: increased contact between the people of western Batangas and the principal vector of the disease, the *Anopheles minimus var. flavirostris*. When the people of western Batangas fled from the towns to escape the fighting and destruction, they typically went to upland areas—the very sort of terrain favored by the anopheline vector of the Philippines. The mosquitoes thus had more opportunities to take their blood meals from, and to transmit malaria to, the human population. The continued shortage of cattle in the region also led to increased contact between anophelines and humans. Deprived of the bovine blood meals they preferred, the mosquitoes again found it necessary to feed more often on people. For a combination of reasons, therefore, malaria transmission was increasing in western Batangas, and the increased rate of transmission, combined with malnutrition, was causing death rates to soar.[72]

★ The Fourth Phase: June 1897–January 1898

The devastating defeats of the past three months and the mounting human costs did not stop the revolution in Batangas. As Aguinaldo withdrew to Bulacan and Rillo stayed on in Batangas as leader of the provincial government-in-hiding, Malvar established his headquarters in the neighboring province of Laguna, on the eastern slope of Mount Maquiling, and prepared for future operations.[73] His initial effort was far from impressive. Malvar had approximately five hundred men with him on Mount Maquiling, and on a nearby peak, Gen. Paciano Rizal also had a large force. In late June, Malvar and Rizal attempted to leave the mountains, with the intention of passing northward to the province of Morong. But, the Spaniards learned of their planned movement from informants and intercepted them near Nagcarlang, driving them back to their hiding places.[74]

After that failure, and for the remainder of the year, Malvar limited himself to occasional forays against Spanish garrisons in Batangas and Laguna. A few guerrilla actions occurred in August and September.[75] Then, in early October, Malvar and Mariano Trias, who held the position of vice-president in the revolutionary government, launched a major attack on the Spanish garrison in San Pablo, Laguna. After dislodging the enemy from their positions, the Filipino troops occupied the town for three days. On the fourth day, however, General Jaramillo, at the head of two relief columns, retook San Pablo after bloody house-to-house fighting.[76] Although technically a defeat, the battle at San Pablo had symbolic value. By occupying a population center for as long as they had, Malvar and Trias were signaling to the Spaniards that the southern Tagalog region was far from pacified.

The battle at San Pablo was noteworthy, too, because of the presence at Malvar's side of two recent recruits to the revolutionary ranks. One was Sebastian Caneo, the pastor of the Colorum Society, a religious brotherhood that was based on the slopes of Mount San Cristobal, not far from San Pablo. Composed largely of peasants, many of whom had recently fled to the uplands to escape the fighting, the Colorum was similar in kind to many other lower-class brotherhoods that proliferated in Luzon at the turn of the century. Caneo, its leader, believed that the revolution against Spain was divinely inspired and marked the onset of a major transformation of the world. To help God's plan along, Caneo had ordered his followers in June 1897 to attack the Spanish garrison at Tayabas, the capital of Tayabas province.

Armed with nothing more than the pieces of rope they wore around their waists, the members of the Colorum marched in a procession to the town, and as they approached the Spaniards, they prepared to throw their ropes, which, according to Caneo, would miraculously tie up the enemy. But the promised miracle did not occur; what transpired instead was the slaughter of many members of the brotherhood.[77]

Now, a few months later, Caneo had resurfaced, this time as the head of one of Malvar's columns. The sources do not tell us how Caneo came to link up with Malvar, but one can imagine the circumstances. At the time, both Caneo's Colorum and Malvar's revolutionary troops were residing in the mountains along the Batangas-Tayabas-Laguna border, and they had ample opportunity to become acquainted, to discover that they had a common enemy, and to begin to cooperate. Still, Caneo, an uneducated man from a humble background, differed from most of the commanders who, up to then, had led Malvar's columns. By enlisting Caneo, Malvar was demonstrating the kind of flexibility—and, it might even be said, the kind of opportunism— he had shown in the Aguinaldo-Bonifacio conflict and would show again in the struggle against the Americans. To keep the good fight going, he was willing to accept help from anyone who was in a position to give it, and Sebastian Caneo, the head of an organization with a membership numbering in the thousands, was obviously in such a position.

Another man who could help—also a prominent participant in the battle at San Pablo—was Aniceto Oruga, whose credentials for command were also somewhat curious. Oruga was a *ladrón*—a bandit—albeit a well educated one. Born about 1860 in Tanauan, Oruga had attended the prestigious Colegio de San Juan de Letran, eventually completing his secondary school requirements at the University of Santo Tomas. At some point after graduation, however, he had run afoul of the law and begun a career as a robber and cattle rustler. Captured, he received a prison sentence of twenty years. Oruga served a few years of his sentence, but in early 1897 he managed to escape from jail with twenty-five other prisoners, killing a guard in the process. Not long afterward, he appeared as the commander of a column in Malvar's forces.[78]

Although Oruga's past was checkered, one can easily imagine that Malvar was happy to gain his assistance. Like gobernadorcillos, bandit leaders like Oruga knew how to use firearms and had experience with command. They were also skilled in hiding from a pursuing force, a talent that was useful to an overmatched army like Malvar's. Finally, as a bandit leader,

Oruga was able to provide Malvar with additional weapons as well as men (the members of his band) who could fire them.

Malvar was not the only revolutionary commander who forged alliances with ladrones. Bandit leaders in Cavite cooperated with both Mariano and Santiago Alvarez in early military operations, including the takeover of the town of Noveleta from the Spaniards, and a number of them received military commissions during the war against the Americans.[79] Alliances like these could be forged because, in the colonial Philippines as in many other parts of the world, the general populace did not necessarily view the members of armed bands as their enemies. Although some ladrones were genuinely nasty characters, guilty of despicable acts, others simply had somehow gotten in trouble with the law and wanted to avoid incarceration. Common men and women in the barrios often offered assistance to such people, and it was not unusual to find local officials—Miguel Malvar's father, Maximo, for one—who were on close terms with the ladrones in their localities and who consequently made only token efforts to capture them.[80] It might be more correct to view these ladrones, or at least some of them, as "social bandits"—that is, Robin Hood–type figures, who were respected and typically supported by the communities in which they operated.[81]

Assisted by new allies like Sebastian Caneo and Aniceto Oruga, Malvar continued to resist. In the final days of October, the revolutionary forces clashed with a Spanish detachment at Tuy. On November 19, Malvar led an attack on Santo Tomas, and on the following day, his troops entered Tanauan, capturing and holding for ransom several prominent men who had cooperated too enthusiastically with the Spaniards.[82] Yet, while Malvar was enjoying some success, the revolution was losing momentum elsewhere. For the past few months, talks had been going on between Aguinaldo and Pedro Paterno, a wealthy Manileño who was attempting to bring about a negotiated settlement. Malvar and Paciano Rizal vigorously opposed the idea of coming to terms with Spain, but by early December 1897 the overwhelming majority of the revolutionary leaders had come to the conclusion that the battle was lost.[83] By the terms of the Pact of Biak-na-bato, agreed to by the Filipinos on December 14 and 15, Aguinaldo pledged to go into exile in Hong Kong in exchange for a grant of amnesty to all revolutionaries and a substantial money payment. On December 27, the Philippine president and a few dozen companions left the Philippines.[84]

The final days of this fourth phase of the revolution were anticlimactic. Before he left, Aguinaldo designated a number of his ranking officers to remain behind for the purpose of convincing the soldiers still in the field to surrender. One of the designated men was Malvar, who was charged with bringing peace to Batangas.[85] For about two weeks, Malvar traveled around the province, rounding up his followers. On January 18, 1898, his task completed, Malvar turned himself in to the Spanish authorities, and shortly afterward, he joined Aguinaldo in Hong Kong.[86]

★ Reflections on the Revolution

A major theme runs through this chapter. Rather than being simply a "revolt of the masses," the Philippine Revolution in Batangas appeared to be, in large measure, the continuation and culmination of at least a decade of political agitation by elite residents of the province. Frustrated by Spanish rule, Miguel Malvar and other members of Batangas's political elite began in the 1880s to challenge it. They formed factions, engaged in power struggles with Spanish priests, and suffered repression for their efforts. When the Philippine Revolution was brought to Batangas by Aguinaldo's troops, such men were among the first to rally to it, and, as the revolution went on, they came to have a formidable influence within the revolutionary government. Rillo and Malvar were key players in the power struggle between Aguinaldo and Bonifacio, and after May 1897, Malvar emerged as one of the staunchest advocates of continuing the fight against the Spaniards.[87]

Such a view of the revolution may prove to be unpopular in some academic circles. A large number of Filipinists persist in believing that the uprising of 1896 was a genuine lower-class struggle and that Aguinaldo's accession to the presidency in 1897 represented a radical deviation in its development. But, in fact, there is little evidence that a chapter of the Katipunan existed in Batangas prior to the outbreak of fighting, and what evidence there is indicates unambiguously that the members of the provincial political elite were the principal agents of change, revolutionary or otherwise. What is more, as I have suggested several times, the situation that prevailed in Batangas may not have been atypical. The sources indicate that the revolutionary movement in Cavite was directed by affluent, usually well educated political influentials, and there is no compelling reason to believe that, with the possible exception of Manila, the nature of the revolution was appreciably different in any other area.

A second theme should be noted. Clearly, Batangas had played a substantial price for its participation in the revolution. Soldiers had been killed and wounded, towns had suffered extensive physical damage, many Batangueños had become refugees. The conflict had been responsible for a food shortage, widespread malnutrition, increased morbidity, and an extremely high level of mortality in several towns.

Up to now, the sacrifice and suffering had been for nothing. But that was about to change.

3

Liberated Batangas

I N April 1898, following a protracted dispute over conditions in Cuba, the United States and Spain went to war, and early on the morning of May 1, Comdr. George Dewey's Asiatic Squadron littered the bottom of Manila Bay with the antiquated tubs that passed for Spain's Pacific fleet. Dewey's action dealt a crippling blow to Spanish power in the Philippines, a fact not lost on Philippine president-in-exile Emilio Aguinaldo, who had been observing the deteriorating diplomatic relations between the United States and Spain with some interest. A revolution that had failed against an undistracted enemy might very well succeed against a distracted one, and after the battle of Manila Bay, the Spanish Army in the Philippines, concerned about an American invasion and seemingly cut off from reinforcements, was very distracted indeed. In mid-May 1898, with the assistance of the U.S. Navy, Aguinaldo returned to the Philippines and to the battlefield. Within a month, he had established a government with himself as its leader and issued a declaration of independence, and by the end of September, his government was in control of much of Luzon. Also in September, in accordance with one of Aguinaldo's decrees, a congress of eminent Filipinos assembled at Malolos, Bulacan, for the purpose of drawing up a constitution for a Philippine republic. They met for several months, and ultimately, on January 23, 1899, the new republican government was inaugurated, with Aguinaldo as president.

So began a period of self-rule for much of the Philippines—a period that, in the case of Batangas, lasted from mid-June 1898, when the province was liberated from the Spaniards, until mid-January 1900. Those nineteen months were, on balance, a time of troubles in liberated Batangas. Rival political factions renewed their squabbling; in western Batangas, economic and epidemiological conditions continued to cause distress; tensions surfaced within the provincial military establishment and between civilian and military leaders. Beyond all that, following the outbreak of war between the United States and the Philippines in February 1899, the people of Batangas had to come to terms with a most unpleasant reality. However much they might have wished it otherwise, the inescapable truth of the matter was that one day soon their province would be invaded by a new enemy and their hard-won freedom would be lost.

★ The Revolution Renewed: The Final Phase

The liberation of the southern Tagalog region occurred quickly. Aguinaldo arrived in Cavite on May 19, 1898, and shortly thereafter issued a proclamation of war against Spain. Many former revolutionary officers rallied to him, among them Mariano Trias, Artemio Ricarte, and Juan Cailles. The province of Cavite was in Filipino control by the end of the month, and many Spanish soldiers were captured.[1]

The situation now facing the Spanish command was almost hopeless. Aware that large numbers of indigenous troops were deserting from the Spanish ranks, Col. Rodrigo Navas, the senior officer in the southern Tagalog region, ordered all the Spanish detachments in the provinces of Batangas, Laguna, and Tayabas to assemble at the three provincial capitals. Navas himself proceeded with a large force from northern Batangas toward Batangas City. At Lipa, however, he and his men encountered stiff resistance, and they sought refuge in the priest's residence.[2]

From June 7 to June 18, the Spanish troops in Lipa were besieged. Initially, the Filipino operations were directed by Paciano Rizal, but after a few days Arcadio Laurel took over, and Laurel himself was subsequently relieved by Eleuterio Marasigan, a native of Calaca and another veteran of the 1896 revolution. As the operations went on, the Filipino besieging force swelled to several thousand. Eustacio Maloles, Malvar's brother-in-law, commanded one large contingent of revolutionary troops, and others were led by Anastasio Marasigan, a leading citizen of Calaca, Brigido Buenafe, a political influential in Batangas City, Valentin Burgos, one of Lipa's wealthy men, and Nicolas Gonzales, the politico from Tanauan who had finally decided to cast his lot with his fellow Filipinos. Noncombatants also offered their services. "Everyone in Lipa, including the wealthy, helped," wrote Teodoro Kalaw, the son of Lipa's incumbent capitán municipal. "Their cattle were butchered, rice and food from their farms were brought in, and their horses were used by the Filipino officials and soldiers." In the end, with his supplies dwindling and his casualties mounting, Navas was forced to surrender.[3]

Spanish arms did no better elsewhere in Batangas. Even before the siege at Lipa had ended, the only other large Spanish force in the province—the approximately 600 *cazadores* garrisoned at Batangas City—had given up to the local forces. At the same time, the Filipinos captured more than 1,000 weapons, 150,000 cartridges, some dynamite, and 60,000 pesos in cash.[4] Many of the Batangueño troops now shifted their attention to the neighboring province of Tayabas, which had not yet been freed from Spanish rule, and led by Eleuterio Marasigan, the hero of the siege of Lipa, and Miguel Malvar, who had only recently returned to the Philippines from Hong Kong, they marched off to the east. Once again, the Spanish defenders held on gamely, but on August 17, after another long siege, Malvar's forces captured the town of Tayabas, the provincial capital.[5]

★ New Order, Old Realities

Once Batangas had been liberated, the provincial leadership turned to the task of putting into place a new system of municipal and provincial government. The characteristics of the new system as well as the procedures to be followed in choosing its administrators were spelled out in two decrees, both apparently composed by Apolinario Mabini, Aguinaldo's chief adviser, and issued by Aguinaldo himself on June 18 and 20. The decree of June 18 provided that, as soon as a town was freed from Spanish control, an election should take place for the municipal chief (*jefe del pueblo*), a delegate of justice and civil registry, a delegate of police and internal order, a delegate of taxes and property, and a headman for each barrio. The electorate was to consist of individuals who were "friendly to Philippine independence," at least twenty-one years of age, and "distinguished for their learning, social position, and honorable conduct." The municipal chief and his assistants would be required to collect taxes, preserve order, and perform essentially the same duties that the capitán municipal and his own subordinates had performed under the Spanish administration. Once the municipal elections had taken place, the chiefs of all the towns were to elect a provincial chief, three provincial councillors, and one or more delegates to the forthcoming revolutionary congress.[6]

The system of local government established by Aguinaldo has been aptly characterized as conservative. By excluding from the electoral process all but the educated and socially prominent, the Filipino leadership had guaranteed that municipal affairs would remain in the hands of the same individuals who had dominated them during the Spanish era. Aguinaldo's reasons for adopting this approach are not difficult to fathom. Himself a member of Cavite's political and economic elites, Aguinaldo was serving notice that his government was committed to pursuing policies palatable to, and winning the adherence of, the members of his own social class. He and other elite Filipinos had fought, and were still fighting, the Spaniards because they wanted to rule; they had no intention of broadening the electorate and sharing power with the lower classes. Nor, for that matter, was Aguinaldo—unlike Bonifacio—interested in introducing the kind of socioeconomic reforms that might have improved the lot of, and consequently have appealed to, a lower-class constituency. From the outset, his government would allow large landowners to consolidate and even to increase their holdings, while it did next to nothing for tenants and the landless. In time, a substantial price would have to be paid for pursuing such a course, but in the short run, the measures adopted had the advantage of ensuring a relatively easy transition from the old order to the new.[7]

In early July, elections were held in Batangas's municipalities, and in town after town the proceedings followed a similar script. On a given day, the eligible voters—a small number of well-off and socially prominent men—gathered in the población to cast their votes. In Balayan, which had more than 15,000 inhabitants before the outbreak of the Philippine Revolution, only 46 men took part, and in Batangas City, with a population of approximately 33,000, 78 eligible voters were in attendance. The meeting was called to order and presided over by a representative of the designated election commissioner, Miguel Malvar, who was unable to attend because he was still preoccupied with military operations in Tayabas. The commissioner's representative read aloud relevant portions of Aguinaldo's decrees of June 18 and 20 in Spanish and Tagalog, and then the voting began.[8]

The men elected to the principal municipal posts were, with few exceptions, individuals who had held power during the final years of Spanish rule. In Taal, Teofilo Atienza, a former capitán municipal and a member of the town's antifriar faction, was chosen as jefe del pueblo; and in Calatagan, San Luis, and Ibaan, the electorate returned to office the incumbent capitanes municipales. In Lipa, the top municipal office went to a former capitán municipal, and in Cuenca and Lobo, to former justices of the peace.[9] The election for provincial officials, which was held in August, produced similar results. Manuel Genato, who had been *alcalde* on the *ayuntamiento** of Batangas City during the last few years of Spanish rule, was elected *jefe provincial*, and the two men chosen to represent Batangas in the revolutionary congress were Gregorio Aguilera Solis, one of Lipa's richest men, and Mariano Lopez, a brother of the sugar baron Lorenzo Lopez.[10]

The transition to the new system of local government was not always effected without incident. In a number of communities, there were complaints about electoral irregularities. According to one letter of protest, the presiding officer at San Jose's election decided, for some unexplained reason, to hold the proceedings from 10:00 P.M. to 3:00 A.M. on a very rainy night, with the result that only a handful of the eligible voters were able to attend. The elections in another town were tainted as well because the supervising official, too ill to travel to that community, ordered the voters to assemble in a neighboring municipality. As in the San Jose elections, few people were able to attend, and the central authorities subsequently voided the balloting.[11]

The problems were most severe in Bauan, a town in which the electoral contests were traditionally bitter and where the contending factions had grown accustomed in the Spanish era to challenging the results. About four months after the elections in Bauan, a number of the town's residents filed protests about Eugenio Aranas, the elected delegate of justice and civil registry, and Andres Buendia, the delegate of taxes and property. The protesters, who included a number of longtime political rivals of both men, claimed

---

*Batangas City was one of the few towns in the Philippines that had an ayuntamiento (municipal corporation) during the Spanish period. The alcalde was the second leading official (next to the civil governor of the province), and like all members of the ayuntamiento, he was appointed. The ayuntamiento made decisions on a number of municipal matters. However, Batangas City also elected a capitán municipal (gobernadorcillo), various *jueces, tenientes,* and so forth, and these officials shared authority with the ayuntamiento.

that Aranas and Buendia had collected excessive fees, ignored the regulations of the central authorities, and otherwise disturbed the tranquility of the town. The two accused men denied the charges, and several of the townspeople, including a number of their political allies, came to their defense. Since Filipino officials had often been found guilty of similar kinds of abuses during the previous regime, one might suspect that the two delegates had actually done some of the things they were charged with doing. Indeed, the evidence was incriminating enough to convince the central government to suspend both of them and to call for new elections. But, we should also recognize that the events in Bauan probably dealt with more than the abusive practices of a few officials. They suggest that, despite the elimination of the Spanish overlords, the bitter factional rivalries of decades past had not been eliminated and that old scores remained to be settled. A new regime may have come to power, but fundamental realities had not been altered.[12]

★ Economic Distress and Social Tensions

Liberated Batangas was beset too by problems of a different order. In the western part of the province much of the land had not been cultivated since late 1896 owing to the lack of work animals and human labor, and just as the new government came to power a food crisis engulfed the region. On June 28, only ten days after the siege at Lipa had been lifted, Santiago Rillo authorized that one thousand pesos be taken from the provincial treasury to pay for rice seed for the residents of Lian and Nasugbu, who were too poor to purchase the seed themselves. About two weeks later, the gravity of the situation was confirmed by Vicente Lukban, who reported to Aguinaldo that hunger was widespread in the towns of western Batangas. Throughout the following months, a stream of letters and petitions detailing the plight of the populace came to the central government from the officials and leading citizens of the region. In Tuy, for example, there was no rice or corn to eat, and the people were subsisting on whatever fruits and vegetables they could find, including the shoots of sugarcane.[13]

As agricultural conditions deteriorated in western Batangas, so did the health of the populace. "Many of our townmates are dying of hunger, fever, malarial chills, skin disease, and foot sores," several residents of Tuy wrote to Aguinaldo in September 1898. Similar observations were made about health conditions in Balayan, Lian, Calaca, and Talisay.[14] An examination of parochial records reveals that death rates in those towns had not declined from the extraordinarily high levels they had reached in 1897. In Lian, severely depopulated since late 1896, 215 burials were registered in 1898, and only 22 baptisms. In Balayan that year, 1,404 burials and 196 baptisms were recorded, and in Calaca, 783 burials and 176 baptisms (see Appendix C).[15]

Faced with an agricultural collapse, widespread hunger, and an epidemiological catastrophe, the communities of western Batangas appealed to Aguinaldo's government for understanding and assistance. In his decree of June 20, Aguinaldo had prescribed the collection of a long list of taxes, most of which had been in effect during the Spanish regime, and had directed that part of the proceeds be used by the municipalities, with the rest being forwarded to the provincial and central authorities.[16] But the residents of western Batangas simply lacked the resources to meet their fiscal obligations. In September, the leading citizens of Tuy, citing the manifold problems that beset their community, petitioned Aguinaldo for a two-year exemption from taxation; nearly identical petitions were later received from Lian and three other towns. Although the central government, itself hard-pressed for money, was reluctant to exempt any communities from fulfilling their fiscal responsibilities, it agreed to suspend tax collection temporarily in Lian and provided a small number of cattle to the people of Tuy.[17]

During this period of economic distress, social tensions began to surface in western Batangas. Robberies were prevalent. Tenants, struggling desperately to feed their families, grew resentful toward unsympathetic landlords. Felipe Gonzales, a tenant farming a plot of land in a barrio of Nasugbu, attacked his landlord, Lucas Advincula, because Advincula demanded a larger share of Gonzales's harvest than the tenant was able to turn over. An even more spectacular disturbance occurred in Nasugbu. In September 1898, some people from the neighboring town of Alfonso in Cavite, intent on improving their lot, invaded and occupied part of the estate of the Spaniard Pedro Roxas, intimidating and displacing many of Roxas's longtime tenants in the process. Municipal officials complained as well that residents of the area were defying their authority. The situation in western Batangas was becoming potentially explosive.[18]

Conditions were not disturbed in the entire province. Although life in eastern Batangas had been disrupted by the recent revolution, the amount of physical destruction had been comparatively limited. What is more, the eastern sector had not experienced any substantial increase in mortality or any noticeable out-migration during the years 1896–98.[19]

At least one town—Lipa, the cultural capital of the province—appeared to undergo something of a revival during the period following the liberation. A weekly newspaper, *Columnas Volantes,* was established. Edited by Gregorio Aguilera Solis, one of Batangas's delegates to the revolutionary congress, it included articles by Baldomero Roxas, Pedro Laygo, Fidel Reyes, and other members of the town's intellectual elite. A new school, the Instituto Rizal, was founded under the leadership of Gregorio Catigbac, a Lipeño who had been suspected of political agitation during the Spanish era. Two new social clubs also appeared—the Club Democrático Independista, with the aforementioned Gregorio Aguilera Solis as its president, and the Cruz Roja de Dama. "The days were filled with seemingly endless activities," recalled Teodoro Kalaw, then a student at the Instituto Rizal and a sometime participant in the cultural programs presented by the Cruz Roja. "No week passed without some important visitor coming to town. With reason was it said then that Lipa was another Athens where the select and illustrious in culture and the arts met."[20]

★ Athens Imperiled

In addition to the economic and epidemiological problems that troubled several of Batangas's communities, an external danger threatened them all. Having recently won their freedom from Spanish rule, the residents of the province were forced to confront the possibility that they would have to fight again, this time against the United States. The country that had vanquished the Spanish fleet at Manila Bay was now, it seemed, unwilling to leave the Philippines to the Filipinos.

Over the years, much has been written about the American decision to acquire the Philippines, although, unfortunately, the existence of a large body of scholarly literature has done nothing to guarantee that we actually understand why American policymakers did what they did. According to one version of the events, Dewey's descent on Manila was primarily a strategic decision, designed to defeat the Spanish enemy, not to secure an Asian empire; according to another, it was an economically motivated act, a logical next step in an emerging policy of acquiring coaling stations and bases that would enable the United States to penetrate the China market.[21] The disagreement among scholars is particularly intense about the role of the U.S. president, William McKinley, in the decision to pursue imperialist goals. In the eyes of some—most notably, Thomas McCormick, H. Wayne Morgan, and Lewis Gould—McKinley took a very early fancy to the idea of taking the Philippines, and once he did, he pursued a consistent, considered policy of promoting that objective. But other historians—Ernest May and David Trask, for example—see the president as indecisive: someone who waffled over what to do with the Philippines for more than five months after Dewey's victory and who came to a decision only after he was convinced that the American public overwhelmingly favored acquisition of the islands. That historians have reached such contrasting conclusions about the president's policies can be explained by the simple fact that the evidence about the man, like the evidence about the Katipunan, is both scant and contradictory. The debate persists because the sources are problematical.[22]

Still, it is clear that in the weeks and months following the battle of Manila Bay, whether by design or force of circumstances, the United States found itself progressively more involved in Philippine affairs. Immediately after Dewey's attack, the president decided to send an expeditionary force to the Philippines, and on May 19, 1898, he issued instructions to the commander of the expedition. The mission, McKinley wrote, had two objectives: to "complete the reduction of Spanish power in the archipelago" and to provide "order and security to the islands while in the possession of the United States." McKinley also indicated that the powers of the American occupying force were to be "absolute and supreme." American troops began to arrive in the Philippines on June 30, and they quickly occupied positions close to the Filipino forces besieging the city of Manila.[23]

Although the Americans and the Filipinos had a common enemy, relations between the two besieging armies showed early signs of strain. The American commanders wanted to occupy Manila, but, heeding the instructions of their president that their powers were to be absolute and supreme, they did not want to do so in conjunction with the Filipinos. So they elected to negotiate secretly with the Spanish governor-general for the surrender of Manila, and eventually a deal was made. The Spaniard agreed to surrender if the Filipino Army were excluded from the city and a sham battle were staged. The battle was for the benefit of Spanish pride, which presumably would be less wounded if Spain appeared to put up a fight before surrendering. On August 13, 1898, the battle took place (at the cost of a few hundred casualties), the Americans took Manila, and as promised, they prevented Aguinaldo's men from entering the city. Aguinaldo himself reluctantly accepted the fait accompli, but some of his generals were irate.[24]

Up to now, McKinley had given no clear indication of his intentions concerning the future disposition of the Philippines, but a clarification would soon be necessary. Spain, suffering defeats on all fronts, sued for peace, and the peace negotiations, which began in early October, forced the American president to announce his objectives. His initial instructions to the American negotiators called for the cession of at least Luzon, but on October 28, he revised them and demanded the entire archipelago from Spain. As on every other key question relating to McKinley, historians cannot agree on why the president acted as he did; some see the revision of the instructions as the logical culmination of a consistent policy aimed at acquiring an Asian empire, and others characterize it as the issue of a weak president's reluctant acknowledgment that the American public overwhelmingly favored overseas expansion.[25] Yet, whatever the president's motives, the United States, now publicly committed to expansionism, was on a collision course with the new Filipino nation.

The only question that remained to be answered was when the collision would take place. By the terms of the Treaty of Paris, concluded on December 10, 1898, Spain agreed to cede the Philippines to the United States. As the U.S. Senate debated the treaty, friction increased between American and Filipino soldiers stationed in the environs of Manila. Negotiating sessions took place between representatives of Aguinaldo and Elwell Otis, the American commanding general, but they solved nothing. Finally, the collision came. On February 4, 1899, two days before the U.S. Senate voted to acquire the Philippines, fighting broke out at the San Juan Bridge, in a suburb of Manila, and the Philippine-American War had begun.[26]

★ Malvar's Army

At the time of the San Juan Bridge incident, Miguel Malvar, the commander of the Filipino Army in Batangas, was at his headquarters at Lipa, too far removed from the field of operations to be of any assistance. Malvar remained in Batangas until the end of April and focused his attention on making defensive preparations within the province and on readying his forces for the fighting, which was initially concentrated in the region north of Manila.[27]

The provincial military organization that began to take shape in this period—in essence, the army that the United States would encounter when it entered Batangas in January 1900—bore Malvar's distinctive stamp. Aguinaldo's decrees relating to military matters gave each provincial commander the freedom to choose his own corps of officers, and Malvar took full advantage of the authority he was granted.[28] Some of the men he appointed were fellow veterans of the revolution. Santiago Rillo and Arcadio Laurel both received appointments as lieutenant colonels, as did Nicolas Gonzales, the municipal official from Tanauan who had joined the struggle against Spain during the siege of Lipa. Other local dignitaries who volunteered their

services were given commissions—including Melecio Bolaños, a former capitán municipal of Rosario, Gregorio Catigbac, the head of the Instituto Rizal,
and Cipriano Lopez, another brother of Balayan's sugar baron Lorenzo
Lopez.[29]

Good revolutionary credentials, elite status, and experience with bandit-
chasing were not the only distinguishing characteristics of the Batangueño
officer corps. The glue that held it together was personalistic in nature,
since many of its members were Miguel Malvar's intimate friends. Martin
Cabrera, one of several Cabrera brothers who held high rank, was Malvar's
compadre, as was Eliseo Claudio, a company commander in the First Maquiling Battalion. No fewer than a dozen ranking officers in Batangas's
military units—including Cipriano Calao and Gregorio Catigbac of Lipa,
Alfonso Panopio of Bauan, and Anastasio Marasigan of Calaca—had been
Malvar's classmates in secondary school, the famous Malabanan school located in the town of Tanauan.[30] The composition of the Batangueño officer
corps mattered. In choosing his chief lieutenants, Malvar depended on existing social relationships: he relied on men he could trust, men he had
known since his youth. As in so much else, the behavior of Batangueños
during this period of crisis was determined by the fundamental realities of
their society.

This is not to say that the realities of late nineteenth-century Batangas
were uniquely Batangueño. Anyone familiar with the twentieth-century
Philippines is well aware of the importance of the old school tie. Studies of
recent Philippine politics have demonstrated that strong political alliances
exist among former classmates at the University of the Philippines, and the
same cohort solidarity is alleged to exist among graduates of the Philippine
Military Academy. Students of Chinese history might point out as well that
Chiang Kai-shek's control over the Nationalist Army rested on a similar kind
of personal relationship: his most trusted lieutenants, the men who dominated his military bureaucracy as well as the secret military police, were
officers who had been his students at the Whampoa Military Academy in the
mid-1920s. Indeed, throughout much of Asia as well as the West school ties
have long served as powerful institutional bonds, holding together not only
military hierarchies but also law firms, boards of directors of corporations,
government agencies, and university administrations.

Another Batangueño officer, Elias Mendoza of Taal, was connected to
Malvar in a different way. Mendoza was something of a curiosity in the
provincial forces. Like Sebastian Caneo, the pastor of the Colorum who was
currently a high-ranking officer in Tayabas, Mendoza was one of the few

commanders in the southern Tagalog region who did not come from an established family. His parents had been musicians, and Mendoza himself had been an itinerant merchant—an unsuccessful one at that—in the years before the Philippine Revolution. When he joined the Filipino Army during the struggle against Spain, his initial assignment had been as a servant in Malvar's retinue. But a bizarre turn of events led to his rapid rise. At one point in the fighting against Spain, some enemy soldiers had captured Malvar's wife, who often accompanied her husband in the field. Fearful about her safety, Malvar offered a ransom to obtain her release. Mendoza volunteered to conduct the negotiations—a tricky business, for if the Spaniards proved to be incorruptible they might decide to take Mendoza prisoner. Somehow, though, he succeeded, and for his efforts he won Malvar's gratitude and confidence and, ultimately, the command of a column.[31]

In these appointments, a common denominator stands out. Whatever else it might have been, the Filipino officer corps in Batangas was, at bottom, *Malvar's* corps. Bound to the local commander by a complex of personal ties—ritual coparenthood, personal gratitude, the old school tie, and former military service—it was responsible to and dependent on him alone. The nature of Filipino society at the turn of the century in a sense determined that the provincial officer corps would be organized in this way. The Philippines had no military schools and no tradition of a standing army: What other principle of institution formation could have been adopted? But a military command organized on such a principle was seriously flawed. The personalistic ties that bound a former classmate like Cipriano Calao, a former servant like Elias Mendoza, and a compadre like Eliseo Claudio to the provincial commander Miguel Malvar did not necessarily bind those three high-ranking subordinates to each other. And it did not bind any of Malvar's officers to Filipino military and civilian officials in other provinces. The army in Batangas accordingly operated like a collection of private armies, each of them led by a powerful warlord who recruited his own followers, exhibited intense loyalty to Malvar himself, and regularly failed to cooperate with other warlords in Batangas or neighboring provinces.

None of the above is meant to imply that individual officers lacked a commitment to the cause they were fighting for. In personal correspondence, many of them repeatedly affirmed their determination to do battle. "We all swear to defend the honor of the country until our last drop of blood has been shed," asserted Capt. Crisanto Borruel, in words that were echoed in other letters written by Batangueño officers.[32] Men of this sort might well feel a special devotion to the cause. Typically well educated, many were familiar with the ideas of European liberal thinkers that had contributed to the political ferment of the preceding decade. Often politically influential, many had supported the factions that had challenged Spanish rule. Invariably members of affluent families, most had already benefited from the policies of Aguinaldo's government, which had pursued policies favorable to the upper rungs, and they stood to prosper in the future too so long as the Filipinos prevailed on the battlefield. Yet, however strong their commitment to independence—and however great their devotion to their own self-interest—few of them would prove to be capable of overcoming the personal animosities, suspicions, and jealousies that surfaced among them.[33]

Another structural weakness of the Filipino Army in Batangas was that, unlike the volunteer army they opposed, their forces included a large number of conscripts. On February 21, 1899, Aguinaldo had issued a decree establishing procedures for military recruitment. Soldiers were to be chosen by lot from among able-bodied men between the ages of eighteen and thirty-five. Only a few categories of individuals were legally entitled to avoid the draft. Men shorter than 1.3 meters in height were exempted, as were various officials; married men and widowers with children were to be selected only after the supply of single males had been exhausted; and rich men could buy their way out of the army by making a cash payment ranging from two hundred to seven hundred pesos.[34] In the following months, in accordance with the official procedures, many young, poor men were conscripted into Batangas's military units; not all of them were genuinely pleased to serve. During the harvest season there was a steady trickle of deserters from the ranks, and following periods of heavy fighting, the trickle turned into a torrent.[35] The high rate of desertion impaired the war-making capacity of Malvar's forces, and it provided a hint about an even more serious problem that would plague the Batangueño leadership throughout the guerrilla phase of the fighting—the occupants of the lower rungs may have been less committed to the struggle against the Americans than the occupants of the upper.

★ Batangueños at War

While Malvar was preparing his troops for the hour of battle, the Filipino troops to the north were absorbing heavy losses. When the war with the United States had broken out in February 1899, Aguinaldo had decided (as he explained in his memoirs) to fight a conventional military campaign against the enemy in order to defend Malolos, the capital of the Philippine

Republic, and to ensure the continuation of the government he had recently established.[36] In addition, although Aguinaldo did not allude to this consideration in his memoirs, it is likely he was inclined to fight conventionally because he feared that if he split his army into guerrilla units he would lose control of it, and his leadership would be challenged by other commanders. But the conventional operations had thus far been disastrous. By the end of March, Malolos had been captured, and in the following weeks the Americans had occupied several more towns in the provinces of Bulacan and Pampanga. To make matters worse, the Filipino high command was rent with conflict, as several ranking officers chafed at the policies and style of Gen. Antonio Luna, Aguinaldo's principal field commander.[37]

Although the U.S. troops focused their attention on the northern provinces during these early months of the war, they made a few thrusts toward the east and the south. In mid-March, an expeditionary force under Brig. Gen. Loyd Wheaton moved eastward, clearing Filipino troops from the vicinity of the Pasig River and thereby assuring the Americans of riverine access to Laguna de Bay, the purse-shaped, freshwater lake located in the heart of central Luzon. About a month later, taking advantage of Wheaton's recent gains, Maj. Gen. Henry Lawton led an expedition to Santa Cruz, on the eastern shore of Laguna de Bay, where the Filipinos had a large concentration of troops. Lawton's force engaged the enemy several times, occupied Santa Cruz briefly, reconnoitered the area, and then returned to Manila.[38]

The foray by Lawton, only a modest success by the general's lofty standards, caused great concern to the Filipino high command, for it seemed to presage the onset of a major American campaign in southern Luzon. In fact, the Americans were not yet planning such a campaign, but the Filipinos had no way of knowing that. To meet the apparent danger, Aguinaldo decided to call into action his forces in the southern provinces. In late April, he ordered Mariano Trias, his second-in-command, to concentrate all available troops from Batangas, Laguna, and Cavite at the town of Muntinlupa in preparation for an offensive against the American garrison at the town of Pasig.[39]

At last Gen. Miguel Malvar and his military units in Batangas were to enter the war against the Americans. By May 7, Malvar's brigade had arrived in the vicinity of Muntinlupa, and about the same time several columns of the Banajao Battalion from Tayabas, one of them commanded by Malvar's old friend Sebastian Caneo, were attached to his command.[40] In the following weeks, the Filipino forces to the south of Manila became, to use the words of General Otis, "boldly demonstrative." Malvar and other commanders in the area launched occasional attacks against American positions,

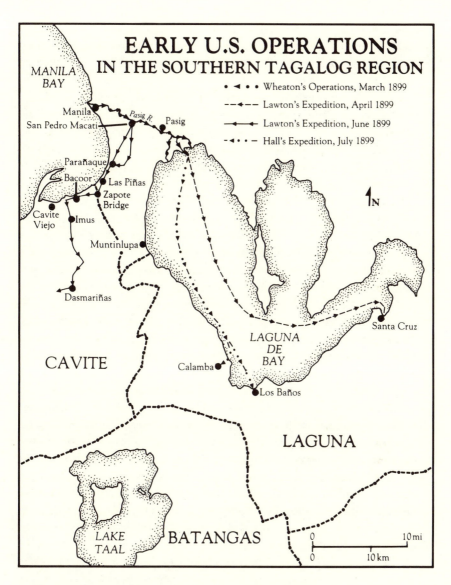

EARLY U.S. OPERATIONS
IN THE SOUTHERN TAGALOG REGION

MANILA
BAY

• ◄ • • Wheaton's Operations, March 1899
––◄–– Lawton's Expedition, April 1899
◄––– Lawton's Expedition, June 1899
–◄ • • – Hall's Expedition, July 1899

Manila
San Pedro Macati
Pasig R.
Pasig

Parañaque
Bacoor
Las Piñas
Zapote
Bridge
Cavite
Viejo
Imus
Muntinlupa

N

Dasmariñas

CAVITE

LAGUNA
DE
BAY

Calamba

Santa Cruz

Los Baños

LAGUNA

LAKE
TAAL

BATANGAS

0   10 mi
0   10 km

3. *Early U.S. Operations in the Southern Tagalog Region*

81

although, for some reason, no full-scale operation against Pasig was undertaken. Over all, Malvar appeared to be pleased with the results. "The Americans are very discouraged by their losses," he wrote to a fellow officer on June 9.[41]

Such optimism was unwarranted. Annoyed at the enemy's activity so close to Manila, Otis ordered Lawton to move again into the southern Tagalog region. Lawton divided the four thousand troops at his disposal into two expeditionary brigades, one commanded by Wheaton and the other by Samuel Ovenshine. On June 10, the two brigades advanced, with Wheaton on the left heading toward Muntinlupa and Ovenshine on the right. Wheaton's men quickly broke through the Filipinos' entrenchments on the Guadalupe Ridge, a few miles south of Manila, but then, instead of ordering the troops to proceed to Muntinlupa, Lawton directed them to join up with Ovenshine's brigade, which was having trouble near Parañaque. Over the next few days, the two brigades, acting in tandem, seized the strategic Zapote Bridge and occupied Bacoor, Imus, and Dasmariñas, three towns in Cavite. Then, as before, the bulk of the American troops were withdrawn, since the U.S. command was still committed to concentrating on the northern campaign. Filipino losses in the fighting were substantial, but, thanks to Lawton's decision to redirect Wheaton toward Parañaque and away from Muntinlupa, the Batangas brigade got off lightly.[42]

For the rest of the year—up to the point, that is, when the Americans were ready to turn their attention to the provinces south of Manila—the fighting in the southern Tagalog region took on a certain predictable rhythm. From time to time, usually after a period of intense activity by the Filipino forces, the U.S. commanders would send a new expeditionary force into the area. The troops would penetrate a bit more deeply into enemy territory, perhaps establish another garrison, and then, after a few days, most of the men would return to Manila. The Filipinos, on their part, would constantly harass the American outposts and occasionally attack them in force, but never succeed in overrunning them.

The Batangas brigade, still reinforced by elements of the Banajao Battalion, figured prominently in this campaign of thrust and counterthrust. During June and most of July, Malvar's men remained in Muntinlupa, where they twice resisted American efforts to send landing parties ashore from vessels operating on Laguna de Bay.[43] Then, at the end of July, a large amphibious force under Brig. Gen. Robert Hall landed at Calamba, farther to the south on Laguna de Bay. Malvar's troops rushed to the town's defense. For several days the Filipinos put up a determined fight, but in the end they were unable to dislodge the enemy. Malvar's losses in those encounters were heavy: in the Banajao Battalion alone, 48 out of 175 men were either killed or wounded.[44]

Although Calamba was now occupied by ten companies of the Twenty-First Infantry under Col. Jacob Kline, the U.S. garrison's position was anything but secure. Malvar ordered additional men from Batangas to join him near Calamba, calling into action, among other units, a large part of the Maquiling Battalion, which up to then had been guarding the coast of Batangas. A portion of Eliseo Claudio's company was transferred to the front at this time, and the remainder, including Claudio himself, was called up shortly afterward.[45] Thus reinforced, Malvar's brigade ringed Calamba with an elaborate system of trenches and applied steady pressure to Kline's regiment. "The insurgents . . . kept up a most annoying fire night after night," recalled the regimental historian of the Twenty-First, "and thus deprived our men of necessary rest and sleep." The environment also took a toll. "The site of the camp is in the trenches around Calamba," wrote a surgeon attached to the garrison.

> For the most part the ground is swampy, consisting principally of rice fields, which, when it rains, are covered more or less with water; at all times it is damp and more or less muddy and swarms with mosquitoes. The Companies had, with few exceptions, absolutely no quarters, the men being obliged to sleep upon the swampy ground, the majority having no blankets, ponchos, or shelter tents. Many slept in deep rice ridges, or tried to, but it was very difficult to find sleep in this manner, especially when annoyed by swarms of mosquitoes, heavy rains, and the . . . noise of insurgent guns.

Under such conditions, the local microparasites thrived: by the end of September, 321 men out of 1,330 were on the sick list, many of them suffering from malaria and dengue fever.[46]

In October, the situation became even more precarious for the Twenty-First. Seeing that the Americans at Calamba had adopted a purely defensive posture and sensing that they were vulnerable, Malvar decided to attack. On October 3, his brigade, assisted by the Banajao Battalion and some of Gen. Mariano Noriel's men, hit Kline's positions from the south and the northwest. For a while, the Filipinos managed to hold Lecheria Hill, just south of the town, from which they had a clear view of the American trenches; but eventually Kline's regiment threw them back.[47]

Malvar did not appear to be discouraged by the reverse. His men staged several more attacks on Calamba in October and maintained the harassment during the following month. Kline retaliated at times, ordering his artillery to shell Malvar's positions several times and launching two assaults of his own against their trenches, but for the most part he remained on the defensive. Meanwhile, the health of his men continued to deteriorate. By the beginning of December, about half the regiment was unfit for duty. According to the surgeon, "An important factor in the deterioration of the health of the command is the nervous strain which the men have been under since being stationed here. They have been almost constantly molested by the enemy, thus depriving them of their sleep; cases of acute delirium, extreme nervousness, irritability of the heart and persistent insomnia have become numerous."[48]

Malvar's troops experienced difficulties of their own during this period. After the heavy fighting of October and November, the rate of desertion increased markedly. Some units were short of supplies, some were not receiving their pay on time, and all were suffering from a high rate of illness. Even so, as Malvar left the front lines in mid-December for a brief rest, he had good reason to be satisfied with the performance of his command. While the Batangueños had not retaken Calamba, they had more than held their own against Kline's regiment.[49]

★ Behind the Lines

While the Batangas brigade was seeing action against the enemy, many Batangueños behind the lines were demonstrating their support for the war effort. Municipalities contributed large sums of money to the local forces and furnished them food, uniforms, cigarettes, and an assortment of supplies. A military hospital was set up at Lipa with funds provided by private donations. When the local boys marched off to battle, the towns held celebrations in their honor, and when they returned from frontline duty, the populace turned out to greet them.[50]

Patriotic sentiments—as well as a fierce determination to resist the Americans—were manifest in the columns of *Columnas Volantes,* the weekly published in Lipa. In issue after issue, contributors stated their intention to continue the struggle to the death. The Filipino goal, asserted one columnist in July 1899, was "Independence or nothing." Another writer discussed the possibility of a forthcoming American invasion of Batangas:

> Uneasiness, to some extent justified . . . , prevails in the populace. Regions which were untouched until recently are being invaded. . . . Where

will all this end? Will we succumb to such pressure? . . . These are questions which one hears frequently, enigmas which every Filipino longs to see deciphered, obviously in favor of our aspirations. But if bad luck sends us precisely the opposite of what we hope for, there are fortunately many mountains and craggy spots [in the province]. No doubt it will be preferable to live in such places, sheltered from the opprobrious flag which usurps our rights, than to live in a village with a chain around one's neck.[51]

In addition to supporting the frontline troops, the people behind the lines made preparations to resist the enemy's efforts to invade the province. Three types of organizations shared responsibility for local defense. The principal burden was borne by units of the regular army, which were deployed at strategic points around the province.[52] These regulars were assisted by a territorial militia as well as municipal militias, which were responsible for constructing trenches, providing for the safety of noncombatants, and fighting—in most cases, with bolos, since rifles were in short supply—in the event of an invasion. Like the regular army units, the militias were officered by members of the local economic and political elites; some were chosen by Malvar himself (who called once more on former classmates at the Malabanan school), but most were appointed by Santiago Rillo, who assumed the position of provincial military governor when Malvar left Batangas to conduct military operations near Muntinlupa.[53]

Between February 1899, when the Philippine-American War broke out, and January 1900, when Batangas was invaded, several plans of provincial defense were drawn up by the Batangueño high command. They differed a bit on details, but shared an unstated operating assumption—that the principal task of both the regulars and the irregulars stationed behind the lines was to protect the province from a *seaborne* invasion. Evidently, Malvar's brigade and the other frontline troops to the north were charged with repelling any enemy movement overland. Consequently, a large percentage of the behind-the-line regular troops were deployed in coastal towns like Batangas City, Lobo, Bauan, Lemery, and Balayan, and most of the trenches were constructed in those places too.[54]

Several times in 1899, these coastal defenders were placed on alert. American naval vessels regularly sailed along the Batangas coast, and more than once they dropped anchor in Batangas Bay and sent a landing party ashore to arrange a conference with local officials. Whenever the U.S. vessels appeared, the regulars and the militia, anticipating a bombardment or an amphibious assault, would rush to the beaches and take their positions in the trenches. But the Americans always refrained from firing, and the Filipinos did so too, although on one occasion an overzealous officer almost launched an attack by mistake.[55]

Yet, if many Batangueños were demonstrating by word and deed their support for the war against the Americans, tensions of a new kind were becoming visible in the province. For one, there was widespread conflict between civilian and military officials. For another, animosity existed among members of the Batangueño officer corps. Although none of these problems would, as yet, cause real damage to the Batangueño war effort, they were adumbrations of a troubled future.

Poor relations between civilian and military officials were a serious problem for the Filipino leadership throughout the archipelago. In part, the friction stemmed from ambiguities inherent in the decrees, regulations, and circulars issued by the central government; in part, from the tendency of local commanders to ignore legal niceties in times of military necessity; and in part, from clashes of strong personalities. Whatever the causes, civil-military conflict appeared almost everywhere, and the central government struggled without success to control it. Circulars were issued requiring municipal officials to furnish assistance to soldiers on leave, but many jefes del pueblo adamantly refused to do so; other circulars instructed military men to pay for supplies provided by the towns, but soldiers often disregarded them.[56]

The conflict was acute in the municipality of Batangas City. In the barrio of Tabangao, located along the coast, residents complained repeatedly about the petty crimes and other abuses committed by the regular troops stationed there. But when the *teniente* of the barrio, Apolonio Belmonte, brought the matter to the attention of the corporal commanding the detachment, the soldier arrested him. Although the teniente was ultimately released, he was so offended by the conduct of the corporal that he submitted his resignation.[57] Meanwhile, the municipal jefe, a pharmacist named Jose Villanueva, was having disagreements of his own with the Filipino Army. He complained again and again to local commanders about illegalities committed by the soldiers, and when he got no satisfaction, he became uncooperative, refusing to allow the men to be quartered in private dwellings in the población. The military authorities viewed Villanueva with suspicion, ostensibly because he, along with the civil governor, Manuel Genato, took part in several conferences with U.S. naval officers between February and December 1899. There is no evidence that Villanueva was the least bit sympathetic to the enemy, his sole objective in talking to the American officers being to induce them to spare Batangas City from bombardment, but the Batangueño commanders in the area refused to give him the benefit of the doubt; instead, they made accusations against him to the central government.[58]

About the same time, enmity arose between Santiago Rillo and Elias Mendoza, two ranking officers in the Batangueño forces. Rillo and Mendoza were men of very different social backgrounds—the former, a political influential from Tuy; the latter, a poor man with a faintly disreputable past—and possibly the ill will between them was a function of the social distance that separated them. Perhaps, as well, Mendoza resented the fact that in January 1899 Rillo had taken over the position of military commander of Batangas City, displacing Mendoza, who had held the post for several months. In any case, the trouble began in late March 1899, when the U.S.S. *Charleston,* a protected cruiser with formidable eight- and six-inch batteries, dropped anchor in Batangas Bay to deliver a peace proposal from General Otis. Rillo had learned of the *Charleston*'s mission a few days earlier from the commander of an English vessel who had called at Batangas City, and he had given his word not to attack the American ship. But Mendoza, claiming that he had "private orders" from Malvar to defend the beaches, refused to honor the arrangement, and as a rowboat flying a flag of truce approached the pier, he and his men prepared to attack. Before they could fire, Manuel Scarella, one of Rillo's aides, appeared and managed to convince Mendoza to desist. So, Otis's proposal was delivered, the Filipinos politely declined, and the *Charleston* sailed away.[59]

The matter did not end there, however. Angry that Mendoza had disobeyed his order, Rillo gave him a severe dressing down. Then Mendoza, insulted at being rebuked, wrote several letters to his sponsor Miguel Malvar, accusing Rillo of being an *americanista*. In subsequent months, the hostility between the two men grew, and something of even greater significance may have taken place. According to Scarella (who, as we shall see, was not a completely trustworthy informant), Malvar's relations with Rillo now started to deteriorate because Malvar, who trusted Mendoza, became suspicious that Rillo secretly favored an accommodation with the enemy.[60]

The Rillo-Mendoza conflict was an early symptom of a developing cancer. One of the basic structural deficiencies of the Filipino Army in Batangas—the lack of cohesion within the officer corps—was suddenly showing itself. If an officer like Elias Mendoza could defy the orders of his superior Santiago Rillo, how many other Batangueño officers might feel justified in doing the same? And if Mendoza's response to a dressing down was to conduct a surreptitious campaign of criticism against the man who rebuked him, was it not likely that others would adopt a similar course?

A footnote to the Rillo-Mendoza episode is in order. There is a strong likelihood that Mendoza's accusations against Rillo were well-founded. In June or July 1899, when Malvar was occupied at the front, the American command received an intelligence report from the southern Tagalog region indicating that Santiago Rillo was anxious to leave the field: "Rillo sends word that if American forces will feign an attack, during absence of Malbar [*sic*], he will surrender with his men and arms. States that the native priests will cooperate in maintaining public order. If this proposition is not satisfactory, requests that some one come down on gunboat to arrange the details."[61]

The U.S. Army never followed up on this alleged overture from Rillo and the sources contain no other reference to it, but in light of his often-curious behavior after the American invasion of Batangas, we would be unwise to dismiss the report as an intelligence operative's invention. In addition to the numerous chinks already spotted in Batangas's protective armor, there may have been a major rent.

★ The Approaching Danger

As 1899 drew to a close, Batangueños sensed that the province's period of freedom was about to end. In October, Malvar, believing that a full-fledged American invasion of the southern Tagalog region was imminent, instructed the troops within the borders of Batangas to be on the alert. Defensive preparations were stepped up in all the coastal towns.[62] In November, Emilio Aguinaldo, his own forces in total disarray, decided to adopt guerrilla tactics; with no conventional army to oppose them in the northern half of Luzon, the U.S. commanders were now in a position to turn their attention to the provinces to the south. In early December, Malvar issued another alert. Local militia units were ordered to report for duty; new defensive plans were drawn up; regular troops were shifted from place to place.[63]

While the defensive preparations intensified in Batangas, speculation about a forthcoming invasion increased. Some residents of coastal communities became alarmed and fled to inland barrios, well out of range of the guns of U.S. naval vessels. But for the moment the majority held firm. "It is not clear that we will succumb," opined one columnist in *Columnas Volantes* in mid-October. Another wrote in late November, "Our desire to uphold national honor and to defend our holy freedom is what makes us determined in our fight with the Yankees."[64]

★ ★ ★ ★ ★ ★ ★ ★ ★

PART TWO

Enter the Americans

4

The Invasion, January 1900

JOHN LELAND JORDAN, a thirty-year-old Tennessean, was not a professional soldier. For most of his adult life he had worked as secretary of the general passenger department of the Nashville, Chattanooga, & St. Louis Railway. But in 1898 the patriotic bug bit him, just as it had bitten so many other Americans of his generation, and he volunteered to fight in the war against Spain. In June 1898 he received a commission as captain in the Fourth Tennessee Volunteer Infantry, but he never took part in a hostile action during that conflict. His regiment did not leave training camp for Cuba until late November 1898, some three months after the fighting with Spain had ended. The Fourth Tennessee remained overseas until March of the following year and then was recalled. Not long afterward, Jordan and his regiment were mustered out.[1]

By now there was another war to be fought, and more officers were needed, so Jordan decided to seek a commission in one of the Federal Volun-

11 and 12. *Departure of the Thirty-Eighth Volunteer Infantry for the Philippines from Jefferson Barracks,*

teer regiments recently authorized by Congress. On August 23, 1899, he was appointed captain in the Thirty-Eighth Volunteer Infantry, commanded by Col. George S. Anderson, a bearded, somewhat portly fifty-year-old West Pointer. For the next two weeks Jordan recruited men for the regiment and then took charge of his company at the regiment's assembly point, Jefferson Barracks in Missouri. The training that followed was extremely rigorous; the troops were needed immediately in the Philippines. Six days a week, the men were drilled into shape—setting-up exercises, school of the soldier, school of the company, school of the battalion, extended order, the manual of arms, target practice, and so on. They endured as well the usual quota of inspections, parades, guard mounts, and details. Late in October, ready or not, these soldiers boarded a train bound for San Francisco, and on November 21, after a bit more training at the Presidio, they sailed for the Philippines aboard two U.S. Army transports, the *St. Paul* and the *Duke of Fife*.[2]

The *Duke of Fife*, which carried Captain Jordan and his company, arrived in Manila Bay on December 26, 1899, and on the following day, the men disembarked and set up a temporary camp on the Luneta, the bay-side park where many Manileños normally came in the early evening to promenade, to be seen, and to exchange gossip. Like any newcomer to a strange place, Jordan took in the sights and sounds around him. American soldiers generally found Manila exotic and exciting, but to Jordan, better-traveled than most, much struck him as familiar. "The native Filipino resembles the native Cuban but is somewhat smaller in stature," he noted on December 28. "I don't think they are as intelligent as Cubans as a rule. The city, country, people and customs are very similar." And if what he found around him was not novel, what he saw in the future was downright disappointing. Having traveled halfway around the world, he and his men were anxious to take part in a bona fide war, but the prospects did not seem promising. "I don't think that there is much chance for any serious or heavy fighting," he wrote, "yet it is believed there will be a great deal of guerrilla or desultory warfare."[3]

Jordan was half right. Eventually he and his men would be exposed to more than their share of guerrilla warfare, but for the moment there was indeed some "serious" fighting to be done. Maj. Gen. Elwell Otis, the commander of the U.S. Army in the Philippines, had been biding his time, waiting for more Federal Volunteers to arrive so that he could begin a full-scale invasion of the southern Tagalog region and eliminate the Filipino forces in Cavite, Batangas, Laguna, and Tayabas. By the end of December, all but three of the new regiments had reached the Philippines, and Otis was finalizing his plans for the invasion. In only a few days, Jordan and his regiment would be on the move; in a few weeks, they would fight in the battles against Miguel Malvar's soldiers in the province of Batangas.

★ Two Brigades

General Otis's plan for the invasion called for a closely coordinated movement by two expeditionary brigades. One was to be commanded by Brig. Gen. Loyd Wheaton, a participant in several earlier operations in the southern Tagalog region, and the other by Brig. Gen. Theodore Schwan, who had led a brief foray into Cavite in October 1899. Both generals were vigorous field leaders and were convinced that the best way to "pacify" the Filipinos was to thrash them soundly on the battlefield. "The people are by no means civilized," Schwan wrote to a fellow officer. "They live as they have lived for centuries. . . . To put the matter briefly, they are in identically the same position as the Indians of our country have been for many years, and in my opinion must be subdued in much the same way, by such convincing conquest as shall make them realize fully the futility of armed resistance, and then win them by fair and just treatment." The immediate superior of both brigadiers was Maj. Gen. John Bates, the recently appointed commander of the First Division of the Eighth Army Corps.[4]

Otis committed more than eight thousand American soldiers to the expedition. Schwan's brigade was composed of two Volunteer infantry regiments, the Thirtieth and the Forty-Sixth, nine troops of cavalry, two companies of Macabebe Scouts,* an artillery detachment, one company of engineers, and a detachment of signal corpsmen; and Wheaton's, of four full infantry regiments (the Fourth, Twenty-Eighth, Thirty-Eighth, and Forty-Fifth), two companies of another (the Thirty-Seventh), an artillery detachment, and support troops. A few days after the invasion had started, moreover, a cavalry squadron was added to Wheaton's brigade. The soldiers already stationed at Calamba and Los Baños—the Thirty-Ninth and ten companies of the Thirty-Seventh—were assigned to the operation as well, but they were to be under the direct command of General Bates, the division commander.[5]

According to Otis's plan, Schwan's brigade was to assemble at San Pedro Macati, a suburb of Manila, proceed southward via Muntinlupa to Biñan, and from there sweep into Cavite, taking Silang, Indang, and finally Naic near the coast. The objective was to establish a barrier across the province

*The Macabebes were mercenaries from the town of Macabebe in the province of Pampanga.

of Cavite and envelop the main elements of Gen. Mariano Trias's army. Wheaton's orders were to concentrate his forces in northern Cavite and initially to act as a containing force, "merely holding the enemy with demonstrations" until Schwan should have placed his troops across Trias's line of retreat. Then Wheaton was to launch a frontal attack against the enveloped enemy soldiers. Once Trias's main units were defeated, the two brigades would continue their advance into Batangas, Laguna, and Tayabas and mop up the forces of Malvar and Juan Cailles. The expedition also aimed to liberate any American and Spanish prisoners of war held in the region.[6]

Whether or not the plan was well conceived—and as we shall later see, it had one basic flaw—these two brigades approached the campaign with major advantages. For one, as we already know, the Filipino Army in Batangas, and probably in the neighboring provinces, was riddled with internal conflicts. For another, the Americans had a superiority in matériel. At this stage of the war, all U.S. infantrymen were equipped with the Krag-Jorgensen rifle, a modern repeating weapon that fired a smokeless cartridge. Some of the Filipinos had magazine rifles too, Mausers captured in the revolution against Spain, but others were armed with outdated, single-shot Remingtons, which used a black-powder cartridge that had the obvious drawback of revealing the position of the firer. Still other Filipino soldiers—perhaps one in three—carried only bolos, of little use except in hand-to-hand combat. Bolomen usually remained in the rear, coming forward to join the fighting when a rifle became available. Furthermore, the Filipinos were terrible marksmen. "Did you ever kill any Americans?" I asked one old man who had fought in Malvar's forces. "No," he replied, obviously amused, "but I killed many birds." The Filipino troops consistently fired high, probably because they had never learned to use the sights on their rifles.[7] Whereas many of the American soldiers had learned to fire weapons as young boys, the Filipinos, with the exception of the veterans of the Revolution, had little experience with firearms. They did not have opportunities to practice firing either because their army was almost always short of ammunition, and the men had to conserve their scarce cartridges for encounters with the enemy.

The Americans were stronger in other respects. In heavy weapons, the U.S. Army, though it did not ship its heaviest artillery pieces to the Philippines, had at its disposal 3.2-inch lightweight field pieces and an assortment of Maxim-Nordenfelt, Hotchkiss, Colt, and Gatling guns, all of which proved to be fairly effective in the fighting in the southern Tagalog region. The Filipinos, by contrast, had few modern heavy weapons, and some of their field pieces were downright primitive.[8] The Americans' superiority in cav-

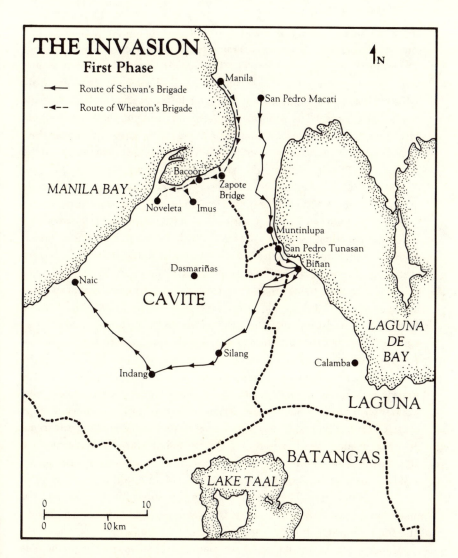

THE INVASION
First Phase

→— Route of Schwan's Brigade
--◄-- Route of Wheaton's Brigade

N

Manila

San Pedro Macati

MANILA BAY

Bacoor

Zapote Bridge

Noveleta   Imus

Muntinlupa

San Pedro Tunasan

Biñan

Dasmariñas

Naic

CAVITE

LAGUNA DE BAY

Silang

Calamba

Indang

LAGUNA

BATANGAS

LAKE TAAL

0   10
0   10 km

4. *The Invasion, First Phase*

alry was likewise telling. Trias, Malvar and the other Filipino commanders south of Manila were forced to face some eight hundred cavalrymen with but a handful of mounted soldiers. The U.S. cavalry was invaluable not only because of its mobility but also because of its shock effect. "I was very afraid of the big horses," one Batangueño veteran admitted to me, and others made similar comments.[9] The American cavalrymen brought their own mounts with them to the Philippines, and these horses were larger and faster than those commonly found in the archipelago. The Americans also controlled the sea. At several points during the expedition into the southern Tagalog region, the U.S. Navy's gunboats shelled coastal towns, and its supply vessels transported needed rations, ammunition, and clothing to the troops.

A final advantage for the Americans was that their Filipino opponents were woefully unprepared to resist a full-scale invasion. The major responsibility for this state of affairs must be assigned to General Trias, the supreme commander of the Filipino Army south of Manila. At the very moment Otis was preparing to invade and at a time when many soldiers and civilians in the southern Tagalog region were bracing for an invasion, Trias became distracted. In mid-December 1899, he and Gen. Artemio Ricarte had hatched a plan for an operation in Manila: a mass uprising by Manila's population and the attempted takeover of the city by the territorial militia led by Ricarte. Clearly it was a terrible time to carry out such a plan, since the American defenses of the city had recently been strengthened, and one may wonder with good reason whether Trias had temporarily taken leave of his senses. Perhaps he had simply become overconfident, having experienced a modicum of success in the preceding months in harassing the undermanned U.S. garrisons in Cavite and Laguna. In any case, the operation went ahead, and on December 29, Ricarte posted notices in Manila calling for an uprising on the following day. The plan fizzled. On December 30 only a few minor disturbances took place in the city, the Americans put them down quickly, and the Filipinos abandoned the operation.[10]

Hence, while he should have been readying his troops for the predictable American offensive, Trias had been preoccupied, and the chief issue of his preoccupation was to be military disaster. As Schwan and Wheaton prepared to advance, a conventional force of no more than three thousand Filipino soldiers waited in Cavite and northwestern Laguna, scattered across the map in the same fortified positions they had occupied for the past several months.[11] Meanwhile, the rest of the men under Trias's orders in the southern Tagalog region—at least five thousand of them, including approximately three thousand troops led by Malvar—remained in eastern Laguna, Tayabas, and Batangas, much too far away to come to Trias's aid. The Americans were to find themselves facing several uncoordinated, widely separated commands in the region. To succeed, Schwan and Wheaton needed only to keep their brigades intact and then to attack in detail the smaller Filipino units they encountered along the way.

What else could Trias have done under the circumstances? Basically, he had two choices. The first was to mass all his troops in the region to meet the Americans. All together, the regular forces under his command were nearly as large as the American brigades that were about to invade, and several thousand militiamen in the area could have been called up as well. By massing his troops, he would at least have given them a better chance in set-piece battles. On the other hand, even if Trias's forces had been massed it is unlikely that they could have held off the invaders. In any conventional contest, the Americans' superiority in matériel and marksmanship was bound to prove decisive. Filipino losses might even have been even higher if Trias had adopted this course; once beaten, a large army would have found it far more difficult to escape the pursuing Americans than would a number of small scattered ones.

Trias's second option—and, in hindsight, the one he should have adopted—was to allow the Americans to enter the region unopposed and to reorganize the local forces along guerrilla lines. To adopt this course was not necessarily to bow to the inevitable, but rather to embrace it—to recognize the impossibility, given the available men and resources, of defeating the Americans in set-piece battles and to choose to fight a guerrilla war at the outset rather than to be forced to fight one later because conventional warfare had proved disastrous. Had Trias chosen this course, he would have avoided serious losses and presented the invading Americans with a far more troublesome enemy than the one they encountered. He might have prolonged the war.

Guerrilla warfare was well known to Filipino commanders: they had resorted to it in 1897, during the final days of the first stage of the revolution against Spain, and Aguinaldo had opted for it again, belatedly, in his own area of operations in November 1899. There is, however, no evidence that Aguinaldo's recent switch to guerrilla tactics had any effect on Trias's approach to the war. What made unconventional warfare unattractive to him at this point was no doubt the same thing that had made it unattractive to Aguinaldo in the early days of the conflict with the Americans: he did not want to surrender control over an area in which a Filipino government was functioning, and he also realized that if he reorganized his forces along guerrilla lines he ran the risk of undercutting his own authority. One failing of the leaders of the Filipino Army was their persistent view of guerrilla warfare as merely the last resort of a beaten army rather than a means by which an inferior army could cope with a superior one, and one consequence of such thinking was to undermine the potential effectiveness of the unconventional approach. Thus, Aguinaldo had continued to fight set-piece battles until his elite units had been decimated, and Trias, in a different theater of operations, was about to repeat the mistake.

Not everything favored the invaders. Most of the U.S. troops were unused to campaigning under a tropical sun, and, weighed down with more than forty pounds of gear, a number would succumb to the heat. They were highly susceptible to many of the microparasites that thrived in that part of the world; in the end, disease would inflict far more casualties on them than enemy bullets. They also had little firsthand knowledge of the territory south of Manila, since their operations in the region had been confined to northern Cavite and northwestern Laguna; and to compound the problem, the maps they used—which were based on Spanish cartographic information—were badly out of date.[12] The Filipinos, by contrast, were fighting literally in their own backyards, and their leaders could, and did, take advantage of their familiarity with the terrain to choose favorable positions for making their stands against the Americans. Still, the relative advantage of their superior knowledge of terrain was arguably more than offset by their inferior matériel and marksmanship. Several thousand miles away, at almost exactly the same time, the Boers were inflicting a stunning rate of casualties on British troops precisely because they were able, with magazine weapons and accurate firing, to take maximum advantage of the opportunities created by their greater familiarity with the veld. By comparison, the Filipinos, with too few Mausers and too little experience in firing weapons, were less dangerous foes.

In retrospect, the success of the American invasion of the southern Tagalog region appeared to be predetermined. This was not to be a contest between armies of comparable strength. There would be few of the dramatic scenes one might find in campaigns in which the result was in doubt—no matching of wits by rival commanders at the climax of a battle, no moments of crisis when the actions of a single company or battalion would determine the outcome of the fighting. This was rather to be a merciless thrashing. The Filipinos would fight bravely but they would lose every set-piece encounter. For Malvar and his forces in Batangas, as for the rest of the Filipino Army in the southern Tagalog region, the price to be paid for the folly of attempting to resist the Americans by conventional means would be substantial.

★ The First Phase

The first phase of the invasion—the operations of the two brigades in north-western Laguna and Cavite against the main forces of General Trias—foreshadowed the type of warfare that would later take place in Batangas. On the American side, there was isolated disorganization, some insubordination, and constant, relentless forward movement. On the Filipino side, there were crushing defeats, crippling casualties, demoralization, and, ultimately, panic.

By January 3, 1900, all the elements of Schwan's brigade had assembled at San Pedro Macati, and the engineers received orders to check out the projected route of march. To their dismay, they discovered that their cartographic information could not be trusted. The maps showed a main road running along the shore of Laguna de Bay to Muntinlupa, but their eyes told them that no such road existed, and the brigade had to spend a day locating a suitable alternate route. Finally, late in the afternoon of the fourth, Schwan gave the orders to march, and some 2,500 soldiers—clad in uniforms of blue and khaki, equipped with Krags, blankets, ponchos, and assorted field gear, and accompanied by dozens of carabao carts and scores of "chinos"* who served as bearers and factotums—moved out along a narrow trail that led southward along the Guadalupe Ridge and eventually intersected a better thoroughfare running from Las Piñas to Muntinlupa. The men hiked a few miles before sunset, camped along the trail for the night, and resumed the march on the next morning. Yet if those 2,500 soldiers were making progress, about 550 others—the troopers of the Fourth and Eleventh Cavalry who were attached to Schwan's brigade—were not. The forage needed for their horses had been delayed en route to San Pedro Macati, and they were obliged to remain behind. The forage arrived on the fifth, and the troopers set out in

---

*The Chinese population of the Philippines, predominantly male, numbered approximately ninety thousand on the eve of the Philippine Revolution. Although a significant number of Chinese merchants and shopkeepers were prosperous, the majority of the Chinese were poor laborers and itinerant traders, and such people were employed by the U.S. Army to transport supplies and to work as servants for officers. On the whole, the Chinese lived separately, and relatively few were integrated into Filipino life. On the Chinese, see Edgar Wickberg, *The Chinese in Philippine Life, 1850–1898* (New Haven, 1965).

pursuit at a gallop, catching up to the rear of the column in only a few hours and then slowing to a walk as they followed the cumbersome carabao carts along the narrow, barely passable trail. Late in the afternoon the head of the column reached Muntinlupa, and shortly afterward the cavalrymen, frustrated by the delays and the slowness of the march, also entered the town.[13]

On the following day, Schwan divided his brigade into two columns for the advance on Biñan, seven miles to the south. One column, which included the cavalry, the artillery, and one battalion of the Thirtieth Infantry, approached Biñan via an inland road that ran along the base of a range of hills. The other, consisting of most of the infantrymen and the slow-moving wagon train, took a road that paralleled the coast of Laguna de Bay. The first column came upon a few hundred enemy troops only a mile and a half outside Muntinlupa and drove them away after a thirty-minute fight. It proceeded to Biñan, and on the outskirts of town encountered several hundred more Filipinos, dug in on both sides of the road; they were a rearguard left behind on the previous day by Gen. Mariano Noriel, one of Trias's ablest officers and the commander of the brigade normally stationed in Biñan. The rearguard's task was to delay the Americans and so protect the withdrawal of the main body of Noriel's brigade to Silang. But they did not slow Schwan's column much, and, according to the Americans' after-action reports, eighteen Filipinos were killed in the fighting, while the U.S. forces suffered only three casualties of their own.[14]

The soldiers in the second column made their way up the beach road without incident and paused for their midday meal at San Pedro Tunasan, about midway between Muntinlupa and Biñan. The town was deserted, and the troops, tired of eating bacon and hardbread rations, proceeded to forage for chickens. "What a time all had chasing them," Sgt. George Gelbach of the Forty-Sixth Volunteer Infantry later recalled. "That dinner at Tunisan [*sic*] was a good one as we had chicken soup with rice in it, also eggs in any style you wish to prepare them. The officers did not bother us as we had fared pretty hard the past few days but it was against the rule to loot a town even for something to eat." After enjoying their meal, the men pushed on to Biñan, arriving there a few hours after the first column's skirmish with Noriel's rearguard. Biñan too had been abandoned, and as the same Sergeant Gelbach remembered it, the soldiers foraged far into the night.[15]

Thus Biñan, Schwan's first objective, was captured quickly, and on January 7, with the cavalry taking the lead, the Americans took Silang with equal ease. Demoralized by the enemy's lightning victories and their own severe losses, Noriel's brigade began to dissolve. About two hundred men retreated

13. Gen. Theodore Schwan and staff en route to Silang, Cavite, January 1900

to Indang, seven miles to the west, for a final stand, but the majority ran away, scattering in all directions. Meanwhile Schwan's cavalrymen continued on, and by sunset, after dislodging the remnants of Noriel's force from fortified positions outside Indang, captured that town as well.[16]

Schwan's brigade was now close to completing its mission, the establishment of a barrier across the province of Cavite. But to the north, in General Wheaton's designated area of operations, something had gone awry. Otis's plan had called for Wheaton's brigade to avoid serious contact with the enemy until Schwan had completed his envelopment, but Wheaton's subordinates, anxious for a fight, could not be restrained. On the seventh, two engagements had taken place near Imus and another near Noveleta, and if the Americans' battle reports are to be believed, Trias's forces had suffered more than 250 casualties. On the eighth, Wheaton's reconnaissance parties found only a few scattered enemy troops in the area.[17] What then had happened to Trias's army? Like Noriel's brigade to the south, it had begun to disintegrate. The only organized body of Trias's forces remaining after the defeats at Imus and Noveleta numbered no more than 300 men, and they retreated hastily in the direction of Naic, the town near the coast that had not yet been occupied by Schwan's brigade. Some other troops attempted to sift through the American lines in small parties in order to join up with Filipino units in the neighboring provinces. But most of Trias's soldiers simply ran away, hid their weapons and uniforms, returned to their homes, and pretended to be innocent civilians.[18]

These occurrences exposed, after the fact, the major flaw in Otis's plan for the invasion of Cavite. Otis had assumed that Trias's army could be trapped and destroyed by the two brigades. However, even if the timing of the operation had been perfect and Wheaton had delayed his attack until Schwan had executed his envelopment, there was no guarantee that the Filipinos would have been caught in the trap. It was always possible for them to do what they did—melt into the countryside and avoid further contact with the Americans.

To the south, the commander of Schwan's cavalrymen, Col. E. M. Hayes, was unaware of developments in Wheaton's sector. After capturing Indang, he had not pressed his advantage because he lacked instructions to proceed farther. On January 8, therefore, the troopers remained in Indang. But late in the day updated instructions arrived from Schwan, and on the following morning Hayes and his men left for Naic. A few miles outside the town, they came across the last organized contingent of Trias's forces, the 300 soldiers who were retreating from the north. The cavalrymen outmaneuvered them in a flooded rice field, killed a few before they scattered, and then occupied Naic.[19]

Hence, Schwan's brigade had finally executed its envelopment. But by now it was apparent that there was no longer a Filipino army in Cavite to envelop. Reconnaissance parties sent out by both brigades in the following days were able to find only traces of Trias's troops. In his official report about the invasion, written a few months after the events, General Bates would pronounce this first phase of the operation a success: "The enemy was completely dispersed, the small advance guard of Trias' force, which had been separated from its main body by Hayes, being probably the only organized body that escaped across the intercepting line."[20] Dispersing the Filipinos, however, was not the same as eliminating them. Trias's troops had been battered, but most had survived, and they would be able to fight another day—albeit in a different way.

If the Filipino soldiers in Cavite had temporarily disappeared from the scene, there was still plenty of fighting to be done. Just as the first phase of the U.S. invasion of the southern Tagalog region was coming to an end, the second phase was beginning. On the same day that Colonel Hayes had his fight outside Naic, another American colonel, Robert Lee Bullard, led more than a thousand soldiers into the province of Batangas and engaged the forces of Gen. Miguel Malvar.

★ Initial Operations in Batangas: Santo Tomas

There was definitely an insubordinate streak in the American officer corps. Though never quite as prominent or as damaging as that in the Filipino officer corps, it was there all the same. American individualism may have contributed to it; so too, perhaps, did jealousy, personality conflict, and disagreement about how wars should be fought. But, at bottom, it was born of ambition—the ambition of long-frustrated professional soldiers to achieve high rank. The classic example of the ambitious, insubordinate American career officer was Colonel Bullard, the youthful, mustachioed commander of the Thirty-Ninth Volunteer Infantry.

Bullard had graduated from West Point in 1885, and after a year devoted to chasing Geronimo, he had settled down to an uneventful life on military posts in the West. Equally uneventful had been a stint as professor of military science at a college in Georgia. As it happened, Bullard had entered military service at one of the dullest periods in the U.S. Army's history: there was little fighting to be done and it was extremely difficult for an officer to

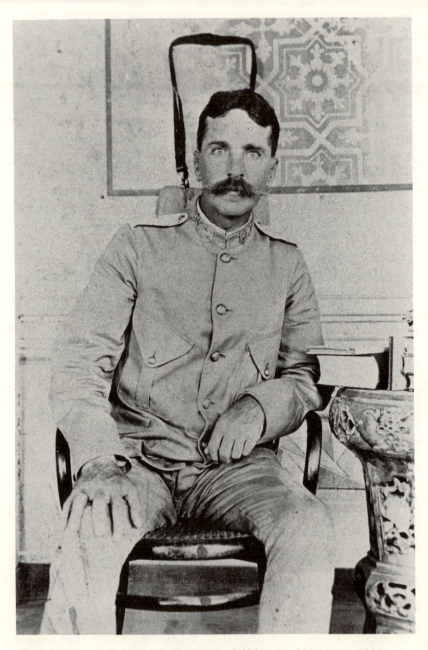

14. Col. Robert Lee Bullard, Thirty-Ninth Volunteer Infantry, c. 1900

progress through the ranks. Bullard's own progress had been unspectacular. On the eve of the Spanish-American War, he was a captain in the Subsistence Department. The campaigns in Cuba had brought only more frustration to Bullard. Although he was appointed colonel of a Volunteer regiment, his unit had languished in training camp while others did the fighting. But the new war in the Philippines and a new commission—colonel of the Thirty-Ninth—gave Bullard a second chance, and he was determined to make the most of it.[21]

Possibly he was too determined. The Thirty-Ninth had arrived in the Philippines on December 7, 1899, and eight days later Bullard moved to Calamba along with one battalion of his regiment. The other two were temporarily assigned to garrisons in the environs of Manila in order to shore up the capital's defenses. Initially, Bullard merely watched and waited. The ill-fated Twenty-First Infantry was still stationed at Calamba, and Col. Jacob Kline remained in charge of the post. What Bullard saw did not please him. Kline's regiment was sick, battered, and demoralized; within the town of Calamba itself, the streetlights could not be lit at night because the enemy shot at them. "Not so good," Bullard commented to a subordinate, "and we must see about that." The situation changed in the last week of December, when the remainder of the Thirty-Ninth joined Bullard at Calamba and Kline's men were finally withdrawn. Now in command of the post, Bullard ordered a careful reconnaissance, and despite the fact that he lacked authorization to undertake large-scale offensive operations in the area, he decided to do so. On January 1, Bullard's troops attacked the Filipino trenches to the northwest of Calamba, dislodged the enemy, and pursued them to Santa Rosa; the following day, his men occupied Biñan after a brief fight.[22]

Bullard won no plaudits for his initiative. The chief problem with his offensive, aside from not having been approved by his superiors, was that it conflicted with General Otis's plans for the invasion of the southern Tagalog region. Unwittingly, Bullard's troops had moved into the very part of Laguna through which Otis was planning to, and did, send Schwan's brigade in a few days. When Otis learned about Bullard's expedition, he was not pleased. "You did right in attacking insurgents' line around Calamba, but should not have pursued," he cabled the colonel on January 3. "You will withdraw your troops to Calamba. . . . Do no move from the vicinity of Calamba without orders from superior authority." Thus upbraided, Bullard ordered his men back to the post.[23]

Back in Calamba, Bullard grew restless. Days passed; the invasion of the southern Tagalog region got under way; Bullard received word that during the invasion he would be under the direct command of General Bates; but he received no orders from Bates to take part in the operations. The enforced idleness was galling. Even more galling was the fact that other officers were now scoring the victories and gaining the glory. Furthermore, as he waited, he observed that to the south of Calamba, on the road leading to Santo Tomas, the Filipino forces appeared to be strengthening their positions. Once again, Bullard succumbed to ambition: in willful disregard of Otis's orders, he decided to attack the enemy and seize Santo Tomas.[24]

What were Miguel Malvar and the Batangueño forces thinking and doing while the Americans were preparing to attack? Malvar was definitely aware that a major operation was being launched by the enemy. Bullard's unauthorized offensive of January 1–2, which had begun with an assault on the Banajao Battalion's position northwest of Calamba, was one indication of the Americans' intentions; the occupation by Schwan's brigade of Muntinlupa and other towns to the north of Calamba was another. By January 5, as Bullard could plainly see, Malvar was repositioning his troops to resist an attack on his native town, Santo Tomas.[25]

From a tactical standpoint, Malvar's plan for the defense of Santo Tomas was well conceived. His initial defensive position was a line of trenches across the main road, approximately a mile south of Calamba. In addition, his troops had prepared several positions to the rear, including an impressive series of earthworks at barrio Biga, where a great iron bridge spanned a gorge some four miles from the población of Santo Tomas. "Here," wrote Charles Summerall, an artillery officer who served with Bullard, "the insurgents had erected fortifications so elaborate as to be of a permanent character. The fortified side of the ravine was about twenty feet higher than the side we approached. Along the crest, deep trenches were cut, and the exterior slope was evenly finished. The deep cut on that side, through which the bridge was approached, was filled by a strong work with two tiers of loop holes, the lower part being supplied with two embrasures for field guns." Finally, to prevent the enemy from attacking the potentially vulnerable right flank of the Biga position, Malvar had deployed a company of the Banajao Battalion slightly to the west of the barrio, at two strategic narrow passes at the base of Mount Maquiling. Malvar believed, or so it was later reported, that his position at barrio Biga was impregnable.[26]

Yet, if his defensive positions were strong, the force that Malvar had assigned to man them was surprisingly small—no more than ten or eleven companies in all. The rest of his troops remained behind at their normal stations—Batangas City, Taal, and other places. Why his troops were so

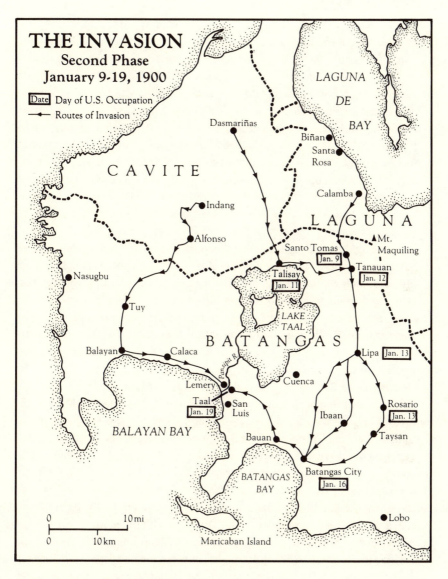

THE INVASION
Second Phase
January 9-19, 1900

Date Day of U.S. Occupation
——◄—— Routes of Invasion

LAGUNA
DE
BAY

Dasmariñas

Biñan

Santa Rosa

C A V I T E

Indang

Calamba

L A G U N A

Alfonso

Mt. Maquiling

Santo Tomas
Jan. 9

Tanauan
Jan. 12

Nasugbu

Talisay
Jan. 11

LAKE TAAL

Tuy

B A T A N G A S

Balayan

Calaca

Lipa Jan. 13

Pansipit R.

Cuenca

Lemery

Taal
Jan. 19

San Luis

Rosario
Jan. 13

Ibaan

BALAYAN BAY

Taysan

Bauan

Batangas City
Jan. 16

BATANGAS
BAY

Lobo

0   10 mi
0   10 km

Maricaban Island

5. *The Invasion, Second Phase: January 9–19, 1900*

dispersed is not completely clear. Possibly Malvar regarded the fortifications at Biga as so formidable that even a relatively small force would be able to hold the position. More likely, his men remained dispersed because he was genuinely unsure about where the Americans would strike. During the past year, after all, Batangas's defensive plans had anticipated a seaborne invasion of the province, and since late December U.S. Navy vessels had been appearing with great frequency off the coast of Taal, Balayan, and Batangas City. Indeed, at one point, the U.S.S. *Mariveles* had even fired a few shots of its Colt gun at Filipino troops on the beach near Taal.[27] So, despite knowing that a major U.S. operation was under way, Malvar was probably reluctant to commit too many of his troops to Santo Tomas. The Americans might attempt to invade Batangas from the sea at the same time their troops were moving overland.

Once again the Filipino Army was undertaking to fight a conventional battle with severe, perhaps insuperable, disadvantages. Defensive plans might be well conceived and fortified positions might be well constructed. Commanders might be brave and resolute and enlisted men might be battle-hardened. But, lacking the ability to protect the Batangas coastline, Malvar was in no position to commit a sufficient number of his troops to the defense of Santo Tomas. Knowing that, as well as the fact that the Filipino forces had to contend with so many other deficiencies, one can conclude only that the chances of the Batangueño defenders were slim at best.

Early on the morning of January 9, Bullard moved against Malvar. He divided his attacking force into three columns. One of them, composed of two companies of the Thirty-Ninth under the command of Capt. William Taylor, deployed to the west of the road connecting Calamba and Santo Tomas. The second, three companies of the Thirty-Ninth led by Maj. George Langhorne accompanied by Lt. Charles Summerall and his heavy weapons, approached the enemy along the road itself. The third, commanded by Bullard and consisting of three companies of the Thirty-Ninth and another three of the Thirty-Seventh, took a route close to Mount Maquiling, to the east of the main road. As it happened, Bullard's column was moving directly toward the position occupied by the company of the Banajao Battalion, which was guarding Malvar's right flank.[28]

In many respects, the fighting followed the pattern established in the first phase of the invasion. At daybreak, Summerall's guns began firing on Malvar's trenches, and Major Langhorne's three companies moved forward briskly along the road. The Filipinos fought bravely for a while, but after suffering heavy losses, they abandoned the position. Regrouping several miles down the road at barrio Tulo, they made another ineffective attempt to repel the Americans and finally retreated to the heavily fortified position at Biga.

Meanwhile, to the east, Bullard's column had been making progress along the base of Mount Maquiling. The men of the Banajao Battalion made an effort to stop the Americans' advance, but they were quickly overwhelmed. Bullard's units were now in a position to attack the Filipino troops at Biga both from the flank and the rear, and, faced with that threat as well as the accurate fire being directed at them from the front, Malvar and his men decided to abandon Biga after less than an hour of fighting. As most of the Filipinos fled westward in the direction of Lake Taal, the Americans moved on to the población of Santo Tomas.[29]

Bullard had won a clear victory: only one of his men had been killed and two had been wounded; on the Filipino side, according to U.S. after-action reports, twenty-four soldiers had died, many more had been wounded, and about sixty had been captured, as had two bamboo cannon, two brass mortars, and an assortment of rifles and ammunition. On this occasion Bullard received praise rather than rebuke for his initiative. Following his victory, Bullard posted some troops in Santo Tomas and returned temporarily to Calamba. Soon afterward he received a telegram from General Bates telling him—as Bullard put the matter in his diary—"to do almost exactly what I had done." He immediately sent Bates a report of his day's activities and received a reply "stating the pleasure of the Division Commander."[30] Apparently some generals were more tolerant of insubordination than others.

The battle for Santo Tomas should have been a warning to Malvar. At barrio Biga, he had held a strong defensive position and had failed. His position had been outflanked, his field guns had been ineffective, and there was no good reason to believe that, given the disadvantages he was forced to contend with, his troops' performance was likely to improve in future setpiece battles with the Americans. Malvar, however, was not yet ready to admit that his forces were outmatched. Conventional warfare would continue in Batangas.

★ Lipa and Rosario

To this point in the invasion, the Thirty-Eighth Volunteer Infantry, the regiment in which Capt. John Leland Jordan served, had played a minor role. It had even been the cause of some embarrassment. On the night of January 2, while most of the regiment was stationed in the vicinity of Bacoor, the men assigned to outpost duty, green troops from Company B, had become frightened and sounded the alarm, and for more than an hour the entire company had fired wildly into the dark. The regiment's commander, Colonel Anderson, investigated the incident personally, and the results of his inquiry appalled him. "I am convinced," Anderson wrote, "that the entire firing was precipitated and brought about by the nervousness of the sentinels." To make matters worse, on the following night a sentinel from Company D, Jordan's unit, mistook one of his own men for a Filipino soldier and killed him.[31] But now, after Bullard's victory at Santo Tomas, Anderson's regiment was to get a chance to do some fighting and make amends. Having learned from Bullard that Santo Tomas's defenders were retreating along the northern shore of Lake Taal, General Bates ordered Wheaton to dispatch the Thirty-Eighth, then at Dasmariñas, to intercept the fleeing Filipinos.[32]

In the events that followed, a crucial part was played by the instructions Anderson received from General Wheaton. They were extraordinarily open-ended. In his written orders, Wheaton instructed the colonel to march immediately to Talisay, the northernmost town of Batangas, and to "attack, pursue, and destroy" any enemy troops he found on the northern shore of Lake Taal. Wheaton did not specify where and when the Thirty-Eighth should stop its pursuit. Equally open-ended were the verbal instructions that the brigade commander conveyed at the same time; according to Anderson, Wheaton "told me to pursue and punish the enemy wherever found and to operate in conjunction with Col. Bullard." Anderson was being given an opportunity to do pretty much what he liked, and, being just as ambitious as the next officer in this army, he was not inclined to waste it. Moreover, whatever doubts he may have had about his interpretation of Wheaton's words were dispelled by his subordinate Lt. Col. Charles Crane, who, on looking over the orders, suggested that "we go to Lipa and Batangas, and from the latter place . . . notify headquarters where we were." This suggestion, Crane recalled, "seemed to please Anderson."[33]

Anderson moved out at a killing pace. The regiment left Dasmariñas at sunset on January 10 and after a six-hour march reached Silang, where the men rested for the night. The next day's hike was exhausting: the sun was scorching and the terrain mountainous; many soldiers ran out of water and began to suffer from dehydration. Anderson pressed on. Just outside the lakeside town of Talisay, a small party of Filipinos ambushed them, but their marksmanship was poor and the Thirty-Eighth absorbed no casualties. The troops then entered the town, and many of them, almost mad from lack of water, charged fully clothed into the lake.[34]

15. *Col. George S. Anderson, Thirty-Eighth Volunteer Infantry,*
November 1899

The next morning, January 12, Anderson's troops marched off to the east, along the northern shore of Lake Taal. They came across a few Filipinos, but only one of them turned out to be an enemy soldier. The men that Bullard had dislodged from barrio Biga three days before had disappeared without trace. In the early afternoon, the Thirty-Eighth entered Tanauan without opposition, and since they had exhausted their rations, they promptly foraged for food. "Plenty of oranges and chicks," Thomas Selm, a private in Company A, noted laconically in his diary.[35]

Although his troops were tired, Anderson had no thoughts of stopping here. And even if he had, they would have been swiftly put to rest by the U.S. Army officer who joined him in his camp. Col. Robert Bullard had again grown restless, and when he saw the Thirty-Eighth march into view, he decided to find out what Anderson proposed to do next. Learning that Anderson planned to go to Lipa, he offered to cooperate, even though he had no instructions to justify such a decision. Anderson accepted the offer, and the two colonels agreed to proceed together to Lipa on the following morning.[36]

Meanwhile, unknown to Anderson and Bullard, decisions were being made by their superiors many miles away. At this stage in the invasion the soldiers of the two brigades had become spread out across the region in no rational pattern, with several units of Wheaton's brigade far closer to Schwan's headquarters than to their own. Obviously, a reorganization was necessary, and on January 12 General Bates issued orders to that effect. Anderson's and Bullard's regiments plus one battalion of the Thirty-Seventh, all of which were already operating in the province of Batangas, were incorporated into Schwan's brigade, and henceforth that brigade would have the task of destroying the enemy in eastern Batangas, Laguna, and Tayabas. At the same time, the Forty-Sixth was transferred to Wheaton's brigade, and thereafter Wheaton's area of responsibility was to be Cavite and western Batangas. In order to carry out the contemplated reorganization and to coordinate his future operations against the enemy in eastern Batangas, Schwan sent telegrams to Anderson and Bullard informing them that he would arrive at Santo Tomas on January 13 and directing them not to "press the enemy" before his arrival.[37] As it turned out, though, Schwan's telegrams did not reach the camp of the two colonels before they left for Lipa.

For the past few months, the residents of Lipa had known that an American invasion of the town was inevitable. The town's newspaper, *Columnas Volantes,* had reported the Americans' successes in the fighting north of Manila, the disintegration of Aguinaldo's conventional army, and the president's flight to northern Luzon. Editorials in the paper had sought to prepare

16. Thirty-Eighth Volunteer Infantry marching from Silang, Cavite, to Talisay, Batangas, January 1900

the people for the trauma of occupation. Still, when word came that the Americans were close to Lipa, the townspeople panicked. "People clustered around the *municipio,* the Club, the *Instituto,* asking for news," recalled Teodoro Kalaw, who was a student at the time. "Families . . . took up their belongings and evacuated from the town to seek safety in the mountains. My own family went to the same country-place which had sheltered us during the fight with the Spaniards."[38]

As the townspeople fled, Malvar prepared to resist the Americans at the barrio of Luta, about eight miles north of the población. Following the disaster at barrio Biga, Malvar had done what he could to rally his forces. He had issued instructions to units stationed further to the south to be ready to fight the invaders, and he had ordered several of his lieutenants to appear at a conference on January 10 to discuss future operations. At that meeting the Batangueño leaders decided to defend Lipa, and over the next few days several commands received orders to send additional rifles and ammunition to Lipa's defenders. For some reason, however, no orders went out to send additional men from other stations to join in the defense of the town. As at Santo Tomas, Malvar was to face the Americans with a surprisingly small force—in this case, fewer than one thousand men. Since Bullard and Anderson had close to two thousand soldiers under their orders, it is clear that Malvar's task was hopeless.[39]

Something about all this smacked of bravado. Malvar would stand up and fight even though his chances of succeeding were negligible. How can such behavior be explained? In his influential study of popular movements in the Philippines, Reynaldo Ileto has suggested that a number of Filipino military leaders of the revolutionary period (Andres Bonifacio, for one) believed that spiritual preparation was as important as military preparation in gaining victories on the battlefield: that their troops could triumph against all odds if their souls were pure and their cause was just.[40] One possible corollary of such an interpretation is that we cannot understand the Filipino Army's actions according to the standard criteria of military performance. Did Malvar exemplify this distinctively Filipino (as opposed to Western) approach to warfare?

Perhaps. But another explanation for Malvar's behavior may be that, like Aguinaldo and Trias, he was acting out a part—acting the way he believed that a leader of a great nation was expected to act. Rather than being an exemplar of a typically Filipino approach to battle, he may have been more an imitator of the Western approach—or at least, of what he believed the Western approach to be. For many leaders of the Philippine Republic, the war against the United States represented an opportunity to demonstrate that their fledgling state was capable of taking its place in the community of nations, and doing that meant that it must show itself capable of fighting according to Western norms. For Malvar to adopt guerrilla warfare, he would have had to acknowledge the impotence of the government he fought for.

The conventional approach may have had something else to recommend it. For the leaders of the Filipino Army were attempting not only to validate their new nation-state, but also to preserve a government that, since Aguinaldo's accession to the presidency, had committed itself to the maintenance and promotion of upper-class interests. Such a government may have appealed to an upper-class Batangueño like Malvar, and his attachment to it possibly led him to decide to stick to conventional warfare. After all, only by continuing to fight conventionally could he ensure that he and his social class retained control over the region's population, its food supply and other material resources, and the legitimating symbols of local office. Seen in this light, the decision to continue conventional warfare may have been as much a function of a class-control strategy as of military imperatives.

There was still another compelling reason to avoid making a change. For Malvar, as for Aguinaldo and Trias before him, the Filipino officer corps was an ongoing cause of concern. The tensions within the corps had been difficult enough to contain in a conventional army; Malvar must have realized that they would become even more troublesome if he switched to guerrilla warfare. A guerrilla force might suffer fewer casualties on the battlefield, but the price to be paid for becoming one might have seemed too high.

★ ★ ★

At 6:00 A.M. on January 13, the Americans began their advance on Lipa, with Anderson's regiment and Summerall's artillery taking the lead and Bullard's men following behind. As the Americans approached Luta, Malvar's troops opened fire on the advance guard, Captain Jordan's company, from a distance of two to three hundred yards. Jordan's men returned the fire. Summerall then opened up with his artillery, and within a few minutes the Filipinos were forced to withdraw. But a half-mile further on, the advance party was again attacked by Malvar's forces, firing from behind a barricade thrown across the road. Jordan's company boldly charged the position, and, supported by the artillery and a few lead companies, succeeded in dispersing the Filipinos. In these two encounters, the Americans killed several enemy soldiers and wounded many more; their own losses were one man killed and another severely wounded.[41]

Although Malvar's troops were scattering in all directions, Anderson decided not to chase them. He believed—incorrectly, as it happened—that the Filipinos planned a last-ditch defense at the entrance to Lipa, and he wanted to keep his forces intact for that anticipated encounter. About a mile from the población, still certain that Malvar's men were lying in wait ahead, he halted for an hour to prepare for the assault. At this unlikely juncture, a courier arrived with Schwan's telegram of January 12, ordering Anderson not to press the enemy. But Anderson had no intention of stopping now—"It was then too late to withdraw from this attack," he later explained—and he ordered the column forward. Meeting no resistance, the Thirty-Eighth entered Lipa shortly after midday. The town was deserted, except for approximately 130 Spanish soldiers—the members of Navas's force, captured some eighteen months earlier—and these men, just released by their captors, waved their hats and handkerchiefs at the Americans and cheered them wildly.[42]

Warfare sometimes has bizarre episodes, and one was about to occur. It began when Colonel Bullard joined Anderson in the población and learned from the Spaniards that a group of Filipinos had left for the nearby town of Rosario two hours earlier with several dozen more Spanish prisoners and a handful of Americans. Actually, the first piece of information was correct, but not the second. The Spaniards had invented the story about the Americans in order to provide an added incentive for the U.S. troops to set off in pursuit. The ever-impetuous Bullard was taken in, and he suggested to Anderson that they make an effort to rescue the Americans. Anderson agreed, and within a few minutes the two colonels had assembled a mounted party of twelve men which, besides themselves, included Lieutenant Colonel Crane and a former Spanish prisoner who consented to act as a guide. Crane, looking back on the events in his memoirs, claimed that he realized (and told Anderson at the time) that "it was very reckless and desperate to pursue a retreating force of uncertain strength with only a dozen men." But Crane went along anyway. "I have never been rash, but I felt that I had to join in this foolhardy dash on Rosario, or show the white feather."[43]

The dash began about 2:00 P.M. The road to Rosario was crowded with the fleeing residents of Lipa, carrying their clothes and valued possessions and, according to Bullard, "crying, screaming, praying, but above all 'hiking' . . . to fields, forests and mountains." The mounted party reached the town in about an hour, and luckily, they found only a small number of Filipino defenders. "I saw four," wrote Bullard, "and shot at them until they were half a mile off on the run. 'Americanos, Americanos!' they cried, and in five

17. *The dash by Colonels Anderson and Bullard to Rosario, Batangas, January 1900, as depicted in the* Detroit Evening News, *June 15, 1900*

minutes every living soul, soldiers, citizens, women and children, even the ponies and carabaos had disappeared, taken to the deep forest that surrounded the town." Not everyone had disappeared, however. Crane, bringing up the rear, came upon some seventy Spanish prisoners in the población, and like their compatriots in Lipa they earnestly professed their love for their liberators.[44]

Crane and the others continued to search for American prisoners but found none. They did find something else of value. When Bullard arrived, he questioned a Spanish officer and learned that the Filipino troops had left behind a large amount of money in the town. The Spaniard led the Americans to a lot owned by a municipal official, and there they discovered a number of wooden boxes filled with silver coins—in all, approximately 20,000 Mexican pesos. They loaded the boxes on two *carromatos,* instructed the liberated Spaniards to escort the money back to Lipa, then set off for Lipa themselves. Arriving there just before sunset, they made another discovery. In their absence, the two regiments had foraged enthusiastically for chickens, pigs, cows, and other edibles (and some of them, it was later charged, had stolen valuables from the vacated houses).[45]

So ended a disastrous day for Malvar's forces and an eventful one for Bullard and Anderson. For their efforts, the two colonels received favorable coverage in the American press. But their superiors—Schwan, in particular—were not so impressed. To some extent, Schwan's displeasure stemmed from his belief that the movement of the two regiments to Lipa and beyond had been premature and had potentially jeopardized the chances of trapping Malvar's troops inside the boundaries of the province of Batangas. Yet, he may also have been jealous of the success achieved by Anderson and Bullard. "I have always believed," Crane later wrote, "that the hike breaking into those provinces of Cavite, Laguna, Batangas and Tayabas was intended to pave the way for a small shower of stars, and that we got into some other man's apple orchard, and spoiled some plans." Bullard's assessment was similar: Schwan, he maintained, "was hunting glory himself as a basis to be a brigadier [in the regular army] and the 39th's col. was getting in his way."[46] Whatever his motives, Schwan decided that some disciplinary action was in order. When he finally caught up to his colonels at Lipa on the evening of the fourteenth, Schwan ordered Bullard to return to the north with one battalion of his regiment, to establish garrisons at Santo Tomas and Tanauan, and thereafter to focus his attention on keeping open the line of communication between Calamba and the troops to the south. "Gen. Schwan thus intended to and did 'sidetrack' me for the balance of this expedition," Bullard commented in his diary. Anderson went unpunished, probably because he could justify his conduct by pointing to Wheaton's earlier instructions, and he was permitted to continue south with the advancing brigade.[47]

★ Batangas City

If jealousy was erupting in the ranks of the advancing army, hints of despair, and a growing sense of realism, could be perceived in the retreating one. Col. Santiago Rillo, commander of the Eastern Zone of Batangas, learned about the debacle at Luta and the American occupation of Lipa only a few hours after the events took place. A practical man, Rillo at once concluded that a change to guerrilla tactics was necessary. Under normal circumstances, Rillo would have had to secure Malvar's approval for any major decision, but because the channels of communication between the Batangueño commanders had been disrupted he decided to act on his own. Late on the thirteenth, he instructed Lt. Col. Mariano Cabrera, leader of the Filipino troops in the vicinity of Batangas City, to station his soldiers in "safe places" for the time being, to conserve ammunition, and to avoid further set-piece battles with the Americans.[48]

For several weeks, the Batangueño forces in the provincial capital had made preparations to fight the Americans. Cabrera himself had drawn up the plan for the town's defense. But after the succession of disasters to the north, Cabrera too had become convinced that it was futile to fight a conventional war against the invaders. Communicating Rillo's orders to Eliseo Claudio on January 14, he made a case for the change in approach:

> The war we make upon our enemies is formal, and because of their greater numbers and the superior means of warfare which they have at their disposal, the result is disastrous to us, even though we sacrifice the lives of our brothers. The most advisable thing to do at the present time in this campaign is to employ ambush warfare; although it is slow in results, it will enable us to attain our independence.

Cabrera then instructed Batangas City's defenders to abandon the población and go into hiding in seven different barrios. Most of the troops did so, although for some reason one unidentified Filipino company commander refused to obey, ordering his men to stay behind and fight the Americans. Even in this moment of extreme danger, the conflicts within the officer corps could not be completely contained.[49]

As the soldiers departed, so did the civilians, equally terrified, it seems, of the approaching American foot soldiers and of a U.S. gunboat, the *Mariveles,* which had entered Batangas Bay and hovered close to shore, well within range of its guns. Pablo Yturralde, a thirty-year-old unemployed pharmacist, took refuge in the seaside barrio of Ylijan, no fewer than ten miles from his normal residence in the población. The merchant Feliciano Cantos took his family to the barrio of Santo Niño, where they went into hiding in the house of his mother-in-law. Francisco Abas, a wealthy landowner and former gober-nadorcillo of Batangas City, began a two-month odyssey which took him first to Talumpoc in the uplands and later to Lagnas, a barrio of the neighboring town of Bauan. On January 15, with the población almost deserted, Manuel Genato, the civil governor of Batangas, and the *consejeros* of the provincial government also abandoned the town's center and fled to the safety of the countryside.[50]

While the town was emptying, informal negotiations took place between the municipal authorities and C. E. Gilpin, the commander of the *Mariveles.* Fearful that the gunboat would bombard the población, the Filipino officials agreed to surrender Batangas City to Gilpin. But when the American sailors attempted to go ashore to take possession of the town, Filipino troops—soldiers from the lone company that had remained behind—occupied the trenches on the beach and raised the Filipino flag. In reply, the gunboat shelled the town. So the diplomatic effort netted nothing, and the sailors de-cided to leave the matter of taking possession of Batangas City to Schwan's brigade. As they waited, the last of the Filipino defenders decided to disobey the orders of their company commander and joined in the exodus from Batangas City.[51]

On the fifteenth, Schwan's brigade began its advance from Lipa toward the provincial capital. The general divided his forces into three columns for the movement, which was expected to take two days. The column on the right under Colonel Anderson took the main road linking Lipa and Batangas City. The center column, led by Col. Cornelius Gardener, went by way of Ibaan. On the far left was a battalion of the Thirty-Eighth under Maj. Charles Muir; Muir's instructions were to swing eastward to Rosario, then due south to Taysan, and finally to take a mountain trail westward to Batangas City. Schwan planned that the center column, which he was accompanying, would be the first to enter the capital, with Anderson acting as a reserve and Muir cutting off the enemy's line of retreat to the east.[52]

Things did not work out that way. Muir made better progress than expected on the fifteenth, and my midmorning on the sixteenth he had come within two miles of the población. At that point his troops stumbled across some Filipino soldiers—most of the company that had belatedly decided to abandon the capital. The Filipinos fired a few volleys from thickets on a ridge and then retreated into fields of dense sugar cane to the north. Muir's men, including Captain Jordan's company, pursued them, and as they did, they witnessed a remarkable sight. "In every direction, in little gullies, in ditches, in corn rows were women and children, old men, dishes, clothing, etc.," wrote Jordan. "Many were on their knees praying, but most of them were lying like leeches on the ground, with heads covered and moaning as if in great distress." These praying and moaning people were refugees from the provincial capital who had fled in fear of the approaching Americans and had been unlucky enough to choose a route that brought them into contact with Muir. The soldiers being chased by Muir's men were even unluckier. In the fighting that ensued, the Filipinos absorbed a number of casualties and more than seventy men were captured. At about 10:30 A.M., the point of Muir's column finally reached the población of Batangas City. The Americans were "tired, wet, and sore," wrote Private Selm, who was there, "but not too tired to hunt chickens."[53]

Another town thus fell to the Americans, albeit on this occasion without serious opposition. In only a week, despite jealousy, professional rivalry, and occasional insubordination, the U.S. Army had taken control of the major towns of eastern Batangas, and in the process had routed Malvar's conventional army and destroyed the local governments which for the past eighteen months had been running Batangas's affairs. The battle for Batangas was far from over, but its conventional phase was drawing to a close. For the rest of the war, the overriding fact of life for all Batangueños would be the presence of American troops in their major population centers.

These considerable achievements had cost the American troops only a handful of casualties, but the campaigning had taken a toll of a different kind. After twelve days of intermittent fighting and almost continuous marching under a tropical sun, many soldiers in Schwan's brigade were ill or exhausted. Uniforms, socks, and undergarments were torn, and shoes were worn out. Schwan decided that his troops needed a rest, and for the next two days, as they waited for new supplies to arrive and for the sick and wounded to be evacuated, the men had an opportunity to enjoy themselves. "Nothing of interest to mention," Private Selm wrote in his diary on January 17. "Took in the town. Went to the old Spanish prison. Also the beach for a swim. . . . Boat arrives. Has got Bull Durham on it. I buy a sack. . . . First [tobacco] we have had in 8 days. It was fine."[54]

One more battle of consequence occurred in the province of Batangas, but

Schwan took no part in it. While his troops were resting and seeing the sights, new instructions from General Bates directed Schwan to leave Anderson's regiment behind to garrison eastern Batangas and to proceed with his remaining troops into Laguna and Tayabas. Schwan left Batangas City on the nineteenth and marched off to more victories in the east.[55] And as he moved out of our picture, some soldiers from General Wheaton's brigade moved into it.

★ Lemery and Taal

While Schwan's brigade had been punishing Malvar's troops in eastern Batangas, Wheaton's was working its way down the western side of the province. On January 16, Maj. William Johnston and three companies of the Forty-Sixth left Indang, with instructions to proceed to Lemery via Tuy and Balayan. Johnston's men met little resistance along the way, but as they approached Lemery on the afternoon of the eighteenth, they were attacked by somewhere between eight hundred and one thousand Filipino troops entrenched on a hillside across the Pansipit River in the neighboring town of Taal. The Filipinos laid down a furious fire, and, to make Johnston's position even more precarious, they had three field pieces. The Americans managed to fight their way into the población of Lemery, but when they attempted to dislodge the Filipinos from their trenches by making a flanking movement, they were unable to ford the river. One U.S. soldier was killed in the fighting and another was mortally wounded. Filipino losses appeared to be light.[56]

As the sun set and the firing stopped, Johnston had an opportunity to survey the situation. It occurred to him that the simplest way for his men to reach the enemy—and conversely, the simplest way for the enemy to reach him—was to cross an old stone bridge that spanned the Pansipit and linked the poblaciones of Lemery and Taal. He became convinced that the Filipinos would attempt to storm the bridge on the following day in order to reach the mountains west of Lake Taal. "Under such circumstances I deem it my duty to hold this bridge as long as ammunition lasts," he wired Wheaton.[57]

Because no Filipino records relating to the battle at Taal have survived, and the reports written by the Americans are silent on the question, we do not know who led the Filipino forces there.[58] It is not known either why the Filipino commander at Taal, whoever he was, decided to resist the Americans by conventional means. But we do know why the Filipinos lost. Notwithstanding their numerical advantage over Johnston's party, their situation was extremely precarious, for only about half of the Filipino soldiers at

Taal were armed with rifles. The rest carried bolos.[59] What is more, although they could probably hold off a frontal assault by Johnston's three companies, they were highly vulnerable to an attack from the rear—that is, from the direction of Batangas City, where U.S. troops were already garrisoned. If such an attack could be launched, the Filipinos at Taal might be caught in a trap.

For most of January 19, Johnston's men remained on the defensive, as the Filipinos, positioned in their trenches and in some of the houses at Taal, fired into the streets of Lemery. Help was on the way, however. On the morning of that day, Johnston had sent a message about his predicament to Commander E. H. Gheen, skipper of the U.S.S. *Marietta*, a gunboat that was lying offshore, and Gheen promptly agreed to ask the American garrison at Batangas City to come to Johnston's aid. Shortly after midday, Gheen communicated with Colonel Anderson, who had been left in charge of the troops stationed in the provincial capital, and Anderson sent Major Muir and three companies of his battalion to Taal.[60]

Muir's men, hiking as fast as they could, reached the outskirts of Taal by 5:30 in the afternoon, and here they met heavy fire. Muir quickly deployed his troops, sending Company C to the south of the main road and Captain Jordan's company to the north. According to Jordan, the Filipinos showed "unusual courage" in the subsequent fighting and remained in their trenches until the Americans were practically on top of them; but in the end they bolted, seeking refuge in the cane fields nearby. Having disposed of the enemy's first line of defense, Muir's forces advanced toward the población, with Company C in the lead.[61]

Time was now working against Muir. It was growing darker by the minute, and his troops were finding it difficult to see. Yet he was reluctant to delay his attack until morning for fear that the Filipinos at Taal would take advantage of the respite to escape. As the Americans reached the población, they found a large enemy force entrenched near the church and across several streets. One platoon from Company C advanced by rushes in the face of a surprisingly accurate fire, and within a few minutes these soldiers had absorbed three casualties and were pinned down. A second platoon came to the rescue, and after a few more volleys and rushes, the company succeeded in taking the trenches and driving their occupants out of the población. Muir's troops could not pursue the fleeing Filipinos because by now it had grown too dark.[62]

As Muir was attacking Taal from the east, Johnston was hitting it from the west, with some assistance from the *Marietta*, which had returned to

Lemery after delivering its message. As the gunboat shelled the Filipino trenches, Johnston and two companies of his command moved across the stone bridge spanning the Pansipit. They cleared it of an abatis and some other obstructions the Filipinos had placed across it and then charged and captured the Filipinos' field battery on the Taal side of the Pansipit. The remaining defenders of the town scattered, and shortly after dark Johnston's men joined Muir's in the población.[63]

So once again the Batangueños had attempted to fight the enemy on the enemy's terms, and once again they had failed. Improved marksmanship and an advantage in numbers had enabled them to give a somewhat better account of themselves. In the two days of fighting at Taal, they had inflicted ten casualties on the Americans—more casualties than the Americans had suffered in the encounters at Santo Tomas, Lipa, and Batangas City combined. But Filipino losses had been even heavier, and they had avoided total disaster only because most had escaped under cover of darkness. Still, at least one beneficial result came of this battle for the Batangueño forces. Their leaders had at last learned the simple lesson that it was futile to fight set-piece battles against the Americans.

★ ★ ★

The U.S. invasion of the southern Tagalog region was not a major episode in the annals of warfare. The battles, such as they were, rarely involved more than a thousand soldiers on either side, and most of them lasted no more than an hour or two. Even in U.S. military history the invasion did not constitute a glorious chapter. The Americans were clear-cut victors, but their victories should not obscure the fact that there was insubordination and even incompetence in the U.S. officer corps, or that the U.S. troops had failed to eliminate most enemy soldiers in Batangas and the neighboring provinces.

If the invasion was neither momentous nor memorable in a strictly military sense, it was revealing all the same. For, in fact, what was most striking about the fighting was not that the American commanders did bizarre things on the battlefield, but rather that, even though they did such things, they were able to trounce the Filipinos so soundly. That result merely underlines a point that has been stated on several occasions in this chapter: from the outset the Filipino troops in the southern Tagalog region suffered from almost insuperable disadvantages. Inferior weapons, insufficient ammunition, poor marksmanship, lack of cavalry and naval power—all of these contributed to the Filipinos' failures in set-piece battles.

And, in addition, lurking just beneath the surface, there were ongoing structural and attitudinal problems in the Filipino Army. Hints of these problems could be detected from time to time in the conventional contests that had just taken place—Malvar's reluctance to switch to guerrilla tactics, the failure of the company commander at Batangas City to follow Mariano Cabrera's order. But, in the unconventional warfare that was to come, they would become increasingly prevalent, and, in time, they would come close to paralyzing the Filipino war effort in Batangas.

★ ★ ★ ★ ★ ★ ★ ★ ★ ★

PART THREE

*Three Views of Guerrilla Warfare,
February 1900–April 1901*

5

With the Americans

WITH THE TAKING of Taal on January 19, 1900, the conventional phase of the battle for Batangas came to an end. As Schwan raced eastward through Laguna and Tayabas, the American troops left behind—the men of the Thirty-Eighth and Thirty-Ninth who were stationed in eastern Batangas, those of Wheaton's brigade who were responsible for operations in Cavite and western Batangas—focused on the tasks of holding the towns already occupied and pursuing the remnants of the local forces. Buildings were rented to house the men. Canteens were opened so that the troops could let off steam. Scouting parties went out daily and exhausted themselves in scouring the mountains, ravines, and outlying barrios of Batangas in search of the enemy.[1]

As the Americans were attempting to mop up the remaining units of the Filipino Army in the occupied provinces, the Filipino forces were undergoing a major transformation. Their military organization had been shattered, their troops battered and scattered. Trias himself was left in "a kind of isolation," unable to locate or communicate with most of his lieutenants. Even so, the Filipino leaders in the region were not ready to quit. "The sacred fire of patriotism that . . . inspired us to fight for the triumph of our Republic" had not, according to Trias, been extinguished. The setbacks could be overcome; the war, they believed, could still be won. To replace the men lost in the recent fighting, they could recruit new men and organize new units. To cope with an enemy that could not be beaten in set-piece encounters, they would turn to unconventional warfare. "The system of guerrillas and our [superior] knowledge of the land in which we saw the first light" would, according to Trias, ultimately bring victory.[2]

In Batangas itself, the reorganization of the Filipino Army into a guerrilla force began overnight. On January 20, four days after Batangas City had been occupied and only one day after the debacle at Taal, Malvar set to work. He decreed that three new "flying columns" were to be created in Batangas City; he named three trusted subordinates—Eliseo Claudio, Crisanto Borruel, and Elias Mendoza—as column commanders, each with the rank of major; and he ordered them to find the necessary soldiers as soon as possible. The three majors swung into action, and in a matter of days the new columns were functioning. The most distinguishing feature of these new units—and this too was decided by Malvar—was their decentralization. Borruel's column consisted of four companies, with two stationed in outlying barrios of Batangas City, one in the environs of Ibaan, and the fourth in Taysan. Claudio's column was positioned in barrios of Batangas City, Lobo, and Taysan. The structure of these new organizations reflected their function; hereafter their principal activities were to be hiding and harassment.[3]

In the aftermath of these changes, the war in Batangas and the neighboring provinces took on a different character. Although Malvar's men concentrated on hiding, they were always on the alert—watching the Americans from a distance, passing on information about their movements to other guerrilla units in the vicinity, planning ambushes.[4] And then, without warning, they struck, usually in small numbers and rarely for more than a few minutes:

> JANUARY 25. A group of about fifty Filipino soldiers attacked two companies of the Thirty-Eighth in mountainous country east of Lipa. A scouting party of the Forty-Fifth was ambushed in the mountains northeast of Nasugbu.

JANUARY 27. Company D of the Thirty-Eighth, escorting a shipment of money, was surprised just outside Taal by a small force of Filipinos. Company B of the same regiment, scouting in a barrio of Bauan, was attacked by approximately seventy-five enemy soldiers.

JANUARY 28. A scouting party of the Thirty-Ninth was fired on near Tanauan.

FEBRUARY 2. One officer and twenty-six men of the Thirty-Eighth, escorting a wagon train, were ambushed about four miles south of Lipa by more than one hundred Filipinos. A party of five soldiers of the Thirty-Ninth was attacked by a large number of Filipino soldiers in the vicinity of Tanauan.[5]

All of these were militarily inconsequential encounters, with no more than a handful of casualties on both sides. But their real significance lay in something other than the duration of contact and the statistics of killed and wounded. By their actions, Malvar's men were signaling to the U.S. Army that the battle for Batangas had only begun.

The American commanders in the southern Tagalog region were somewhat slow to comprehend the possible consequences of the enemy's change in tactics. At the outset most were certain that the new guerrilla enemy could be defeated as easily as the old conventional one. In a report to General Bates on February 7, Maj. George Morgan, stationed at Taal, exuded confidence: "I think that, with the exception of a few of the leaders, there will be few of the insurgents around here a month from now." Colonel Anderson, in command of the garrison in Batangas City, gave an almost identical assessment. And so did General Schwan. On February 8, after his brigade had occupied the principal towns of Laguna and Tayabas, he had returned in triumph to Manila and left General Wheaton in charge of all the U.S. forces in the southern Tagalog region. Eight days later, in a self-congratulatory letter to a fellow general, he wrote, "Although the predatory bands into which . . . the insurgent forces have degenerated are giving occasional trouble, these, I trust and believe, will be extirpated in short order. The pacification of the territory . . . will then be complete."[6]

But a few soldiers knew better, and one of them was Capt. John Leland Jordan of the Thirty-Eighth. In the weeks following the battle at Taal, he and his company had done much scouting in Batangas's rugged countryside, and they had also fought a few skirmishes with Malvar's men, including one at Talumpoc, a barrio of Batangas City, in which his men had captured one machine gun and two brass field pieces. Jordan was as aware as any American officer of the Filipinos' deficiencies on the battlefield, but he had emerged from his recent experiences with an appreciation of their doggedness. "From present indications," he confided to his mother, "there will be considerable fighting yet. Small parties of Filipinos[,] about 50 to 100[,] are continually ambushing wagon trains, . . . and we will perhaps have some difficulty in rounding them up."[7]

★ The Men at the Top

During the first fifteen months of Batangas's occupation by the U.S. Army, three different American commanders were entrusted with the task of finding a strategy to cope with this new guerrilla enemy. The first was Loyd Wheaton, one of the leaders of the recent invasion. From the start, Wheaton was convinced that the only way to eliminate armed resistance in the field was to pursue the enemy relentlessly. When a subordinate suggested that each regiment stationed in southwestern Luzon be assigned a sector in which it alone should conduct operations, Wheaton became incensed. Each station, he ordered, should chase the enemy wherever he went, "without regard to geographical limits." As time passed and the resistance in the region continued, Wheaton grew irritated. In early April 1900 he wrote to one regimental commander:

> The importance of the greatest practicable activity in scouting the country and exterminating all hostile bands is urged. All concentration or organization of guerrilla bands will be prevented when it is known that such effort is being made. The greatest severity consistent with the laws of war is enjoined when armed parties of hostiles are encountered.[8]

Wheaton was not in charge for long. On March 29, 1900, the War Department reorganized the U.S. forces in the Philippines. It gave a new name to the American military organization in the islands—the Military Division of the Philippines—and it divided the division into four departments. The Department of Southern Luzon, one of the four, was itself subdivided into four districts. Batangas fell into the Second District, along with Tayabas, Laguna, and the island of Polillo. Wheaton remained as commander of the Second District until April 17 and then left to assume command over the Department of Northern Luzon. With no brigadier general available to replace him, the U.S. command chose William E. Birkhimer, colonel of the Twenty-Eighth Volunteer Infantry, as temporary head of the Second District.[9]

Birky, as he was called (but never affectionately) by the soldiers who served under him, was ten years younger than Wheaton but also a Civil War veteran. In March 1864, as a boy of sixteen, he had joined the Fourth Iowa Volunteer Cavalry, and he served with that unit until August 1865, when he was mustered out of service. Afterward he went to West Point (he graduated with the class of 1870) and accepted a commission in the artillery corps. A lackluster military career followed, during which Birkhimer became a competent artillery officer and developed a reputation as an expert in military law. At the time of the outbreak of the Philippine-American War, he was, like Robert Bullard, only a captain. Service in the Philippines was a welcome tonic. Although he was assigned as judge advocate to General Lawton's division, Birkhimer spent most of his time in the field. On May 13, 1899, he showed courage in a battle at San Miguel, Bulacan, and for his efforts he eventually received a Congressional Medal of Honor. Two months later, he was appointed colonel of one of the Volunteer regiments recently authorized by Congress—the Twenty-Eighth.[10]

Short and bespectacled, Birkhimer looked more like a schoolmaster than a soldier. Humorless, egoistic, and unforgiving, he was very unpopular. Matthew Steele, a major who served under him when he took charge of the Second District, called him a "nasal-toned fool." "Birkhimer," Steele wrote, "seems to consider it his chief end in life to annoy people." Robert Bullard, commander of the Thirty-Ninth, described him as "cold-blooded and selfish." The enlisted men found him to be a martinet. According to Pvt. Dan Campbell, who served with the Twenty-Eighth, Birkhimer "had his own ideas about what was necessary to maintain a strict discipline, which, to most of us, seemed entirely unreasonable." If he spotted a man with a legging unhooked, he assessed a stiff fine (usually, a month's pay); if a soldier's shirt were open at the throat or if his cot were sloppily arranged or if he committed any of a dozen other trivial offenses, he could expect the same treatment. When the men of the Twenty-Eighth learned one day that their colonel was taking a leave, they were, as Private Campbell wrote in his diary, "tickled to death to see him go."[11]

If there was a key to understanding Birkhimer's conduct, it was ambition. Like Schwan and Bullard and so many other long-frustrated career officers, he was driven by a desire to achieve high rank. Yet he went about the task in a ludicrous way. He tried too hard. He seemed to see himself (or was it that he wanted to be seen by others?) as a reincarnation of Stonewall Jackson or William Tecumseh Sherman. A sampling of the orders Birkhimer issued to his regimental commanders gives a flavor of the man:

APRIL 22, 1900. Let there be no abatement of energy until the defeated, cowed and terrified enemy abandons his bandit and ladrone habits, and bows submissively in complete subjection to the authority of the United States.

APRIL 24, 1900. What we want to do here is to root out and suppress or kill off these evil-doers. To do this requires ceaseless energy on the part of commanders, the sending out to work day and night of small parties. The banditti and ladrones should not feel safe for one moment. Our small parties should be among them and on top of them always.

MAY 3, 1900 (to the commander of the Thirty-Seventh Infantry). I am much disappointed at apparent inertness [of] your regiment. . . . You must seek these malefactors and assassins, not wait for them to commit crimes and then follow at [a] distance as they retreat. Send out small parties under energetic officers. Let evil doers have no rest. Let them never feel sure for day or night that the American soldier is not at their elbows with the fatal bullet. Do not let officers or men get the idea that they are in garrison life, but rather that no species of warfare the American troops ever engaged in required such persistent activity as that now confronting them here. Do not permit your regiment or the troops under you [to] fail.[12]

Despite such exhortations, Birkhimer did fail in ending the resistance in southwestern Luzon and, for the moment, in winning promotion to a brigadiership. His temporary assignment was simply too temporary. On July 2, 1900, Brig. Gen. Robert H. Hall took over as commander of the Second District, and Birkhimer returned to his regiment.[13]

Robert Hall was almost sixty-three when he took charge. A graduate of the U.S. Military Academy (class of 1860), he had served in the Tenth Infantry during the Civil War and taken part in more than twenty battles. After the war, he had various assignments in the West and a seven-year stint as adjutant of the Military Academy. Gradually, Hall climbed the ranks—major in 1883, lieutenant colonel in 1888, colonel in 1893. When the Spanish-American War broke out, he was appointed brigadier general of Volunteers, but he took no part in the fighting, since the troops he commanded never left Florida. In early March 1899, he arrived in the Philippines and immediately assumed command of the Third Brigade in Gen. Arthur MacArthur's division. His brigade captured Antipolo and Morong in June 1899, and Calamba in late July. Subsequently, he was placed in charge of the First Brigade of that same division, and then, after the reorganization of the U.S. military organization in the Philippines in March–April 1900, of the First District of the Department of Southern Luzon, which included the provinces immediately north of Batangas.[14]

Compared to his predecessor, Hall was a cautious commander. Whereas Birkhimer had his eye on advancement, Hall seemed more interested in retirement—he was scheduled to leave the service in sixteen months, and he no longer held illusions about gaining glory. One of his first orders set the tone. After an attack on an American escort party near Tanauan, soldiers from the nearby garrison had burned a house in which they found enemy supplies. Hall was critical of his men's actions. "Conditions reported do not justify you in burning house in which uniforms and cartridges were found," he wrote to the commanding officer at Tanauan. One can imagine that if Birkhimer had still been in charge the destruction of the house would have been overlooked. Whereas Birkhimer had constantly urged his subordinates to step up the pace during the rainy season, Hall ordered his regimental commanders to slow it down. He clearly had doubts about the value of continuous scouting: the results achieved did not appear to justify the effort, and what is more, the men were so exhausted from their treks through the bush that they were succumbing to illness in alarming numbers. He instructed his officers to devote more attention to gathering information about the enemy through the use of spies and to restrict their offensive operations to "expeditions having in view a definite object." In other words, the troops should remain at the post unless the station commander was certain about the location of the enemy.[15]

For the remainder of the rainy season, the scouting activities of the men in the Second District decreased noticeably, and even after the onset of the dry season, the troops were somewhat less active than they had been under Wheaton and Birkhimer. This is not to say that Hall was a total failure as head of the Second District. As we shall see, there were some victories, some captures of Filipino military leaders. Yet it seems that the successes came in spite of Hall's leadership rather than because of it.[16]

By late March 1901, Hall's health began to fail, and he asked to be relieved. He was granted sick leave on April 5, and in mid-April he left the district.[17] The man who replaced him as commander of the U.S. troops in Batangas and the neighboring provinces was, as it turned out, a much more aggressive soldier than Hall. But the story of that man—Samuel Sumner—belongs in another chapter.

★ In the Ranks

During the period February 1900–April 1901, the U.S. command normally stationed two thousand to twenty-three hundred officers and men in Batangas. During the first eight months of the occupation, troops from three Volunteer regiments were posted there—the Twenty-Eighth, the Thirty-Eighth, and the Thirty-Ninth. In time, regular units replaced the Volunteers. The First Cavalry was assigned to Batangas in September 1900, and they were later joined by elements of the Eighth Infantry, the Twenty-First Infantry, the Fourth Infantry, and the Sixth Cavalry. By mid-March 1901, all the Volunteer regiments had left the province.[18]

To fight for their country in the Philippines, these soldiers received a minimal salary. The monthly pay of a private was $15.60—less than half the salary of a steelworker in Andrew Carnegie's employ, less than a third the salary of a male schoolteacher in rural America. True, the soldiers had no expenses for lodging, but their quarters were hardly luxurious, most of them typically being housed in the priest's residence or in public buildings. True, their meals were free, and, so long as the troops were in garrison and the Army's supply network was functioning efficiently (which was often not the case), the menu was satisfactory enough, with the men receiving beef and mutton imported from Australia and fresh vegetables. In the field, however, the fare was abominable—hardtack and stewed tomatoes, bacon and embalmed beef, a revolting brand of canned salmon (the men called it goldfish), coffee, a soup made of bouillon cubes. Occasionally the cooks concocted a dish made from wild sweet potatoes.[19]

What were the American soldiers like? The enlisted men, regulars and Volunteers alike, were generally young (many were still in their teens, most in their twenties), white, single, and relatively uneducated. Most, including those in the regular units, had received little training—generally less than six weeks. The infantry troops had learned to march and had taken part in a few field exercises; the cavalry had practiced riding and saber exercises; they all had some target practice with their Krag-Jorgensen rifles.[20]

These boys and men had enlisted for a variety of motives. Simple patriotism was the crucial consideration for a large number. Frank Rose, who served with Schwan's expeditionary brigade, joined up because "the U.S. needed men." Others used different words—"I though it the thing to do," "I answered President McKinley's call for Volunteers," "I was a good American"—but the underlying motive was the same.[21]

Many, however, were prompted by less lofty reasons than love of country.

18. Soldiers from Companies A and D, Thirty-Eighth Volunteer Infantry, Batangas City, 1900

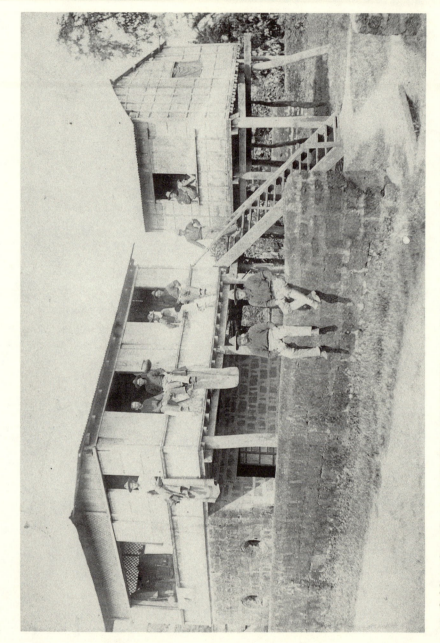

19. Soldiers from Company K, Thirty-Eighth Volunteer Infantry, at their barracks, Lipa, Batangas, 1900

140

Frederick Presher, for one, wanted to escape from a tedious job. On May 1, 1900, eighteen-year-old Presher was plowing a field on a truck farm in Wanamassa, New Jersey, and as he did so, he decided that he was tired of farm life. So he set down his plow, packed his bags, went to New York City, and enlisted in the army. Four months later, after a modicum of training and a long sea journey, he arrived in Bauan, Batangas, where he served for almost two years as a member of the First United States Cavalry. Allen Mummery, an infantryman, enlisted for essentially the same reason as Presher—in Mummery's own words, "to get away from the farm and to see some of the world." Georges Le Vallée, a Canadian, signed on with the Sixth Cavalry in order to escape from an overbearing father. Others sought adventure. For Claude Line, on the other hand, enlistment was a means of demonstrating his manliness. "Every trip on the train I made, someone on the train said, 'Butch, ain't you going to get a Chinese pigtail?'" Line never got his pigtail—his unit served in the Philippines rather than in China—but he did take part in some of the toughest fighting of the Batangas campaign.[22]

At the outset, when Volunteer regiments were stationed in Batangas, only a few of the officers were career men. Usually, the colonels, lieutenant colonels, and majors were, and the captains, lieutenants, and second lieutenants were not. In the ranks of the noncareer officers, there were a large number of businessmen, lawyers, and college students. Most of them had served in the Army during the Spanish-American War, but only a handful had ever seen combat. The Volunteer officers were older than the enlisted men, but far from old. Colonel Bullard had turned thirty-nine in January 1900, and the average age of the three battalion commanders who served under him was thirty-three. When the regular units began to arrive in Batangas in September 1900, an older, more experienced, more "professional" officer corps came with them. Curiously, though, the professional officers did not appear to perform any more effectively than the Volunteers.[23]

A large number of these officers and men (Volunteers and regulars alike) evidently brought to the Philippines, as part of their cultural baggage, the preconceived notion that the brown-skinned Filipinos were uncivilized and inferior. Like most of their compatriots, they applied to the Filipinos the racial stereotypes that white Americans of that generation applied to blacks and other non-Caucasians. Soon after their arrival, they applied the racial epithets as well. Many referred to Filipinos as niggers. (Others called them gugus, a word of indeterminate origin that bears an eerie resemblance to *gook*, used by U.S. troops to refer to Vietnamese during the Vietnam War.)[24]

One thing they did not bring to the Philippines was self-doubt. As they set out, they were confident of victory; they also seemed certain that they were engaged in a noble undertaking. Such confidence and certainty were to be expected. Americans of Theodore Roosevelt's era had an overwhelming—perhaps naive—faith in their country, their leaders, their political system, and their future; soldiers who served in the Philippines naturally shared that faith. Beyond that, these soldiers had volunteered: no draft board or lottery system had forced them to go. Understandably, therefore, the American army that fought in the Philippines at the turn of the century was far more enthusiastic about its task than the one that fought in Vietnam in the 1960s and 1970s.[25]

★ Frustration

For the U.S. soldiers stationed in Batangas the war was frustrating. The Batangueño forces generally restricted their offensive operations to ambushing small units and escort parties and conducting hit-and-run raids on the American posts. With great regularity, they disrupted the Americans' communications system by cutting down telegraph wires.[26] Hence, the Americans faced an elusive enemy—one who was willing to fight only when he had a decisive advantage and who, when he lacked such an advantage, was content to hide.

One of the frustrations faced by the U.S. soldiers in Batangas was their inability to distinguish guerrillas from noncombatants. According to Captain Jordan, "Several times when a small force stops in a village to rest the people all greet you with kindly expressions, while the same ones slip away, go out into the bushes, get their guns, and waylay you further down the road. You rout them & scatter them; they hide their guns and take to their houses & claim to be amigos." Frederick Presher, the young ex-farmer from Wanamassa, had similar experiences. In early December 1900, one of the First Cavalry's scouts reported that he had seen some Filipino soldiers, so Presher and the other cavalrymen stationed at Bauan saddled up and galloped off in pursuit. But when they arrived at the place where the enemy had been spotted, they found only a group of farmers working in the fields. Presher and the others suspected, but could not prove, that the farmers were enemy soldiers. "They are 'quick change' artists in changing from insurgents to ordinary hombres," Presher wrote in his diary. During the January invasion, Colonel Bullard even witnessed a "quick change":

> From Santo Tomas hill I could with glasses see this transformation going on. It was wonderful and fully explained the ease with which our friends,

the enemy, have, when beaten, been able to escape destruction at our hands. He has not marched away and escaped the fierce American. He has shed all signs of the soldier, grabbed a white flag and some agricultural tool and gone to work, hard, in the nearest field and shouted "viva America" when the hot American soldier again comes in sight. I caught many wearing two suits, one military, the other, underneath, civilian, so as to be ready for the quicker transformation.[27]

Such a campaign was also enervating. In order to flush out the Batangueño guerrillas, the U.S. troops set out on "hikes" into the bush. During March 1900, the company commanded by Captain Jordan undertook a mission every night. Typically, they marched about a dozen miles, entered a town, and searched every house for weapons, documents, and other evidence of guerrilla activity. Typically, too, they found nothing.[28]

When the rainy season began in May, the campaigning tested the U.S. forces even more. The roads turned into a muddy mush; weapons misfired; powder got wet; many U.S. soldiers fell ill. Birkhimer, with his eyes fixed on a brigadiership, minimized the difficulties and urged his men to pursue the enemy constantly: "The rebels hate rain and its inconveniences ten times more than we do; . . . They think rain knocks us out. Teach them differently."[29]

The American fighting men taught the Batangueños nothing of the sort. Day after day, the U.S. troops set off on hikes; and most of the time, they failed to make contact. The report of a scouting expedition that took place in June 1900 gives a sense of what it was like.[30]

At 8:00 P.M. on June 11, Capt. Ross A. Nichols, two fellow officers, and sixty-four enlisted men, all from the Thirty-Eighth Volunteer Infantry, accompanied by a surgeon, two hospital men, and several pack mules, set out from their station at Batangas City. Their destination was Laiya, an outlying, seaside barrio of the town of San Juan de Bocboc. Nichols's superiors had received intelligence (probably from local informants, but the sources are not clear on the point) that the Filipinos were planning to land supplies at Laiya, and Nichols's mission was to stop them.

From the outset, there were difficulties. They started off on the Lobo trail, a winding road that was barely passable in the dry season. "A light rain was falling at the time we started," Nichols later wrote, "and the roads were muddy and slippery, which made marching very tiresome and consequently very slow." After ten hours of hiking, they had traveled only seven miles, but the men were exhausted, so they made camp and rested. At 3:00 P.M. on the twelfth, they again moved out along the Lobo trail, continued on it for a few

20. *A supply train transporting troops and rations from Batangas City to San Jose, Batangas, 1900. The poor quality of the roads, particularly in the rainy season, led not only to resupply problems but also to difficulties in conducting field operations.*

more miles, and then, in the vicinity of the barrio of Calumpit, they proceeded onto another trail that led to Laiya.

The new road was nearly overgrown with trees and bushes, and several mules became entangled in the vegetation and their packs fell to the ground. At one point, a mule slipped off the trail, and in order to rescue him, "it was necessary to let him down with ropes a nearly perpendicular bank, a distance of one hundred feet." By now, after enduring so much poor weather and hard marching, some of the men had become ill, and the pace of the expedition slowed to a crawl. The detachment finally reached Laiya at noon on June 13.

Nichols made a permanent camp at Laiya, gave his men a rest, and then diligently looked for indications of enemy activity. From his outpost, he had a clear view of the sea for several miles. "If there had been any attempt to land arms," Nichols reported, "I would certainly have known about it." He saw nothing.

On June 15, Nichols, a lieutenant, and thirty men left the camp at Laiya and headed north toward San Juan. At the time, there was no U.S. garrison stationed in that town, and the Americans believed that Batangueño military units frequented it. No doubt Nichols hoped to catch the enemy unprepared and salvage something from his expedition. Just south of the población, the detachment spotted three Filipinos in the distance. Nichols believed that they were "insurrectos," probably because they fled when the Americans approached. A chase ensued, but the three men got away. Nichols and his men then proceeded on to the población, where, as in Laiya, they found no sign of the enemy. After spending the night there, they returned to Laiya on the sixteenth.

On the seventeenth, with his rations running low and with a growing conviction that he was wasting his time, Nichols decided to return to Batangas City. He had originally intended to march his men along the coast to Lobo, and then take the Lobo trail back to the provincial capital. But he decided to change his plans when he discovered that the coastal route was, if anything, slower and more treacherous than the inland route he had taken to Laiya. Time was now of the essence, since ten of his men were sick. (Several, according to Nichols, had temperatures of 105!) So he and his men retraced their steps. As before, a steady rain slowed the rate of march and took a toll on the men's health. Late in the afternoon of June 18, they arrived, wet and exhausted, back in Batangas City.

Including the side march to San Juan, Nichols's group had covered approximately 120 miles in their seven-day expedition. And what had been accomplished? "No attempt to land arms or ammunition was made by the insurgents," Nichols wrote in his report. "Nor was there any indication that any force of insurgents were [sic] in the vicinity." To be sure, there were casualties, but they were all on the American side. Several of Nichols's men required hospitalization.

When the rains abated in mid-November (and Hall's directive no longer applied), the scouting became somewhat easier—but never easy. Batangas is a mountainous province, and the Batangueño forces, aware that the Americans had difficulty in maneuvering in elevated terrain, established many of their camps in the uplands. And so, as the many personal letters, diaries, and official reports written by U.S. soldiers in Batangas make clear, the frustrations continued. Another example, briefer than the last, will make that point.[31]

In mid-January 1901, Frederick Presher's unit, Troop K of the First Cavalry, set out on a hike from Bauan. Presher wrote a bit about it in his diary:

> After going up the Bauan-Taal road for about 5 miles [we] turned left and went over a trail towards the hills near the coast. There was no road, only a trail that was sometimes hard to find. The country here is very rough, surprisingly so, for where the surrounding country appears almost level when viewed from a distance a closer view shows deep fissures in the earth's surface, not gradual slopes but deep gashes in the earth's surface some many feet deep, some of them having sides almost perpendictular [*sic*].

To traverse such terrain, the men dismounted and then the horses and troopers, on their own, maneuvered as best they could. After a while, well up in the hills, the troops came to a small barrio, which they decided to search. Presher's unit followed a set procedure in searching a barrio. They rode as close to it as they could without running the risk of being spotted and quickly surrounded it; then the captain, first sergeant, and trumpeter rode into the barrio; and if these three encountered no resistance, the troop conducted a house-by-house search. On this occasion, the plan of operations was not effective. As the troopers were in the midst of their search, a man suddenly ran out of one of the houses and dashed for the brush. Presher was certain that the man was an enemy soldier. A trooper fired at him but evidently missed because, according to Presher, "the 'gugu' kept on going and jumped into a clump of bushes headfirst and disappeared." The troop then resumed the search but found no other evidence of the enemy. In the end, tired and dirty, the soldiers made their way back to Bauan with nothing to show for their efforts.

This type of campaigning took a psychological as well as a physical toll. Already predisposed to view the Filipinos as racially inferior, the American soldiers came in time to view them as savages and to hate them—combatants and noncombatants alike. "They cannot even be said to be half civilized, but must be classified as barbarous," wrote Captain Jordan. He was exasperated at the continued hostility of the civilian population:

> As a rule the women and children hate the U.S. soldiers and in their language, a kind of dog language, they frequently abuse us. They think

we are very ignorant because we can't understand them and because we catch their soldiers in civilian garb and turn them loose because we can't prove who they are. We cannot have a spy & scouting system because our men are all large, and they are small, coppered or brown color, and use an unpublished dog tongue, and will under no circumstances reveal [the] whereabouts of any of their soldiers.

George Anderson, the commander of Jordan's regiment, echoed his captain's assessment. "They are rank barbarians, not much above our better class indians," he wrote to his sister. After an ambush in which two American soldiers were killed, Robert Bullard commented acidly, "The men feel bitter. It is the same old story—if U.S. troops are strong it is 'mucho amigo'; if weak, it is cruel death."[32]

The frustrations of the campaign might help to explain the frequent use of torture by U.S. troops in Batangas. As in other parts of the Philippines but perhaps more often, the U.S. soldiers in Batangas engaged in a form of torture known as the "water cure" in order to extract information from captured enemy soldiers and suspected supporters of the resistance. A syringe was inserted into the mouth of the prisoner or suspect, and he was forced to swallow water until his stomach became distended and he experienced the sensation of drowning. "It got results," one veteran of the Batangas campaign later recalled. After a few hours of this treatment, the waterlogged individual invariably provided information.[33] Someone even composed a ditty entitled "The Water Cure in the P.I.," sung to the tune of a popular song of Civil War vintage:

Get the good old syringe boys and fill it to the brim.
We've caught another nigger and we'll operate on him.
Let someone take the handle who can work it with a vim,
Shouting the battle cry of freedom.
Chorus: Hurrah. Hurrah. We bring the Jubilee.
Hurrah. Hurrah. The flag that makes him free.
Shove in the nozzle deep and let him taste of liberty,
Shouting the battle cry of freedom.
We've come across the bounding main to kindly spread around
Sweet liberty whenever there are rebels to be found.
So hurry with the syringe boys. We've got him down and bound,
Shouting the battle cry of freedom.
Chorus.

21. *Filipino prisoners at Nasugbu, Batangas, c. 1900*

22. *Filipino prisoners at Batangas City, 1900*

148

Oh pump it in him till he swells like a toy balloon.
The fool pretends that liberty is not a precious boon.
But we'll contrive to make him see the beauty of it soon,
Shouting the battle cry of freedom.
Chorus.
Keep the piston going boys and let the banner wave,
The banner that floats proudly o'er the noble and the brave.
Keep on till the squirt gun breaks or he explodes the slave,
Shouting the battle cry of freedom.
Hurrah. Hurrah. We bring the Jubilee.
Hurrah. Hurrah. The flag that makes him free.
We've got him down and bound, so let's fill him full of liberty,
Shouting the battle cry of freedom.[34]

Also common in Batangas was the practice of destroying Filipino property to punish acts of resistance. After an attack on one of their patrols,
the U.S. troops usually burned the houses in the nearest barrio. If the Americans found evidence that a noncombatant had contact with the Batangueño
forces, they often burned his or her house as well. Initially, such destruction
was prohibited by the U.S. command in the Philippines: American troops
were authorized to burn Filipino houses only if they had been used as
barracks by the enemy. But the troops disregarded the prohibition. In December 1900, General MacArthur, now head of the Division of the Philippines, decided to change the official policy; thereafter U.S. soldiers were freer
to retaliate against communities that assisted the enemy. In Batangas,
however, the principal consequence of that decision was to bring policy in
line with practice.[35]

Predictably, too, there were accidents. On June 20, 1900, Maj. John
Parker of the Thirty-Ninth led a detachment to Trapiche, a barrio of Tanauan, where, according to information provided by a "friendly native," they
would be able to find Sergio Trinidad, a Filipino officer who owned a house
there. The Americans reached Trapiche at 7:00 P.M. and could find no sign of
Trinidad. Someone in the barrio told Parker that the Batangueño officer had
gone north, but Parker was dubious. He and his men feigned pursuing
Trinidad to the north and then doubled back to Trapiche later that night.
When they returned, they saw what appeared to be two men in Trinidad's
house; one ran away; the Americans fired, and they killed the person who
remained in the house—a young boy. "I regret unspeakably that such an
accident should have occurred," Parker wrote in his report, "but so long as

insurgents play the spy and try to cover themselves behind women and in disguise as 'Amigos,' that long such accidents are liable to occur."[36]

The Americans were not the only ones guilty of atrocious behavior during the Batangas campaign. "A few days ago," Captain Jordan wrote to his mother in April 1900, "one of our men got a little careless and went out of town about a quarter of a mile unarmed. He was missed. We made search, found him with his head cut off and terribly mutilated. The Filipinos carried his head away as a trophy—an example of their civilization." Malvar's men also shot Americans who were in the act of surrendering and severely mistreated prisoners of war. The abuses grew so prevalent that Malvar issued a proclamation calling for swift punishment of any Filipino soldiers who violated the laws of warfare. But the proclamation went unheeded, and atrocities continued unabated. This was, on both sides, an ugly guerrilla war.[37]

★ Contacts

Although the Americans usually chased the enemy in vain, there were, all the same, occasional contacts. During the fifteen-month period February 1, 1900–April 30, 1901, U.S. troops engaged in more than 150 hostile actions in the province of Batangas. Three points about these contacts should be made. First of all, most were initiated by the Filipinos; in effect, Malvar's men were dictating the level of the fighting at this stage of the campaign. Second, the contacts occurred in virtually every part of the province. In this war without fronts, the Filipinos were apt to strike anywhere; they might be hiding anywhere. Third, almost all of the engagements that occurred in Batangas during these fifteen months were little more than skirmishes—small-scale actions that lasted only a few minutes.[38]

Of these skirmishes, the ones started by the Filipinos followed familiar patterns. Generally, one or two companies of Malvar's men attacked a small group of Americans—an escort party, a wagon train, a scouting party. After firing a few shots, the Filipinos scattered. Also, from time to time, a Filipino unit sneaked into an occupied town, briefly attacked the American garrison, and then withdrew.[39] Most of these Filipino-initiated engagements might technically be classified as ambushes. But they were not so described in the American after-action reports. A directive issued by Maj. Gen. John Bates, commander of the Department of Southern Luzon, explains why: "The use of the word 'Ambushed' or 'Ambuscade' is wrong, in that it indicates lack of precaution on the part of our officers and men, which is not the case. The use of these words is therefore liable to misapprehension and criticism, and should be avoided." In another order, Bates suggested strongly that the word *attacked* be used in reports, except when an American unit had been "surprised through its own lack of proper precautions," and he added that if U.S. troops had actually been surprised in this manner, "an investigation and report will be made in regard to the carelessness that will be inferred from the fact of the party being ambushed."[40] Thereafter, the Americans were attacked frequently, but never ambushed.

Of the American-initiated skirmishes, most might be best characterized as accidental. Typically, American troops on a hike stumbled upon a group of Batangueño soldiers. These encounters ended in a few seconds; at the first opportunity, the Filipinos slipped into the bush. The U.S. garrisons in Batangas employed a number of local people to act as informants and guides during this period, but they rarely provided the Americans with useful information about the location of Filipino troops (and on a number of occasions, the guides appeared to mislead the U.S. troops on purpose). These Filipinos had good reason to be less than completely cooperative, of course; they knew that the Filipino troops would kill anyone who led the Americans to their hiding places.[41]

Only a handful of the engagements that occurred in Batangas during this period—a dozen at most—might properly be classified as battles, albeit minor ones. One, which took place on July 17, 1900, involved Colonel Birkhimer.[42] Eleven days earlier, a Filipino force estimated at five hundred had attacked the U.S. garrison at Taal, wounding six American soldiers and setting fire to many of the houses in the población. Following the attack, Birkhimer had pursued the Filipinos without rest, and finally, on July 16, a reconnaissance party had spotted them, dug in on the old Bauan road, not far from the town of San Luis. Anxious for a fight, Birkhimer devised a plan, enlisting the assistance of Lt. Edward Simpson, commander of the *Villalobos,* a gunboat patrolling on Balayan Bay. Birkhimer's men, a detachment of the Twenty-Eighth, would first attack the Filipino trenches, attempting to drive the enemy to the west—in the direction of the sea, where the *Villalobos* was waiting with its two six-pounders. If the Twenty-Eighth succeeded in doing that, the Filipinos would be caught in a crossfire, and Birkhimer reckoned that the Americans would be able to inflict considerable damage.

Early on the morning of July 17, Birkhimer launched his assault on the enemy, shouting at his troops: "Drive them out men. Show them what you can do. Let the damn niggers know that they are up against the Twenty-Eighth. Show them you're Yankee soldiers. Charge." The result was a stunning victory, with the Filipinos falling into the trap Birkhimer had set for them and suffering heavily from the combined fire of the Twenty-Eighth and the *Villalobos*. According to Birkhimer's report of the action, thirty-eight Filipinos were killed, including two officers. The Americans also captured ten serviceable rifles and some hospital supplies, and they destroyed a large amount of military stores. Overnight, Birkhimer became a hero. "He is the champion insurrecto exterminator in the islands," wrote Frank Carpenter, a fellow officer. Hall, the district commander, recommended him for a brevet, but for some reason the star did not come.

Another action that might qualify as a battle took place near Nasugbu, in the northwest corner of the province. On October 21, 1900, a detachment of twenty men, led by Capt. George Biegler of the Twenty-Eighth Infantry, was attacked as it was returning to its station at Balayan. The attacking force included no fewer than four hundred men, and throughout the four-hour battle they controlled the high ground. Nevertheless, the Filipinos fared poorly. In his report of the battle, Biegler suggested, in passing, why that was so: "The insurgents used black powder, at least in part, and we were able to locate them at once." In the end, two men in the American detachment were killed and four were wounded; the Filipinos, according to Biegler's estimate, suffered approximately one hundred casualties.[43]

The results of battles such as these—battles in which the Filipinos had a striking numerical advantage—lead to but one conclusion. As the engagements that occurred during the American invasion of the province had shown, the Batangueños were no match for the Americans in conventional warfare. Even in the skirmishes the Filipino forces invariably absorbed a far higher rate of losses. According to the U.S. Army's after-action reports, the Filipinos suffered at least one thousand casualties in the actions that occurred during the period February 1, 1900–April 30, 1901; on the American side, there were no more than one hundred casualties. The reports indicated further that during the same period the U.S. troops captured in excess of one thousand Batangueño soldiers or suspected soldiers, hundreds of weapons, thousands of cartridges, and huge quantities of enemy supplies. Of course, the reported counts of Filipino casualties were, without question, a bit inflated; in the war in the Philippines, as in the more recent conflict in Vietnam, ambitious American officers occasionally padded the counts in order to improve their chances of promotion. Even so, they provide at least a rough measure of battlefield realities; Filipino accounts of some of those same engagements have also survived and, on the whole, the casualty figures mentioned therein are fairly close to those found in the American reports.[44]

Yet, if the battlefield statistics indicated that the Americans were succeeding, other figures hinted that they were not. Many American troops were succumbing to disease, exposure, and simple fatigue. The Thirty-Ninth Volunteer Infantry, which had taken part in the invasion of southwestern Luzon in January 1900 and was subsequently stationed in Batangas and Laguna, had an "official" strength of 49 officers and 1,230 enlisted men. By the end of September 1900, after several months of campaigning in the rain, only 31 officers and 748 men were available for duty; most of the others were sick. During its fourteen months of service in the Philippines (almost all of it in southwestern Luzon), the Thirty-Ninth lost 111 soldiers. Only 13 were battlefield casualties; the others died from typhoid fever, malaria, and a variety of other diseases.[45]

★ Garrison Life

The U.S. soldiers stationed in Batangas did not spend all their time chasing the enemy. Back in the garrison, frustration gave way to tedious routine: reveille (at 5:30 or thereabouts, depending on the post), assembly, mess, drill, fatigue duty, mess again, and so on, day after day. Garrison life was filled as well with inspections, guard mounts, parades, and endless details. "It is the dreary duty of garrison work that the soldier detests," Private Presher wrote in his diary.[46]

In their free time, to break the deadening monotony, the garrisoned soldiers wrote letters to family and friends and participated in bull sessions with their fellow soldiers. ("Lay around the quarters and discuss the political campaign that is about to come off," Pvt. Thomas Selm wrote in his diary on September 29, 1900. "Who will be the president is the question. If the soldiers had their say it would be McKinley and not some other slob.") They played baseball and games of chance, especially craps and poker.

They also drank liquor, and, as the surviving court-martial records reveal, many of them frequently consumed far more of it than they could handle. Those records tell us, for example, that on May 10, 1900, three soldiers from the Thirty-Eighth Volunteer Infantry—Sgt. Albert Jamison and Cpls. Harry Hogarth and William Clements—were drunk and disorderly on the streets of San Jose, and after being found guilty of the offense, all three were given stiff fines. We learn too that Pvt. George Cusack of Troop K,

First Cavalry, stationed in Bauan, was found inebriated on January 25, 1901, and, as a consequence, was required to forfeit part of his pay. Cusack did not appear to learn his lesson, however, since he was court-martialed four more times for drunkenness, and on two of those occasions he was drunk while in the field.[47]

Once drunk, the men were liable to get into even more trouble. Brawls between intoxicated men were common, and drunk soldiers were likely to become involved in altercations with Filipino merchants and other residents of the town. Drunkenness also brought to the surface some of the feelings of anger and resentment that the enlisted men felt toward commissioned and noncommissioned officers. An incident in Santo Tomas was fairly typical. On April 19, 1900, Pvt. Julius C. Netterberg of the Thirty-Ninth Volunteers, having imbibed a good deal, was making an excessive amount of noise in his quarters, and his sergeant, Karl A. Guetzlaff, asked him to quiet down. Netterberg replied, "Oh, go fuck yourself, you son of a bitch," or words to that effect, and he was soon brought up on charges for his choice of verbs and nouns.[48]

Most of these free-time activities took place among soldiers, but the garrisoned troops also interacted regularly with the townspeople. Many of the enlisted men patronized the local prostitutes, a form of social contact for which they usually paid twice. (The prostitutes, complained the surgeon at Lipa, "are a constant source of venereal infection of the troops of this command. . . . Every few days some man enters the Hospital by way of this place, to say nothing of those who are treated in Quarters.") Some of them established lasting relationships with local girls—commonly, poor ones who were given part of the soldier's pay in exchange for the companionship they provided. The soldiers were also in frequent contact with the owners of bars and retail stores, owners and operators of stalls in the local market, laundresses, whom they paid to clean their clothes (and who were sometimes available for sexual favors as well), and men from the town with whom they gambled. Beyond all that, the troops socialized with local people at the cockfights on Sunday, at concerts held in the towns by the regimental bands, and at fiestas and other celebrations.[49]

Such intercourse was not limited to the enlisted men. A large number of U.S. Army officers, including many who privately expressed contempt for Filipinos in their diaries and correspondence, maintained social relations with municipal officials, schoolteachers, and other important residents of the towns. In May 1900, Silvestre Yturralde, a leading citizen of Batangas City, invited a group of U.S. Army officers to his son's wedding, and, according to the groom, the Americans behaved impeccably. Charles Crane, an officer stationed at Lipa, was entertained by several of that community's most prominent figures, including Toribio Catigbac, whose talented daughters provided musical entertainment.[50]

It is tempting, of course, to be cynical about these Filipino-American interactions since they were obviously based on something other than affection and mutual respect. Most of the American enlisted men interacted with the residents of the towns in order to secure things that they wanted— female companionship, alcohol, access to gambling establishments, and cheap labor; the officers attempted to keep on good terms with local influentials in large measure because they depended on such people to govern the towns. The Filipinos had their own agendas. Many of them—the prostitutes and other women who consorted with the Americans, the owners of drinking establishments and other shops, the men who gambled with the troops— were attracted by the large amounts of ready cash the soldiers had at their disposal. Elite Filipinos who entertained U.S. officers in their homes were probably trying to convince the occupying army of their good will, even while they continued to send money and supplies to the guerrillas in the field. Still, fragile as these relationships may have been, they played an absolutely vital part in the daily lives of the U.S. soldiers stationed in Batangas: the simple fact of the matter was that, much of the time, by their own choice, the garrisoned troops were in the company of Filipinos.[51]

And, the vast majority of these daily interactions were civil, even cordial. One reason for the civility was the U.S. Army's approach to misconduct in the towns. Whereas U.S. soldiers were rarely brought up on charges stemming from abusive behavior toward Filipinos in the field, they could not expect leniency for such misconduct once they returned to the garrison. In part, the stricter approach was adopted in order to enforce proper military discipline; it was also adopted because, theoretically at least, one of the Army's principal responsibilities was to guarantee the safety of the residents of the towns. As a result, the garrisoned troops quickly discovered that they ran a real risk of punishment for any abusive acts that they committed against the local populace.[52]

The garrisoned troops were not always well behaved. The court-martial records tell of Americans abusing the residents of the towns, often when they had had too much to drink or when they were refused credit by local merchants. On February 15, 1900, for example, William Norris, a private in Company E of the Thirty-Eighth Volunteer Infantry, hit a Chinese resident of Lipa with eggs; he was fined one dollar. About a month later, Pvt. Harry Ward was guilty of "violently taking a banana from a native woman"; his fine

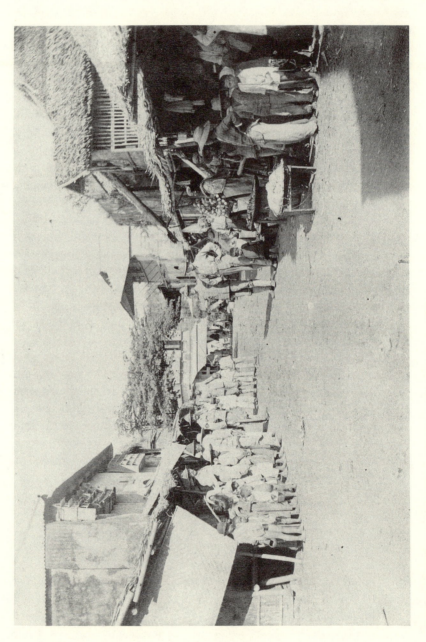

23 U.S. troops at the local market, Taal, Batangas, c. 1900

was five dollars. Some incidents resulted in injury. In June 1900, Pvt. George Avery beat up a Lipeño; he was fined one month's pay and confined for a month. In July, Pvt. Thomas Calligan pummeled another man in Lipa; his fine was twelve dollars.[53] Soldiers were also prosecuted for stealing Filipino property: one destroyed an image of the Virgin Mary in the Rosario church and took away a piece of ivory from the head, and another removed a gold-embroidered cloth from a house in Batangas City.[54]

On occasion, there were genuinely atrocious acts as well. One afternoon, shortly after the occupation of Lipa by the U.S. forces, Pvts. Frank Detterman and Robert Phillips of Company F of the Thirty-Eighth Volunteers got drunk and decided to leave their quarters. John Otter, a fellow soldier, later recounted a brief meeting he had with the two men before they left. "I was in the yard cooking chickens, and [Detterman] and Phillips came around there. They were pretty drunk and talking to me, and Frankie said, 'Boys, let's go and get a nigger.'" Several hours later, the two men returned, boasting that they had killed an unarmed Filipino, and on the following day the dead man's body, with a bullet wound in the temple, was discovered close to another company's quarters. Both Detterman and Phillips were tried and convicted for the killing, the first receiving a four-year prison sentence and the second a ten-year sentence.[55]

The diaries, personal letters, and reminiscences of the American soldiers also make clear that most abuses committed by the garrisoned troops went unreported and unpunished. Among other things, the enlisted men frequently stole edible items from the local people in order to supplement the army's unappetizing rations. Homer Cook, a bugler in the First Cavalry, discussed such activities in his reminiscences:

> Our food was not good or plentiful. So we done some foraging. One night I was one of four. So we started out after taps at 10 P.M. and went along the Batangas River to some barrios. . . . We had some limbs with knots on one end, like golf clubs, about 5 or 6 feet long. We would slip in under [the] trees where the chicks roosted and hit a chicken on the head. This particular night we had 4 chickens when the dogs woke the natives. We taken a path along the river to the rear of our quarters. The natives [were] after us, [so] we ducked in the cane field and waited till the natives went by, took our chickens and went to our quarters. . . . We had chicken the next day. This was a common occurrence.[56]

Nelson Bishop, who served in the Thirty-Ninth, recorded a number of other abusive actions in his diary:

DECEMBER 1, 1900. A sentry on post intoxicated with vino, out in the street without hat or belt, ransacking every thing carried and molesting every native passing.

DECEMBER 3, 1900. Natives at morning prayer, a soldier goes up and smashes the side of the shack in with the but [*sic*] of his gun.

DECEMBER 4, 1900. A native taken from his house and dealt with blows from an officer's fist and soldier's guns on suspicion of being guilty of theft.[57]

More serious still, and likewise unpunished, were the actions taken by soldiers after they learned of the death of Alexander Cooper, the man whose decapitated body was found near Batangas City. Infuriated, a number of men in Cooper's regiment, the Thirty-Eighth Volunteers, retaliated by setting fire to a large section of the town.[58]

What conclusion can be drawn about the conduct of the garrisoned soldiers? Obviously, they were guilty of abusive behavior—more abusive behavior, in fact, than the military justice system ever became aware of. Obviously, they committed atrocious acts too. On the other hand, because of the Army's policy of punishing soldiers for misconduct in the occupied towns, most of their day-to-day contacts with Filipinos appeared to be friendly enough. The record of the garrisoned troops was, in short, a decidedly mixed one—far from unblemished, but better than the record of those same soldiers in the field, and probably better than most students of the war have given them credit for.

★ Hearts and Minds

In addition to hiking, getting bored, and sometimes getting into trouble, the U.S. soldiers in Batangas devoted some attention to policies that were designed to win over the populace. The policies had been formulated by Major General Otis, who believed that by establishing schools and municipal governments in occupied towns he might convince Filipinos of America's good will, win their friendship, and thereby expedite the task of pacifying the archipelago. Hence, throughout the Philippines, the U.S. Army organized schools, detailed soldiers to act as teachers, and even instructed military district commanders to act as regional superintendents of education. To coordinate the school work, Otis established on March 30, 1900, a Department of Public Instruction under the direction of Capt. Albert Todd.[59]

Otis and his subordinates were taking steps to reorganize local governments as well. In July 1899, Col. William A. Kobbé, at Otis's request, drew up a plan establishing a procedure of municipal organization in pacified areas. That plan, slightly amended, became General Order No. 43, issued in August 1899. Each town was to be governed by a municipal council composed of a president and headmen from each barrio. The president was to be elected by a voice vote of the residents of the town and approved by the local U.S. commander. Headmen were to be chosen by residents of their barrios. The council was to collect taxes and perform other duties; however, no municipal ordinance could be enforced until it received the local commander's approval.[60]

Early in 1900, Otis decided to replace General Order No. 43, in part because he felt that Kobbé's plan was inadequate for the organization of large towns. He appointed a board to draft a new plan of municipal organization, and that body composed General Order No. 40 (1900 Series), issued on March 29, 1900. The new plan still provided for relatively strict supervision by the Army. Commanding officers were to audit municipal accounts and oversee other municipal activities. The plan also stipulated that each municipality was to elect, by secret ballot, a mayor and a municipal council. The electorate was to be limited to males twenty-three years old or over who had one of the following qualifications: previous service as capitán municipal, gobernadorcillo, teniente, or cabeza de barangay; annual payment of thirty pesos in taxes; or the ability to speak, read, and write English or Spanish. The most obvious effect of setting such qualifications was to limit the franchise to a small percentage of the residents—to essentially the same kind of people who had dominated the towns during the late Spanish period.[61]

One scholar who has written at length about the U.S. Army's activities in the Philippines has argued that policies such as these won many friends and thus played a major role in winning the war.[62] Perhaps they had an impact in some parts of the Philippines, but in Batangas they were a relative failure. True, the U.S. commanders in Batangas attempted to carry out these policies. On January 17, 1900, only a day after U.S. troops had occupied Batangas City, Gen. Theodore Schwan issued a proclamation in that town in which he assured the residents that the Americans came "not in the spirit of ruthless invasion, but in the spirit of peace and good will to all good citizens, and with the object of establishing good government."[63] Shortly after the issuance of General Order No. 40, Colonel Birkhimer, then in charge of the Second District, sent a copy of it to all the regimental commanders serving under him and commented, "It is greatly to be desired that the minds of the people be inclined favorably to putting this scheme of municipal government into operation. . . . We must win these people by showing them our firmness and good faith." And, indeed, the U.S. Army did establish municipal governments in most towns in the province in 1900.[64] However, the American commanders' commitment to Otis's policies and their subordinates' execution of them did not guarantee that the Batangueños would switch their allegiance. By day, under the scrutiny of the U.S. officers, municipal officials enforced sanitary regulations and dutifully performed other official tasks. By night, they cooperated with Malvar. In some towns (Batangas City, for instance, which I examine in chapter 7), the townspeople were so hostile to the occupying army—and so fearful of antagonizing the Filipino forces still in the field—that they refused to take part in municipal elections.

Equally ineffectual were the Army's educational policies, which, according to a number of U.S. Army officers stationed in other parts of the Philippines, contributed to civilian acceptance of U.S. rule.[65] Yes, schools were organized in Batangas and Filipino children enrolled in them, but not always so many. A report written in late August 1900 indicates that in Tanauan, with a population of about 18,000, the U.S. Army had organized 27 schools with a total enrollment of approximately 900. In neighboring Lipa, population 40,000, there were 3 schools and only 190 pupils; and in Bauan, with a population equal to Lipa's, there were 3 schools with a total enrollment of 100. Furthermore, school buildings were inadequate and overcrowded, only a limited number of textbooks were available, and many of the teachers were incompetent.[66] It would be difficult to argue that the U.S. Army's educational efforts in Batangas did any harm, but it would be equally difficult to argue that they did much good, or that they won many friends for the Americans in the province.

★ A Sense of Failure

Energetic campaigning, repeated successes in engagements, and efforts to win hearts and minds were not enough: the U.S. Army had not come close to winning the battle for Batangas. Victories on the battlefield were offset by losses in the hospital ward. The establishment of schools and municipal governments did not win the support of the noncombatant populace. Malvar and thousands of his men remained in the field. The American soldiers stationed in Batangas recognized their failure. Many had started out believing that the campaign in southwestern Luzon would end quickly; many were encouraged by the successful invasion and the subsequent mopping-up operations. Robert Bullard, the colonel of the Thirty-Ninth, was one who shared the initial optimism. But, in March 1901, just as he was leaving south-western Luzon, he wrote in his diary, "A year ago, . . . I believed that the insurgents were going to pieces. They are no more in pieces today than then."[67]

Yet if the American soldiers sensed their failure, they were unwilling to accept it. The problem, some thought, was that up to now the U.S. Army had not been harsh enough with the enemy. In their diaries and letters, and even in a few official reports, the U.S. troops stationed in southwestern Luzon began to discuss the need for a sterner approach. As might be expected, Birkhimer came to this conclusion earlier than most. In late October 1900, he put the matter baldly in a letter to his superiors:

The trouble . . . is not our lack of military power exerted against a foe that will face us, on any terms they might choose. The great problem is to meet and overcome the foe that will not, as a foe, face us. The strength of the latter should not be underestimated. It is a very powerful foe in a military sense: that is, it wears out our troops chasing a phantom, for, even when parties of armed insurrectos are certainly and definitely located, the facility with which they can perform the chameleon act, by throwing away their arms under the bushes or grass . . . and blandly greeting us as good amigos, utterly defeats our best trained and most skillfully conducted operations, or at least that is likely to be the result, and generally it is so.

It seems to me that the people have less respect for the United States authority than they had six months ago. They still have the same appreciation of their incapacity to meet its military power, but they have learned what they did not know, that it can be evaded, and how this can be done. I say this with profound regret.

It is submitted that the thing to be done, the object that must be attained is to render harmless that element of the male population which the Tagalog authorities utilize for military purposes. There are two ways of doing this, first, to kill off the males; second, capture and deport them under such conditions as to render them harmless for all time hence.

Either plan properly put into execution would accomplish the object sought; innocent will suffer; but so our innocent friends suffer now, their only offenses being friendliness for us; but this is a case where the principle of self-preservation is worked in favor of the dominant nation. Considerations affecting individuals must give way before the overruling necessities of the United States government, and regrets at being compelled to resort to this course are lessened by the knowledge that the individuals who may adversely be affected constitute that class from which the enemy, disregarding the laws of war, seeks to carry on against us an insidious, evasive, assassin-like system of hostilities.[68]

The U.S. command in the Philippines was not willing to go this far—at least, not yet. As Hall's tenure as district commander came to an end, there was no hint that there would be any change in the American approach: more schools would be established; the hikes would continue; so too, unofficially, would the torture. And so would the frustrations.

6

With the Batangueño Guerrillas

DID YOU FIGHT against the Americans?" I asked old Emilio Vergara. Yes, he told me, he had taken part in occasional hit-and-run raids against wagon trains and small patrols. Vergara then described for me one of the actions in which he participated—an attempt to ambush a wagon train, escorted by a small party of foot soldiers and cavalrymen, just outside the town of San Jose. The unsuspecting Americans walked and rode right into the trap. The Filipinos fired three rounds at them, but their shots missed, and once the Americans regrouped and assumed the offensive, the Filipinos retreated in disarray. Vergara himself was lucky to escape. The cavalrymen spotted him and chased him through a forested area and into a field of tall cogon. Out of breath, he lay hiding in the cogon. The Americans searched the field but were unable to find him, although at one point he was almost trampled by one of their horses.[1]

Most of Emilio Vergara's days in that long-ago war were not so memorable. Offensive operations like the one outside San Jose were rare; most of the time, Vergara and his fellow soldiers hid from the enemy. The commander of his column, Antonio Mandigma, had several well-concealed camps in the forests around Lipa, and the troops constantly moved from one to another in order to avoid capture. Mandigma was not a coward, Vergara assured me; he merely recognized that the Filipinos, with inferior weapons and insufficient ammunition, were outmatched. But if the Filipino forces were at such a disadvantage, why did they continue to resist for more than two years? "The leaders told us that if we held out long enough, the Americans would get tired and go home," Vergara told me, and there was just a hint of sarcasm in his voice.

Vergara, hiding in the vicinity of Lipa, obviously viewed the war from a different angle than Birkhimer or Jordan or the thousands of other American soldiers stationed in Batangas. In this game of cat and mouse, Vergara, the Batangueño guerrilla, was the mouse—small, quick, shifty, and always terrified of being caught in the open, as he was briefly on the day of the ambush near San Jose. And like the game of cat and mouse, this contest between Americans and Filipinos in the hills, forests, ravines, and outlying barrios of Batangas was ultimately unfair; the mouse could taunt his enemy and he could hide, but there was no way he could inflict serious damage. So here, in sum, was the dilemma of the Batangueño guerrilla; for if the war was frustrating for the American soldiers, for Vergara and his comrades it was, from a military perspective, virtually hopeless. Aware that they could not win by a resort to arms, they harassed and hid and, while they did so, they prayed that the decision-makers back in Washington would grow weary of the enterprise and call the boys home.

Stranger things have happened in the history of warfare, but at this stage of this war, such a strategy was bound to fail. Even before the Americans had set foot in Batangas, they were too close to victory to abandon the conflict. The resistance in Batangas and a few other provinces was a nuisance, and the longer it persisted, an embarrassment; and the campaigning itself was terribly testing; but none of this was likely to cause the American command or the American fighting man to lose heart. Nor could the Batangueño guerrillas realistically expect the American public to grow war-weary and to pressure the McKinley administration to end the fighting. The war was fairly popular back home, even though a group of determined, well-connected anti-imperialists sought to make it otherwise. Some Filipino leaders still in the field, including Aguinaldo, encouraged their followers to believe that the Filipino Army needed only to hold out until November 1900, when the American people would go to the polls to choose their president. If, the argument went, William Jennings Bryan, the vocal critic of imperialism, won the election, he would call off the war of conquest and set the Philippines free. But this too was chimera, for no sensible person gave Bryan a chance against McKinley, and as it turned out he was soundly thrashed.[2]

All this seems far more obvious today than it possibly could have to the Batangueño forces in February 1900. Licking their wounds in the forests of Batangas, they might well have believed that they still had a chance. But how long could such beliefs last? Would they still be willing to fight after a year in the bush—a year of being chased after and shot at for a cause that seemed with each passing day less likely to triumph? And how would they feel after Aguinaldo had been captured, and Trias and some of their local leaders had surrendered? Clearly, it was only a matter of time before hope would be exposed as illusion, and when that happened, extraordinary measures would be needed to keep the war going.

★ The Man at the Top

Once the Filipino forces in southwestern Luzon had opted for guerrilla warfare—or ambush warfare, as they preferred to call it—Mariano Trias's control over the troops in Batangas disappeared. From his headquarters in Cavite, Trias concentrated on organizing resistance in that province and on resurrecting Artemio Ricarte's plan of fomenting a mass uprising in Manila. (The uprising was scheduled to take place in early July 1900, but Ricarte was captured, and it all came to nothing.) Occasionally, Trias issued orders of a general nature to his subordinates in Batangas and passed on the decrees of his own superior, Emilio Aguinaldo, now on the run in northern Luzon with the Americans in pursuit. But the burden of carrying on the good fight in Batangas (and in most of Tayabas as well) fell squarely on the shoulders of Miguel Malvar.[3]

The first fifteen months or so of the U.S. Army's occupation of the region Malvar spent mostly at a hideout in the mountains, several miles west of the población of Tiaong, Tayabas. In addition to being well concealed, the hideout was situated almost precisely at the point on the map where the three provinces of Batangas, Laguna, and Tayabas met. The location allowed Malvar to remain in contact with the Filipino forces in all three provinces.[4] When Malvar was not in his headquarters, he was on the move, traveling about the southern Tagalog region to confer with his lieutenants and to check on the status of his army. He knew that the American commanders

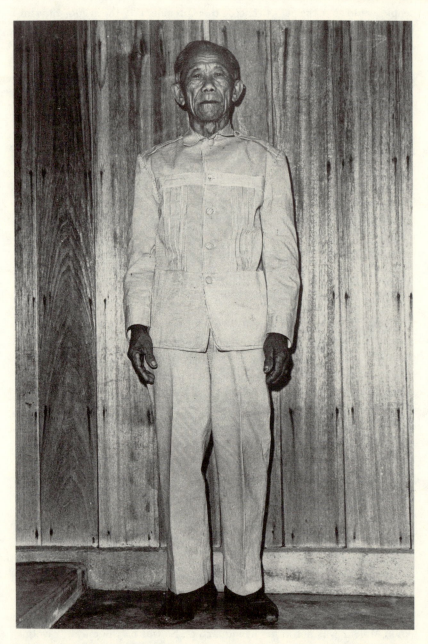

24. *Severino Magsombol, Batangueño veteran (in uniform), c. 1970*

placed a high priority on capturing him and that they immediately dispatched scouting parties whenever they received word of his whereabouts. Hence, he rarely spent more than a few nights in the same place, and wherever he went, he wore disguises. "Goes about the country with an indian shirt and trousers cut off or rolled up to the knees," one U.S. intelligence officer reported, "and if captured will affect being a very simple, inoffensive and ignorant native who knows nothing, and will give a wrong name. . . . Miguel Malvar is said to have frequently visited Manila wearing a new U.S. campaign hat. He passed through American troops with a rooster under his arm, and has ridden a carabao through Santo Tomas and Lipa, stopping at Lipa to talk to the Presidente without being detected."[5]

There were close calls. Late in May 1900, Malvar and a few members of his staff went to the Eastern Zone of Batangas to hold discussions with various commanders and inspect conditions. Malvar attended a brief meeting in Cuenca and another which lasted more than a day in Sampaga, a barrio of Batangas City. He then moved on to the barrio of Talumpoc, where he stayed for only four hours; to Bilogo, where he spent a day; and finally to the house of Gregorio Aguirre in San Ysidro, a small barrio in the jurisdiction of Taysan. There he found Maj. Crisanto Borruel, Aguirre's brother-in-law, who had been out of action for several weeks, recovering from a severe illness. Exhausted from his travels, Malvar rested in Aguirre's house for three days and conferred with Borruel.[6]

On the afternoon of the third day, a man from a neighboring barrio came to the house with the information that Americans were nearby. In fact, there were thirty-three of them, the members of a scouting party led by Capt. J. S. Powell of the Thirty-Eighth Volunteer Infantry, on their way back to Batangas City from San Juan de Bocboc. Malvar and his retinue mounted their horses and barely got away. Borruel, too ill to flee, was not so fortunate: the Americans took him into custody and later deposited him in the military prison at Batangas City.[7]

As time passed and such incidents multiplied, Malvar's reputation grew to heroic proportions. Soldiers who served under him claimed that Malvar owed his ability to elude pursuers to the fact that he had an *anting-anting*, an amulet that gave him magical powers. So long as he wore his anting-anting, they maintained, bullets could not hit him; even if the enemy managed to corner him, Malvar could become invisible and escape. What people believe to be true is, of course, just as important as the truth itself, and we would be unwise to laugh away such statements about Malvar's powers. Like many heroes of the revolutionary period, he appeared to have charismatic qualities, and they surely counted with his followers.[8]

Another thing that counted was Malvar's determination. His published manifestoes indicated that he was prepared to remain in the field indefinitely in order to achieve "a government of the Filipinos by the Filipinos," and in his private statements on the subject, his doggedness was equally evident. According to Bernardo Marques, a lieutenant colonel who was close to Malvar, "he had given his word that he would never surrender as long as a gun remained in the field." Malvar's brother-in-law, Eustacio Maloles, made almost identical remarks. Fully committed to the cause and willing to endure the hardships of guerrilla life, Malvar was one commander who seemed to command respect.[9]

Although some of Malvar's organizational decisions earlier in the war may have been questionable—for one, his reliance on personalistic criteria in creating his officer corps—his ability to solve the formidable problems that faced him at the beginning of the guerrilla campaign was nothing short of remarkable. His first major task was to complete the reorganization of the local forces, so badly mauled during the American invasion. To do so, he elaborated on the changes that he had initiated in late January 1900. He placed his colonels—Santiago Rillo, Martin Cabrera, Melecio Bolaños, and the others—in charge of specific geographical areas, or zones, in which several columns were stationed. Each column was commanded by a major, was composed of three or more companies led by captains, and was itself assigned to a designated sector, typically, the geographical limits of a town. Within that sector, individual companies were responsible for their own areas of operations, usually a few barrios.[10]

His second was to feed the approximately three thousand troops under his command in Batangas. Although the Filipinos suffered from a lack of weapons and ammunition—no more than two-thirds of the Batangueño troops were equipped with rifles and the supply of cartridges was limited—the shortages did not extend to food. From the outset there were plentiful supplies of rice, corn, fish, and other foodstuffs. In February 1900, Malvar established a system of taxation in the province, designed to raise the money needed to cover the expenses of his troops. All noncombatants over the age of fourteen were required to pay a minimum weekly tax: 4 *cuartos** for single males, two for single females, six for married couples. The rich were ordered to contribute according to their means (some gave more than one hundred

*Four *cuartos* were equal to one *real;* eight *reales* equaled one peso.

pesos a year). In addition, after each harvest, landowners were obliged to contribute a tenth of their rice and corn to the Filipino Army. Malvar instructed local commanders to appoint one man in each barrio to serve as a tax collector, and the collectors were required to turn over the proceeds of their collection to military administrators. So long as noncombatant support for the war effort remained strong—and as the next chapter will show, it remained so for about a year—the system worked reasonably well, and the troops were well fed.[11]

In addition to completing the reorganization of his army and providing for their sustenance, Malvar had to confront the problem of fighting the Americans, now by unconventional means. His approach to guerrilla warfare was elegantly simple. Most of the time, his troops were expected to do three things: to ambush the enemy, to disrupt their supply and communications networks, and to hide. Most contacts with the enemy were to be brief, most units making contact were to be small, and, before launching any ambush, commanders were required to make certain that they stationed men along roads which the enemy might use to send reinforcements and that their own troops had easy access to escape routes. Such operations were intended to annoy and demoralize the Americans, not produce a decisive battlefield result, and Malvar did not want his own forces to absorb heavy losses in them.[12]

In his instructions to the troops, Malvar emphasized maintaining good relations with the civilian population. Column commanders were required to secure the cooperation of the local civil government—which is to say, of the very same officials who were chosen in the elections supervised by the U.S. Army—in keeping the peace, capturing common criminals, collecting taxes, recruiting soldiers, and procuring weapons. Malvar understood that the ability of his troops to resist by unconventional means depended on keeping the support of the noncombatants, and he aimed to ensure that the noncombatants would not come to view the demands of the guerrillas as unnecessarily burdensome. Hence, large columns were to be stationed in the vicinity of populous towns, with sufficient resources to provide for their needs, and smaller columns in the vicinity of less densely populated ones. In addition, company commanders were instructed to recruit new troops and collect taxes only from certain designated barrios, lest communities be subjected to exactions from more than one command. "All commanders will make sure," Malvar wrote, "that the civil authorities are in agreement with the military authorities (and vice versa), avoiding the situation in which anyone suffers loss to his person or his family." And he went on: "All commanders and good citizens will ensure that all misunderstandings are resolved because they only weaken the united front and solidarity of interests that are needed for the attainment of our independence."[13]

Malvar's view of guerrilla warfare was far from unique. Since time immemorial, guerrilla forces have focused on small-unit, hit-and-run raids against the enemy and endeavored to keep on close terms with the civilian population; in other theaters of the Philippine-American War, other Filipino commanders were taking the same approach.[14] Malvar was doing, in effect, what any effective guerrilla commander had to do: adopting the tactics of the social bandit.

To assert that Malvar, the onetime bandit-chaser, was now acting like a bandit is intended neither as a slight nor as a confirmation of the view, subscribed to by soldiers like Colonel Birkhimer, that the Filipino troops, one and all, were mere ladrones. The fact remains though that, much of the time, the actions of guerrillas are remarkably similar to those of social bandits. The most crucial difference between the two is attitudinal: guerrillas view their authority as legitimate and aspire to control the state, whereas bandits recognize that their position outside the state is probably permanent.

While Malvar intended to, and did, place primary emphasis on small-unit actions, he also mounted large-scale operations from time to time. His reasons are unclear. One explanation, suggested by a statement he made about a general offensive launched later in the war, is that he believed a periodic large-unit action necessary to gain the attention of the U.S. public and to make them aware of the costs of continued occupation.[15] Generally, however, such large operations were botched.

One persistent headache for Malvar was coordinating the maneuvers of his guerrilla forces. The Batangueño military units were stationed in inaccessible, outlying areas—places where they could not be easily discovered by American scouting parties. Yet Malvar had trouble finding them too, and because of that it took an inordinate amount of time for his army to execute his orders. After issuing instructions, Malvar had first to locate his zone commanders—no easy task in itself, since they frequently moved around their zones. The zone commanders had then to find the column commanders, who in turn had to find their various company commanders. By then, several days would have passed, and a few more would pass before all these widely dispersed units could be marched to an assembly point. If all went well, it took no less than a week for the Batangueño forces to mobilize in preparation for a large-unit action.[16]

And, as in the past, there were personnel problems too. In early March

1900, Malvar ordered his troops in the vicinity of Batangas City—three columns under Majs. Eliseo Claudio, Crisanto Borruel, and Nicomedes Yrineo—to assemble in the town of Taysan in preparation for a surprise attack against the enemy. The three commanders arrived on March 12 and set up camps close to Taysan. Before they could execute Malvar's plan, Yrineo suddenly, and for no apparent reason, ordered his troops to march away. (Throughout the war, Yrineo demonstrated a real talent for insubordination, and he was forever in trouble with his superiors.) Yrineo's disappearance placed Claudio and Borruel in an awkward position, and they decided to hold a meeting with their officers to consider their options. Three courses of action were discussed. First of all, they could carry out the attack anyway, even though they were not at full strength; second, they could try to locate Malvar and request new orders; and finally, they could return to Batangas City. The discussion dragged on for five hours, and in the end, the officers voted to abort the mission and return to their zone.[17]

On the return march, the two columns ran into more trouble. They left Taysan at 3:00 P.M. on March 14 and proceeded to the barrio of Mataasnalupa, where they rested for a few hours. Just after sunset, they moved out again, with Claudio and Borruel in the vanguard along with the company of Capt. Fernando Garcia. When that party reached the barrio of Panghayaan, they encountered an American scouting party, and a firefight broke out in the dark. The Filipinos had an overwhelming numerical advantage, but they gave a poor account of themselves. Most of Borruel's men ran away without firing a shot. Only the two companies led by the Buenafe brothers (Eulalio and Juan) and one platoon from Garcia's company put up a fight, and after about two hours of ineffective firing they too retired from the field. All things considered, it was a dismal performance—a poorly coordinated operation, an aborted mission, humiliation in battle. The only consolation was that the casualties had been light: one soldier slightly wounded in the foot.[18]

A month later, Malvar tried again, now placing Briccio Casala in charge of an operation against the U.S. troops stationed in Batangas City. This action too was aborted, largely because Eulalio Buenafe's company failed to show up at the designated assembly point. At least Buenafe had a reason for noncompliance: most of his troops had fallen ill, and they were in no condition to fight.[19]

Malvar did not give up, and in time some of his plans for large-unit actions were carried out—among others, the attack on Taal in early July 1900 in which several U.S. soldiers were wounded.[20] Without exception, however, the results were disappointing, the Filipinos absorbing a higher number of casualties than the Americans. In retrospect, it seems evident that Malvar was a bit too impatient at this stage of the conflict. His guerrilla army simply lacked the capacity to undertake large-scale operations; even small-unit actions were beyond the capacity of some columns at this point. He would have been wiser to have concentrated on tightening his control over his decentralized, often insubordinate forces and to have deferred large-unit actions until his troops were prepared for them.

★ In the Ranks: A Troubled Guerrilla Army

And what was happening down in the ranks during this phase of the war? The story of the San Miguel Column, which operated in the town of Lobo and in three outlying barrios of Batangas City, provides a revealing view.

Malvar had organized the San Miguel Column in October 1900 out of troops that had previously been stationed in the jurisdiction of the provincial capital, and he had chosen his compadre Eliseo Claudio as its commander.[21] Born in Manila about forty years earlier, Claudio had come to Batangas as a functionary in the Spanish colonial administration and subsequently had married Faustina Zaraspe, a few years his junior and a member of one of Batangas City's affluent families. Appointed a *regidor* (alderman) on the ayuntamiento of Batangas City in the early 1890s, Claudio held that post until the end of the Spanish regime, and in that capacity he was charged with overseeing the municipal accounts. Claudio also operated a printing establishment in Lipa, and he and his wife owned sizable estates in UaUa (today, Wawa), a seaside barrio of Batangas City. A veteran of more than year of fighting against the Americans, Claudio had held the rank of major since January 1900.[22]

Claudio's command consisted of three undersized companies with no more than 150 men in all. His three company commanders were Tomas Ramirez, a member of the principalía of Taysan who was already past sixty years of age, Manuel Scarella, a creole in his late twenties who had served in the Spanish Army, and Felix Farol, a well-educated resident of Batangas City who was likewise in his twenties. Claudio's immediate superior was Col. Damaso Ybarra, a Caviteño who had succeeded Santiago Rillo as head of the Eastern Zone of Batangas when Rillo had come down with tuberculosis.[23]

All things considered, Lobo seemed an ideal area of operations for a guerrilla force. The terrain around the town was mountainous; the mountains were thickly forested; and the roads in that part of Batangas were, in the words of one late nineteenth-century observer, "tortuous paths over which a person cannot travel on horseback without arriving at the end of his journey with his clothes in a very great state of deterioration."[24] Taking into account the remoteness and relative unimportance of the town (it had no more than six thousand inhabitants), the U.S. command had decided initially not to station a garrison there. Detachments were subsequently assigned to the town from time to time but never for an extended period. On the whole, Claudio and his men were able to roam as they pleased.[25]

Claudio had another advantage. At this stage of the war, when noncombatant support for the resistance was strong, the Batangueño forces received excellent intelligence about the movements of the U.S. troops. As soon as an American unit moved out on a hike (and often, even before the movement had begun), informants alerted all the Filipino troops in the vicinity. Claudio received intelligence from a wide range of sources: municipal officials, barrio lieutenants, native priests (who were now in charge of all the parishes in Batangas because the Spanish friars had departed), even clerks employed by the U.S. garrison. Thus forewarned, Claudio's troops had little difficulty in eluding any American patrols that ventured into their assigned area of operations, and they also had frequent opportunities to conduct ambushes.[26]

If the opportunities were there, the means were not. Rifles were always scarce in this guerrilla army, and the longer the fighting lasted, the more scarce they became. Some Filipino weapons were captured by the Americans; some were rendered useless by the elements; and some were even turned over to the Americans by guerrillas who succumbed to the U.S. Army's tempting offer of thirty pesos for each serviceable rifle delivered in person by a Filipino soldier.[27] The Filipino command, of course, made every effort to increase their supply of weapons. Ybarra ordered the troops to scour the barrios and seize any rifles in private hands, and Malvar instructed recruiting officers to excuse men from military service if they delivered a rifle and fifty cartridges to the Filipino Army. Such measures brought a handful of weapons into the army's arsenal in the following months, but not nearly enough to offset the losses. The troops in Ybarra's zone were so short of weapons that they often had to shift rifles from one unit to another in order to carry out military operations. And if for any reason the weapons failed to arrive—as occasionally they did—the operations had to be scrapped.[28]

The shortage of ammunition was just as serious, and again extraordinary measures were adopted to overcome the deficit. Most of the food consumed by the Americans came in tin cans, which the troops discarded. The Filipino command decided that these discarded cans could be used to manufacture cartridges, and so the guerrillas were ordered to collect as many tins as possible and forward them to the army's arsenal. Claudio's men dutifully collected the cans and passed them along, and a large number of cartridges were eventually turned out. To make gunpowder, the Filipinos were equally inventive, concocting a home-made powder from matches smuggled into the province and various locally procured components. The ammunition produced was occasionally unreliable, and it had the added drawback of generating position-revealing black smoke, but it at least gave the Filipinos an opportunity to fight from time to time.[29]

The problems of the Batangueño forces went far beyond shortages of matériel. Human deficiencies hurt the Filipino cause more, and especially the constant, demoralizing conflict within the Batangueño officer corps. Something was clearly eating away at the gut of this army, and it was doing just as much damage as the bullets and incendiary tactics of the enemy. There was too much backbiting and caviling and chewing-out and sulking, and all of it added up to a draining problem of morale.

A number of things appeared to trigger the conflicts—the excessive ambition of certain officers, clashes of personalities, rivalries that had existed before the war. At bottom, though, most of them stemmed directly from the structural deficiencies of the officer corps that Malvar had created in Batangas. The local commanders had already revealed their disputatious tendencies during the period of conventional fighting, but with the transformation of the Filipino Army into a guerrilla force, the problems became infinitely more serious. Now, Malvar's command was nothing more than a loose collection of local units, each of them functioning as the private force of a local magnate. Under the circumstances, many of these magnates developed an inflated sense of their own worth and resisted any challenge to their authority, especially if the challenge came from an officer from another town or another province.

Relations between Claudio and Ybarra were particularly acrimonious. A Caviteño, Ybarra had earlier served in his native province, but he had fallen out with General Trias and was reassigned to Malvar's sector. In solving that problem, however, the Filipino command had created another, since Batangueño officers like Claudio resented an outsider's being elevated over them. Ybarra had some objectionable human qualities too. A former telegraph operator, he suddenly found himself in a position of authority and obviously enjoyed the experience.[30] From his pen issued a constant stream of orders on matters big and small, and if a subordinate failed to comply at once, Ybarra began to fume. In his own way, Claudio was just as difficult. Few more intelligent men served in the Filipino Army, and few were more disorganized or deliberate. And Claudio was very proud—an acknowledged leader in his community who had grown accustomed to being treated with respect, a man who would not allow himself to be dictated to by an upstart like Ybarra.

Claudio's deficiencies soon became a cause of conflict. Shortly after Claudio took command of the San Miguel Column, Ybarra informed him that an American patrol would be passing near Lobo and ordered him to attack it. Claudio was unable to do so because—as he later explained to the colonel—he had become embroiled in administrative matters and had not yet had time to meet with his lieutenants to discuss ambush procedures. So an opportunity was lost, and Ybarra was not pleased. About ten days later, Claudio left the jurisdiction of his command without his superior's approval and went to the barrio of Bilogo in Batangas City on personal business. Ybarra was now incensed. "In order to teach discipline and respect for authority to your forces," he wrote to Claudio, "there is no better method than setting a good example." In his view, Claudio, by disobeying orders and infringing on the jurisdiction of another column, was not doing so. He added that Malvar wanted his guerrilla army to ambush the Americans frequently, and that up to now Claudio's column had been insufficiently aggressive. Claudio returned to Lobo in short order, but his relations with the zone commander did not improve.[31]

At the same time Claudio was having problems with one of his company commanders. Capt. Manuel Scarella, the creole who had served in the Spanish Army, was a rather worthless sort—cowardly, dishonest, totally self-interested. During the Spanish-American War, he had taken part in the defense of Manila, but when the Americans had occupied that city, Scarella had decided to offer his services to Aguinaldo and had received a commission in the Filipino Army. For no obvious reason, Malvar had a high regard for Scarella; and for more obvious reasons, Scarella had a high regard for himself; but just about everyone else in the Batangueño forces, with the possible exception of his brother Lino, found him loathsome and unreliable. In mid-1900, when Scarella served in a different column, Santiago Rillo became convinced that the man planned to surrender and ordered someone to kill him. Rillo then reconsidered the matter, decided that the evidence was not conclusive, and let Scarella live. If he had not, he would have spared the Filipino Army a lot of trouble.[32]

In October 1900, Malvar informed Scarella of his appointment as commander of the second company of Claudio's column, which was to be stationed in three barrios of Batangas City—Ylijan, De la Paz, and Ysla Verde (the last, a small island off the province's southern coast). The men of the second company immediately assembled at their station, but Scarella was nowhere to be seen; it took him no less than a month to report for duty. In the meantime, he sent excuses—he was obliged to attend to some job in the zone headquarters; several officials had failed to provide him horses, and that had delayed him further. Scarella, it seems, had excuses for every occasion.[33]

When he did show up, he was worse than useless. In late November 1900, Celestino Gutierrez, the municipal president of Lobo, informed Claudio that an American wagon train had left Lobo bound for Batangas City, that it would be returning from the provincial capital in a few days, and that on its return it would pass through the barrio of Ylijan. Ylijan was in Scarella's sector, and Claudio promptly ordered his captain to ambush the Americans on their return journey. Scarella's company failed to do so, and Scarella wrote back to his superior to explain why. When he had received Claudio's order, he reported, he had conferred with his troops about setting up the ambush, and they had begged him not to do it. Most were recent conscripts, they had little experience in using firearms, and, according to Scarella, they were not ready for the battlefield. Scarella also pointed out that Colonel Ybarra had given strict instructions to avoid ambushes near barrios that had not yet delivered rice to the tax collectors, and no collection had occurred in Ylijan. What he failed to point out was that, if the troops were poorly trained and the rice in Ylijan uncollected, he himself was largely to blame, since it had taken him so long to arrive at his post.[34]

Claudio saw that Scarella's company was of little military value so long as Scarella remained in command. He grew troubled too by the captain's other failings. Scarella consistently disobeyed Claudio's orders, and he distributed most of the money and rice collected in his area of operations not to the troops but to a coterie of favorites and to himself. So Claudio determined to get rid of Scarella, and on December 28, 1900, he sent one of his lieutenants to Ylijan to take command of the second company.[35]

But Claudio made one mistake. He failed to discuss the matter first with his own superior, Ybarra, and the result was another clash between Claudio and the zone commander. When Claudio's lieutenant arrived at Scarella's headquarters, Scarella proved unwilling to be relieved. He played for time and meanwhile sent a letter to Ybarra explaining that he would not leave unless the colonel ordered him to do so. Claudio became suspicious, and he dispatched his own letter to the zone commander informing him of Scarella's shortcomings and belatedly asking him to relieve the captain. Sensing that trouble was fast approaching, he paid a visit to his compadre Miguel Malvar to convey New Year's greetings and to discuss his problems with Scarella.[36]

Trouble was approaching in the person of Damaso Ybarra. When he learned of his column commander's attempt to relieve Scarella, Ybarra wrote an angry letter to Claudio, accusing him of insubordination; Scarella had, after all, received his assignment from Malvar, and higher authorities alone could remove him. Ybarra made it clear that he had no intention of making any change, and he lectured Claudio that "any actions that you consider to be of benefit to the service must be discussed and approved by this command before execution." Claudio's reply was equally intemperate; Ybarra, he maintained, made accusations without first investigating the situation. Battle lines were being drawn.[37]

An outright break was avoided, thanks in part to Malvar's intervention. Convinced that Claudio had grounds for acting as he did, Malvar persuaded Ybarra to investigate the charges against Scarella, and on January 25, 1901, the zone commander called the captain to his headquarters. Scarella came and promptly submitted his resignation, no doubt because he realized that his record could not stand up to scrutiny. So round one went to Claudio: he got rid of his deficient company commander. But round two went to Ybarra, for he now ordered Claudio to withdraw his second company (formerly Scarella's) from the three Batangas City barrios, and he then removed those barrios from Claudio's jurisdiction. In the end, the only clear loser in the affair was young Scarella, and in March 1901, he severed his ties with the Filipino Army by surrendering to the Americans.[38]

Conflicts like these were by no means confined to Claudio's column. Briccio Casala, a commander in the vicinity of Taysan, was on equally poor terms with Ybarra. In late August 1900, troubled by the high prices the Batangueño troops were obliged to pay for meat and other food items, Ybarra had issued a proclamation strictly regulating the sale of all foodstuffs in his zone. He prohibited the sale of eggs, cattle, chicken, and various other products in occupied towns because the Americans had been bidding up their prices. Casala felt that the proclamation was ill-conceived, since it placed an inordinate burden on the inhabitants of those towns, and he refused to enforce it. "I will not obey orders of this type and others which hurt our people," he explained to Claudio. And then there was Nicomedes Yrineo, another major in Ybarra's zone, who got along with no one. Claudio complained that Yrineo recruited soldiers and collected taxes outside the area of his jurisdiction; Ybarra upbraided him for disobeying orders; and there were complaints about Yrineo from an officer in Laguna, who claimed that the major and his men had committed depredations in that province. At the very top of this guerrilla army there were tensions too. Malvar quarreled constantly with Mariano Noriel, one of the leaders of the Filipino forces in Cavite, and at one point Trias was obliged to intervene to reconcile the two.[39]

Conflict within the officer corps is a problem in any army; in this case, it was especially serious because in a real sense Malvar's officer corps *was* his army. As in the past, large numbers of common soldiers in the Batangueño forces were pressed into service by recruiting officers and by patrons, and they were unenthusiastic about the cause they were defending. "We were fighting because our officers told us to fight," Emilio Vergara told me. "We obeyed our leaders. There was no alternative. If we did not obey, we would be punished."[40]

One alternative did exist, however, and many Batangueño soldiers discovered it. In one company of Major Claudio's command, the rate of desertion was generally close to 10 percent a month, and in columns that saw more action, the rate was higher still. In planting and harvest seasons, when human labor was needed in the fields, most units experienced such heavy losses that Malvar's army found it almost impossible to mount any operations at all.[41] So the leaders were discontented, and the followers were often uncommitted, and under the circumstances, it was something of a miracle that Malvar's forces had managed to hold out so long.

★ Contacts

Although the shortages of matériel, the recurrent clashes between officers, and the other problems severely reduced the effectiveness of Malvar's army, they did not paralyze it. Claudio's men went to the aid of other columns on a few occasions; they moved around in order to avoid U.S. scouting parties; they set up a few ambushes, and even executed one. All in all, they did little fighting, but in that respect they were not unique: at this stage of the conflict, a number of Malvar's columns fought infrequently, if at all.

Had it been up to Tomas Ramirez, the captain of Claudio's first company, prosecution of the war might have been more vigorous. More than twice as old as Claudio's other two company commanders, he had at least twice their energy. Ramirez was a rare breed in Malvar's army, an able field commander who liked nothing more than a good fight and who was always on the lookout for the enemy. Ramirez's men got their first taste of battle in late November 1900, and indirectly they owed their opportunity to Manuel Scarella. Ramirez spotted the very same party of Americans whom Scarella had refused to attack. They were near the barrio of De la Paz, and, on his own, Ramirez ordered his company to ambush them. The odds were solidly in the Filipinos' favor—Ramirez's unit had a three-to-one numerical advantage, and almost all of his men were armed with rifles—and this time the ambush worked. They captured two horses and assorted supplies, wounded one American (a civilian packmaster named Daniel Welch, who died a day later), and escaped the fray with no losses of their own.[42]

In the following months, Ramirez continued to show a fighting spirit, although through no fault of his own he took part in no more engagements. In December the Americans scouted almost constantly in Claudio's zone, burning several barrios in which they found evidence of noncombatant contact with the guerrillas. Ramirez became very angry. He received Ybarra's permission to retaliate, but the Americans left the area before Ramirez was able to prepare an ambush. The next month, Briccio Casala, having received information that the Americans planned to burn several barrios in Batangas City, asked Claudio to send some of his troops to participate in a combined attack against the would-be incendiaries, and Claudio nominated Ramirez's company. Ramirez appeared at the designated meeting point but Casala did not, and the operation had to be scrapped.[43]

Claudio's other company commander, Felix Farol, lacked Ramirez's initiative and aggressiveness. Farol did everything he was asked to do, and he did it competently enough, but he was incapable of making decisions on his own. When something unexpected happened—and in unconventional warfare, it too often did—Farol found it necessary to write to Claudio for instructions. Should he admit to his company two men from the Taysan Column who had presented themselves at his headquarters? Should he attack the Americans if they conducted a reconnaissance in his area? Would it be permissible for him to serve a goat and green vegetables to the troops for Christmas dinner? Farol was not the sort of man who would be likely to take advantage of opportunities that came his way, and in practice, he did not. His company took part in no battles.[44]

Here then was a column that had fought exactly one time between October 1900 and April 1901, had suffered no battlefield casualties, and had inflicted but one on the enemy. Claudio's troops had hidden well and had thereby contributed to the enemy's sense of frustration, but they had done little of substance to win the war. Still, to put the matter in perspective, even if they and all of Malvar's forces had harassed the Americans incessantly, victory would have been beyond their grasp. The Batangueños could prolong the war, but they could not win it; Aguinaldo's decision to fight a conventional war at the outset—and the destruction of the elite units of the Filipino Army that ensued—had seen to that.

Although Claudio's column absorbed no casualties on the battlefield, sickness took a steady toll. The Batangueño troops, no less than the Americans, were afflicted with malaria, typhoid, dysentery, and many other debilitating maladies, and they sought medical treatment from both local physicians and hospitals in the field. Unfortunately, though, medication like quinine was always in short supply, and the field hospitals were too small to house patients for long periods. When the men became too ill to take part in military operations, they were usually given temporary passes to return home in order to regain their health.[45]

The granting of such a pass was equivalent to discharging a man from the service. The sickest men died, and the ones who recovered generally did their best to avoid further involvement in the fighting. Captain Farol's company lost ten men to illness between November 8 and December 15, 1900—a loss of 20 percent of the company in less than six weeks. The record of Ramirez's company was only slightly better. Even Claudio succumbed to illness, and in April 1901, Malvar granted him an extended leave.[46]

★ Other Activities

In this kind of war, intercourse between combatants and noncombatants was to be expected, and in towns like Lobo, where U.S. troops were rarely in evidence, it was extremely frequent. The local forces regularly raised recruits to fill vacancies in the ranks. Aguinaldo's earlier decree on recruitment was still in effect: as before, recruits were to be chosen by lot, and men were to be permitted to buy their way out of military service. Also in effect were Malvar's regulations instructing company commanders to recruit men only from the barrios in which they operated. Yet nothing ever seemed to go according to the book in Malvar's army. Generals and colonels might issue orders, but majors and captains, operating well out of sight, often ignored them. Sometimes officers recruited men outside the jurisdiction of their commands; sometimes the lotteries were not held at all, commanders conscripting any able-bodied men they happened to spot; and sometimes men bought their way out of military service not by paying the amounts prescribed by decree but by bribing the soldiers conducting the lottery. Such abuses brought complaints, and these in turn led to orders by the high command to right the wrongs. But the pernicious practices persisted—at the cost of some civilian support for the resistance.[47]

While they struggled to police themselves, Malvar's forces also made an effort to restore law and order in the province. Banditry was widespread during the war, and although some of the bandits (such as Aniceto Oruga) were acting in concert with the guerrillas, others were simply nasty characters, guilty of rape, robbery, and the like. The American troops and the municipal police appointed by the Americans attempted to capture these criminals, but with little success. The Filipino forces appointed their own officials—generally military officers, but on occasion, prominent local citizens—to pursue and prosecute the malefactors, and their appointees made more headway. One reason for their success was that they operated with greater freedom in the barrios, because the Batangueño guerrillas controlled the bush; a second was that barrio people trusted them more. In any event, if the townspeople were victimized—if a horse were stolen or a house burglarized—they tended to seek satisfaction from the Filipino shadow officials.[48]

If the aggrieved got satisfaction, the accused did not necessarily get the kind of justice normally dispensed by the colonial state. As soon as an investigating officer became convinced of a person's guilt, the case was closed, and sentencing swiftly followed. The accused had no opportunity to confront his or her accusers; and he or she never got a day in court. Furthermore, once found guilty, a person could expect a punishment out of proportion to the seriousness of the crime: robbers might lose their eyesight; adulteresses might lose their lives.[49]

Apologists for the U.S. Army often pointed to such punishments as evidence of the enemy's inhumanity, but their critique was unfair. The dispensing of justice is a vexing problem for a guerrilla force. For most of recorded history, states have relied on four basic kinds of punitive sanctions to deal with violators of the law—fines, imprisonment, corporal punishment, and death. But guerrilla organizations in places where the majority of the population is poor have a narrower range of choices. Fines of any magnitude cannot be exacted, since most malefactors cannot afford to pay them, and imprisonment is no option, since a guerrilla army cannot maintain prisons. Thus, as severe as the guerrillas' sentences—corporal punishment and death—may have seemed, they were really the only kinds of sanctions available to them.

The troops' contact with the civilian population took other forms. Claudio periodically allowed his officers and men to visit their families, and Claudio himself went to Batangas City to see his ailing wife. Malvar was accompanied in the field by his wife and children, and other officers—Manuel Scarella among them—enjoyed the company of their girlfriends. These women provided more than companionship to the troops: some ran errands, some provided information, and a few even served as tax collectors.[50]

The soldiers kept in touch with family and friends by correspondence as well. Servants and couriers traveled between town and field, carrying messages both personal and military in nature. Thus, Enrique Claudio—Eliseo Claudio's teenage son—kept his father abreast of family matters, forwarded the latest Manila newspapers, and sent him several boxes of his favorite brand of tobacco. One of Claudio's close friends sent him bacon and dried fish and also news of the latest cockfights. Still another correspondent was Celestino Gutierrez, the president of Lobo, who, in addition to reporting on municipal affairs and the movements of U.S. troops, supplied Claudio with goat, a Batangueño culinary specialty.[51]

While intercourse between guerrillas and noncombatants occurred more often in towns like Lobo, where U.S. units seldom patrolled, it was by no means confined to them. On November 12, 1900, several weddings took place in Lipa's splendid cathedral, located in the town's plaza, scarcely a hundred yards from the buildings in which the U.S. troops were billeted. At one, Marcos Mendoza and Victoria Calingasan, both from the barrio of Tambo, were married. As at most weddings in the Philippines, the families of the couple chose two distinguished residents of the town to serve as sponsors. According to custom, the sponsors incurred a moral obligation to assist the newlyweds, especially if they encountered financial difficulties. For that wedding, the sponsors were Paulino Ynciong and Serafin Manalo. On the same day, Eugenio Tibayan and Fausta de Leon, both from the barrio of Mataasnacahoy, were married, and their sponsors were Gregorio Lat and Petra Lumbera. Ynciong and Lat were more than simply men of means; the first was then a lieutenant colonel in the Filipino Army, and the second a major.[52]

Ynciong seemed to derive pleasure from participating in these ceremonies and from so openly defying the Americans. Between February 1900 and April 1901, he was a sponsor at no fewer than ten weddings in Lipa; Lat served in that capacity in four.[53] This was a curious war indeed, with the Americans exhausting themselves in searching the bush while their enemies paraded in formal attire through the center of the province's principal town.

★ Disturbing Developments

Behind the acts of bravado, concern mounted over events that were occurring outside the province. Only a few days before the Mendoza-Calingasan nuptials, a presidential election had taken place in the United States, and McKinley had decisively defeated Bryan, the Democrat and anti-imperialist.

So Aguinaldo and other military leaders could no longer rally the troops by claiming that the United States would soon concede independence to the Philippines. If independence were to be achieved, the Filipinos would have to win it on their own.

McKinley's victory had other consequences. Now assured that the Americans were in the Philippines to stay, more than a hundred well-known Filipinos—including Trinidad H. Pardo de Tavera, Cayetano Arellano, and other members of Manila's indigenous upper crust—assembled in the capital on December 23, 1900, to form the Federal party, an organization that aimed to cooperate with the Americans in bringing peace to the Philippines. *Federalistas* subsequently traveled around the archipelago speaking in favor of U.S. policies and attempting to convince Filipino soldiers to surrender. In January 1901, moreover, a Federal party chapter was organized in Lipa, and chapters sprang up in other Batangas towns in the following weeks.[54]

Meanwhile, the military situation outside Batangas grew steadily worse. By the end of January 1901, the Americans had essentially eliminated armed opposition in the provinces north of Manila and on several islands in the Visayas. Then came shocking news. On March 15, 1901, Gen. Mariano Trias, Aguinaldo's second-in-command, surrendered to the Americans along with approximately 130 of his Caviteño troops. In an open letter to his countrymen, Trias explained that he had done so because "the people were demanding peace and seeking some means of securing that tranquility lost on account of the war. . . . It was my duty to listen to the voice of my brothers." He now called upon all Filipinos to put down their arms and place their faith in American rule: "If the country is to advance with firm steps to the height of happiness and prosperity it needs nothing less than energetic and powerful assistance; and for this purpose, there is nothing better than [the assistance of] the United States, which, I am convinced, has no other aim than to unite its forces with ours for the intellectual and commercial progress of the Filipino people." Only eight days after Trias's surrender, the Americans captured Emilio Aguinaldo at his camp at Palanan in the highlands of Isabela. Suddenly, the Filipino Army was leaderless.[55]

These events drove home a basic point about the Batangueño resistance. Malvar's theater of guerrilla operations was, after all, only one of many in the Philippines, and the ability of his forces to continue to resist could be undermined by reverses elsewhere. For one, the loss of leaders like Aguinaldo and Trias was a blow to the morale of the Batangueño soldiers and their noncombatant supporters; for another, the Americans' success in other theaters meant that they would be able to devote an ever-increasing percentage of their attention and resources to pacifying Batangas and the rest of southwestern Luzon. Some Batangueños now looked into the future and were frightened at what they saw. According to Alfonso Panopio, a former colonel in the local forces but more recently a member of the Federal party, further resistance could lead only to the destruction of the province; many more Americans would come and they would commit all sorts of *barbaridades*.[56]

As the reverses multiplied, the Federal party stepped up its efforts in Batangas. In late March, Panopio and several other Federalistas met with Malvar and attempted to persuade him to surrender. Malvar heard them out, rejected their arguments, and reaffirmed his commitment to the cause of independence. Other Batangueño officers were not so steadfast. Cipriano Lopez, the commander of the guerrillas in the vicinity of Balayan, turned himself in, and several leaders of the Lipa forces began to discuss surrender terms.[57]

A final development was one that Trias had alluded to in his letter to his countrymen. A perceptible transformation had taken place in the attitude of the civilian population toward the resistance. The growth of the Federal party in Batangas was one sign of the change. Claudio's company commanders observed another; beginning in mid-December 1900, the amount of money and food turned over to the tax collectors in Lobo dropped sharply. The drop may have been due in part to a scarcity of rice in the region brought about by the shortage of work animals and the disruptions caused by warfare, but it also likely resulted from a decline of enthusiasm for the Filipino cause. In any case, the commanders did not have enough cash to pay the salaries of the troops, and the San Miguel Column experienced food shortages for the first time.[58]

This attitudinal change was equally as serious as the reverses in the field. To keep the resistance alive, Malvar needed the continuing assistance of the noncombatants; he needed them not only to pay their taxes and contribute rice and corn but also to give information about the enemy, hide his men when they were being pursued, and provide a score of other services. And now, just as the situation in the field was becoming critical, the Batangueño general appeared to be losing his hold over his civilian supporters. In a war such as this one, the story of the noncombatants is every bit as significant as that of the men in the field, and it will bear some examining.

7

In the Towns: Batangas City

ONLY A FEW DAYS after the Americans had occupied Batangas City, a handful of the townspeople trickled back into the población. Among the first were Florencio Caedo and Diego Gloria, two men who had served as minor functionaries in the provincial government both under the Spanish regime and the Philippine Republic. They did not appear to be pro-American at this point, but they were self-serving, and no doubt they wanted to stake out their claims to any jobs that might be available. Bureaucrats the world over seem to have a talent for moving easily from one employer to the next, and the Filipino variety of this peculiar breed was no less talented.[1]

Such men were the exceptions, though. For about a month the town remained deserted, except for the American soldiers who occupied the priest's residence and a few large private houses. Most of the townspeople remained in hiding, afraid not only that the Americans might treat them badly but also

185

that the local forces might interpret their return as an indication of pro-American sympathies. But in mid-February 1900, convinced that their fears were largely unfounded and tired of life on the run, they began to return, and by the end of the month most of the houses were again occupied and the población was alive with activity.[2]

★ An Appearance of Normality

On the surface, at least, life in Batangas City returned to normal. Most of the men resumed their work in the fields. Those engaged in sugar production immediately faced arduous labor, since the cane harvest normally began in March. Not long after that, it would be time for cultivators of lowland rice to prepare their seedbeds and for the growers of upland rice to begin plowing in preparation for the broadcast sowing in May. For all these cultivators the labor in the fields would prove to be more time-consuming and enervating than usual because of the shortage of carabaos.[3]

People engaged in nonagricultural work likewise returned to the job. Ynocencio Aguilera and hundreds of others from seaside barrios set off in their bancas to fish in the nearby waters. Pedro Sarmiento, a butcher, and scores of shopkeepers, male and female alike, reopened for business in the población. As always, large numbers of women and girls supplemented the family income by engaging in embroidery, weaving, and other cottage industries.[4]

Life in the town resumed normal rhythms in other ways. Children played their favorite games—*tangga, tubigan, pico,* and many more. Young couples courted and married. Women gave birth, raised the children, and performed household chores. Men traded stories, raised their fighting cocks, and played monte and other games of chance. As before, Thursday was market day, when people from the barrios flooded the población to buy and sell, and Sunday was the Lord's day and also the one when the men went to the cockpit and gambled away their hard-earned pesos.[5]

Despite the presence of the American troops, the residents of Batangas City were free, most of the time, to travel about the countryside. Pedro Sarmiento regularly circulated in the barrios to purchase pigs and other animals. Anacleto Magtibay traveled to San Juan de Bocboc to oversee his landholdings. Jose Babasa and Mariano Yturralde, both landlords, went to Manila after the harvest to sell their sugar, and local merchants also went there to buy goods and transact other business.[6]

Yet appearances can be deceiving, and in this case they definitely were.

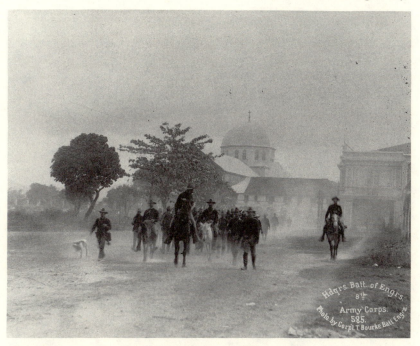

25. *U.S. troops occupying Batangas City, January 1900*

Something else was going on in Batangas City and in the other towns of the province, and it was going on day after day and right in front of the unseeing eyes of the American army of occupation. In scores of ways the noncombatant population of Batangas was covertly supplying and otherwise supporting Malvar's men, and for about a year their activity remained constant. The principal suppliers and supporters were the wealthy, the politically promi-nent, and the well educated—people of the same kind as the leaders of the military units. Let us first see what they did, and then why they did so.

★ Resistance

Sixty-one years old at the time of the American occupation of the province, Fermin Arceo was a wealthy man, the owner of a residence in the población of Batangas City, some agricultural property in one of the outlying barrios, and a large hacienda in Quilo, a barrio of Ibaan.[7] During the year and a half since the liberation of the province from the Spaniards, Arceo had, in addition to attending to his landed wealth, served as a sheriff of a sort, empowered by

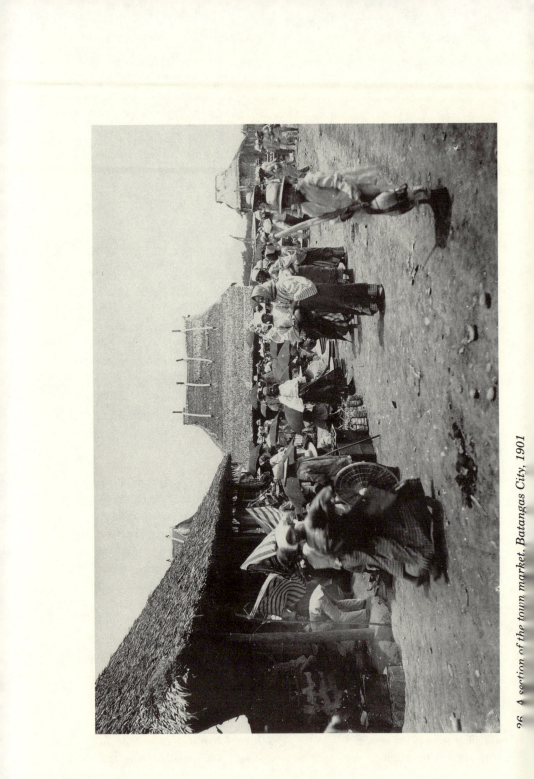

26 *A section of the town market, Batangas City, 1901*

Malvar to pursue and punish the many robbers and other lawbreakers who were operating in the towns of Batangas City, Ibaan, Taysan, San Jose, and Lobo. When the Americans arrived, he was conducting business at his hacienda in Quilo, and he decided to remain there and see what happened.

In this kind of conflict, however, watching from the sidelines was impossible. Inevitably the war touched people, and before they knew it and whether or not they liked it, they were transformed from observers into players. For Fermin Arceo, observation gave way to participation about a month after the American invasion, when Briccio Casala, only a company commander at the time, came to his house, accompanied by 80 well-armed guerrillas. Casala asked for directions to Banaybanay, a *sitio* in the town of San Jose, and Arceo gave him a guide. A few days passed and Casala returned to Arceo's house, now accompanied by several other officers and about 150 armed men. Arceo provided a meal for the troops, and as they ate, they told Arceo about their recent battle with the Americans at Banaybanay.

Not long after that, Arceo had dealings with another Filipino officer, Mariano Cabrera of Taal. Malefactors were causing trouble in Ibaan, and Malvar's lieutenants expected Arceo to catch them. Cabrera dispatched seven soldiers to assist Arceo, but the troops did not remain long; soon after they arrived, the Taal forces suffered heavy casualties in a fight with the Americans, and Cabrera decided that he needed the men more than Arceo did. In April, Arceo rendered assistance of another kind to the Filipino cause—he donated fifteen pesos to support the war effort.

Late in April, Arceo had his first contact with the Americans. A U.S. infantry detachment from San Jose came to his hacienda, occupied his residence and his warehouse, and confiscated a rifle, two horses, and other possessions. With no roof to shelter him in Quilo, Arceo was obliged to return to his house in Batangas City, and he remained in the provincial capital for the rest of the war. Still, he continued to assist Malvar's men. In August 1900, Briccio Casala sent him a letter asking for a contribution of fifty pesos, a large sum even for a wealthy man, but Arceo paid the money, and later that month he also gave five cavans of palay to Casala and ten cavans to an agent of Martin Cabrera. In September, another Batangueño officer requested money to buy hats for his men, and Arceo gave five pesos. For the rest of the year, Arceo continued to have dealings with the Filipino troops, although he gave them no more cash.

This war in the Philippines appeared to be different things to different people, and one reason they saw the war so differently was that they saw it from such different angles. The angle of vision of the American soldier, searching and destroying and cursing the rains, was obviously not the same as that of the Batangueño guerrilla, ambushing and hiding and praying for miracles. And all the combatants, Americans and Filipinos alike, saw the war from a far different perspective than someone like Fermin Arceo, obeying the regulations of the Americans by day and assisting Malvar's men by night. The battle for Batangas was the sum of all these perspectives, and if Arceo's war was less exciting and ultimately less dangerous than Emilio Vergara's war, it was no less important, given the crucial role that noncombatants always play in unconventional conflicts.

Potenciano Hilario, another of Batangas City's prominent men, viewed the war from approximately the same angle as Arceo, and he too played a key role in it. A distinguished member of the town's political elite, Hilario had, like Eliseo Claudio, served on the ayuntamiento of Batangas City in the early 1890s. He was, as well, a member of the economic elite; the Spanish property assessment of 1891 showed that Hilario was the owner of two houses on Bustos Street in the población, both valued at twenty-five hundred pesos. He was in his fifties and a widower.[8] During the town's occupation, Hilario played a clever double game. He tried to convince the American authorities that he was a peaceful man and a friend of the United States, but at the same time he aided the Filipinos in the field.

For a while, Hilario was successful in deceiving the Americans. A few months after the arrival of the U.S. troops, Felipe Calderon, the author of the Philippine Republic's Constitution but now a collaborator, came from Manila to the province with the mission of convincing Col. Santiago Rillo to leave the field. Col. George Anderson, the commander of the U.S. garrison in Batangas City, asked Hilario, his apparent ally, to contact Rillo and set up a meeting. Hilario complied and a conference took place, although Rillo decided not to surrender. About the same time, another U.S. Army officer characterized Hilario as "disposed to help" the Americans.[9]

Not so. Even after he had arranged the meeting between Calderon and Rillo, Hilario kept in touch with the Batangueño colonel and at various times sent him chocolate cakes, fish, and cigarettes. When Rillo was replaced by Damaso Ybarra, Hilario gave the new commander a large supply of goods. At one point, he journeyed to Manila to procure some cloth for Ybarra; he also delivered medicine needed by ailing soldiers. When the Filipino forces in the area captured Americans, Hilario provided food for the prisoners. Late in 1900, he raised money in the town to buy Christmas presents for the troops, and he gave twenty-five pesos to the family of Briccio Casala to meet their expenses.[10]

In the long run, the Americans stumbled upon the fact that Hilario was acting duplicitously. In a battle near Lipa, a Filipino officer was killed, and on his body U.S. troops found a letter written by Hilario, boasting that he had hoodwinked Colonel Anderson into thinking that he was an americanista. Unamused, the Americans threw Hilario in jail and kept him there until the war was over.[11]

Other leaders of the community contributed too. Early in February 1900, Melchor Babasa, one of Batangas City's wealthiest men, sent a message to the Filipino forces warning them that on the following day three hundred American soldiers would be converging on Talumpoc, a barrio about six miles to the east of the población. At the time Santiago Rillo had his head-quarters at Talumpoc and several hundred soldiers were with him. Thus forewarned, Rillo's men put up a good fight against the Americans, although in the end they ran out of ammunition and were forced to retreat, leaving be-hind one machine gun and two brass field pieces. Other members of the eco-nomic elite of Batangas City—Jose Rea, Leoncio Arceo (Fermin's brother), and Vicente Olmos, for example—provided similar warnings about Ameri-can military operations. Many prominent families entertained Filipino sol-diers in their homes and hid them when they were trying to escape from pursuing Americans. Physicians like Domingo de los Santos treated ailing or wounded men. Jose Villanueva, a pharmacist and also Batangas City's mu-nicipal president under the Philippine Republic, provided medicine to the troops from a drugstore he owned in Manila. Vicente Soriano, formerly cabeza de barangay of the barrio of San Miguel, acted as a sometime guide and messenger for Maj. Nicomedes Yrineo, and his residence served as a storehouse for the army's weapons and supplies and as a meeting place for the town's leaders when they wished to discuss resistance activities. The list of services rendered by members of Batangas City's economic and political elites is endless.[12]

Support for the resistance was not limited to individuals at the apex of society and local politics. All Batangueños over the age of fourteen were obliged, some against their will, to pay the prescribed weekly taxes and to turn over a tithe of their harvested rice and corn to the Filipino Army's collectors.[13] No taxation system works perfectly, and the one that operated secretly in Batangas City during the Philippine-American War was no excep-tion. As was the case in the vicinity of Lobo, Filipino tax collectors often demanded payments from barrios that did not fall within their tax territory. Some residents of the town were too poor to meet the weekly payments, others were able to evade the collectors, and a few collectors found their duties so dangerous and onerous that they resigned. One even ran away. Still, for about a year most of the adults in the provincial capital paid their taxes, and for much of that time the troops in the area had enough rice, fish, cigarettes, and clothing to meet their needs.[14]

In other towns of the province, covert support for the resistance was just as strong. In Lipa, Valerio Calao, president of the municipal government established under American auspices, and members of the town's leading families (Catigbac, Africa, Solis, Roxas) made large contributions of money, rice, cigarettes, and other supplies to Filipino commanders. The chief tax collector for Malvar in Lipa, Quintin Castillo, actually lived in the población and conducted his business with impunity. Another director of Lipa's tax collection effort was Father Angel Ylagan, a Filipino priest and one of many native clerics in Batangas who assisted the local forces. The most celebrated was a priest from the Taal area, identified in the sources only as Father Castillo, who joined Malvar's army in the bush, taking with him the revered image of the Miraculous Virgin of Caysasay. Afterward, large numbers of people trekked to the hills to see the image and to worship, and many gave contributions, most of which were passed on to the guerrillas.[15]

All these activities—the payment of war taxes, the feeding and hiding of soldiers, the running of errands, the treatment of wounded men—occurred in towns occupied by U.S. troops. Although American soldiers like Captain Jordan sensed that Batangueños were hostile and complained about their lack of cooperation, and intelligence officers occasionally unearthed evidence of contact between Malvar's men and the residents of the towns, it was almost a year before they realized that intercourse on such a scale was taking place.[16] One might wonder how the Batangueños were able to fool the Americans so adeptly and so long. Had the Americans been misled by surface appearances—misled into believing that because the townspeople offered no overt opposition they were not worth worrying about? Perhaps. But perhaps, too, it was relatively easy for the Batangueños to mislead an army that was devoting so much of its attention to chasing the enemy's main forces and so little to understanding the nature of the conflict. By failing to perceive the bonds linking the men in the field to the people in the towns, the U.S. command itself insured that the resistance would continue. It was, as students of the Vietnam War will recognize, not the last time that U.S. commanders attempted to win an unconventional war by conventional means.

If support for the resistance was strong during the first year of the town's occupation, relations between the townspeople and Malvar's troops did, from time to time, show signs of strain. The fault lay squarely with the military

men, some of whom demonstrated a capacity for matching—and even out-
doing—the Americans in their mistreatment of noncombatants. Tax collectors who exacted payments outside their area of operations caused grumbles
and more than a few complaints. So did commanders who demanded items
for their personal use. Colonel Rillo, who had a sweet tooth, constantly asked
for chocolates, and Damaso Ybarra, Rillo's replacement, demanded and received a saddle, riding clothes, and a mount. Another irritant was the practice of forced conscription; no parent is happy to see a son dragged off to serve
in the hills, and no landlord is happy to be deprived of the services of an able-
bodied laborer. The parents and landlords could buy the conscripts' freedom,
but the required cash payments were substantial.[17]

Some of the actions of Malvar's men caused outrage in the community.
Shortly after the Americans had occupied the province, a group of Filipino
soldiers ransacked the house of Doña Ramona Aguilera, an elderly resident
of the neighboring town of Bauan, fired shots at the inhabitants, and stole
about one thousand pesos. Doña Ramona was highly respected and well-
connected. One of her daughters was married to Vicente Agregado, a lawyer
in Batangas City, and another to the fisherman Anacleto Magtibay. Both
sons-in-law were alienated by the soldiers' actions. Agregado became less
willing to comply with requests made by Filipino commanders, and Magtibay, frightened and disillusioned, decided to move his wife and children
from their residence in the barrio to a friend's dwelling in the población.[18]

Another incident had similar consequences. Lino Scarella, the brother of
the insubordinate Manuel and himself a major, attempted to take unfair
advantage of his position. In October 1900, he went to the home of Mariano
Arce in the barrio of Pinamucan, demanded sexual favors from the woman of
the house, and threatened to shoot Arce if he were refused. Arce, who
informed the Americans about the affair more than a year later, did not
reveal where the hot-blooded major spent that night, but he did indicate that
because of his fear of Scarella he—like Magtibay—left the barrio and entered the población.[19]

Obviously, the Filipino forces were not alone in committing such excesses
in Batangas. American soldiers in the field frequently stole from noncombatants, destroyed their property, occupied their homes, insulted them, beat
them up, administered the water cure to them, and otherwise abused them.
But, just as obviously, Malvar's men could not afford the luxury of being as
unlovable as the Americans, for they depended for their very survival on the
food, supplies, and other assistance they received from the towns. So here
was a problem of major proportions for the Filipino Army in Batangas—and

one that worsened as the war went on. Some mistreatment of noncombatants can be expected of any army. In Malvar's, it was even more difficult to
control for several interrelated reasons: because his forces were so widely
dispersed, because local commanders consequently operated without regular supervision from higher authority, and because, even when orders from
above were received, many of those commanders were inclined to ignore
them. And so, almost inevitably, the abuses continued, and in the long run,
the Filipino troops in Batangas paid a price for them.

★ Why Resistance?

Initially, however, relations between guerrillas and civilians were good in
Batangas and support for the resistance was widespread, and the time has
come to examine why that was so. It is much easier to describe people's
actions than to explain their motives, and in this case, the task of explanation is complicated by the number of individuals involved and the limitations
of the sources. The province of Batangas had approximately 300,000 inhabitants, and in Batangas City alone there were in the vicinity of 33,000. The
documents, voluminous though they are, relate largely to the elites of the
province, and even so tell us about the motives of only a fraction of such
people, almost all of them male. On the "masses," there are only fragments of
evidence.

Even by restricting the focus to male, elite Batangueños, one encounters
a serious problem of interpretation. Most of what we know about events in
Batangas City during the war is derived from declarations made by prominent residents of the southern Tagalog region between February and June
1902. These people made the declarations in response to an offer made by
Brig. Gen. J. Franklin Bell, then the American commander in the region. The
general agreed to pardon local leaders for all assistance they had rendered to
Malvar's forces during the war if they made complete and truthful statements about what they had done. There is no evidence that the Americans
used force to extract the declarations. It is clear, however, that several of the
declarers were frightened of the U.S. Army officers who took their statements, and also that a number were less than truthful about their involvement with the Filipino Army, probably because they feared punishment for
their actions in spite of Bell's promise. Some claimed that they had done little
or nothing to help the resistance whereas, in reality, they had done a great
deal. Occasionally declarers lied about the activities of other people, because
they wanted to incriminate and cause trouble for their enemies.[20]

More to the point, a number declared that they had provided assistance only because the Filipino forces would have harmed them if they refused. Dalmacio Serrano, who served as tax collector in the barrio of Santa Clara for several months in 1900, said, "If in those months I was the instrument of the insurgents in the collection of taxes from the townspeople, it was not because I supported them, but rather because I feared them, since at that time the insurgents thought nothing of assassinating, of committing arson, and of abusing people and carrying them away to the hills."[21] Can we believe statements such as these? Possibly, some of these people genuinely wanted to avoid involvement but were unable to adopt a neutral stance because of their fear of reprisals. As Serrano indicated, and other records confirm, the troops often threatened the use of force, and sometimes used it, to cow the luke-warm and the refractory. On the other hand, perhaps the men were lying, hoping to deceive the Americans about their motives. While we cannot dismiss the possibility that a percentage of the elite residents of the town were coerced into supporting the men in the field, we cannot be certain how large a percentage it was.

If fear was one motive, it was not the only one. An overwhelming majority of the declarers did not attempt to avoid responsibility for supporting the resistance. Many indicated that they were enthusiastic about it, and a number of these, Potenciano Hilario and Jose Villanueva among them, explained why. They aided the Filipino Army, they asserted, because they remained committed to the ideal of independence.[22] Such assertions echoed sentiments long expressed by upper-class Batangueños. During the months before the American invasion of the province, editorial writers in *Columnas Volantes* had declared their faith in the concept of popular sovereignty, and since the days of the revolution against Spain, the leaders of Batangas's military units had made declarations to the same effect. To some extent, the commitment of these Batangueños stemmed from their familiarity with the liberal notions that had been circulating in the Philippines for almost two decades. To some extent, it stemmed from their deeply felt belief that they were fully capable of directing their own affairs. Before the arrival of the Americans, these men had done exactly that for more than a year, and it would have been surprising indeed if they had decided overnight to accept American sovereignty. In addition, it should be recognized that the government these men were supporting was one that had consistently promoted upper-class (which is to say, their own) interests. To fight for independence, then, was also to fight for their own continued well-being.

Beyond these considerations, there was another, unstated but perhaps equally compelling: something that might be called the nephew/neighbor factor. The commanders in the field were, in fact, the friends and relatives of the elite residents of the town. It was understandable that Silvestre Borbon, a prosperous landowner from the barrio of Mahabang Dahilig, offered assistance to Maj. Nicomedes Yrineo; Borbon was Yrineo's godson. Ramon Canin often entertained Filipino soldiers at his home in the barrio of San Jose, and two of the men he entertained were his sons, Rufino and Leopoldo, both officers in the Taysan Column. Hilario, the player of the double game, was a long-time acquaintance of both Santiago Rillo and Briccio Casala. Alejo Acosta, who delivered a large shipment of rice to the Filipino forces, had been Rillo's business partner before the outbreak of the Philippine Revolution. Another staunch supporter, Leoncio Arceo, was one of Malvar's closest friends; and two others had been classmates of the general at the Malabanan school.[23] And so it went. Bonds such as these, similar to those that originally tied the Batangueño officer corps to Malvar, made it a virtual certainty that the leading men of Batangas City would play an active role in the resistance.

Of course, the nephew/neighbor factor did not guarantee that they would play this role forever. Their loyalties were to individuals, not to the army as a whole, and if the individuals were killed or captured or if they surrendered, these relatives and friends might be less willing to assist the Filipino forces. Noncombatants might also become disillusioned with the resistance. Contact with commanders and soldiers who were not within their nephew/neighbor network might occasion disillusionment, especially if such men took unfair advantage of their positions and committed abuses (as Lino Scarella and others did). The inability of the Batangueño military units to win victories against the Americans might produce the same result. Still, at the outset, the bonds of family and friendship were extremely strong, and so too was the support of the town's leaders for the guerrillas.

And what about the occupants of the lower rungs of the political and socioeconomic ladders? How committed were they? According to Teodoro Agoncillo, the Filipino resistance was essentially a mass-based phenomenon, and the same view can be found in the writings of Renato Constantino, undoubtedly the most popular historian in the Philippines today. Describing the guerrilla phase of the Philippine-American War, Constantino has written, "The people supported their fighters, *wholeheartedly* contributing arms, money, food and other supplies and, most important of all, information about the enemy and safe sanctuary in their midst." And again, a few pages later: "The determination and ferocity with which the Filipino masses *spontaneously* and at great odds continued the resistance for almost a decade after

Aguinaldo had sworn allegiance to the United States proved that he had misread his countrymen" [italics mine].[24]

For Batangas, however, the evidence cannot support such generalizations about the attitudes of the "masses," aggregated or disaggregated—at least, not for the period February 1900–April 1901. The documents tell us that most of Batangas City's peasants and day-laborers paid their taxes to the Filipino Army, but not whether they did so wholeheartedly or spontaneously; and in the absence of documentary proof, many interpretations of their participation in the resistance are plausible. The poor may have been coerced into contributing to the war effort by Malvar's tax collectors or by the Filipino soldiers. Or perhaps they were pressured into paying by their patrons—by landlords or other big shots in the community—just as poor Emilio Vergara had been pressured by Antonio Mandigma into fighting against the Americans. Granted, the nephew/neighbor factor may have caused some of the poor to support the resistance enthusiastically—they too had friends and relatives in the field. But this consideration would not have been as compelling for such people as it was for elite Batangueños, since many of the common soldiers (the nephews and neighbors of the masses) served only because they had been conscripted.[25]

Personal interviews provide tantalizing hints about lower-class attitudes and an additional reason for doubting the generalizations of Agoncillo and Constantino. "The town's leaders helped us very much," an old veteran from the town of San Luis told me. "Did the common people help too?" I asked. "They didn't help so much," he replied. "If there was a battle, they would hide. Most of all, they wanted to continue working." Other Batangueños who had fought in or lived through the war gave almost identical assessments of nonelite attitudes toward the war effort.[26] It must be acknowledged that nonagenarians speaking about events that occurred in their tender years are far from unimpeachable sources. Still, their recollections cannot be discounted. They suggest, even though they do not conclusively prove, that many occupants of the lower rungs were less enthusiastic about the resistance than the elites of Batangas.

If that was so, there were good reasons why it was so. The peasants who remained in the paddy had no more cause to be enthusiastic about the war against the Americans than those unfortunates who had been conscripted into the Batangueño forces. Their lot had not improved under the Philippine Republic, and there was no reason to believe it would improve if, by some queer turn of events, the Filipino Army ultimately managed to expel the invaders. This war may have been many things to many people, but one thing it clearly was not was a struggle for social justice. Victory would not bring land for the landless or equitable taxes or a larger role for peasants in local government. The only obvious consequence of a Filipino victory would be the return to power of a group of men who had consistently disregarded the aspirations of the common people.

What then can we conclude about the attitudes of the Batangueño lower classes? Yes, they often manifested hostility to the Americans. But one should not deduce from this that they sympathized with the local forces. Hostility to one side is not the same thing as sympathy with another. Yes, most participated in the resistance—they paid their taxes, gave a tithe of their harvests, provided information and shelter to the troops—but it is not clear that their participation was wholehearted and spontaneous. On the other hand, it cannot be proved beyond doubt that they were half-hearted and unspontaneous about the war effort; the interviews are suggestive, hardly conclusive. If we can conclude anything at all, it is that we know too little to generalize with confidence about the attitudes of the Batangueño masses.

★ Collaboration

While support for the resistance was widespread, although not necessarily wholehearted or spontaneous, for more than a year, some people did not take part in it. As we have seen, the very poor were unable to pay the minimal weekly taxes, and some others, rich and poor alike, managed to avoid the tax collectors. It should be noted, too, that the Filipino forces generally made no demands on the sick and the handicapped.[27] And finally, at the far end of the spectrum, there were collaborators—individuals who cooperated with the Americans.[28]

In the long run, nearly everyone in the province of Batangas collaborated in one way or another, for when a resistance fails, as this one did, most of the vanquished are obliged to come to terms with the victors. Yet if the majority of Batangueños might technically be classified as collaborators, important differences marked the timing of and the motives for collaboration. Some individuals cast their lot with the Americans long before others. Some collaborated because they had been wronged by the Filipino forces, some because they recognized that continued resistance was futile, some for financial reasons.

During the first year of the American occupation, there were no more than a handful of collaborators in Batangas City and other towns in the province. Batangueños were understandably wary of the Americans; even those who were lukewarm about the resistance were not yet ready to trust, or side with, men they did not know. More important, anyone who even appeared to be on close terms with the Americans ran the risk of punishment at the hands of the Filipino troops—the destruction or loss of property, kidnapping, even death.

One of the town's early collaborators was Manuel Arguelles, the onetime man on the make.[29] Shortly before the outbreak of the Philippine-American War, Aguinaldo had appointed him colonel in the Army, and Arguelles had served on the staff of Gen. Antonio Luna. But, after a short time in the field, Arguelles decided that the Filipino forces were too weak to defeat the Americans. That became evident in April 1899, when Aguinaldo chose him to head a commission to negotiate with General Otis. When the Americans offered to concede the Filipinos a measure of autonomy (but not independence), Arguelles indicated that he found the offer acceptable, and he urged his government to accept it. Luna then branded him a traitor and arrested him. A military court convicted Arguelles and sentenced him to life imprisonment.

After Luna's death, Aguinaldo reversed the decision, ordered Arguelles's release, and in September 1899, restored him to his former rank. Yet he could not restore the man's enthusiasm for the Filipino cause. A few months later, Arguelles went to Manila, turned himself in, and began openly to assist the Americans. In December 1900, he was one of the organizers of the Federal party, which spoke in favor of U.S. colonial policies and urged Filipinos still in the field to surrender.

Arguelles probably chose to collaborate because he was convinced of the futility of further resistance. His unhappy experiences with the Filipino Army, especially his incarceration, might have contributed to that conviction. Perhaps he also realized that he stood to gain a good deal from helping the Americans—favorable treatment by U.S. officials, even a position in the colonial administration. Yet, whatever the reason, it should be emphasized that at this stage Arguelles was an exception. Many other people from Batangas City might also have felt that the war was unwinnable, but they were in an unfavorable position to collaborate. What chiefly distinguished Arguelles from the others was that during the occupation of his native town he was in Manila. Comparatively safe in that city, he was freer to assist the enemy.[30]

A collaborator who remained in the province ran an enormous risk. One who proved willing to do so was a man of Chinese descent whom the Americans called Leung Sui. Probably that was not his name. The archival records relating to the Chinese residents of Batangas are largely intact, and there is no reference to a Leung Sui in them. (But a census of Chinese residents taken in 1895 includes one Sy Lengco, a day-laborer living in Batangas City, then thirty years old, who had come to the Philippines from China in March 1890.) In any case, Leung Sui had a grievance against the Filipino forces. Earlier, Malvar's troops for unknown reasons had held him prisoner and abused him. Once the man gained his freedom he rendered, according to one American officer, "open and valuable assistance to the United States troops." Among other things, he served as a guide, leading the Americans to several caches of Filipino supplies in the mountains. But his career as a collaborator was short. On March 8, 1900, Marcelo de Castro, a soldier in the Filipino Army, stabbed him to death in the central market of Batangas City.[31]

Even if a person were only suspected of collaboration, he or she might be dealt with severely. Mariano Roxas, also from Batangas City, had been arrested by the U.S. troops, held for questioning, and released. The Filipino forces in the area then came to the debatable conclusion that Roxas had gained his freedom by agreeing to spy for the Americans. On March 25, 1900, two Filipino soldiers went to Roxas's house, asked him to come outside, and killed him.[32] On several occasions, the Filipino forces took carabaos, horses, and other valuable possessions from suspected collaborators.[33]

Acts like these helped to convince the populace to keep their distance from the Americans. So did the warnings that the Filipino troops gave to noncombatants who showed pro-American leanings.[34] It was understandable, therefore, that when the Americans scheduled elections in March 1900 to choose Batangas City's municipal officials, only a handful of men decided to participate, and none of those elected proved willing to serve. The commander of the Batangas City garrison rescheduled the elections for April, but the results were the same. The U.S. Army's educational effort in the town was no more successful. The garrison opened three primary schools, but as of late August 1900 only eighty-four pupils had enrolled; the townspeople were evidently reluctant to permit their children to attend the schools, lest their permission be interpreted as a preference for the Americans.[35]

Even so, the U.S. Army was able to find a few more collaborators in the provincial capital during the first year of the occupation. A number of men served as guides, and several more acted as informers, telling the Americans about the location of Filipino troops and supplies. One of the collaborators was a captured Filipino soldier, who helped the Americans in order to avoid prolonged incarceration. Others might have collaborated simply to supplement their income; poor people often take great risks for a meager financial reward.[36] But for at least a year, collaboration was rare in Batangas City and elsewhere in the province.

★ Signs of Change

Beginning in late December 1900 or thereabouts, several changes occurred in Batangas City. As Claudio's lieutenants had observed in Lobo, there were signs that noncombatant support for the resistance was waning. In Batangas City, the waning was most pronounced in the población and in nearby barrios. Juan Gutierrez, the Filipino Army's tax collector in the población, discussed the matter in his declaration to General Bell: "In 1900, it was much easier to collect taxes, and in large amounts, but little by little they diminished, until by April 1901 it was difficult for me to collect anything, because the majority of the residents refused to pay, giving me only promises. Later, I was obliged to stop collecting, out of fear of being reported to the Americans." Several other tax collectors, though not all, told a similar tale.[37]

At approximately the same time, the number of collaborators increased markedly, particularly among the elite residents of the población. In early February 1901, a chapter of the Federal party was organized in the provincial capital, and a few dozen members of the town's political elite joined, including several men who earlier had been staunch supporters of the resistance. In March, many residents of the town—Fermin Arceo among them—took an oath of allegiance to the United States, an act that Americans and Filipinos alike viewed as a rite of passage. In May, the Americans tried again to establish a municipal government in Batangas City, and this time the eligible voters participated in the election and the government was organized. Jose Villanueva, the pharmacist who had provided medicine for the Filipino troops in the past, was elected municipal president, and most of the municipal councillors had earlier played prominent roles in the resistance.[38]

These changes occurred for a combination of reasons, some of which I have already touched upon. A number of the townpeople had evidently soured on the resistance because of mistreatment by Filipino troops; others had grown tired of their constant demands.[39] Such men and women had not necessarily developed any affection for the Americans, but they had come to the conclusion that the Filipino forces behaved just as badly and that it made no sense to support them.

Even if the general populace wanted to assist the troops, conditions in the countryside were now making it much more difficult for them to do so. First of all, a new wave of rinderpest had struck the cattle population of the Philippines, killing large numbers of the already-scarce work beasts and placing a greater burden on humans to prepare the soil for cultivation. The rapid spread of the disease was attributable, at least in part, to the fact that the U.S. Army requisitioned cattle and carabaos to haul heavy loads during troop movements, thereby placing healthy beasts in close contact with infected ones. Cattle were also seized by Filipino military units for food, rustled by bandits, and destroyed by U.S. troops in the field.[40] Meanwhile, the supply of human labor was depleted, since many able-bodied men were in the hills. The shortage of animal and human labor combined to reduce rice production throughout the province, as did the fact that the total amount of rice acreage had decreased, because people were disinclined to cultivate their plots in heavily contested areas. Hence, most families had much less rice at their disposal than in normal times and were hard-pressed to comply with the demands of the tax collectors.

Events outside the province had an effect as well. McKinley's reelection in November 1900 caused at least a few residents of Batangas City to wonder whether a Filipino victory was possible. The work of American civilian policymakers in the Philippines caused more than a few to wonder whether victory was necessary. In early June 1900, the Philippine Commission, empowered by McKinley to enact legislation for the pacified regions of the archipelago, arrived in Manila. The commission spent a few months investigating conditions, and then, on September 1, it began to legislate. To some extent, its laws built upon programs already begun by the military authorities. The commission's municipal code, legislated into effect in January 1901, resembled in several ways the Army's General Order No. 40—the electorate was limited to the wealthy, the educated, and men with previous governmental service, and the municipal governments were still to be subject to outside supervision. However, the supervising authority was no longer to be the U.S. Army, but rather a three-man provincial board, two of whose members were to be elected, and the obvious effect of that change was to concede Filipinos far more control over local affairs. In addition, the commission committed itself to a complete restructuring of public primary education in the Philippines, something far beyond the unsystematic educational efforts of the military authorities. It decided to adopt English as the language of instruction, to hire one thousand trained American teachers to supervise the instruction, and to establish schools in every town of the archipelago. As the people of Batangas became aware of the acts and pronouncements of this body, it became clear that the Americans had no intention of imposing a Carthaginian peace on the Filipinos. True, American rule would not be the same as rule by Filipinos, but it promised to be far less oppressive than rule by the Spaniards. Here then were compelling incentives to assist the Americans in putting an end to the battle for Batangas, and by so doing, to bring to the province the promised benefits of civil government.[41]

The reverses suffered by the Filipino forces in the field also had a devastating impact on the attitude of noncombatants in Batangas toward the resistance. Because of these reverses, a number of Batangas City's residents were forced to conclude that continued resistance served no useful purpose. Also, potential collaborators now realized that the risk of collaboration was no longer so great, especially if they lived in the población under the protection of the U.S. garrison. Under the circumstances, there was another risk to be considered; for if the Americans were to win the war, those who continued to assist the Filipino military units or who refused to assist the Americans might face punishment at the hands of the victors. One man who decided to switch sides at this time was Graciano Babao, a loyal supporter of the Filipino forces during the first year of the town's occupation. But, in early 1901, "convinced that it [was] impossible to make war against a nation as large and strong as the United States," he went to Manila, took an oath of allegiance to the United States, and then returned to Batangas City to take part in the organization of the local Federal party chapter.[42]

But what about the nephew/neighbor factor? If many residents of Batangas City now refused to support the Filipino forces and if some chose the course of collaboration, were they not abandoning their relatives and friends? Some were, but perhaps they felt that their actions were justifiable in light of the changed circumstances. If the war were lost, it made no sense to prolong it and thereby increase the chances that their nephews/neighbors might be killed. So it was that Ramon Canin, the father of two Batangueño officers, joined the Federal party in February 1901, and after that did his best to convince his sons to surrender. For Canin, it was necessary to abandon his sons in order to save them.[43]

The men who now joined the Federal party and who cooperated with the Americans in other ways cannot simply be characterized, one and all, as traitors. The point merits emphasis because it calls into question the conventional wisdom about the Federalistas. In Philippine history textbooks, they are generally depicted as spineless and self-serving, interested above all in preserving their accumulated wealth and in gaining positions in the U.S. colonial administration.[44] Some of the Federalistas of Batangas City fit the textbook stereotype. One need think only of Diego Gloria and Florencio Caedo, those two opportunistic petty bureaucrats who had come back to town immediately after the arrival of the Americans. The two were among the first residents of Batangas City to join the Federal party, and later they were rewarded with positions in the provincial bureaucracy. But these men appeared to be exceptions. Many of the leading Federalistas had earlier been enthusiastic supporters of the resistance. Ramon Canin and Graciano Babao were two such individuals, as was Crisanto Borruel, who had served as a major in the Batangueño forces until his capture in May 1900. The same might be said about the men who became members of the town's municipal council in May 1901. Among the councillors were Vicente Olmos, Melchor Babasa, and at least a dozen others who in earlier days had rendered valuable services to the Filipino troops. That these men had become collaborators is true enough; that they were spineless and self-serving is not.[45]

These changes were gradual: over the course of several months thousands of men and women made thousands of individual decisions about their role in the resistance, and in the end the sum of their decisions came to something new—a lower level of support for Malvar's troops and an increased level of collaboration. There was, however, nothing predetermined about the result; any person with his or her eyes open could surely see that Batangas was in a state of flux in the first few months of 1901, but there was no way to predict how that man or woman would read the various signs and what decision he or she would come to. Moreover, if by April 1901 a new pattern had at last become visible, that did not mean that the old pattern had been erased. For every person who decided to collaborate, there were still dozens who continued to support the resistance.

Indeed, to some degree, things were still in a state of flux. Appearances could always be deceiving in this war in the Philippines, and a person who appeared on the surface to be a collaborator might, underneath, be something quite different. Consider the case of Jose Villanueva, a supporter of the resistance in 1900 who emerged the next year as the head of the Federal party in Batangas City.[46]

Villanueva's route to collaboration was anything but direct. According to his own account, he was elected to the position against his wishes, and he accepted only because he realized that his refusal would anger the Americans. But, at the same time, Villanueva knew that the Filipino forces despised the Federal party and threatened to kill its members. Caught in the middle, he decided to write to Briccio Casala, now a lieutenant colonel, and in that letter, he made a remarkable suggestion: if the Filipino Army did not want him to be a Federalista, then Casala should send soldiers to the town and kidnap him. By offering himself as a candidate for kidnapping, Villanueva hoped to convince Casala that he was not an americanista and to avoid the risk of being killed. Convinced, Casala told him that he should continue to serve in the Federal party; he evidently figured that as head of the local Federalistas Villanueva could provide him with information. Ostensibly a collaborator, Villanueva was in reality something akin to a double agent.

But in the following months, Villanueva became a collaborator. Gradually he came to the conclusion that most Batangueños wanted the war to end. He also decided that it was necessary to put an end to the anarchic conditions then prevailing in the province. When he was elected municipal president in May 1901, he did not ask Casala's permission, and when Casala subsequently asked him to contribute, he refused. He then made frequent appeals to Casala, the Buenafe brothers, and other local commanders to surrender, and he provided intelligence to the U.S. garrison.

Hence, a new pattern of noncombatant behavior was slowly emerging in Batangas City, and if some collaborators collaborated more wholeheartedly than others and if many men and women continued to contribute enthusiastically to the guerrillas, all of them, regardless of their angle of vision, could see that something had changed. The resistance had sustained a major reverse. Some of Malvar's principal noncombatant supporters—wealthy, educated, influential, politically prominent individuals—had defected; the war effort had lost their financial and moral support as well as their prestige. And the pattern that was becoming visible in Batangas City could also be discerned in most of the other towns of Batangas. The only noteworthy exceptions were Santo Tomas and Lipa, and even Lipa was beginning to waver.[47]

★ Epidemiological and Demographic Developments

During the first fifteen months of the U.S. Army's occupation of the province, as relations between noncombatants and Malvar's guerrillas were undergoing a gradual transformation, changes of a very different kind were taking place in towns like Batangas City. Beginning shortly after the arrival of the U.S. troops in the province and continuing for more than a year, there was a substantial jump in the level of mortality in at least half a dozen towns of Batangas. In Batangas City itself, the number of burials recorded in the parish registers increased from 965 in 1899 to 1,986 in 1900; in Ibaan, from 433 to 770; in Lipa, from 1,277 to 2,476; in San Jose, from 390 to 833; in San Juan, from 580 to 1,373; and in Taysan, from 234 to 594. (See Appendix D.)

Although crude death rates for those towns cannot be calculated with precision, it seems clear that all of them exceeded 60 per thousand, and three (Ibaan, San Juan, and Taysan) may have been as high as 100 per thousand.[48]

Predictably, as the death rates rose in those towns, birth rates began to decline. According to Batangas City's parish books, the number of baptisms fell from 1,713 in 1899 to 1,306 in 1900 to 1,223 in the following year. In San Jose, the figures were 508, 436, and 254, and in Taysan, 436, 391, and 138.[49] As in other mortality crises, the depressed birth rates reflected not only a high incidence of terminated pregnancies but also the decision on the part of many married couples to defer family expansion until times had improved.

Clearly, then, Batangas was again experiencing a demographic disaster, but just as clearly, not all the province was sharing that unfortunate experience. As a glance at the map will reveal, all six of the aforementioned towns that suffered a sizable increase in mortality are located in the eastern part of the province. An examination of the parish records for the towns of western Batangas indicates that there was, on balance, a slight *decrease* in the level of mortality in 1900.[50] What seemed to be happening was that eastern Batangas, which had been spared serious population losses during the period of the Philippine Revolution, was now being exposed to some of the same epidemiological and environmental conditions that had earlier devastated the western section of the province.

As in the past, the principal killer in the province was almost certainly malaria. Two developments contributed to the increased incidence and virulence of the disease. First of all, as we already know, the entry of U.S. troops into Batangas in January 1900 had produced panic among the populace, and most of them had fled from the población and nearby barrios to outlying upland areas, where they tried to hide from their human enemies and found themselves within easy flying range of the anophelines who lived in that elevated terrain. When those people returned to their homes several months later, many carried in their bloodstreams the infective plasmodial parasites that they received from the mosquitoes, and in short order they fell victim to malaria. Second, the cattle population had been decimated by disease and warfare, with the ineluctable result that the anophelines in the region were increasingly seeking out humans for their blood meals.[51]

But, if all that was so, why was it that only the eastern section of Batangas experienced a mortality crisis in 1900? Most likely, the western part of the province suffered less because it had already come to epidemiological terms with the malaria-transmitting anophelines. Having endured one prolonged malaria epidemic, the residents of the western towns had developed a certain level of immunity to the disease and their chances of survival were reasonably good. Those from the east, with no comparable level of immunity, were bound to succumb in much larger numbers.

★ ★ ★

So, by April 1901, two developments were reaching a climax. One was demographic. The number of malaria deaths was soaring in eastern Batangas, due in large measure to the combined effects of a new outbreak of rinderpest and the population withdrawal that took place at the time of the U.S. invasion of the southern Tagalog region. The second was behavioral. Enthusiasm for the resistance was waning among the noncombatant population, and collaboration was becoming more common.

The deteriorating situation in the towns posed a dilemma of major proportions for Miguel Malvar, the man who was about to assume full command of the southern Tagalog resistance. To rally the men in the field after Trias's surrender and Aguinaldo's capture would be a herculean task in itself, but obviously it would not be enough. It would be necessary too for Malvar to rebuild his base of support among the noncombatant population. Incredibly, in the following months, Malvar came close to reviving the Batangueño war effort.

★ ★ ★ ★ ★ ★ ★ ★ ★

PART FOUR

On Their Own

8

A Second Wind, April–November 1901

THE THIRTEEN MONTHS that transpired between the capture of Emilio Aguinaldo and the surrender of Miguel Malvar are, without question, the most celebrated period in Batangas's history. Long after most of the Philippines had been pacified, the Batangueño guerrillas held out, sustained by a substantial sector of the noncombatant population. In that period, the province of Batangas came to symbolize the Filipino resistance, and the name Miguel Malvar became synonymous with Filipino defiance. But, as is always the case with lost causes, the price to be paid for valor of this kind was high. To quash the resisters of the southern Tagalog region, the U.S. Army resorted, in the end, to extreme measures. Had the Batangueños been less dogged, they would have suffered less.

The two chapters that follow tell the story of those heroic/tragic thirteen months. The first, covering the period April–November 1901, focuses on

Batangueño persistence. By April 1901, as the preceding narrative has shown, the Filipino war effort in Batangas was in decline, badly hurt by the reverses suffered by the Filipino forces outside the province as well as the alienation of a sizable number of Malvar's elite supporters. Over the course of the next few months, however, Malvar was able to reinvigorate the southern Tagalog resistance to a certain extent. He slowed down considerably, although he never halted, the tendency of elite Batangueños to abandon the resistance. More important, his policies strengthened the ties between his guerrillas and lower-class Batangueños, and as time passed, the local forces came to rely increasingly on the contributions of humble barrio-dwellers.

This is not to say that he accomplished anything that was likely to alter the ultimate outcome of the Filipino struggle against the United States, for a close scrutiny of the military map of the day revealed that, at the time the Batangueño resistance was reviving, few sparks of life remained in the Filipino war effort in other parts of the archipelago. Nor did it mean that Malvar's military units in Batangas were experiencing success against the Americans on the battlefield. Actually, from a purely military perspective, what seemed to be happening between April and November 1901 was not appreciably different from what had occurred during the first fifteen months of the U.S. Army's occupation. On the American side, the troops continued to scour the bush, but without noteworthy or even noticeable success; on the Filipino, most units were paralyzed by weapons shortages and debilitating maladies. Still, to revive noncombatant support for an obviously failing war effort was a remarkable feat.

The second chapter deals with the part of the battle of Batangas that has received far more attention from historians than any other: the period between December 1901, when Brig. Gen. J. Franklin Bell introduced a new plan to pacify the southern Tagalog region, and mid-April 1902, when Malvar turned himself in. By and large, the literature to date has concentrated on Bell's controversial pacification measures, most writers holding the general responsible for a massive loss of life in the province as a consequence of his policy of "concentration," the confinement of civilians in delimited areas in order to prevent them from aiding the guerrillas. My own account covers some of the same terrain but comes to very different conclusions.

★ Malvar Takes Charge, Mid-April 1901

Almost a month had passed since Trias had surrendered, and in the interim, there was no little confusion in the ranks of the Filipino leadership about how to proceed in the war against the Americans. Reports had circulated among the guerrillas in the southern Tagalog region that various generals were on the point of leaving the field and that mass surrenders had taken place in other parts of the Philippines; so many unconfirmed stories were making the rounds, in fact, that most commanders were unsure about exactly who was directing the war effort.[1] So on April 12 Malvar, aware that the resistance was in desperate trouble, issued a proclamation designed to provide direction to his "brothers and companions in the struggle."[2]

The Batangueño general began by announcing that, in accordance with a decree issued by Aguinaldo in June 1900 establishing an order of succession and until a general assembly of military leaders could be held to discuss the issue further, he, Malvar, had assumed the position formerly held by Mariano Trias: second-in-command of the revolutionary army and commander of the provinces of the Southern Department. He took this step, he claimed, with great reservations. "Realizing my unworthiness, I feel that I lack the strength to perform this difficult job. I would gladly turn it over to another, if not for my hope that all of you will give me assistance, because without it I can accomplish nothing more than the lowest-ranking soldier [can accomplish]." Likening himself to a humble beggar who, "in spite of illness, continues walking on to the end," he vowed to persevere in the war against the Americans.

Malvar then turned to other subjects. As we have seen, one striking feature of Aguinaldo's government had been its consistent promotion of the interests of the upper rungs at the expense of the lower, and one result of such policies had been the government's apparent failure to attract widespread support among lower-class Filipinos. Malvar signaled his intention to change that state of affairs:

> Let us do away with the untrue stories that the uneducated will be weeded out afterwards, because any brother in the field who has learned to ignore dangers to his life in defending the fatherland; whose good conduct has been shown in protecting the chastity of women and the lives, honor, and property of noncombatants, native or foreign; who has organized and trained a unit or company; and who cannot be disparaged by his compatriots; such a man is a well-spring of knowledge.
>
> Yes, be reassured, and answer the call of the fatherland and be prepared for a just reward.

Henceforth, the contributions of humble Filipinos to the war effort would be appreciated.

Malvar's proclamation of April 12 is noteworthy on at least two counts. First, it marked the initial step in the Batangueño leader's elevation to the command of the entire Filipino Army. In the next few weeks, Malvar began to issue orders to officers in the Southern Department, and on July 13, 1901, after attempting without success to organize the general assembly he had referred to in his April proclamation, he assumed the position of supreme commander of the "Liberating Forces" until such a meeting could be arranged.[3] In reality, Malvar's new title was somewhat more impressive than the range of his authority. Although he issued many directives to officers in other areas, the effective limits of his influence did not extend much beyond the geographical boundaries of the southern Tagalog region. As Aguinaldo had discovered earlier, once the decision had been made to adopt guerrilla tactics, the overall commander of the Filipino Army lacked the power to enforce compliance with his wishes outside the immediate area of his operations.

Second, as I have already suggested, the proclamation of April 12, 1901, marked a change of direction in the southern Tagalog resistance. Whereas Aguinaldo had concentrated on gaining the favor of Filipinos of means, Malvar, having recently lost the support of part of his elite following, was delivering a message intended to appeal to the occupants of the bottom rungs. And if the content of the proclamation was bound to resonate with a lower-class audience, the same was true of the form. As Reynaldo Ileto has shown, the language used by Malvar in his April proclamation was remarkably similar to that found in the manifestoes and writings of Andres Bonifacio and several other leaders of popular uprisings of earlier days. That is to say, he employed some of the same words and symbols that had proved to be so effective in mobilizing the peasantry during the initial stages of the struggle against Spain. Hence, Malvar's characterization of himself as a humble man and a beggar echoed words used by Apolinario de la Cruz, the key figure in a popular movement in the southern Tagalog region in the 1840s, and other passages in the proclamation were reminiscent of the writings and speeches of Bonifacio and Apolinario Mabini. "In fact," Ileto writes, "it is Malvar speaking in light of the masses' perceptions of the qualities that a meaningful, popular struggle should have."[4]

The proclamation of April 12, 1901, presents the historian, as well as the reader, with a difficult and possibly insoluble puzzle. How can the change signaled by the proclamation—Malvar's break with Aguinaldo's policy of ignoring the peasant masses—be explained? One possible explanation is that it reflected Malvar's genuine inclination toward men and women of humble origins. Long before Malvar had assumed command of the regional resistance—indeed, since the early days of the revolution against Spain—he had shown himself to be far more disposed than most of his superiors to cultivating close relations with the lower classes. He had, for instance, forged an alliance of a kind with the Colorum leader, Sebastian Caneo, an alliance that had continued despite the opposition of upper-class officials in the revolutionary government.[5] Yet, while all that may be so, we should not ignore another, somewhat more cynical line of explanation. Malvar's past was filled with examples of his political maneuvering—his use of surrogates to carry his banner in municipal elections; his risky decision to back Bonifacio during the struggle for control of the revolutionary government. Even his alliance with Caneo and the Colorum might be interpreted as a political maneuver, since it was forged at a time when the revolution against Spain was close to defeat and the revolutionaries needed all the help they could get. In light of this track record, it is certainly possible that the change marked by the proclamation of April 12 was the product of political calculation rather than inclination or conviction—that Malvar was adopting a new tack in order to win a new base of support and to reenergize the resistance.

Which view of Malvar should one accept? Was he motivated by opportunism or conviction or perhaps a bit of both? Unfortunately, the evidence on the matter is too ambiguous to permit us to come to a firm conclusion. All we know for sure is that, beginning in April 1901, the southern Tagalog resistance was transformed.

In addition to making an effort to rally the peasantry, Malvar attempted by other means to rejuvenate the resistance in the region. A few days after issuing his proclamation, he turned his attention to the problem of bolstering the morale of the local guerrillas. As the membership of the Federal party had expanded in Batangas and the neighboring provinces, Federalistas had escalated their appeals to soldiers and civilians to abandon their support of the guerrillas. These collaborators, Malvar wrote to Eliseo Claudio on April 20, were spreading "false information" intended to "demoralize the people."[6] To counteract the propaganda of the Federal party, Malvar began in late April to spread some of his own. Periodically, he sent the troops circulars which contained a modicum of factual information and a large amount of invention about happenings inside and outside the Philippines. The troops were told that Trias had not really surrendered to the Americans but had been tricked into attending a meeting with American officers and then captured; that the United States was about to become embroiled in a war with a major power; that Malvar had approximately seven thousand rifles in his native region and many more in other provinces under his command; that the Filipino forces had vast stocks of ammunition; and that some newspapers in New York were opposed to the war and were counseling the U.S. government to grant independence to the Philippines. Of all these items, only the last had any basis in fact. The circulars, Malvar explained to Claudio, were intended to "prop up the spirits of the people and the army" and to reinforce their resolve to resist the enemy.[7]

Malvar adopted other tacks. On April 28, he circulated a lengthy list of instructions to his subordinates in the Southern Department. The document contained more than twenty specific regulations to be followed by the troops serving under him, but at bottom, it had three objectives: to standardize, rationalize, and otherwise improve the operations of Malvar's military units; to eliminate the kind of behavior that had been causing conflict between the civilian population and the guerrillas; and to promote recruitment into and resupply of his army.[8] In effect, Malvar was attempting to do with his army essentially what he was trying to do with the populace at large: strengthen his control and increase thereby the possibility of keeping the resistance alive.

So, for example, Malvar instructed his lieutenants to engage the enemy in battle only when they had had an opportunity to set up an ambush and held a decisive advantage in numbers; to avoid attacking the Americans near populated areas—in particular, areas in which the inhabitants had given strong support to the guerrillas—because of the enemy's practice of burning all houses located in the vicinity of a Filipino ambush; to pay soldiers and officers no more than their prescribed salaries; to submit requests for promotions through the proper channels; to draft on average no more than one unmarried man from each one hundred inhabitants of a town; to collect no more than the prescribed amount of taxes from the citizenry; to keep detailed records of income and expenditures; and to punish severely any "abuses on the part of the military." Such abuses, Malvar asserted, "are detested by the people and dishearten the good sons of the Philippines, detracting from the true spirit of the Revolution to the detriment of the Fatherland and the Cause that we defend." Malvar also offered a commission in the Filipino Army to anyone who was able to organize a guerrilla unit or supply rifles to the local forces; indicated his willingness to forgive soldiers who surrendered rifles to the enemy if they turned over an equal number of weapons to the Filipino forces by the end of August; required noncombatants to plant rice, corn, sweet potatoes, and several other crops that could be used to feed the troops; and finally, in an effort to arrest the tendency to collaborate with the

enemy, decreed that "those who serve as spies for the invader or who volun-
tarily lead him to [the Filipino Army's] camps" would be killed.

Malvar was taking charge, and in the process of doing so, he was adopting
a wide range of innovative approaches to deal with the problems at hand. He
offered the carrot, wielded the stick, and, all the while, sought to convince his
followers that their prospects for success were far more promising than they
really were. In the months that followed, he did more of the same, circulating
more propaganda, issuing additional lists of instructions to his lieutenants,
and continuing to cement his ties with the lower classes.[9]

★ Rejuvenation, Early to Mid-May 1901

On May 2, 1901, the members of the Philippine Commission, the chief policy-
making arm of the U.S. government in the pacified parts of the archipelago,
held a meeting in Batangas City to celebrate the establishment of civil
government in the province of Batangas. Representatives from eleven towns
took part, among them many of the leaders of the Federal party in the
province. William Howard Taft, the president of the commission, began the
proceedings by expressing his appreciation to the assembled Batangueños
for attending, and then the attendees launched into a discussion of various
matters, including the special bill establishing the new provincial civil government. As the session neared its conclusion, Taft announced the names of
the men who had been chosen by the commission to serve as provincial
officials: Diego Gloria and Florencio Caedo, the two professional bureaucrats
from Batangas City, fiscal and secretary, respectively; R. D. Blanchard, an
American, treasurer; and Felix M. Roxas, a Manila-based lawyer and a
member of the Federal party, governor.[10]

The ceremony at Batangas City was, we now know, something of a sham.
Taft and his fellow commissioners had decided to place Batangas under a
civil administration not because they believed that the province had actually
been pacified but because the commander of the U.S. Army in the Philippines, Arthur MacArthur, had lobbied vigorously for it, arguing that the
change might help to bring about some surrenders. In a letter to Secretary of
War Elihu Root, Taft admitted that he and his colleagues were "a bit doubtful" about the exercise, and his fellow commissioner Bernard Moses confirmed the assessment in a diary entry written on the day of the ceremony.
"On the part of the natives, very little enthusiasm was manifest," Moses
observed. "[Batangas City] presents a very sorry spectacle. Its buildings are
dilapidated and in many cases deserted. Its people are afraid of themselves

and terrified by the bandits that render insecure the neighboring country."[11] (The qualms of Taft and Moses would turn out to be justified; in July, after observing a step-up of resistance activities in Batangas, the commission opted to return the province to full military control.)[12]

Approximately ten days after the ceremony in Batangas City, a meeting of a very different sort was held in a remote barrio of Rosario. Miguel Malvar was in attendance, as were most of Batangas's military worthies—Nicolas Gonzales, Martin Cabrera, Arcadio Laurel, Dalmacio Hernandez, Damaso Ybarra, Briccio Casala, Melecio Bolaños, Anastasio Marasigan, and several other men who commanded one or more columns. The Batangueño general had assembled his lieutenants in order to consult with them about the political situation and to attempt to reach a consensus about their future course of action. Malvar began the meeting by reaffirming his commitment to the cause of Philippine independence. He would continue to fight, he asserted, "until the liberation of the country was accomplished." He then solicited the views of the others about continuing the war. Several reported that their troops were short of ammunition and provisions, and some were troubled by the success of the Federalistas in undermining support for the resistance. But, in general, there was agreement that the good fight should go on, and all but a few of the local leaders elected to remain in the field. The only important exception was Colonel Bolaños, the former municipal official of Rosario, who turned himself in a few weeks later.[13]

Here, then, in an outlying barrio of Rosario was a ringing rebuttal to the message that the Americans had attempted to convey in the public ceremony at Batangas City. The military barons of Batangas, the men of influence who led the private armies that made up Malvar's command, were committing themselves and their men to continuing the struggle. In retrospect, their decision to do so may seem bizarre and illogical, especially in light of what we know about the battlefield realities of the day—the recent reverses, the recurrent shortages, the steady toll taken by malaria and other maladies. But, in fact, the Batangueño actors were following the dictates of a more compelling logic—one that required compadres, friends, and neighbors to stand together despite overwhelming odds and the appeals of something we call common sense to do otherwise. Malvar's army had been built on personalistic foundations in the first place, and it would continue to have such a character.

About the time Malvar was receiving a vote of confidence from his officer corps, there were strong indications that the guerrillas were receiving renewed support from the noncombatant population, something clearly needed if the local resistance was to have even a remote chance of surviving. Three processes were at work. Towns which had consistently provided a high level of support to the resistance continued to do so; towns which had wavered in their support now began to stabilize; and in both types of communities, there was evidence of a greater commitment by lower-class Filipinos to the war effort. We cannot be certain why the noncombatants came to adopt the course they evidently did, but more than likely there was a connection between their behavior and the policies that Malvar had recently introduced. Some men and women may have been influenced by the propaganda efforts and some may have been frightened by the threats. Almost certainly, a number of individuals who occupied the lower rungs of the provincial socioeconomic ladder were won over by Malvar's appeal to them.

Consider the town of Santo Tomas, the birthplace of Miguel Malvar, which had assisted the guerrillas fairly consistently in the past. In June 1901, just before Santo Tomas held an election to choose a new municipal president, Dalmacio Hernandez, the commander of the guerrillas operating in the town's vicinity, had a meeting with the barrio lieutenants and instructed them to vote for Marceliano Villegas, a man Hernandez trusted. The lieutenants agreed, Villegas was elected, and the new president proceeded to cooperate fully with Hernandez in the following months—furnishing him with intelligence about U.S. troops movements, turning over to him the proceeds from the cockpit and games of monte, supervising the collection of money and palay in the town, and doing much, much more. The barrio lieutenants assisted Villegas in his tax collection efforts, communicated regularly with Hernandez, and gave him useful information.[14] In effect, Santo Tomas was holding fast, providing approximately the same level of assistance to the guerrillas in mid-1901 that it had a year earlier.

Meanwhile, the situation had become more satisfactory (from the point of view of the guerrillas, that is) in towns like Batangas City and Lipa, which had faltered in their support during the early part of 1901. Although the municipal president of Batangas City, Jose Villanueva, refused to cooperate with the local forces and while contributions from residents of the población were now infrequent, between May and November 1901 there was no observable decline, and possibly even an increase, in the assistance provided to Malvar by the barrio-dwellers of the town: in eighteen of the twenty-two barrios for which we have information, men and women continued to pay their weekly taxes, give the troops a tithe of their harvests, and run errands for them.[15] In Lipa, where the Federal party had also made inroads, the downward spiral was reversed by the town's new municipal president, Gregorio Aguilera Solis, the well-known man of letters and longtime friend of the resistance. Most of the town's wealthy residents remained reliable contributors to the cause, and Aguilera managed to enlist the full cooperation of Lipa's barrios. In July 1901, at a meeting with barrio officials, the new town president declared that the Filipino soldiers were "working for the good of all" and urged the officials to sustain them. The officials appear to have taken their superior's words seriously, for, as the documentary record demonstrates, an elaborate tax collection bureaucracy was set in place in Lipa's barrios, which kept the local guerrillas well supplied up to December 1901. As several tax collectors later admitted, "All the people donate[d]."[16]

Most striking was that an ever-growing share of the help that Malvar now received from the noncombatants of Batangas came from the very sort of people he had appealed to in his April proclamation. Let us look at some of the evidence on that point. In February 1902, in a declaration to General Bell, municipal president Jose Villanueva recalled that, some seven months before, he had had a conference with Gen. Adna Chaffee, MacArthur's successor as commander of the U.S. Army in the Philippines. Chaffee warned Villanueva that, if the principales of Batangas did not bring about the immediate establishment of peace, the U.S. forces would be forced to adopt extremely harsh measures. Villanueva replied that "the end of the war did not depend on the town's principales, who wanted peace," but on Malvar's willingness to give up the fight. He also maintained that Malvar and his guerrilla forces "did not need the assistance of the rich, as was believed, because they collected enough in the barrios and, in the ultimate extreme, from the members of the *Colorum*." According to Villanueva, the Colorum now had thirty thousand members, and at one point in the war its members had given Malvar three thousand pesos.[17]

The Colorum—the peasant-based religious society led by Sebastian Caneo—had originated, as we know, on the slopes of Mount San Cristobal on the Laguna-Tayabas border, but, as Villanueva's account and other records make clear, it had spread by 1901 to Batangas and other provinces in the region. Increasingly, as the Americans came to understand, this lower-class organization became a vital element in the southern Tagalog resistance. In mid-November 1901, after learning that a Filipino soldier killed near Taal had been carrying documents relating to the Colorum, one American officer commented, "This sect seems to be stirring up a system of fanaticism, and may give [us] much trouble." Shortly afterward, a U.S. Army intelligence report indicated that there were branches of the Colorum in every barrio of Batangas.[18]

Another declaration provides even a few hints about lower-class attitudes during this phase of the resistance. Florencio Caedo, the bureaucrat from Batangas City who had become an active americanista, claimed that he had learned from discussions with "poor laborers" that they "were waiting for the arrival of independence, just as the Jews awaited that of the Messiah, and that they were in error about the aims of the American government." As a consequence, in October 1901 Caedo advised Villanueva, Batangas City's president, to send one or two men to the cockpits or to other gathering places each Sunday to tell the people of "the good and sincere intentions of the United States and the impossibility of achieving independence by force of arms."[19] If Caedo's statements are to be believed, they indicate that Malvar's appeal to the lower rungs had been successful.

The rejuvenation did not extend to every town in Batangas, however. In the western part of the province, where the local forces had virtually ceased to operate, there is little evidence of civilian support for Malvar at this stage of the war; in Bauan, the guerrilla leaders were unable to secure the election of the municipal president they favored; and in Lobo, the application of extreme military pressure by the U.S. troops caused a swift decline in civilian assistance to the guerrillas.[20] Collaboration also remained a problem, despite the repeated warnings from Malvar and other military men that civilians who assisted the Americans could expect punishment (and also despite the fact that one of the province's most visible collaborators—Camilo Ylagan, the municipal president of Taal—was captured by the guerrillas in early May 1901 and held prisoner for several months).[21]

Indeed, a new motive for collaboration was becoming evident in the final acts of the battle for Batangas. Some members of the local political elite were beginning to view cooperation with the Americans as a means of promoting partisan political ends. The phenomenon could be observed most readily in Balayan, where a long-standing rivalry existed between Manuel Ramirez, a former gobernadorcillo, and the powerful Lopez clan. In April 1900, the town had elected Felix Unson, a relative of the Lopezes, as municipal president. But Unson was removed by the U.S. military authorities because he had communicated with the guerrillas, and in March 1901, Ramirez was appointed in his place. Ramirez believed that gaining the approval of the Americans was a useful means of improving his political fortunes, and so, once in office, he provided intelligence to the garrison, revealing, among other things, that certain Filipinos in Mindoro were shipping cattle to Batangas for the purpose of selling them and passing on the proceeds to Malvar. In the end, though, even the good will of the U.S. troops proved to be insufficient to keep Ramirez in office. When a new election was held in Balayan in late September 1901, he was thrashed by the candidate of the Lopez family.[22]

Hence, as before, noncombatant support for the war effort in Batangas was neither universal nor universally enthusiastic. But clearly the crisis of early 1901—the crisis of declining contributions and steadily increasing collaboration—had been passed. The level of noncombatant support had begun to stabilize in Batangas in the months following Malvar's assumption of command of the Southern Department, and it would remain high until Bell's "concentration" measures effectively eliminated intercourse between the guerrillas and the civilian population.

Of course, the fact that the *level* of support had stabilized did not mean that the *pattern* of support had returned to what it had been during the early stages of the resistance. Whereas at the outset the commitment of upper-rung Batangueños to the cause had been strong and that of lower-rung Batangueños suspect, now, due to a combination of factors, the situation had been altered. Although Malvar had succeeded in slowing the stream of defections from his elite noncombatant supporters as well as from his officer corps, one could no longer say that the upper rungs constituted the backbone of the war effort. At the same time, Malvar had managed to solidify his relationship with the lower classes, and, above all, with the barrio-dwellers who made up Caneo's Colorum. The resistance had been rejuvenated, but it was a different kind of resistance indeed.

★ The Offensive Resumes, Late May 1901

About six weeks earlier, when Brig. Gen. Robert Hall had been relieved of his command, the Second District of the Department of Southern Luzon was abolished, and the First District, which had hitherto embraced Cavite, Morong, part of the province of Manila, and a section of western Batangas, was enlarged to include all of Batangas, Tayabas, and Laguna.[23] The reorganization brought the entire southern Tagalog region under the command of a single man—the previous commander of the First District, fifty-nine-year-old Samuel Storrow Sumner.

Sumner's tenure as commander of the expanded First District had begun inauspiciously. Seemingly convinced that the guerrillas were ready to admit defeat, he suspended operations for more than a month and concentrated his efforts on arranging negotiations between the commanders still in the field and various Filipinos who were entrusted with the task of inducing them to surrender. Mariano Trias himself and several members of the Federal party

27. Samuel S. Sumner, c. 1898

persistently appealed to Malvar and his lieutenants to come in, and, as it turned out, a few surrenders of consequence were orchestrated—most notably, those of Cipriano Calao and Gregorio Catigbac, two leaders of the guerrilla forces in the vicinity of Lipa. But, as the month of May drew to a close, Sumner reluctantly concluded that further negotiations would be useless, and he began to make preparations to resume military operations against Malvar.[24]

Malvar's new antagonist, Samuel Sumner, was the son of one of the most colorful U.S. Army officers of the Civil War era—Maj. Gen. Edwin V. "Bull" Sumner, a courageous soldier with a booming voice, white whiskers, and an absolute devotion to duty. One of the ranking commanders of the Army of the Potomac, the elder Sumner had fought ably at Seven Pines, and bravely, albeit (in the judgment of most authorities) stupidly, in a losing cause at Fredericksburg, when he had carried out Ambrose Burnside's orders to the letter and sent wave after wave of Union soldiers to certain death in an effort to storm Marye's Heights. Shortly after the Fredericksburg debacle, Sumner was relieved of command, and not long after that he contracted a serious case of pneumonia. His final moments were a commentary on his character. Lying gravely ill on his sickbed, Bull Sumner suddenly roused himself and called out, "The II Corps never lost a flag or a cannon!" An attendant came to his side and offered him a glass of vine. Sumner took a sip, pronounced the words "God save my country, the United States of America," and promptly died.[25]

Bull's son had made his own modest mark in the U.S. Army. In June 1861, at the age of nineteen, he had received an appointment as a second lieutenant of cavalry in the Union forces, and, over the course of the next four years, he was breveted for bravery on three occasions. When the war was over, Sumner held the rank of captain in the regular army. In the decades that followed, he served as a cavalry officer at more than a dozen posts, seeing some combat during the Indian campaigns and rising steadily through the ranks—major in 1879, lieutenant colonel in 1891, colonel in 1896. Two years later, with the outbreak of the war against Spain, Sumner volunteered to fight in Cuba. He served creditably in that campaign, playing a key role in the taking of San Juan Hill, and in February 1901, thanks in part to the support of Theodore Roosevelt, another veteran of the San Juan Hill assault, he was finally appointed to a brigadiership. Since coming to the Philippines, the mustachioed, rather youthful looking Sumner had done a more than respectable job. By sheer persistence, the troops under his command had worn down Mariano Trias's forces in Cavite, and ultimately, their efforts had contributed to Trias's decision to surrender in March 1901.[26]

But the assignment he was about to undertake—that of attempting to subdue Miguel Malvar—was to come close to erasing the mark he had made to date. By November 1901, Sumner would be branded an incompetent and relieved of his command. Such an estimate of the man was, in truth, terribly unfair. Sumner was far more adaptable than he was ever given credit for, accomplished far more than his critics ever realized, and would have surely achieved more if he had received the complete support of higher authorities. To some extent, Sumner was victimized by circumstances beyond his control—by pressures exerted on the U.S. Army by critics in the United States, by military events in other parts of the Philippines. Although the contemporary criticisms of Sumner were not totally without foundation—the district commander did contribute in certain ways to his own downfall—the harsh judgments need to be tempered and his actions understood in the context of the times.

Sumner's plans for his first offensive against Malvar indicated that he was not inclined, at the outset, to depart radically from the approach used thus far in the region. Having been frustrated in his efforts to bring about Malvar's surrender through negotiation, Sumner informed his departmental commander on May 23, 1901, that he was going to launch a major campaign against the guerrilla forces of Malvar and Juan Cailles by assigning approximately a thousand men from Cavite to temporary duty in Batangas and Laguna. The beefed-up American forces would then begin to scout constantly and attempt to break the enemy's will to resist. "It is hoped," Sumner wrote, that "this active campaign will force the surrender of most of the insurrectos, with their arms[,] and may result in the surrender of the two or three important leaders still out." The operations were to continue only up to July 1, for by then the rainy season would have reached its peak and the roads and trails would have become impassable and the streams unfordable. In effect, Sumner was proposing to do in Batangas and Laguna almost exactly what he had done in Cavite a few months earlier—to conduct a short, vigorous offensive in the hope that it would tip the balance.[27]

The active campaign that Sumner had proposed began in the final days of May, when the additional men he had requested—an assortment of infantrymen, cavalrymen, artillerymen, and Macabebe Scouts—were assigned to Batangas and Laguna. For the next month, they repeatedly criss-crossed Batangas in search of Malvar's forces, concentrating on the high ground and the remote barrios that the guerrillas were known to frequent. At the same time, the American units normally stationed in the region accelerated their own operations against the guerrillas, sometimes participating in joint maneuvers with the new troops and sometimes acting alone. It was enervating work in an inhospitable environment, the kind of campaigning that can sap the energy and wreck the health of even the fittest men. And in the end, many miles were marched, many barrios were searched, the health of many men was ruined, and the hoped-for victory did not occur.[28]

One part of Batangas that received attention during this period was the mountainous area around Lobo, where the forces of Eliseo Claudio and Briccio Casala had long operated. As I indicated in chapter 6, the troops in the Lobo region, troubled by insubordination, morale problems, and weapons shortages had conducted few operations against the Americans in recent months. But it galled the American commanders in Batangas that such a sizable sector was controlled by the Filipinos, and some were anxious to rectify that state of affairs as soon as possible. "Reports have shown," wrote Col. T. C. Lebo, stationed at Batangas City, "that . . . the enemy have made

Lobo a congregation place and base for themselves. The high mountains between here and there make a good stronghold for the insurrectos where they feel that there are no troops at their back, and as facts have shown they have not been slow to avail themselves of this advantage, and have been in these mountains in forces of various sizes."[29]

In early June 1901, shortly after the arrival of the troops from Cavite, a Filipino informer told John W. Craig, post commander at San Juan de Bocboc, that large numbers of guerrillas had assembled both in Lobo's población and in Ayas, an outlying barrio of the same town. Craig contacted Capt. Augustus P. Blocksom, leader of the cavalry detachment from Cavite, and those two drew up a plan. Blocksom's troopers, then at Batangas City, were assigned to proceed to the población of Lobo by two different trails, one across the mountains and the other along the beach. Meanwhile Craig's men were to approach Ayas along a very steep, narrow path that led from the beach, the only route by which the barrio could be reached. Craig recognized from the outset that the operation would be extremely difficult. His troops would have to ascend the path on foot, since it was not suitable for horses, and it would be necessary to travel at night in order to avoid being spotted by the local residents.[30]

Like so many American operations in the campaigns against Malvar, this one produced minimal results. On the night of June 8, Craig and a party of sixty-one men boarded a launch at San Juan de Bocboc and proceeded to a point on the coast some five miles from the trail leading to Ayas. They marched along the beach to the path, and then up the path to Ayas, arriving there about 10:00 A.M. on the following morning. By now, Craig had only twenty-five men with him, the others have succumbed to the heat and the effort of climbing the steep trail. The Americans discovered a large enemy barracks, some uniforms, and about fifty rounds of ammunition, all of which they promptly destroyed. But not a single Filipino soldier was in sight. After a brief rest, the detachment continued on to the población, where they finally linked up with Blocksom. "My men's shoes were completely worn out upon arrival at Lobo and their feet were in such a condition that they could not walk," Craig later reported.[31]

In the meantime, Blocksom had divided his forces in two, sending half the troopers under Lt. Charles Rhodes along the beach route and leading the other half himself along the mountain trail. Rhodes, who kept a diary, described the hike:

> JUNE 9. We made our start at 12:00 midnight. . . . We found our route, over which we had never been, very long, rough, and difficult. Long—

because we had to follow the coast-line in its irregular course. We were delayed two whole hours, getting over certain salt marshes, our pack mules getting in quick sands which required tedious work. In addition, my troops had to head several jutting promontories into the sea, where the water was as deep as my horse "Dixie's" belly. There was also one quite high promontory, necessitating dismounting and walking the animals. But finally we arrived at the isolated coast-town of Lobo about 12:00 noon, having marched 28 miles, over one of the worst trails I have ever traversed.

Rhodes discovered that Blocksom's troopers had reached the población about an hour earlier and had rounded up about three hundred men, all of whom were attending Sunday mass at the Lobo church. After lunch, Rhodes and the Filipino scouts attached to the cavalry detachment went through the crowd of captives and picked out four who, according to Rhodes, had "the tell-tale signs of insurrecto soldiers." In the end, the four suspects were deposited in prison, and all the other men were released.[32]

Elsewhere in Batangas, the Americans' stepped-up operations were invariably just as disappointing. They also suffered a serious reverse. On June 10, Capt. William Wilhelm of the Twenty-First Infantry, acting on an intelligence report, led a small detachment to Sapac, a barrio of Lipa, where a number of rifles were supposedly hidden. About daybreak, just as the Americans reached the barrio, they were overwhelmed by a much larger enemy force—part of the Santo Tomas Column, under Col. Dalmacio Hernandez. At one point in the fighting, as the Americans were absorbing heavy punishment, one of Wilhelm's men managed to break through the Filipino lines and carry news of the encounter to the Lipa garrison. Reinforcements hurried to Sapac, but they were too late. Two American officers, one enlisted man, and a native scout had been killed; Wilhelm and an enlisted man were mortally wounded; and two others had received lesser wounds.[33]

The events at barrio Sapac stunned Sumner, driving him to the realization that a quick victory in the southern Tagalog region was beyond his grasp. On June 18, in a special report to his superiors, he admitted that conditions in eastern Batangas were serious:

The operations of this command have demonstrated that a well organized force of considerable strength control this country and are paid and subsisted by the inhabitants. General Malvar exercises supreme command and the country of which Tanauan is the center is governed and controlled by a Colonel Gonzales who seems to have the best organized and equipped command under Malvar's control. While we have found several of his camps and destroyed them, it has been impossible to overtake this force or damage it to any extent. It has been found almost impossible to gain any information owing to fear or sympathy of natives. . . . They pay a regular tax and every barrio is a supply depot for the insurrectos whose homes and relatives are in their midst.[34]

Such conditions seemingly called for new measures, and in that same report, Sumner advocated them. According to intelligence recently received by the Americans, Malvar had ordered his chief lieutenants to attend a meeting in mid-July to discuss the future of the resistance. "It would seem advisable," Sumner wrote, "to take advantage of the intervening month and impress on Malvar and his followers and friends the futility of further opposition." Specifically, he recommended that, once the soldiers on special assignment were withdrawn from Batangas, an even larger force—a thousand infantrymen and five troops of cavalry—be sent to replace them. With the additional men, Sumner intended to establish strong garrisons at Lipa, Tanauan, Santo Tomas, and San Pablo, and from those bases, to send out field columns that would be expected to remain in the bush indefinitely. The columns would be permitted to occupy any barrio "as protection against weather or for Military purposes" and to destroy any "that are used by the enemy or furnish supplies." Sumner also indicated that other stringent measures might be introduced: "I would arrest all the men and bring them to the several posts, force them to surrender arms or give information and if necessary send all prominent men out of the country and let it be known that they will be held till the active Insurrectos come in and surrender their arms."

Sumner's advocacy of such measures is notable, especially in view of the later criticism of his prosecution of the war. Conceding the failure of his initial offensive, he was now prepared to countenance policies toward the noncombatant population that were more severe than any heretofore sanctioned. Up to this point in the conflict, the U.S. command had officially frowned on the burning of Filipino property, except in retaliation against hostile action or in the case of buildings that were used as barracks by enemy soldiers. The directives of the generals had been frequently ignored, and throughout the battle for Batangas it was common for the American troops to destroy houses and even entire barrios in the immediate vicinity of places where telegraph wires were cut and caches of enemy supplies were found.[35] Still, it made a difference that the army's policy on burning was somewhat restrictive, and, by proposing to relax it, Sumner was explicitly endorsing a massive increase of property destruction. "I am aware," Sumner wrote about his recommendation, "that this is a severe and stringent measure and will entail hardships and suffering on the inhabitants, but it seems the only practical means at hand to bring these people to a realizing sense of their present attitude towards the Government and will[,] I believe[,] bring a speedy end to the present unsettled and dangerous condition of affairs in this section."[36]

His comments about the detention of noncombatants likewise suggested that he was willing to depart from previous practice. Since the early days of the U.S. occupation of the southern Tagalog region, the Americans had conducted frequent "roundups" of civilians—the recent one in Lobo, for example, during the combined operation led by Craig and Blocksom—in which the male inhabitants of a community were detained and interrogated, and suspected guerrillas and guerrilla-supporters were sent to prison.[37] Now, it appears, Sumner favored tightening the screws further by holding the leading men of localities in custody until the guerrillas decided to turn themselves in.

Sumner was demonstrating, in short, his willingness to act, and more than that to act harshly. At the same time, as the quotation in the earlier paragraph strongly suggests, he harbored real qualms about the course he was pursuing. Such ambivalence was understandable. Sumner—or any other commander who might have been given the task of ending Malvar's resistance—faced a classic Hobson's choice. For, in an unconventional conflict such as this one, in which the guerrilla forces were proving to be so difficult to defeat, the goal of military success was fundamentally in conflict with traditional notions of acceptable, or even conscionable, military conduct. A commander committed to quick victory often had to order actions that others might deem inhumane; one committed to upholding certain standards of military behavior, on the other hand, had to be willing to endure the consequences of a continued stalemate. Sumner had opted for victory, but the implications of his choice bothered him.

The policies Sumner advocated were neither expeditiously nor fully implemented. Someone up the chain of command—almost certainly Sumner's immediate superior, Brig. Gen. James F. Wade—watered down his recommendations, although the sources provide not the slightest hint about why the watering down occurred.[38] Three alterations of consequence were made. First, Sumner's troop requests were delayed. Even though the units on temporary assignment from Cavite were removed from Batangas by the end of June, replacement troops did not arrive until the middle of July. Second, while the replacements included all the infantrymen Sumner had asked for—ten companies of the Twentieth Infantry commanded by Col. W. S. McCaskey—not a single additional cavalryman was sent.[39] Deprived of those mounted forces, Sumner was in no position to apply the kind of pressure on the guerrillas that he evidently wanted to.

Finally, the recommendations he had urged upon his superiors about conduct toward noncombatants were rejected. Clear evidence of the rejection could be observed in the orders that Sumner issued to Colonel McCaskey on July 19 about the new offensive to be launched against Malvar's guerrillas in Batangas:

> When out on expeditions, the troops are authorized to use any shelter at hand to protect them from the weather; care will be taken not to destroy or damage private property, and no houses, property, or food will be destroyed except quartels [*sic*] actually occupied by the enemy, or food collected for their special use.
>
> In case the troops are fired on from any barrio, it will be burned unless advisable to preserve it for our future use.[40]

Such instructions merely authorized McCaskey to abide by existing policies. They contained not a syllable of the "severe and stringent" measures Sumner had proposed a month earlier—the destruction of barrios that sheltered or supplied the guerrillas, the holding in custody of local leaders. The point to be made here is that, however critical one may be of Sumner's conduct of the campaign against Malvar, it must be recognized that the district commander was not a free actor. Sumner was hamstrung by the constraints under which he was forced to operate.

So, with fewer men at his disposal than he would have liked and without the authority to introduce the policies toward noncombatants he deemed necessary, Sumner initiated his second major offensive against Malvar. As before, the troops marched many miles and suffered heavy abuse from the elements, and, as before, their contacts with the guerrillas were infrequent. This is not to say that their efforts failed to make an impression on Malvar's forces—as we shall see, important surrenders and captures did take place, and the operations of the remaining guerrilla units were severely disrupted—but the progress was far too slow to suit American tastes, and the disappointment of many U.S. officers was palpable.

One of the most disappointed officers of all—and surely the most frustrated—was Samuel Sumner himself. Writing to General Wade on August 2, he drew a dreary picture of conditions in his district: the fact that Malvar's influence was unchallenged in most of Batangas; the failure of the U.S. troops to gain reliable information from the populace; the Americans' frustration in pursuing an enemy whose preference was to avoid contact unless military success was guaranteed; their inability to travel through the region without running the risk of capture. "The amount of country actually controlled by us," Sumner admitted, "is about as much as can be covered by the fire from our guns." Once again, therefore, he lobbied for stronger measures to deal with the opposition that he faced—the destruction of all means of supply in the countryside, the burning of all barrios suspected of harboring enemy soldiers, the deportation to Guam of all priests who supported the guerrillas, even the closing of all ports in Batangas and Laguna until the resistance had ended. He also urged that a bureau of information be established in the region, with "plenty of funds to employ spies," so that the U.S. forces could gather accurate intelligence about the enemy.[41]

But again, for reasons never stated, Sumner's recommendations were not implemented.

★ The View from the Hills, Late June–Early July 1901

Since the end of May, when the Americans had stepped up their activity in the area around Lobo, Eliseo Claudio's San Miguel Column had been subjected to constant harassment. Initially, thanks to intelligence about U.S. troop movements provided by Lobo's parish priest and several leading citizens of the town, Claudio's men had managed to elude their pursuers— including the units led by Craig and Blocksom that had combined to launch the unsuccessful surprise attack on them in early June.[42] But later that same month, all three companies of the San Miguel Column, together with the entire command of Briccio Casala, were cornered and forced to fight near Talumpoc, a barrio of Batangas City. The losses had been heavy, and, as the after-action reports of the Filipino commanders reveal, the survivors of the battle had been physically exhausted by the experience and their supplies of food and ammunition had run out.[43]

To make matters worse, the growing frequency of American operations in the vicinity of Lobo had caused no little strain between the townspeople and the guerrillas. On June 30, one of Claudio's company commanders sent word that men in the town had been pressured into taking an oath of allegiance to the United States. About the same time, the cabezas of Lobo stopped their tax collection efforts. On July 7, irate about the lack of financial support from the town, Claudio ordered the new municipal president, Julian Ramirez, to take steps to ensure that the cabezas would do their jobs. Two days later, in his written reply, Ramirez flatly refused to comply, claiming that he had no jurisdiction in the matter and suggesting that the military men should speak to the cabezas themselves. The municipal president also refused to honor the requests of Claudio's lieutenants for fresh recruits and protested when the local forces, suffering from shortages of personnel, subsequently entered the town and impressed young men into military service. Ramirez, it seems, had concluded that, with the Americans so much in evidence, the risks of cooperating with the guerrillas far outweighed any possible benefits, and so, on July 10, he informed Claudio that he wanted to resign from his job.[44]

What is striking in retrospect about the events recounted above is their implication that the U.S. military effort in Batangas was succeeding, albeit slowly. Even though the Americans rarely saw their enemy, the few contacts that did occur obviously inflicted damage. Furthermore, the longer Malvar's men were forced to hide out in the hills, the more likely it became that their health would be ruined by the elements; and the more difficult the Americans made it for the civilian population to supply Malvar, the more difficult it became for Malvar to mount offensive operations of his own. Ironically, the Americans were largely unaware of the progress they were making. Possessing little reliable knowledge of the mind-set of the enemy, they had no inkling that their patrolling was causing so much disruption and undermining so effectively the morale of both the guerrillas and their noncombatant supporters.

Subsequent developments confirmed the fact that Sumner's operations were causing the guerrillas major problems. As of mid-July 1901, the column commanded by Eliseo Claudio was in sorry shape. Tomas Ramirez's unit was suffering from a severe shortage of weapons: according to a report filed by Ramirez, only nine men out of a twenty-seven-man detachment stationed at Talahib, a barrio of Batangas City, were equipped with rifles. Meanwhile, sickness had thinned out the ranks of Felix Farol's command. Farol informed his commander on July 13 that approximately half the men in his company were too ill to travel, and it was consequently impossible for him to link up with Claudio. Eleven days later, only ten soldiers in Farol's company were fit for duty. At the end of July, Claudio's guerrillas were thrown into total confusion when a company of U.S. infantrymen was stationed in Lobo; the presence of the American garrison made it more difficult than ever for noncombatants to supply the local forces.[45]

In the next month, the situation worsened. On August 6, at barrio Jaybanga, some nine miles northeast of Lobo's población, an American patrol had a six-hour battle with a large Filipino force made up of Claudio's command and elements of Casala's San Rafael Column. The Americans destroyed a number of buildings used by the guerrillas and a quantity of ammunition, captured several ponies, and killed ten Filipinos, including two from Felix Farol's company. Disheartened by the outcome of the encounter, Claudio decided to suspend all operations against the enemy for the foreseeable future. Writing to Malvar on August 19, he described the sad condition of his forces: two rifles had been lost to the enemy at Jaybanga; seven more had been rendered inoperable; his soldiers had no more than ten to fifteen rounds of ammunition apiece. Claudio then informed his chief that, because of the shortages of weapons and ammunition, he had adopted the following expedient: two-thirds of the approximately one hundred men under him were ordered to go into hiding; the weapons of the hiding men were to be turned over to the ones who remained in the field; and those remaining troops were divided into three detachments of ten to eleven men who would be stationed in secure locations in the vicinity of Lobo.[46]

Claudio's decision to go into hiding was fortuitous. Just as the San Miguel Column was being disbanded, General Sumner, having received reports after the battle at barrio Jaybanga that the Batangas City–Lobo–San Juan region had become a stronghold of the guerrillas, ordered that U.S. military activity in the area be intensified. "It is my intention," he informed his superiors, "to continue operations in this section as far as conditions will permit. I believe the population in the mountains are either active Insurrectos or completely under the control of the Insurrectionary forces."[47]

And so, by the end of August 1901, the battle for southern Batangas had once again taken on the characteristics of a game of hide-and-seek. While the U.S. troops pursued the guerrillas, attempting to carry out the instructions of the district commander, the now-reduced San Miguel Column concentrated almost all its energies on avoiding contact with the pursuers. Claudio communicated regularly with his troops and stayed in touch with various residents of Lobo—among them, his old friend Celestino Gutierrez, who had succeeded Julian Ramirez as municipal president and now used his influence to induce some of the townspeople to make contributions of rice to the guerrillas. But for all intents and purposes, the San Miguel Column had temporarily ceased to exist as a military force.[48]

Elsewhere in Batangas, Malvar's forces experienced equally formidable difficulties. The troops of Martin Cabrera, operating in the vicinity of Taal, Lemery, Bauan, and San Luis, complained about the lack of serviceable weapons at their disposal.[49] Cabrera's command was afflicted with the same sort of behavioral cancers that could be found in Claudio's: the repeated refusal of commanders to obey the orders of superiors; the inability or unwillingness of officers to coordinate the operations of their units; and the tendency of some of the men to alienate the noncombatant population.[50] Then, disaster struck. Only July 26, acting on intelligence provided by a collaborator in Bauan, Lt. John Hartman and fifty-two members of the First Cavalry surprised and captured thirty-four soldiers of the Flying Column of Bauan, seizing twenty-two serviceable rifles in the process. Nineteen days later, Martin Cabrera himself, only recently elevated by Malvar to the rank of brigadier general, was brought in by another cavalry patrol.[51]

There were other setbacks. At the end of July, Juan Buenafe, one of the guerrilla chiefs of Batangas City, was captured by Lieutenant Hartman; on August 13, Col. Julian Panganiban, one of Nicolas Gonzales's trusted men, surrendered near Tanauan; and on August 25, one of Batangas's leading figures in both the revolution against Spain as well as the struggle against the Americans, Col. Arcadio Laurel, also turned himself in.[52] In neighboring Laguna, Juan Cailles decided to leave the field at the end of June, and exactly a month later, Emilio Zurbano, a leader of the resistance in Tayabas, did the same.[53]

All in all, then, the condition of Malvar's forces was anything but satisfactory. By the end of August 1901, most columns were understrength, and all of them had been reduced to hiding from the Americans. One should not conclude that Malvar's determination to fight had diminished or that the noncombatants of many towns were losing heart or that the guerrillas remaining in the field were on the point of giving up; but Sumner's recent offensive had clearly taken a substantial toll.

★ Sumner and His Critics, Early September 1901

Just as Samuel Sumner, hamstrung though he was, was beginning to cause genuine distress to Malvar's guerrillas, the ranking U.S. Army officer in the Philippines, Adna Chaffee, was coming to question the district commander's competence. Chaffee had his reasons. He had no indication—nor did Sumner—that progress of any sort was being made in the southern Tagalog region. He was also under pressure, as anti-imperialists in the United States continued to wage their campaign against America's conduct of the war in the Philippines. Under the circumstances, Chaffee and the War Department were anxious to end the fighting as rapidly as possible, and they were

28. Adna Chaffee

increasingly irritated about the ongoing guerrilla activity in Sumner's district. Chaffee gave the first hint of dissatisfaction in a letter to Adj. Gen. Henry C. Corbin on September 2:

> The disturbance in Wade's Department has contracted practically to Batangas Province, but there no serious impression has been made on Malvar's party, generally supposed to be from five hundred to six hundred strong scattered in the mountains and brush. Small parties have been struck, some surrenders made, but nothing done yet to press Malvar hard enough to get a squeal out of him, except that he asserts as do others who know him, that have come in, that he will never surrender.
>
> Campaigning there now is very difficult and while I have urged Wade and Sumner to be active and to give Malvar no rest, it results mainly in filling our hospitals with sick men, principally bowel cases.[54]

Just as doubts about Sumner's ability were beginning to surface, the district commander decided to abandon his advocacy of the severe measures he had thus far been pushing for. He too had reasons. Having failed on several occasions to gain approval for his policies, he had evidently resigned himself to the notion that a radical departure from the currently sanctioned approach to warfare was beyond the realm of possibilities. One could detect a definite change in tone in a report Sumner sent to departmental headquarters on September 4. After reviewing the situation in Batangas and eastern Laguna, he made only two limp recommendations about how to proceed: he advised carrying on "such an active campaign" as to compel Malvar and his followers to surrender, and he renewed his call for the creation of a bureau of information in the district.[55]

Far from advocating the kind of escalation of pressure against the civilian population that he had urged upon his superiors in previous communications, Sumner now firmly opposed such a course. "The policy of our Government as well as the dictates of humanity forbid our waging a relentless and cruel warfare against the inhabitants regardless of age or sex," Sumner wrote in that report of September 4. "We must seek some more humane means of ending the struggle." He also rejected, albeit for ostensibly practical reasons, the adoption of one measure expressly intended to neutralize civilian support for the guerrillas—the policy of forced "concentration," which had been used with some success in the pacification campaigns on the island of Marinduque and in northern Luzon.[56] "The country," he explained, "has a population of several hundred thousand which precludes the possibility of inaugurating any system of concentration or any thorough control of the food supply."

Sumner's flip-flop, understandable though it was in the light of his recent experience, could not have been more badly timed. By abandoning his call for harsher policies at the very moment that Chaffee was pressing for immediate results, he was conveying the impression—a false one, I would argue—that he was, by nature, insufficiently aggressive. In warfare, as in daily life, timing plays a decisive role, and in this unconventional war it would contribute mightily to Samuel Sumner's troubles.

Over the course of the next few weeks, Sumner put into operation the modest policies he had discussed in his latest report. On September 23, he announced the establishment of a bureau of information in the district, and on the following day he instructed his subordinates in Batangas to intensify operations against the guerrillas. Small detachments were to do the bulk of the work, occupying barrios for three days or so and then moving on to others. "It is desired," he wrote, "that this be done so that the enemy will not know for any length of time the location of all our troops and it is thought that this will prevent them from using these barrios to their own advantage."[57] In doing all this, Sumner was under no illusion that his policies were likely to bring immediate results. In a letter written on September 28, he even conceded that harsher measures—the burning of barrios, the destruction of food, the subjection of the populace to personal torture—might be more efficacious, but he made it clear that such an "inhumane" course was now unacceptable to him.[58]

This is not to say that these measures were necessarily unacceptable to the troops who served under Sumner. There was always a sizable gap between official policy and day-to-day practice in this war in the Philippines, and not a few of Sumner's subordinates turned out to be inclined to fight the battle for Batangas according to rules that could be found in no departmental directive. One who demonstrated this type of initiative was Col. A. B. Wells, the post commander at Batangas City. Having managed to capture Juan Buenafe, one of three brothers who commanded guerrilla units in the vicinity of the provincial capital, Wells approached the mother of the prisoner and promised to release her son if she could induce her other two boys to come in.[59] Nothing came of the offer, but the failure did not stop other U.S. Army officers from using family ties to promote their pacification efforts. Shortly afterward, E. S. West, the newly appointed intelligence chief in Sumner's district, threatened to deport another captured officer, Martin Cabrera of Taal, unless the prisoner agreed to bring about the surrender of his brother Mariano.[60] Lt. P. A. Connolly, in charge of the U.S. Army post at San Jose, had more success with pressure of a different kind. Aware that the leaders of the local guerrilla forces were men of property, he fastened upon the tactic of seizing their landed estates. "As a result of many seizures of their property," he boasted in late September 1901, "they have manifested a desire to agree upon a surrender."[61] Finally, despite the explicit prohibitions, there was the usual quota of random violence and abusive behavior that one tends to associate with guerrilla conflicts—beatings of bystanders, torture of suspects, unauthorized destruction.[62]

Whether the troops in Sumner's district were following his orders or willfully disregarding them, the fact remains that none of them believed that they were making substantial progress in pacifying the southern Tagalog region. True, in any given week, there were minor successes—a victory in a skirmish near Lipa on September 21, the capture of several Filipino officers near Santo Tomas five days later—but inevitably there were reverses too, among them the hacking to death of Tomas Diocampo, a Filipino guide who had furnished valuable information to the Americans, by a guerrilla officer in Bauan on September 28.[63] This was hardly the sort of record that was likely to win the approval of a commander like Chaffee, who wanted the resistance to end immediately.

And then, on the distant island of Samar, an event occurred which would ultimately prove to be Sumner's undoing. On the same day that Tomas Diocampo died in Bauan, the forces of Vicente Lukban launched a surprise attack on the U.S. garrison at Balangiga, killing more than forty Americans.[64] The Balangiga massacre, as it was called, was more than simply a stunning victory for the Filipinos; it was also a turning point in the unconventional phase of the Philippine-American War. For it provided the incentive, as well as the excuse, for Chaffee, the now-embarrassed director of the U.S. war effort, to insist upon a more severe approach toward the remnants of the Filipino Army that continued to resist, and it also had the effect of making him even more intolerant about the seemingly sluggish pace of Sumner's pacification efforts in the southern Tagalog region. Only two days after the events at Balangiga, Chaffee wrote to Corbin, "We are making very slow headway in Batangas, Laguna and Western Tayabas. . . . I am afraid that Sumner has not the vigor that the situation requires."[65]

The criticism of Sumner mounted in October 1901. William Howard Taft, the civil governor of the Philippines, had no use for either Sumner or his immediate superior, James F. Wade. "General Wade is incompetent and General Sumner who is under him is not very much better," Taft wrote to Secretary of War Elihu Root on October 14.[66] Meanwhile, Chaffee was close to giving up on the district commander. "Sumner . . . has accomplished nothing much of consequence," he commented to Corbin on October 25. "Unless he does something soon I shall put someone else in command of his Brigade."[67] Not long afterward, he decided to do exactly that. On November 1, the U.S. Army in the Philippines was reorganized, with the First District of the Department of Southern Luzon being incorporated into a new administrative unit known as the Third Separate Brigade of the Department of North Philippines. Loyd Wheaton took charge of the department, displacing Wade from that theater of operations. Sumner was permitted to stay on temporarily as commander of the Third Separate Brigade, and during his final weeks on the job, his troops escalated their activity, scoring a victory near Bauan and destroying several guerrilla camps. But the belated success did not influence Chaffee. On November 30, on Chaffee's instructions, Sumner was obliged to relinquish his command to Brig. Gen. J. Franklin Bell.[68]

★ Guerrilla Woes and Malvar's Plans, October–November 1901

As the U.S. high command glowered and grumbled and grew ever more frustrated, their enemy in Batangas continued to experience difficulties of their own. The heavy rains of September and early October had given the local forces a needed respite from military operations and an opportunity to hide, regroup, and impress new recruits into service. Eliseo Claudio's San Miguel Column, for example, which had been disbanded after the disaster at barrio Jaybanga in August, had reorganized and redeployed by mid-October 1901.[69] Still, Claudio's column, like most of the others, remained incapable of conducting sustained offensive operations because of the persistent short-ages of weapons, ammunition, food, money, and assorted supplies, and at least some of those deficiencies were attributable to the fact that a number of barrio officials were either unwilling or unable to comply with the requests of the local forces. Claudio, his subordinates, and his noncombatant supporters tried to deal with the problem in various ways—by appealing to the patrio-tism of the citizenry, by issuing veiled threats, even by attempting to raise additional funds through door-to-door solicitations by soldiers carrying ven-erated religious objects.[70] But the shortages continued, and they became even more serious in November when the U.S. forces, stepping up their patrolling in the vicinity of Lobo, discovered and burned several caches of guerrilla supplies.[71]

Faced with similar kinds of problems in most of his columns, Malvar redoubled his efforts to energize the resistance. As before, he issued lists of instructions, intended both to enhance the effectiveness of the guerrilla units and to dissuade the populace from assisting the Americans. One directive, which testified to the ongoing shortage of weapons, required his officers to organize units armed with bows and arrows; a second ordered the politico-military heads of all towns, zones, and provinces to establish arsenals where cartridges could be manufactured and reloaded; still another, aimed at al-leviating the food shortages, obliged all males above the age of fourteen to grow a minimum of two thousand sweet potato plants, two hundred squash plants, and a specified amount of at least one other crop each year. Malvar also instructed his troops to punish severely anyone who provided informa-tion to the Americans to the prejudice of the Filipino war effort or any soldier who negotiated with the enemy or induced his subordinates to acknowledge the sovereignty of the United States.[72]

Malvar's lieutenants needed little prodding to deal harshly with soldiers or civilians who cooperated with the occupying army. In the last few months of 1901, several prominent collaborators were killed by the guerrilla forces: Tomas Diocampo, mentioned earlier, whose gruesome death in Bauan was surely intended to convey a message to the local citizenry about the consequences of assisting the enemy; Alvaro Nazareth, an interpreter employed by the U.S. forces in Tanauan, who was stabbed to death in that town's public market; and Maximo Cabatay of Batangas City, a man merely suspected of collaboration because of his close connection to a well-known americanista, who was shot by one of Briccio Casala's officers.[73] Such killings may have helped to convince a certain percentage of the populace that collaboration was a dangerous course, but it should be recognized that the guerrillas' use of what some might characterize as terror tactics was not alone responsible for the support they received: Malvar's earlier appeal to the lower rungs had considerably broadened the base of his support in the southern Tagalog region.[74]

In addition to attempting, by word and deed, to strengthen his army and combat collaboration, Malvar made preparations to do something more. Realizing that the Filipino Army had adopted a defensive posture for several months, he decided in the first half of November 1901 to launch a major offensive against the Americans. "I gave the order that once a year there should be a general movement," he later explained. By going on the attack, however briefly, he wanted to demonstrate to the American public that the Filipino people "were protesting with rifles." Once the large-scale offensive had taken place, he planned to revert to ambush warfare, with the Filipinos avoiding all fights with the enemy and conserving ammunition except on the occasions when they had at least a three to one numerical advantage.[75]

Hence, on November 11, 1901, just as Sumner was making his final push against the guerrillas in the southern Tagalog region, Malvar wrote to his lieutenants that on either December 7 or 8, a simultaneous attack would be launched against a thousand towns in the Philippines. Insisting, as Andres Bonifacio had once insisted at the time of the revolution against Spain, that the Filipinos were capable of achieving victory so long as they were unified and received God's help, he called on his men to assault the Americans with every weapon at their disposal, including bows and arrows. These orders filtered down the chain of command, and steps were taken to carry them out.

By the end of November, the guerrilla forces in Batangas were prepared and deployed, waiting for Malvar's signal to launch the general attack.[76]

★ ★ ★

Eight months had now passed since Aguinaldo's surrender, and the struggle for Batangas was far from over. The Americans had defeated Malvar's troops in almost every battle, but there had, in fact, been few battles of consequence. Their constant patrolling had done real damage, but most of the damage was hidden from view. In some towns, American pressure tactics had severely disrupted the delivery of money and supplies to the guerrilla units, but in most a sizable percentage of the populace continued to support Malvar. And now, to add insult to frustration, the guerrilla forces were finalizing plans for a mini-offensive of their own. Such was the situation in Batangas on the eve of J. Franklin Bell's arrival.

9

Concentration and Conquest

IN HIS DAY, J. Franklin Bell, the director of the final act of the battle for Batangas, was a controversial figure, and he is no less so today. No one denies that he was successful. In fewer than six months, Bell managed to hound or starve most of Malvar's army into submission and to shatter the network of noncombatant support on which the guerrilla forces relied. What has caused controversy, however, has been his methods of achieving that success, and, in particular, his adoption of the so-called concentration policy. Similar in concept to the approach adopted by Gen. Valeriano Weyler in Cuba and also to that of the British in the Anglo-Boer War, the concentration policy was designed to isolate the guerrillas who were fighting the U.S. Army from the noncombatants who were assisting them. Noncombatants were urged to enter "zones," designated areas in designated towns where they were expected to remain so long as the fighting continued; meanwhile, outside the zones, the U.S. troops were free to operate under minimal restraints. According to Bell's critics, the policy was flawed in two principal respects: it resulted in an astoundingly high level of civilian mortality in the zones of concentration and led to widespread abuses on the part of the U.S. military.

Such criticism of Bell and his policies began to surface in 1902, shortly after Malvar's surrender. In May of that year, U.S. Senator Augustus O. Bacon of Georgia, a vocal opponent of the war in the Philippines, read on the Senate floor a letter from an American army officer who claimed that a "corpse-carcass stench" filled the air in the zones, and that "at nightfall clouds of vampire bats softly [swirled] out in their orgies over the dead." Although administration spokesmen issued denials, the charges were repeated by anti-imperialists, along with others about atrocities committed by the U.S. troops during the last stages of the fighting in Batangas.[1]

Scholars have been harsh on Bell as well. Writing in the 1920s, the Filipino historian Teodoro M. Kalaw condemned Bell's campaign: "Life in the zones was very hard for the poor *reconcentrados*. Their health was undermined by diseases. Absence from their farms deprived them of the bare necessities of life. According to the official data, the death rate in Batangas during those months reached appalling figures."[2] More recent accounts by Filipino scholars—for example, those by Gregorio Zaide and Renato Constantino—essentially agreed with Kalaw's assessment.[3] So did Leon Wolff and Stuart Creighton Miller, two American historians. According to Miller, "Bell deserved the epithet 'butcher' for his systematic devastation of Batangas. Moreover, as one of the few West Pointers among the leading generals in the Philippine war, Bell lent greater respectability to methods that should have been considered unprofessional."[4]

But Bell has also found apologists. One of the first was John R. M. Taylor, the U.S. Army's official historian of the Philippine-American War. In his five-volume study, *The Philippine Insurrection against the United States,* he praised Bell's actions in Batangas and asserted that conditions in the zones had been far from dreadful: "No one died of starvation within these districts, although some 300,000 people were at one time gathered within them; nor is there any reason to believe that anyone experienced serious hunger. The most serious discomfort experienced by anyone within these areas was caused to the mestizo ruling group, whose members bitterly resented the blow to their prestige in being treated like everyone else."[5] Two contemporary defenders have been John Morgan Gates and, to a lesser extent, Brian Linn. In Gates's view, Bell's campaign in Batangas was "a credit to the American Army in the Philippines and a masterpiece of counter-guerrilla warfare." Gates has also argued that the zones were not at all unhealthy: "Army physicians furnished medical care free of charge, and the public health measures undertaken in the zones resembled those in typical American garrison towns. Schools were also provided, and all the benevolent and humane actions that had characterized American operations in the Philippines since 1898 were evident in the zones of reconcentration."[6]

The following chapter, which deals in large part with the man and the measures that have aroused so much controversy, will satisfy neither Bell's critics nor his defenders. That Bell and the troops who served under him were guilty of questionable conduct seems clear enough; equally clear is the fact that mortality rates in the zones of concentration were extraordinarily high. But, while all that can be demonstrated and while it also cannot be denied that Bell's policies contributed to the mortality crisis that occurred, it would be wrong to hold Bell and the U.S. Army solely, or even largely, responsible for that massive population loss. In fact, the situation in Batangas was far more epidemiologically complicated than either Bell's defenders or his critics have thus far suggested, and some of the leading players in the demographic drama have never received their due.

★ J. Franklin Bell

Forty-five years old at the time of his reassignment to the Third Separate Brigade, J. Franklin Bell was one of the remarkable success stories of the Philippine-American War. A West Point graduate (class of 1878) and a cavalry officer, he had first served in the Indian campaigns, but when the Indian wars ended, his career had stalled. Bell even considered resigning his commission. In 1898, he received orders to serve with the U.S. military units occupying Manila, and when the Philippine-American War began, Bell was drawn into the fighting. Serving under Arthur MacArthur in central Luzon, Bell made headlines (and later won a Congressional Medal of Honor) for his bravery in battle. In one action, he and a scouting party charged a much-larger enemy patrol, and Bell single-handedly captured three Filipino soldiers; in other encounters, he performed equally spectacular feats. Having won fame on the battlefield, Bell moved on to another theater. Appointed provost marshal general of the city of Manila in July 1900, he came quickly to the attention of the newly arrived Philippine Commission, which (as noted above) had been sent by McKinley to introduce civil government into the pacified parts of the archipelago. William Howard Taft, the commission's president and later the first American civil governor of the Philippines, was

29. *J. Franklin Bell*

impressed. "[Bell] has shown himself so useful here and is so well acquainted with the people and the country," Taft wrote to Secretary Root in early 1901. He praised Bell as well for his command of Spanish and his success in clearing the capital of "insurrectos." With support from soldiers and civilians alike, Bell was appointed brigadier general in the regular army in February 1901 and placed in charge of the First District of the Department of Northern Luzon.[7]

Bell's service in northern Luzon was similarly celebrated. Taking over from Gen. Samuel B. M. Young, who had made progress against the Filipino forces in the Ilocos region but had not managed to subdue them, Bell moved at once to end the resistance. One measure that proved to be effective in this campaign was Bell's policy of concentrating civilians in selected towns—the policy that, with some modifications, he was later to employ in Batangas. Bell discussed his reasons for adopting it in a dispatch he sent to subordinates on April 12, 1901:

> Notwithstanding the utter hopelessness of obtaining any substantial benefit by continuing the present insurrection, the professional peace-desiring [Federal] Party in this district has not assisted the United States in any substantial way in bringing the present hostilities to a close. The guerrilla warfare is continued by the substantial aid and comfort given to the insurrectos by the same people whom we are protecting and who are enjoying a certain amount of prosperity due to our magnanimity. They have never felt the full hardship of War and their professions of a desire for peace are merely words and do not come from a full realization of the discomforts and horrors of a war that is waged in earnest and with full vigor. It is confidentially believed that if the people realize what war is, they will exert themselves to stop the system of aid and contributions to the insurgents by the non-combatants and thus bring hostilities to a close. It is believed that the time has now come to adopt such measures with those so-called "Amigos" as to cause them to feel the absolute necessity of using their active influences in suppressing the insurrection as well as to stop all possible sources of aid.
>
> With that object in view, it is contemplated to cause all the people of the barrios to move into the towns with all their supplies and not return to them without written permission from the military authorities. Any person found in the barrios ordered to be abandoned, after ten days' notice, will be treated as insurgents. It is also proposed to have all ports of the district closed. Your views as to the practicality of carrying out each of the above measures is desired.

> In view of a possibility of a shortage of supplies, it is very desirable to
> have the people bring everything with them.

Relying on such measures as well as on the extensive use of native troops, the
constant patrolling by U.S. units, and the liberal use of the torch, Bell was
able to bring about the surrender of almost all of the guerrilla forces in the
Ilocos region by early May 1901.[8]

His star on the ascendant, Bell had now become, next to Frederick Funston (the U.S. general who captured Aguinaldo), the closest thing to a real
American hero that the Philippine-American War had thus far produced.
Loyd Wheaton, who was head of the Department of Northern Luzon before
taking charge of the newly created Department of North Philippines, had
enormous respect for Bell. So did Chaffee. And so too did Taft, who corresponded with Bell after the general had taken charge of operations in the
Ilocos region. In October 1901, as the criticism of Sumner's prosecution of the
war against Malvar was mounting, Taft offered Elihu Root an assessment of
what was needed to pacify Batangas: "If General Chaffee would insist that
General Bell or General Funston be sent down into Batangas, I think that
affairs would take on a very different hue. General Bell, especially, I think
would make things so uncomfortable for the people who are supporting the
insurrection that the men in the field would soon be brought in." When
Chaffee came to the conclusion that Sumner had to be relieved, he and
Wheaton naturally turned to J. Franklin Bell.[9]

Tall and physically powerful, Bell came to his assignment with more than
a record of achievement and a reputation for relentlessness. He also brought
some cultural baggage. Like most of the U.S. military men who served in the
Philippines, he seemed convinced that the Filipino people were, by and large,
both backward and benighted. "The number of people who realize that the
natives of these islands are unfit to govern themselves is growing greater all
the time," Bell wrote in October 1900. "I know, from ample experience, that
they are totally unfit and will be so for many years." In discussing the
Filipino character several months later, he was just as unflattering: "They
are the most skillful dissimulators on earth, and many of our officers, fresh
from the States, had the wool so completely pulled over their eyes as to be
incompetent to cope with these able deceivers. They have a great many good
qualities but a wonderful lot of customs and habits which must be trained
out of them before we should ever be able to make a creditable people of
them."[10]

Here, then, was the man who was about to take charge of U.S. military
operations in the southern Tagalog region—a brave, able, somewhat ethno-

centric, aggressive, relentless, and perhaps ruthless brigadier. And of course he had been chosen for the job precisely because he was that sort of man. En route to his new command, Bell stopped in Manila to receive instructions from his superiors, and before moving on, he discussed his new assignment with Bernard Moses, a member of the Philippine Commission. "He stated that he was under specific orders which, while they seem necessary, do not furnish him an especially agreeable task," Moses noted in his diary.

> He is sent to Batangas to make peace, and he proposes to do it even if the peace which he establishes must be the peace of desolation. He seemed to be in a somewhat reflective and subdued frame of mind in the presence of an undertaking which may bring destruction to a once rich province and great suffering to a large body of people. While the task is not of his choosing, it is clear that although he may expect to be vilified and have to bear the responsibility of action in many cases which he cannot control, still he seemed to have a deep determination to carry out his orders and to end rebellion in Batangas.[11]

★ Bell's Directives

Bell assumed command of the Third Brigade on November 30, 1901, and devoted his first week on the job to studying the problems that confronted him. "I interviewed every prominent intelligent Filipino within my reach who had the reputation of really desiring peace," he later wrote; and, while he listened, he doubtless kept in mind the briefing his superiors had given him a few days earlier. His investigation, such as it was, convinced him—or, perhaps to be more accurate, confirmed him in his view—of the need to introduce measures in the southern Tagalog region similar to the ones he had adopted in northern Luzon. "It became apparent that the only way that I could possibly succeed in putting an end to insurrection within the territorial limits of the brigade would be by cutting off the income and food of the insurgents, and by crowding them so persistently with operations as to wear them out."[12]

Before Bell had a chance to spell out the policy he had in mind, however, the initiative shifted, albeit momentarily, to Malvar. On December 7, the Filipinos launched the offensive that Malvar had been planning since the second week in November, attacking the U.S. garrisons at three towns in Batangas—Lobo, Lipa, and Tanauan—as well as those at a number of other points in the southern Tagalog region. On December 8, the American troops stationed at Taal and Lobo came under fire, and the latter town was actually occupied by units from two columns of Briccio Casala's command, including the San Miguel Column of Eliseo Claudio. The next day, Lobo was retaken by the Americans and more fighting occurred at Tanauan.[13]

With the exception of the second fight at Lobo, the Filipinos fared badly, and their operations did little to convince anyone, least of all the Americans, that they were a credible offensive force. In the battle at Lobo on December 9, for example, the Americans were able to reoccupy the town largely because two experienced company commanders, Felix Farol and Fernando Garcia, proved incapable of coordinating their efforts; at one point in the fighting, Farol was obliged to withdraw when he discovered, to his shock, that Garcia had summarily abandoned the strategic position he was supposed to occupy, leaving Farol to fend for himself.[14] Although Casala continued to urge the soldiers and civilians in that section of Batangas to maintain the offensive, most of the local forces now found themselves running for their lives. The Americans sent out scouting parties constantly in the final weeks of December 1901, affording Malvar's men little opportunity to rest.[15]

In the meantime, Bell had begun to issue a series of circulars to the station commanders in his brigade, revealing his plans for pacifying the southern Tagalog region. The first important directive, dated December 8, 1901, outlined his policy of concentration, intended to shut off the guerrillas in the field from their sources of supply:

> In order to put an end to the enforced contributions, now levied by insurgents upon the inhabitants of sparsely settled and outlying barrios and districts, by means of intimidation and assassination, commanding officers of all towns now existing in the provinces of Batangas and Laguna, including those at which no garrison is stationed at present, will immediately specify and establish plainly marked limits surrounding each town bounding a zone within which it may be practicable, with an average sized garrison, to exercise efficient supervision over and furnish protection to inhabitants (who desire to be peaceful) against the depredations of armed insurgents. These limits may include the barrios which exist sufficiently near the town to be given protection and supervision by the garrison, and should include some ground on which live stock can graze, but so situated that it can be patrolled and watched. All ungarrisoned towns will be garrisoned as soon as troops become available.

Technically, Bell's circular did not compel the people of Batangas and Laguna to relocate to the zones, but the brigade commander made it clear that anyone who chose to remain outside them was running a substantial risk:

Commanding officers will also see that orders are at once given and distributed to all the inhabitants within the jurisdiction of towns over which they exercise supervision, informing them of the danger of remaining outside of these limits and that unless they move by December 25th from outlying barrios and districts with all their movable food supplies, including rice, palay, chickens, live stock, etc., to within the limits of the zone established at their own or nearest town, their property (found outside of said zone at said date) will become liable to confiscation or destruction.

In order to accommodate the large numbers of people who would be confined in the zones, Bell ordered that residents of outlying districts be permitted to move their houses if that were feasible or to construct temporary shelter on any vacant lots in the zones.[16]

Other directives issued in December 1901 elaborated on the system of control that Bell and his superiors intended to introduce. In an effort to prevent the guerrillas from receiving food and other supplies from outside the region, the Army closed all ports in Batangas and Laguna, and Bell ordered as well that, after January 1, 1902, no merchandise could be transported by land between towns in those two provinces. Travel by noncombatants outside the zones was to be strictly regulated: no person was allowed to leave a town without a special written pass from the commanding officer, and no such passes were to be given to able-bodied males except in cases of extreme necessity. "Any able-bodied male found by patrols or scouting detachments outside of protected zones without passes will be arrested and confined, or shot if he runs away." Only one noteworthy exception to these rules was initially to be permitted: at the station commander's discretion, residents of the zone would be allowed to gather standing crops outside the zone, but only when accompanied by patrols or detachments of soldiers.[17]

In addition to regulating the movement of people and restricting the movement of supplies, Bell intended to cripple the southern Tagalog resistance by striking directly at certain categories of individuals who, he believed, were providing Malvar with the bulk of his support. Aware that most municipal and barrio officials had long acted as agents for the guerrillas, he issued a circular on December 9 directing all station commanders to arrest and bring to trial all presidents and chiefs of police against whom sufficient evidence could be found to convict them of violating their oaths of allegiance. He also singled out native priests for harsh treatment. "It may be considered as practically certain that every native priest in the provinces of

Batangas and Laguna is a secret enemy of the government and in active sympathy with the insurgents. These are absolutely our most dangerous enemies." They too were to be brought to trial if the Army could muster sufficient evidence, but even if only a "well founded suspicion" existed against them, they were to be confined and held in custody. A similar approach was to be adopted in dealing with other wealthy and influential residents of the town. Bell's rationale for taking these steps was straightforward:

> To arrest anyone believed to be guilty of giving aid or assistance to the insurrection in any way or of giving food or comfort to the enemies of the government, it is not necessary to wait for sufficient evidence to lead to conviction by a court, but those strongly suspected of complicity with the insurrection may be arrested and confined as a military necessity and may be held as prisoners of war in the discretion of the station commanders until receipt of other orders from higher authority. It will frequently be found impossible to obtain any evidence against persons of influence as long as they are at liberty, but once confined, evidence is easily obtainable.[18]

Subsequent directives targeted the same categories of individuals for rougher treatment. On December 18, Bell ordered all station commanders in Batangas and Laguna to arrest and confine immediately any priests who had not yet been taken into custody and made clear that they could be released only when they had completely turned against the guerrillas and used their influence to work for peace. Five days later, he directed that, on January 1 or as soon thereafter as was practicable, station commanders in Batangas and Laguna were to arrest all municipal and barrio officials, principales, members of the police force, and any other members of the community suspected of aiding or sympathizing with the resistance, except for those who had previously demonstrated their loyalty to the United States by guiding American troops to enemy camps, denouncing secret agents of the enemy, or performing other public acts that committed them irrevocably to the side of the Americans. The purpose of such measures was, in Bell's words, "to place the burden of the war on the disloyal and to so discipline them that they will become anxious to aid and assist the government in putting an end to the insurrection and securing the re-establishment of civil government."[19]

The approach Bell was adopting—the application of extreme pressure to the elites of the region—was based on an analysis of the sociology of the southern Tagalog resistance that was at least half a year out of date. Elite Batangueños still constituted a major source of support for Malvar and his army, as they had since the early days of the revolution against Spain. But Bell failed to see, or at least appreciate the importance of, the changes that had taken place in the resistance since the removal of Aguinaldo and Trias from the scene: Malvar's self-conscious courting of the lower rungs since his assumption of command, the growing reliance of the guerrillas on the contributions of poor barrio-dwellers, and the important financial role that Sebastian Caneo's Colorum had assumed in the local struggle. Bell's imperfect understanding of provincial realities is discernible in some remarks he made to an assembly of officers in early December 1901:

> To successfully deal with the common people, the head men, their leaders, the *principales,* are the ones we need to influence. The common *hombre* is dominated body and soul by his master, the *principale.* He is simply a blind tool, a poor down-trodden ignoramus, who does not know what is good for him and cannot believe an American. We cannot appeal to him direct. It is impossible. You can no more influence him by benevolent persuasion than you can fly. He is going to do whatever he is told to do by his master or his leaders, because he is incapable of doing anything else.[20]

Bell's misunderstanding of provincial realities did not necessarily undermine his program of pacification. At this point in the conflict the guerrilla forces had been sufficiently weakened and large numbers of people from all rungs on the socioeconomic ladder were sufficiently tired of the struggle that the entire package of new measures adopted by Bell, including one based on a misconception, was enough to drive the remnants of Malvar's army from the field. Still, it should be emphasized that, because of Bell's imperfect understanding, the victory that would be achieved once Malvar's guerrillas were neutralized was to be less complete than Bell's boosters would later claim it was. Throughout Bell's campaign, there were hints, sometimes very strong ones, that, however successfully the U.S. Army was dealing with the local guerrillas and their elite supporters, the lower classes were not dutifully falling into line; and even after the battle for Batangas was declared over by the Americans, the authorities had occasional skirmishes with groups that resembled Caneo's Colorum.

The final important component of Bell's plan to pacify the southern Tagalog region was strictly military: he called for a step-up in the campaign against the guerrillas. Having turned most of Batangas and Laguna into virtual free-fire zones by concentrating the noncombatants in the towns, Bell was determined, as he told General Wheaton in a report, to search "each ravine, valley, and mountain peak for insurgents and for food, expecting to destroy everything I find outside of towns[;] all able-bodied men will be killed or captured." He was also determined that the troops in his brigade be given the greatest possible latitude in pursuing the enemy:

> Subordinate commanders and young officers of experience should not be restrained or discouraged without excellent reason, but should be encouraged to hunt for, pursue, and vigorously operate against armed bodies of insurgents wherever they may be found. . . . Except when the advantage in position and numbers is overwhelming on the side of the enemy, our troops should always assume the offensive and advance on and pursue them vigorously.[21]

To assist the troops in dealing with the remaining guerrillas in the region, Bell directed that, for the duration of the campaign, the fighting would be conducted in strict accordance with General Order 100, A.G.O., 1863 series. A guide to land warfare drawn up during the American Civil War by the distinguished political theorist Francis Lieber, General Order 100 included a long list of instructions governing the conduct of an occupying army. It proscribed certain types of behavior (rape, murder, the inflicting of additional wounds on a disabled enemy soldier, and so on), laid down rules about the treatment of prisoners of war and various other matters, and permitted an army to deal harshly with both spies (who were to be executed) and guerrillas (who were to be treated like "highway robbers or pirates").[22] Since December 1900, the U.S. Army in the Philippines had been using General Order 100 as its general guide to military conduct, but it had not adopted certain of the more extreme measures that Lieber had seen fit to include—for example, the right of an army to retaliate against an enemy guilty of assassination and other misdeeds. Now, Bell indicated that retaliation was permissible, although he added the somewhat ambiguous qualification that "no station member will put any one to death as a matter of retaliation for assassination . . . without obtaining authority from a superior commander, nor will the death penalty be inflicted in any case without similar authority." Bell probably intended that qualification to imply that no execution was to take place without his own express approval, but the wording was vague enough to be misinterpreted. A later directive, which spelled out the procedure to be adopted in cases of retaliation, was likewise ambiguous on the question of who was authorized to order executions:

> The Brigade Commander . . . announces for the information of all concerned that whenever prisoners or unarmed or defenseless Americans

or natives friendly to the United States government are murdered or assassinated for political reasons, and this fact can be established, it is his purpose to execute a prisoner of war under the authority contained in Sections 59 and 148 [of General Order 100]. This prisoner of war will be selected by lot from among the officers or prominent citizens held as prisoners of war, and will be chosen when practicable from those who belong to the town where the murder or assassination occurred.

There is no evidence that the U.S. Army resorted to retaliation during Bell's campaign, and, for what it's worth, Bell stated categorically that retaliation did not occur, but if that was indeed the case, the wording of the circulars did little to promote such a result.[23]

So now, at last, the U.S. troops in Batangas were free to do the sort of things that hardliners like Birkhimer had advocated since the early days of the occupation. Noncombatants were to be concentrated; food found outside the zones was to be destroyed or confiscated; people found outside the zones were to be captured or killed; the troops were free to pursue the enemy relentlessly and make life more than miserable for the wealthy and influential residents of the towns. Observing Bell's actions from his office in Manila, Adna Chaffee was pleased by the new face of warfare in the southern Tagalog region. He wrote to Corbin on December 18, "I can't say how long it will take us to beat Malvar into surrendering, and if no surrender, can't say how long it will take us to make a wilderness of that country, but one or the other will eventually take place."[24]

★ The War in the Hills

During the first month of Bell's tenure in the southern Tagalog region—the period when he was spelling out the policies he would later pursue—substantial progress was made by the U.S. troops on the battlefield. In the area around Bauan, the cavalry forces commanded by Capt. John Hartman were constantly in motion, undertaking a total of forty-four separate expeditions against the enemy in the month of December 1901, capturing thirty-nine enemy soldiers, and confiscating one hundred rifles. Also in December, the troops stationed at Batangas City had a few engagements of consequence in the environs of that town, and scouting parties in the Lipa mountains and in the hilly terrain around Nasugbu and San Juan de Bocboc destroyed tens of thousands of pounds of palay and inflicted damage on the guerrilla forces.[25]

In January, though, the campaigning began in earnest. Between January 1 and April 30, 1902, Bell kept approximately half of his eight-thousand-man brigade regularly in the field in the southern Tagalog region, assigning the rest to guard the civilians crowded into the zones. His plan of operations, which he explained to Wheaton in a telegraphic report written in late December 1901, was to devote his primary attention to the mountainous parts of Batangas and Laguna, which the remnants of Malvar's guerrilla army were known to frequent:

> I expect to first clean out the wide Lobo peninsula south of [the] Batangas, Taisan, and San Juan de Boc Boc road. I shall then move command to the vicinity of Lake Taal and sweep the country westward to the ocean and south of Cavite; returning through Lipa, I shall scour and clean up the Lipa Mountains; swinging northward, the country in the vicinity of San Pablo, Alaminos, Tanauan, and Santo Tomas will be scoured, ending at Mount Maquiling, which will then be thoroughly searched and devastated. . . .
>
> Swinging back to the east, the same treatment will be given all the country of which Mount San Cristobal and Mount Banahao are the main peaks. These two mountains, Mount Maquiling, and the mountains northeast of Lobo are the main haunts of the insurgents. . . . I shall keep the country full of scouting detachments and give the insurgents no peace.[26]

Just as Bell had planned, the first expedition of 1902 was launched in the mountainous country around Lobo, the site of Eliseo Claudio's activities for most of the war. Bell assigned approximately 1,800 soldiers to the operation, placing Col. A. B. Wells in charge of slightly more than half of the expeditionary force and Col. T. J. Wint in command of the rest. On the night of December 31, the troops took up their positions along a line stretching from Batangas City to Mabato, an outlying barrio of Rosario, and on the morning of the following day, they began to move in unison in the direction of Lobo, keeping in contact with each other as much as possible and searching the countryside for any signs of people, animals, shelter, and food supplies. Wells's command spent seven days in the field, marching to Lobo and then back again, and Wint's a total of eight days. During the course of the expedition, the U.S. troops had several brief engagements with the enemy and killed a number of men. In addition, the soldiers led by Wells managed to destroy in excess of 500 tons of rice and palay, hundreds of bushels of corn, hundreds of hogs and chickens, and more than 6,000 houses, 200 carabaos, 800 head of cattle, and 680 horses; Wint's men burned about 900 tons of palay and killed hundreds of animals.[27]

Of course, some physical destruction on such an expedition was preordained, since a principal stated objective of the campaign was to deprive Malvar's guerrillas of all sustenance and to starve them into submission. But much of the devastation occurred for the simple reason that Bell's subordinates wanted to destroy and Bell chose not to upbraid them for doing so. Although one of his circulars specifically instructed the troops to carry back to the zones all rice and other edibles that could feasibly be transported in order to meet the food requirements of the concentrated noncombatants—and Bell sometimes included words to the same effect in the orders he issued to his officers before sending them out on expeditions—that course was adopted infrequently in the first six weeks of 1902.[28] If the officers in the brigade attempted to justify their actions, they invariably explained that the severity of the terrain precluded the removal of the food; but most of the time, they offered no explanation of any kind. And Bell, on his part, did not press them for one.[29] The predictable result of such behavior was ecological destruction on a massive scale.

The area around Lobo suffered most of all. Immediately after the Wells–Wint expedition had finished its work, several companies of U.S. troops trekked through the mountainous country between Lobo and San Juan, killing several hundred more animals and burning many more tons of palay. On January 12, a scouting party mounted another operation in the Lobo mountains which resulted, after 19 days in the field, in the destruction of 308 head of cattle, 57 carabaos, numerous other animals, and about 250 tons of palay. Other elements of Bell's brigade launched two more expeditions into the same general area in January, and both resulted in a staggering amount of devastation as well.[30]

As southern Batangas was being laid waste by Bell's brigade, a similar process was beginning to take place in other parts of the province. In mid-January, an expeditionary force in the mountains near Lipa burned hundreds of tons of palay and killed hundreds of animals, and several weeks afterward, huge caches of food supplies were discovered and destroyed in the vicinity of Lake Taal and in several upland barrios of Batangas City.[31] Systematically and ruthlessly, large sections of Batangas were being turned into the wilderness that General Chaffee had earlier written about, totally lacking in food supplies, domesticated animals, and human shelter. Such devastation of the countryside would, as we shall see, do a good deal more than deprive the remaining guerrillas of food; it would also contribute directly to the mortality crises that occurred that year.

In addition to ravaging the countryside, the U.S. troops were guilty of more than a few other outrageous acts. Freed from most of the prohibitions under which they had earlier operated and pressed by Bell to get quick results, many officers and enlisted men appeared to feel that, so long as they were successful, their actions were likely to be condoned by higher authorities. One of the most successful—and one of the most often-praised—officers in Bell's brigade was Capt. John Hartman, who was stationed in Bauan and who permitted as well as encouraged a number of abusive practices in the cavalry troop he led. On December 26, 1901, Hartman left the post with a detachment of his troopers, accompanied by about fifty prominent citizens of Bauan, who had agreed to assist Hartman in pacifying the area. One of the troopers taking part in the day's activities was Pvt. Frederick Presher, and Presher described in his diary what transpired on that day:

> Our objective seemed to be a deep ravine near Durangao in which a number of rifles was supposed to be hidden and altho' the ravine and the surrounding country was search[ed], the native volunteers assisting[,] not a rifle was found.
>
> Finally, one lone gugu was found hiding in the long grass near the trail. He was taken before the Captain for questioning but he could not or would not talk so the Captain told Sergt. Hufeld, Pvt. Baylor and myself to take him and see if *we* couldn't make him talk.

According to Presher, they took the Filipino down to the bottom of the ravine, where there was a pool of dirty water, threw him in, and held his head under water. The Filipino would not talk, so they ducked him again until he nearly drowned. Every time they allowed the man to come up for air, Sergeant Hufeld would ask, "Quiere habla[r]?" But the man would not speak. Finally, the sergeant gave up, kicked the fellow in the rear, and told him to leave. The Filipino staggered away, and, to hurry him along, the sergeant fired a shot over his head.[32]

Even more tolerant than Captain Hartman of conduct of this sort was a second lieutenant named F. B. Hennessy, who was assigned to the 17th company of Ilocano Scouts, one of the units of native troops that served in Bell's brigade. Much of what we know about Hennessy's activities in the final act of the battle for Batangas is derived from two official investigations into his conduct by U.S. military authorities. Although he was never formally prosecuted and although there was conflicting testimony about his actions, at least one of the investigating officers in the Philippines, the judge advocate general in Washington, and even General Bell conceded that Hennessy had probably committed a large number of the acts attributed to him. Following is a sample of the testimony against this officer:

Q. What is your name?

A. Doroteo Baldonado.

Q. When were you arrested?

A. In December last year.

Q. Where [were] you arrested?

A. At a place called [Malagonlong], a barrio of Lipa.

Q. Who arrested you?

A. American soldiers.

Q. Where did they take you?

A. To the headquarters of the Ilocano Scouts here in Lipa.

Q. What did they do to you then?

A. They gave me the water cure, and I was slapped and kicked and ill treated also.

Q. Who gave you the water cure? American soldiers or the Scouts?

A. Lieut. Hennessy of the Scouts was the one that gave me the water cure.

Q. How [was] it given to you?

A. The water was poured down my throat through a rifle barrel.

Q. Was Lieut. Hennessy present all the time the water cure was being given you?

A. Yessir, he was sitting in a chair and every once and a while would kick my stomach with his feet.

. . . .

Q. Were you an insurgent when they arrested you?

A. No sir.

Q. Why did they arrest you?

A. They said that I was an insurgent—and they ill treated me and abused me so badly that I finally told them I was an insurgent. But I never was an insurgent.[33]

Hennessy's treatment of Baldonado was, if the documentary record of the investigation of that U.S. Army officer can be believed, anything but atypical of his conduct. Between December 11 and 18, 1902, when testimony about Hennessy's actions was taken in Lipa, more than a dozen Filipinos came forward to report that they had received the water cure either from Hennessy or from soldiers, both American and Ilocano, who served under him.

Furthermore, Hennessy's men were charged with committing other types of torture (the tying up of prisoners by their elbows and knees for long periods, the administering of severe beatings, the exposure of prisoners to the sun for several days); Hennessy, another American soldier, and several Ilocano Scouts were accused of rape; there were allegations that Hennessy and his soldiers had burned several barrios of Lipa without cause; and, last but not least, Hennessy was charged with beating, torturing, and killing Vicente Luna, the municipal president of Rosario and the father of Malvar's adjutant Luis Luna, setting fire to Vicente Luna's residence, and then throwing his body into the flames of the burning house.[34]

Lieutenant Hennessy was, it seems, a far from average member of Bell's brigade, and it would be both misleading and unfortunate if the foregoing discussion of his actions and purported actions conveyed the impression that all, or even most, American soldiers serving with Bell engaged in the kind of atrocious acts that he evidently engaged in. But the commission of abusive acts by U.S. military men was anything but rare in this final act of the battle for Batangas. The evidence about their occurrence is simply too extensive to discount.[35]

As the discussion of Hennessy has already suggested and as a great deal of other documentation confirms, outrages were also committed upon the residents of Batangas by the indigenous troops who were assigned to Bell's brigade—both by the Ilocano Scouts who served with Hennessy and perhaps more often by several companies of Macabebe Scouts from Pampanga. On January 23, 1902, in a barrio of Batangas City, a Macabebe identified only as Pedro was alleged to have raped a woman named Maria Marasigan. Nine days later, in Ibaan, a Macabebe Scout by the name of Saturnino Cunanan apparently raped two women and committed murder, and on February 14, in Tanauan, several Macabebes were alleged to have raped two girls and killed an ailing guerrilla who was attempting to turn himself in. Similar incidents were reported throughout Bell's campaign.[36] Although the Macabebes were usually cleared of the charges leveled against them, few of the Americans who served with them doubted that they had done what their accusers said they did. Bell's immediate superior, Loyd Wheaton, for one, was well aware of the Macabebes' behavior in the field. In February 1900, following the invasion of the southern Tagalog region, Wheaton had received reports that certain Macabebe units had looted the town of Magallanes and raped some of the women. His reaction was revealing. "The outrages upon women at Magallanes," Wheaton wrote, "were committed by Macabebe Scouts, who were, in these outrages, conducting themselves in their usual and customary manner. From my observation of the conduct of these savages, I am of the opinion that they harm more than they benefit our cause."[37] One can only wonder, then, why a man who felt that way about the Macabebes would have approved the assignment of so many of them to Bell's brigade.

Some of the most effective practices of the U.S. troops during these final months of the battle for Batangas could not be characterized as abuses or atrocities, although they represented a significant departure from previous procedures. A circular issued by Bell in late December 1901 instructed station commanders to bring all captured enemy soldiers to trial before provost courts for violation of the laws of war unless they rendered suitable services to the Americans. As it turned out, the service that most of the captured men would be expected to (and often did) render was to provide the U.S. troops with intelligence about the location of enemy soldiers, weapons, and supplies.[38] Another practice that proved to be popular among post commanders during this period was the incarceration of relatives of prominent guerrilla leaders. Briccio Casala's sister was jailed in an effort to bring about her brother's surrender, and a similar fate befell the parents of Nicolas Gonzales and the sons of Tomas Ramirez. Faced with an enemy who engaged in such tactics, a number of the remaining guerrilla commanders instructed their families to join them in the hills.[39]

As the military pressure exerted by the U.S. forces increased, the assistance provided by volunteers and captured soldiers became more common, and the guerrillas' food supplies disappeared in flames, Malvar's army began to fall apart. In the area around Bauan, where Capt. John Hartman's troopers had been hard at work, the local forces were broken quickly. On January 4, 1902, the police of Bauan captured Maj. Francisco Castillo and Maj. Geronimo Leynes. On January 6, Maj. Arcadio Villanueva surrendered; on January 11, Capt. Miguel Cuevas; and two days later, Lt. Col. Jacinto Dimaculangan. At the end of January, Captain Hartman reported with satisfaction that "all insurgent forces pertaining to Bauan have either been captured and confined or have surrendered."[40]

The guerrilla forces were collapsing elsewhere. On January 13, the U.S. forces at Taal received the surrender of Col. Anastasio Marasigan along with 21 members of his officer corps and 245 enlisted men. Three days later, 2 leaders of the guerrilla units operating in the vicinity of Lipa intimated that they were willing to discuss surrender terms, and by February 7, most of the Lipa forces had turned themselves in. Meanwhile, on January 20, Lt. Col. Briccio Laqui surrendered at Cuenca, and three commanders of the Batangas City columns—Damaso Ybarra, Eulalio Buenafe, and Lucio Buenafe—

followed suit on January 29.[41] Such tangible results buoyed the spirits of the leaders of the U.S. war effort. "So far as resistance is concerned, practically none exists at this time," Chaffee boasted to Corbin. "They have ceased to fight."[42]

Still, not all of them had ceased to hide. More stubborn than the aforementioned units were the forces of Eliseo Claudio. A few days after Malvar's brief, unsuccessful offensive in early December 1901, Claudio's superior Briccio Casala, who was still bent on taking an aggressive stance toward the Americans, attempted to organize an attack on Taysan and ordered Claudio to send a company to take part in that operation. The attack did not materialize, however, because on December 16, a U.S. cavalry detachment, acting on intelligence provided by civilians, surprised the assembled Filipino forces at barrio San Ysidro, killing several, dispersing the rest, and pursuing them to the mountains.[43] On the same day that the fighting took place at San Ysidro, the remaining two companies of Claudio's command, led by Claudio himself, reentered Lobo, having learned that the American detachment normally stationed in the town had left on an expedition to the nearby mountains. Claudio's orders, received from Casala on December 15, instructed him to burn Lobo to the ground so that the Americans would not be able to use it as an outpost in the future; but when he assembled the town's principales to inform them what Casala had in mind, they managed to convince him to adopt a less draconian course: to destroy the priest's residence, the school, and the municipal building, but to spare the rest of the town. Those buildings were destroyed on December 17, and Claudio stayed on in Lobo for several more days, meeting with the principales on other occasions, including Christmas Eve, when a party was held at the residence of Lorenzo Marasigan and music was played until the early morning hours. The Christmas Eve celebration in Lobo was the last hurrah of the San Miguel Column. With the coming of the new year, Bell's brigade would launch its first major expedition into the Lobo peninsula, and Eliseo Claudio's forces would literally disappear from view.[44]

Exactly what happened to the San Miguel Column in January and most of February 1902 can only be guessed at. The documentary record of Claudio's command—which has thus far provided us with much of our information about the activities of Malvar's guerrillas during the Philippine-American War—ends abruptly in late December 1901, just as Claudio and his men left Lobo, one step ahead of Colonels Wells and Wint. No doubt, the members of the San Miguel Column suffered severely in the following weeks, as the Americans kept up the pressure and destroyed all potential sources of sustenance, and some of them were killed or wounded in the skirmishes that the officers of the Third Separate Brigade described in their periodic reports to General Bell. By mid-February, in any case, there were signs of demoralization in the ranks, as soldiers from at least two of Claudio's companies turned in large numbers of rifles, bolos, and other weapons. On February 24, a second lieutenant and a sergeant from the San Miguel Column were captured; on February 25, another lieutenant surrendered; and on the following day, Claudio himself was brought in by a detachment of volunteers.[45]

By the end of February, therefore, Malvar's army in Batangas was perilously close to defeat. Many guerrilla leaders were no longer in the field, many weapons had fallen into American hands, and large portions of the province—the entire section west of Lake Taal, the southern part, much of the east—were essentially pacified. For the officers and men of the Third Separate Brigade, only two tasks of consequence remained to be accomplished in Batangas: eliminate the only remaining large commands in the province, those of Dalmacio Hernandez and Nicolas Gonzales, which operated in the vicinity of Santo Tomas and Tanauan; and bring in Miguel Malvar.

★ Life and Death in the Zones

While the remnants of Malvar's army were being chased, starved, and broken, the civilians concentrated in the zones were undergoing various kinds of hardships. One group of noncombatants that Bell had singled out for harsh treatment were men of wealth and influence, and in the last days of December and the first weeks of the new year, station commanders in most towns in Batangas deposited hundreds of such individuals in jail, often in facilities that were too small and too poorly ventilated to accommodate them. In Lipa, it was later charged, more than six hundred prisoners were confined at one time in a single room, and even the people who challenged the charges conceded that the number may have exceeded four hundred. During the weeks and months that these local worthies passed in confinement, many were tortured and beaten—including a large number of Lipeños who were unlucky enough to be interrogated by Lieutenant Hennessy and his Ilocano Scouts—and at least a few appear to have died from the beatings they received.[46]

The incarceration and the beatings produced results. In short order, many of the prisoners decided to perform the kind of services that were known to satisfy their captors and win their own release. In Batangas City,

Fermin Arceo, after thirty-three days in jail, volunteered to spend his waking hours trekking through the barrios of Taysan, Ibaan, and Batangas City, attempting to find Filipino soldiers and convince them to give up. His brother Leoncio, whose prison stay was nineteen days, agreed to do the same, and in January 1902, he served as the principal intermediary in the negotiations that led to the surrender of the guerrilla leaders Lucio and Eulalio Buenafe. Vicente Yturralde, who once had given considerable sums of money and large amounts of palay to the Filipino Army, won his freedom by inducing the commander of a company of bolomen to surrender and by leading the U.S. troops to a cache of weapons. Felix Aguirre also served as a guide for the Americans, and Juan Gutierrez, a onetime tax collector, made an effort to convince Briccio Casala to leave the field. Slowly but surely, then, these former supporters of the resistance were being transformed into some of its most dangerous allies. Knowing all that they knew about the guerrillas' operating procedures and hiding places, they were uniquely well qualified to frustrate the efforts of Malvar's shrinking army to avoid their enemy and prolong the war.[47]

They were also well qualified to provide vital information to the Americans about the system of noncombatant assistance that had evolved during the years of American occupation, and after a period of incarceration, they were willing to provide it. In Lipa, Batangas City, and Santo Tomas, many of the community leaders wrote lengthy declarations, confessing to the Americans about their own involvement in the resistance as well as about the help that their relatives, neighbors, friends, and acquaintances had provided to Malvar. As my earlier discussion of these declarations pointed out, not all the declarers always told the truth about the extent of their role (or that of their relatives, friends, and neighbors) in the war effort, and some of them, ever alert to the possibility of promoting their own interests and hurting those of their economic or political rivals, took advantage of the opportunity to implicate their enemies in activities that those people definitely did not take part in. Still, whatever the omissions and the flaws, the picture that emerged from the declarations was close enough to reality to enable the Americans to root out the overwhelming majority of Malvar's elite supporters and to destroy that part of the resistance support system that Bell aimed to destroy.[48]

The suffering in the zones was not confined to the well-off and influential. While the U.S. Army made a determined effort to defend its handling of the policy of concentration in Batangas, often pointing to a report made by Col. Arthur Wagner which concluded that "the common people in the camps are actually more happy and comfortable than they were in their own villages," the sad reality was that conditions in the zones were anything but satisfactory. Mortality statistics compiled by the municipal governments of Batangas in 1902, which have been preserved in the published volumes of the first American census, make clear beyond a shadow of a doubt that death rates soared in the province during the period January–April 1902, when the civilians were confined. The municipalities reported that a total of 8,344 people died, with 69 percent of the deaths coming in the final two months of confinement. If we assume that the population of the province was about 298,000 at the time, the "annualized" crude death rate for the period of concentration works out to be 84 per thousand.[49]

Such figures may underestimate the full impact of the zones, however, since they do not account for the people who contracted illnesses within the zones and died after their release. If the 2,741 Batangueños who died in May 1902 are added, the revised figures are 11,085 dead and an annualized crude death rate of 89.[50]

Those are incredibly high figures, more than twice as high as might have been expected in normal times in the late nineteenth-century Philippines. Yet even they do not provide a true picture of the mortality crisis that occurred. For, if one looks more closely at the geographical pattern of death in Batangas (by studying the surviving parish registers) one discovers that, as in the demographic catastrophe of 1900, the increase in mortality was far more dramatic in the eastern part of the province than in the west. In Lobo and San Juan, for instance, the annualized crude death rate for the period of concentration may have exceeded 200 per thousand, and in Batangas City, Lipa, and Taysan—all eastern Batangas towns—it was almost certainly more than 100 per thousand (see Appendix E). In the western Batangas towns of Balayan and Calaca, by contrast, the figures were close to normal.[51]

The principal cause of death in Batangas, as before, appeared to be malaria, and again the marked increase in malaria deaths can be attributed to a combination of factors.[52] First of all, there are indications that several towns in Batangas suffered from severe shortages of food, especially rice, during at least part of the period of concentration. Rice production had already declined as a consequence of the absence of human labor due to military service and the absence of work beasts due to rinderpest. Now, the situation had worsened because the policy of concentration initially made it impossible for most residents of Batangas to cultivate their land and also because the ongoing epizootic of rinderpest and the destructive practices of

Bell's brigade had almost wiped out the bovine population in the region. In addition, thanks to those destructive practices, mammoth quantities of stored, standing, and recently harvested palay had gone up in smoke.

Aware of the problems, Bell made an effort in late January 1902 to stop the needless destruction, and thereafter, sizable quantities of the palay uncovered by the troops were transported back to the zones. He also instructed station commanders to require the concentrated people to cultivate plots within the zones and to encourage them to plant food on any plot "not situated so far within the mountains as to render it impossible to give laborers any protection." Finally, he arranged to have the Commissary Department supply rice to any towns that experienced shortages.[53] Despite the decrease in destruction, the increase in cultivation, and the shipment of more than six million pounds of rice to Batangas by the Commissary Department during the months of concentration, several towns ran short of rice. At Taal, a station commander named E. F. Willcox reported that the 30,000 Filipinos who were crowded into an area that normally accommodated a sixth of that total "were suffering from want of food." In Lipa, where 43,000 people were confined, rice was sometimes scarce.[54] The shortage of rice and the nutritional deficiencies resulting therefrom may have contributed not only to the sudden virulence of malaria, but also to the susceptibility of the populace to other diseases, for nutritional deficiencies compromise human immune systems, and compromised immune systems are no match for microparasites.

Ironically, the people who were able to keep food on their dinner table may have been even more at risk than those who were not. Supplied with rice by the military authorities when the local stores became exhausted, many people in the zones were obliged to eat imported, thiamine-deficient polished rice rather than the locally grown, hand-pounded, more nutritious varieties that were the normal fare of barrio-dwellers. With a diet that was suddenly thiamine-deficient, they ran the very real risk of contracting beriberi.

Another factor that contributed to the increase in malaria deaths was the aforementioned shortage of bovines in the province. By most counts, between 75 and 95 percent of the cattle population of the province had died by mid-1902, succumbing either to rinderpest or the ravages of warfare.[55] So, the local anophelines, deprived of the bovine blood meals they favored, found it necessary to bite human beings. The result was a rise in the incidence of malaria in eastern Batangas, where the overall level of immunity to the disease was lower.

The last factor of consequence was the policy of concentration itself. By confining large numbers of people in areas that formerly had housed much smaller populations, the U.S. Army was vastly increasing the chances of disease transmission. With several families now typically being accommodated in a single small nipa house, the vectors of disease had a plethora of suitable hosts, and the accompanying microparasites were being passed from one host to another at a much accelerated rate. In fact, the risk of contracting malaria was now considerably greater not only for residents of the población and lowland barrios, who were likely to be nonimmunes, but also for people who normally lived in the uplands, who could have been expected to have acquired a measure of immunity to the disease. The former were at increased risk because the community suddenly included a larger pool of human hosts with infection-producing microparasites in their bloodstreams. The latter were endangered for the simple reason that there were so many susceptibles in their midst. Nonimmunes present a grave threat to people with acquired immunity to malaria because, once those susceptibles become infected, they tend to have extremely high parasite counts. The anophelines that bite the susceptibles become heavily infected themselves, and the large doses of sporozoites they subsequently inject have the capacity to swamp the acquired immunity of human hosts.[56] Under such circumstances, all that was needed to transform increased risk into an epidemic was the presence of anophelines to transmit the microparasites from host to host, and as we already know, those mosquitoes happened to be seeking out humans with great urgency.

Although malaria was the chief agent of death during the period of concentration, it was not the only one. Measles also was an effective killer, as were dysentery and various enteric disorders.[57] The nutritional deficiencies suffered by the concentrated civilians added to the killing power of those diseases, and transmission was facilitated by the crowded conditions prevailing in the zones. In the case of dysentery (both bacillary and amoebic) and other gastrointestinal disorders, poor sanitary practices in the towns also contributed to the spread of disease. Sanitary conditions normally left a good deal to be desired in the provincial Philippines, but they appear to have been woefully deficient during the period of concentration, thanks in no small measure to the U.S. Army's practices. In early May 1902, for example, a U.S. Army surgeon assigned to Lipa reported to his superiors that the "town as a whole is in an extremely dirty and unsanitary condition" and that the Army's own waste removal procedures were "a constant menace to the health of the community." Another officer elaborated a few days later: "I find excreta, dead animals, slop, stable manure, and other filth by the Army have been dumped from 100 to 300 yards from the spring which furnishes drinking water for the entire town. . . . I am surprised that any officer should have allowed such vile filth to be dumped on ground where it is liable to contaminate the water supply."[58] Such hygienic conditions not only expedited the transmission of disease during the last few months of warfare, but also added to the health problems of Batangueños in the months following the conflict.

So Batangas was again experiencing a mortality crisis—a mortality crisis that was, at bottom, a malaria epidemic. Its causes were complicated. Rinderpest and warfare had decimated the cattle population; the malaria-transmitting anophelines were forced to get their meals from people; and the people that the mosquitoes bit, already weakened by malnutrition, often succumbed to the microparasites they received. The role of J. Franklin Bell in this demographic catastrophe was far from unimportant. His troops' operations contributed to the rice shortage and helped to kill the cattle; his policy of confining civilians led to an accelerated rate of disease transmission. But to hold the man or his policies alone responsible for the crisis that occurred would be unfair. Bell was only one human actor in a drama not exclusively about humans. In the appalling demographic crisis that gripped Batangas in the first five months of 1902, some of the key players were mosquitoes, microparasites, and carabaos.

★ Malvar's Surrender

The final scenes of the battle for Batangas were somewhat anticlimactic. Shut off from his civilian supporters in the zones, suffering military reverses in Laguna as well as Batangas, his food supplies gone, his army disappearing, Miguel Malvar was a badly beaten man. But, while his health and that of the family members who accompanied him were failing, while he was obliged to move constantly in order to avoid capture, and while he had become separated from his escort, Malvar was not prepared to quit. Friends, former comrades-in-arms, and prominent Manila-based politicos repeatedly tried to make contact with him in the hills in order to negotiate his surrender, and in February 1902, a seemingly promising peace initiative was launched by Luis Luna, Malvar's recently surrendered adjutant. But on every occasion Malvar refused to meet the would-be negotiators, and somehow he managed to elude his uniformed pursuers as well.[59] Meanwhile, both Dalmacio Hernandez and Nicolas Gonzales were demonstrating a similar kind of defiance, although the strains of the struggle were showing. According to one source, Gonzales was forced to "resort to frightful disciplinary measures in order to hold his men."[60]

Tantalizingly close to victory, J. Franklin Bell was unsure about how to proceed. On the one hand, he seemed to appreciate the utility of negotiating with Malvar. "Far more guns will be obtained through Malvar's surrender than could possibly be obtained through his death, capture, or escape from the islands," he wrote to Wheaton on February 15.[61] But, on the other, as one unsuccessful negotiating effort followed another, Bell came to feel that the Manileños who were taking the lead in the peace offensive—representatives of an organization known as the Peace League—did not know Malvar well enough to gain his trust. In late February, at the request of those Manileños, Bell suspended operations in the area around Rosario, where Malvar was thought to be, in order to create a "quiet zone" where negotiations might take place. But the plan came to nothing, and at the end of March, Bell convinced Chaffee to undertake a major troop movement in that section of Batangas.[62]

In the end, perhaps fittingly, the military pressure applied by Bell produced the sought-for results. On April 4, a scouting party captured Dalmacio Hernandez near the summit of Mount Maquiling, and a few days later, Cipriano Calao and Gregorio Catigbac, two former colonels in the Lipa forces, led an army of no fewer than five hundred Filipino volunteers into the mountainous country in eastern Batangas that Malvar was known to frequent.[63] Malvar's situation was completely hopeless. He had no staff officer, no clerk to write his orders, and no serviceable weapon. He was surrounded by American soldiers and native volunteers. His wife, who was nursing his two smallest children, was running a high fever and had not eaten for several days. Malvar also realized that, if the war were to go on, the people in the region would be unable to begin the planting of rice in May and many would die of hunger. So, on April 13, believing that he could hold out no longer, he sent word to Luis Luna, asking for a chance to talk. Three days later, after receiving assurances that he would be treated fairly by the Americans, he marched into Lipa and surrendered to General Bell.[64]

Once Malvar had come in, most of the remaining guerrilla leaders in the region followed suit. Later in the day on April 16, Nicolas Gonzales had a meeting with General Bell in Tanauan, offered to surrender, and subsequently brought in the remainder of his troops. Briccio Casala turned himself in on April 30, and some lesser figures held out for a few more days.[65] In the meantime, Bell had taken steps to return Batangas to civilian control. Most political prisoners were quickly released from prison. Station commanders were instructed to release civilians from the zones, and by the end of April, they had returned to their homes. The ports of the province were reopened.[66] By the first week of May 1902, the battle for Batangas was over.

Epilogue

THE BATTLE MAY HAVE BEEN OVER, but the dying was not. The level of mortality in Batangas remained high throughout May 1902, as many people succumbed to maladies (particularly malaria) contracted during the period of forced concentration. Then, in the final days of that month, U.S. military authorities detected a still more deadly disease, cholera, in an outlying barrio of Tanauan.[1]

In fact, the outbreak of cholera in Batangas was hardly unexpected. The disease had been ravaging Asia since 1900 and had first been reported in Manila in March 1902. Although American civilian and military officials had taken steps to contain its spread—the burning of the houses of cholera victims (an ill-conceived measure that did nothing to arrest the transmission of the infection); the removal of sick persons to hospitals; the isolation of individuals who had been in contact with victims; the strict enforcement of sanitary regulations; the restriction of population movement—the containment policy had failed, principally because the Americans were unable to monitor effectively the human traffic in the provinces. In some cases, the disease was spread by U.S. troops; more often, the carriers of the cholera vibrios were Filipinos who managed to sneak through the Americans' *cordon sanitaire*.[2] By early April, cholera had made its way to neighboring Laguna, and military officers in Batangas were bracing themselves for its arrival into their own province.[3]

Conditions for the transmission of cholera in Batangas were ideal. Sanitary practices during the period of concentration (in part the deficient waste removal procedures of the occupying army) had compromised water supplies, as in the case of Lipa. Compromised water supplies served as convenient conduits for cholera vibrios. Furthermore, the trying experiences of the preceding months—the forced relocations, the massive property destruction, the increased exposure to disease, the suffering that attended the loss of loved ones, and the many other traumas—had taken a severe physical and psychological toll on the populace. Thus debilitated, many of them were easy targets for the new epidemiological invaders.

They were easy targets for another reason. The ongoing food crisis, which had been exacerbated by the incendiary tactics of Bell's brigade during the final campaign, had become more acute. Col. George S. Anderson, commander of the garrison at Lipa, wrote on June 8, "I assure you that in spite of the fact that some natives hold small stores of palay here, a vast number of the people are in actual want, and charity must soon be resorted to." The situation in San Juan was more serious. "Emergency," the post commander wrote to his superiors on June 15. "Natives suffering acutely notwithstanding rice already distributed."[4]

Several developments were responsible for the escalation of the food crisis. First, the cattle were still dying from rinderpest, and, to compound the problem, the pool of human labor was still depleted as a result of the heavy loss of life and high rate of morbidity during the past several months.[5] Because of the shortage of work animals and agriculturists, only a small percentage of the cultivable land was being cultivated. In addition, the U.S. Army's cholera-control measures had reduced food stores in the region, for, by attempting to restrict human traffic, they interfered with the normal trade patterns between areas which produced surpluses and those which were dependent on outside supplies. Finally, there were the locusts. Clouds of the insect pests began to appear in Batangas in mid-June, and they continued to plague the province through September, inflicting huge losses on the already-reduced rice crop.[6] As before, the Americans attempted to meet the needs of the populace by distributing rice, but the supplies were often slow in arriving, and throughout July and August 1902, reports were received that several towns were suffering from a lack of food.[7] Almost certainly, malnourishment elevated death rates in Batangas during the cholera epidemic.

The inevitable result of all these conditions—the introduction of the cholera vibrios, the poor state of sanitation, the debilitated psychological state of the populace, the escalating food crisis—was an awful human tragedy. The cholera epidemic of 1902 was a collective nightmare for the inhabitants of the southern Tagalog region, far more devastating in its demographic impact than the more written-about period of concentration that preceded it. The new disease struck quickly and ruthlessly, wiped out entire households and came close to eliminating entire barrios, and just as quickly disappeared. In Batangas itself, it did its damage in the two months of June and July 1902. And while it lasted, death was everywhere.

While the epidemic was raging and after it was over, a number of officials made efforts to estimate the toll. The commissioner of public health, who viewed the events from Manila, reckoned that 2,330 Batangueños had died from cholera through September 1, 1902. The following year, a new commissioner revised the figure upward to 2,430. The military authorities, who led the government's efforts to stop the spread of the disease, found about 5,000 deaths in Batangas. But the highest figures of all were those compiled by the governments of the individual municipalities; in all, they counted 10,383 cholera victims.[8]

No one who knew anything about the epidemic had much confidence in the numbers. One American who expressed his doubts frequently was G. C. Saffarrans, the post commander at San Juan and a conscientious keeper of records. In late July, he complained to his superiors that "not more than one fourth" of the actual number of deaths were being reported. "One month ago municipal authorities asked me for permission for cholera corpses to be buried in barrios where they died instead of being brought to the cemetery and having to pay [the] padre's fee. . . . Have every reason to believe corpses [are] being disposed of at night in barrios." Saffarrans's impressions were widely shared by his fellow officers. The ranking army surgeon in the Philippines wrote in the same month, "With the increase of the epidemic the proportion of recorded cases has very much dropped, and it is probable in the whole archipelago not more than one fifth of the cholera cases are now being reported."[9] As it happened, the people's desire to avoid paying the church's burial fee was not the only reason for their failure to report the deaths of family members. A more compelling one was their objection to the measures adopted by the authorities to stop the spread of the disease: quarantine, the assignment of the infected to hospitals, the burning of soiled clothing, and others. Hence, for not the last time, American Army officers found themselves in a Catch-22: if they attempted to enforce the regulations, they got no reports; and if they got no reports, it was impossible to enforce the regulations; and the only way to be assured of getting more reports was to stop enforcing the regulations.

If the statements made by the American officers are not sufficient reason to question the received statistics, the statistics themselves should make us suspicious. According to the municipal authorities, only 113 of the 10,383 cholera victims in Batangas were children under the age of one.[10] That figure seems incredibly low. As on many matters, medical authorities are in sharp disagreement about the incidence and effects of cholera among infants. A number suggest that the incidence is low and hint that breast-feeding might explain the phenomenon. Others—above all, researchers studying cholera El Tor in the Philippines—maintain that the rate of infection is high among infants, although most appear to be asymptomatic carriers. In any case, what studies of both classic and El Tor cholera generally agree upon is that the mortality rate among infants can be expected to be fairly close to that among the population at large.[11] During the cholera epidemic of 1902, it was, according to the statistics, about one-quarter of its expected rate. Most of the families of infant victims of cholera were not reporting the deaths to the municipalities.

Almost ninety years after the events, it is impossible to make an accurate estimate of the number of cholera victims in Batangas. The figure of 10,383 is certainly too low. On the other hand, it would be rash, without better evidence, to assert that we should multiply the official totals by four or five, as the aforementioned army officers suggest. My estimate is that at least 20,000 Batangueños were killed by cholera in 1902. And even that figure would understate the total contribution of the cholera epidemic to Batangas's demographic crisis. Birth rates in late 1902 and early 1903 would also have suffered, since a high rate of terminated pregnancies can be expected among women contracting cholera.

Yet, to a certain extent, figures such as the ones discussed above fail to convey a true sense of the catastrophe that transpired in Batangas during the cholera epidemic. What was it really like for the poor, bewildered people of San Juan, the town that had endured the highest mortality rate in the province during the months of concentration, to experience the loss of no fewer than 1,000 more townmates—about 10 percent of the population—during June and July 1902? Or for the residents of the remote municipality of Calatagan to lose approximately 600 of their friends, neighbors, and relatives—at least a fifth of the town's inhabitants—in that same two-month period?[12] The sources tell us very little about the emotional dimension of the crisis. The American military authorities, on their part, frustrated by the failure of their efforts to control the spread of the disease, manifested little sympathy for the plight of the Batangueños, and, if anything, they appeared to hold the Filipinos responsible for the enormity of the losses. Discussing the high rate of mortality in Calatagan, Bell remarked, "Most of the natives, being ignorant and superstitious, the latter involving fatalism, had no faith in [the cholera-control] measures and were much opposed to the restrictions involved."[13] An Army surgeon in Lipa offered a slightly different analysis: "Such quarantine must always be ineffectual through the duplicity of the native character and the ignorance of the masses."[14] What both officers failed to point out was that the measures adopted by the Americans, often unnecessarily severe, may have been largely to blame for the Filipinos' unwillingness to cooperate.

The cholera epidemic of 1902 was the culminating episode in a period of crisis mortality that had begun in Batangas in 1896. Although it did not occur within the chronological limits of the conflict in Batangas and while it clearly was not caused by the war—cholera was pandemic in Asia at the time—one can hardly deny that it had an intimate connection to the Philippine-American War. Wartime health and sanitary conditions facilitated the spread of the disease; food shortages, partly created by the war, made the malady more lethal; and the cholera-control measures of the U.S. military authorities made a bad situation worse. Once again, while we cannot hold the Americans solely responsible for the high death rates in Batangas, we cannot discount their role either.

As 1902 gave way to 1903, the province of Batangas finally returned to a semblance of demographic normality. Mortality rates tapered off, as no new epidemics appeared. Birth rates picked up. But the combined demographic effects of the epidemiological crises of the preceding six years could not be easily overcome—a fact that was made clear by the results of the first American census, which was taken in March 1903. The enumerators were able to find a total of 257,715 people in Batangas, or approximately 55,000 fewer people than had been counted in the province at the time of the last complete Spanish census in 1887. Even though the American census-takers probably missed as many as 10,000 Batangueños in their count, there can be little doubt that the province had suffered a crippling loss.[15]

★ The Accommodation of the Elites

Although the Americans received little cooperation from the local populace in their cholera-containment campaign, the same could not be said about their efforts to establish civil government in Batangas. As we have already seen, with the introduction of the concentration policy in Batangas and the application of extreme pressure to "persons of influence," more and more members of Batangas's economic and political elites had decided to make their peace with the American regime. They revealed the location of hidden weapons, helped to arrange the surrender of their nephews and neighbors, and pledged their allegiance to the government in Washington. Once Malvar had surrendered, accommodation became almost universal among elite Batangueños.

How can the accommodation of these Batangueños be explained? To begin with, pure pragmatism played a part. After Malvar's surrender, most inhabitants of the province, rich and poor alike, had little choice but to come to terms with their new rulers.[16] The process of accommodation was also facilitated by the Americans themselves, who made a decision to deal charitably with their defeated foes. Although hundreds of Batangueños were held in confinement at the end of the war on charges ranging from collecting taxes for the guerrillas to killing suspected collaborators, most were set free by early June 1902, and all but a handful of the rest were liberated shortly thereafter, the beneficiaries of an amnesty proclamation issued on July 4 by President Roosevelt.[17] Among the many former guerrillas who escaped punishment as a consequence of this benevolent approach were two stalwarts of the San Miguel Column, Eliseo Claudio and Tomas Ramirez, both of whom were being investigated for murder. Malvar himself was not prosecuted. The U.S. authorities also rewarded Filipinos who rendered assistance in pacifying the province by appointing them to posts in the colonial service.[18]

Once resigned to alien rule, Batangueños quickly discovered that the American colonial regime had a good deal to offer. American-supervised schools gave Filipinos of all social classes the opportunity to learn English, arithmetic, and other subjects. Although the schools never effected the kind of radical social engineering that U.S. colonial administrators wished to see, they won many friends for the Americans. Also appreciated were American programs of road, bridge, and port construction, which facilitated travel as well as commerce. Beyond all that, the system of local government established by the Taft Commission had attractions for elite Filipinos. By initially restricting suffrage to Filipinos with wealth, education, and previous governmental service, the U.S. colonial regime provided an opportunity for the existing elites—including, of course, the leaders of the recent resistance—to retain their dominant positions in communities. Such benefits were no substitute for independence, nor could they completely erase the painful memories of Bell's campaign, but they served to mollify a sizable segment of a once-hostile populace.[19]

And so, seemingly overnight, the traditional leaders of Batangueño society—the same people who had been the major figures in Malvar's resistance—came to terms with the new realities. In Lipa, long a center of resistance activity, the man chosen in April 1902 to be vice president of the municipal government was Gregorio Catigbac, once a colonel in Malvar's forces but now a willing agent of the U.S. regime; Cipriano Calao, another former colonel, served as chief of police. Catigbac would be elected municipal president in 1905 and two years later became a delegate to the newly created Philippine Assembly. Another key figure in Lipa's postwar political life was Gregorio Aguilera Solis, formerly the leader of the town's covert resistance, who was elected provincial governor in 1905. In Batangas City, Briccio Casala, another war hero, would be elected to the municipal council in 1903, and he was joined the following year by Lucio Buenafe. Lucio's brother, Juan, began his public service as inspector of municipal licenses in 1904 and eventually rose to the position of municipal president. Martin Cabrera of Taal, the former brigadier general, became a member of the provincial board in 1908, and he was replaced two years later by Luis Luna, Malvar's onetime adjutant. The town of San Jose chose Fernando Aguila, a major in the resistance army, as its municipal president in 1904. Nicolas Gonzales, a major figure in both the Philippine Revolution and the Philippine-American War, was to be elected municipal president of Tanauan and, later, provincial governor. While it is within the realm of possibility that one or two of these officials may have been figureheads rather than true political heavyweights, most were definitely men of standing and substantial influence.[20]

Miguel Malvar, for his part, did not return to political life. Shortly after his surrender, he and General Bell concluded an agreement requiring him to reside in Manila for a year in exchange for a payment of 1,800 pesos to cover living expenses. Malvar received the money, but he was still residing in

Santo Tomas in early September 1902, and it is unclear from the historical record whether he fulfilled his part of the bargain. In subsequent years, Malvar devoted his energies to agricultural work, producing abaca, oranges, and sugar cane, and building a poultry business. His enterprises prospered, and when he died in October 1911, the victim of a liver ailment contracted during his years in the hills, he owned approximately a thousand hectares of productive agricultural land on Mount Maquiling.[21]

Even though Malvar did not hold office under the American regime, he and his family eventually reached an accommodation with the former enemy. Four of Malvar's sons received their university education in the United States—Bernabe at Cornell, Marciano at the University of Pennsylvania, Maximo at the University of Chicago, and Miguel, Jr. at Purdue—and his brother, Potenciano, served both as governor of Laguna and a member of the Philippine Assembly. In his final days, Malvar himself came to be considered something of a friend of the Americans. A day after the famous Batangueño's death, W. Cameron Forbes, then governor-general, confided in his diary that the onetime guerrilla leader was "a very strong and fine Filipino." In 1922, another governor-general, Leonard Wood, approved an act of the Philippine legislature establishing an intermediate school in Santo Tomas as a memorial to Malvar.[22]

We should not conclude that elite Batangueños had become blindly subservient to the American regime. A number of Batangas's political figures were extremely critical of U.S. rule, and many openly agitated for Philippine independence, as did almost every Filipino politician from 1905 on.[23] A few of them may have gone a step further. Beginning in late 1909, reports were received in Manila from agents of the Philippine Constabulary to the effect that Ananias Diocno, Felipe Agoncillo, Briccio Casala, and other Batangueños were conspiring with Japanese officials to mount an uprising in the Philippines. Although several of the reports were later shown to have been fabricated and while the chief of the Constabulary, Harry H. Bandholtz, considered others to be grossly exaggerated, we cannot dismiss the possibility that a certain number of elite Batangueños may have continued to harbor revolutionary sentiments.[24]

However subversive such elite Batangueños may have been, they appear to have been exceptional; for most individuals of this kind, the battle was over, and a new approach was necessary. And because they recognized and accepted the new regime, the end of the war, like the war itself, brought little change in political leadership in Batangas. Prewar politicos had become agitators and revolutionaries; agitators and revolutionaries had become wartime leaders; and wartime leaders now became the core of the postwar provincial political elite. Of course, the political leadership would not always be the same in Batangas; in time, as new families entered the ranks of the well-to-do, some of them would be able to crack into the ranks of the politically influential. The nature of local politics would not remain the same either; because of the new type of elections introduced by the Americans and the gradual expansion of the electorate, leaders would have to develop new techniques to gain and maintain control.[25] But, for about two decades following the battle for Batangas, the families who controlled provincial politics were essentially the ones who had directed the anti-American struggle.

★ Disturbances in the Hills

While the accommodation of the elites helped to bring a measure of stability to Batangas in the years immediately following the Philippine-American War, life in the province was not uniformly peaceful during that period. Batangas was officially returned to civil government on July 4, 1902, but the Philippine Constabulary, now charged with the responsibility of keeping the peace, was obliged to work overtime at the job, especially in the upland areas of southwestern Luzon.

One major source of trouble was the Colorum, the lower-class organization that had provided Malvar with financial support during the last stages of the battle for Batangas. While the U.S. command considered the Colorum to be dangerous, Bell's brigade had focused its attention during the final campaign on neutralizing the opposition of the indigenous upper class. Consequently, even though the U.S. forces captured a number of the leaders of the Colorum (including Sebastian Caneo) during the period December 1901–April 1902, they did not inflict serious damage on the organization.[26] Once the inhabitants of the region were permitted to leave the zones of concentration, the Colorum began to function again, and by late 1902 there was unrest in the mountainous territory on the Batangas–Laguna–Tayabas border, the longtime center of Colorum activity. The Colorum continued to grow in the southern Tagalog region during subsequent years, and in the first few months of 1910, Constabulary agents filed reports that members of the society were "preparing for insurrection and taking contributions."[27]

At the same time, the Constabulary units stationed in Batangas had to cope with several hundred troublemakers they referred to as ladrones. Like the ladrones of the late Spanish period, these individuals were not necessarily, one and all, hardened criminals.[28] True, the bands to which they belonged were often guilty of questionable behavior: they rustled carabaos, extorted money from barrio-dwellers, resorted to violence. A number of them even employed terror tactics, as W. Cameron Forbes discovered on a visit to the southern Tagalog region in 1904: "When I called in Batangas a few days ago they told me there were several men in the hospital whose lips had been cut off and faces otherwise mutilated by the ladrones because they were suspected of having given information as to their whereabouts to the troops."[29]

As was the case in prewar Batangas, however, some of the bands received support from the inhabitants of the province. One that was popular was led by Aniceto Oruga, the ladrone-turned-revolutionary, who had risen to the rank of lieutenant colonel during the Philippine-American War. Captured in January 1902, he was sentenced to two years of hard labor because of his involvement in the war, but the U.S. authorities later released him and Oruga returned to the hills and organized a band.[30] Following an attack on Taal by ladrones affiliated with Oruga in January 1905, Col. D. J. Baker reported that "most of the townspeople remained quietly in their houses, but some openly fraternized with the bandits." Another Constabulary officer admitted that the people were "sympathizing with and aiding" the armed bands.[31] At the very least, Oruga's men should be considered "social bandits"; one can even make a case that their activities were a continuation of the earlier resistance.

The armed bands of the postwar period had another connection to the earlier resistance. According to the Constabulary reports, many of the bands, including Oruga's, professed allegiance to Macario Sakay, head of a revolutionary movement based in the mountains of the southern Tagalog region. Formerly a barber in Manila and an early member of Bonifacio's Katipunan, Sakay had been an active participant in both the Philippine Revolution and the Philippine-American War. Captured in 1901 and later set free, Sakay continued to oppose U.S. sovereignty. Sometime in 1902, he emerged as head of the "Republic of Katagalugan," a revolutionary organization that aimed to revive the spirit of the original Katipunan. Expressing ideas similar to those in Malvar's proclamation of April 1901, Sakay called for unity among all Filipinos in the struggle against the Americans and decried the tendency of the upper classes to look down on the lower. By 1905, Sakay had developed a following among the rural populace of southwestern Luzon, and the bands that were affiliated with his republic were beneficiaries of the relationship.[32]

Concerned about Sakay, the bands that followed him, and the growing rural unrest, the Philippine Commission decided in late January 1905 to suspend the writ of habeas corpus in both Batangas and Cavite, and in subsequent months, it ordered that the inhabitants of several barrios of Taal, Tanauan, Santo Tomas, Nasugbu, and other towns be concentrated "in order to protect peaceable citizens and to prevent the furnishing of supplies to the ladrones."[33] Intensified military operations by the Constabulary, assisted by U.S. Army units, resulted in the capture, killing, or surrender of most of the leaders of Sakay's republic. Oruga was captured in 1905; Sakay surrendered in July 1906, and he was later tried and executed.[34] Still, the elimination of these men did not end the rural disturbances in Batangas and the rest of the southern Tagalog region. Bands continued to roam the hills and millenarian organizations continued to gain adherents.[35]

The unrest described above was not unique to Batangas or to the revolutionary period: bands and lower-class movements of many types had long existed in the Philippine countryside. But, unique or not, it was a strong indication of rural dwellers' ongoing dissatisfaction with the world as they found it. Spanish colonialism had offered them little; Malvar's resistance had briefly raised hopes; American colonialism had forged an alliance of a sort with the elites but made no effort to meet the needs of poor peasants. And so, in a real sense, Bell's defeat of Malvar had resulted in a most incomplete victory; beyond the poblaciones frequented by the elites, there was another Batangas inhabited by the occupants of the lower rungs, and it remained unsettled and ultimately unsatisfied.

★ The Victor's Perspective

For the victorious U.S. Army, and for the general who led the final campaign, the immediate aftermath of the battle for Batangas had a bittersweet quality. Although Bell received the congratulations of President Roosevelt and the members of his brigade could take satisfaction in their defeat of Malvar, the general found himself under attack in the months following his victory, and both he and his subordinates were obliged to defend their actions in official investigations.[36]

Questions about the U.S. Army's actions in Batangas had first been raised in late January 1902, shortly after reports about Bell's concentration policy had appeared in the American press. Several newspapers had characterized the general's measures as inhuman, likening Bell to "Butcher" Weyler in Cuba. "Who would have supposed," asked the *Philadelphia Ledger,* "that the same policy would be, only four years later, adopted and pursued as the policy of the United States in the Philippines?"[37]

The criticism abated after a few weeks, but then, some disturbing revelations brought Batangas back into the public's view. On April 7, 1902, a member of the Senate Committee on the Philippines, which had been holding hearings on conditions in the islands for several months, revealed that he had recently learned about the existence of a report critical of the U.S. Army's conduct of the war. The report had been written in December 1901 by Maj. Cornelius Gardener, the provincial governor of Tayabas. The committee asked the War Department to turn over the document, and it was promptly furnished, together with another report, also composed in December 1901, by Florencio Caedo, then provincial secretary of Batangas. Both documents suggested troubling things about the war in the southern Tagalog region. Gardener claimed that the resistance against the United States in Tayabas had essentially ended by mid-1901, implying that the escalation of U.S. military operations in the province during Bell's campaign had been unnecessary. He charged as well that the U.S. forces operating in Tayabas had been guilty of atrocious behavior, including the burning of an extensive amount of property and the administration of the water cure. "The course now being pursued in this province, and in the provinces of Batangas, Laguna, and Samar," he wrote, "is in my opinion sowing the seeds of a perpetual revolution, or at least preparing the people of these provinces to rise up in revolution against us whenever a good opportunity offers." Caedo described the sad state of agriculture in Batangas, warned about the possibility of famine, and asserted that the province had already experienced a massive population loss. "The mortality," he wrote, "caused no longer by the war, but by disease, such as malaria and dysentery, has reduced to a little over 200,000 the more than 300,000 inhabitants which in former years the province had."[38] While Caedo's report (written *before* the introduction of Bell's concentration measures) exaggerated the population decline, it provided the American public with one of the first hints that Batangas was experiencing a demographic crisis.

Other disturbing moments occurred in May 1902. Senator Augustus Bacon read on the Senate floor the famous letter about mortality in the zones. A U.S. soldier who had been stationed in Batangas told the Senate Committee on the Philippines that he had observed American troops administer the water cure in the province. That same committee included in the record a collection of documents relating to the Lopez family of Balayan which suggested, among other things, that the U.S. Army in Batangas had resorted to torture.[39]

The revelations were followed in short order by two investigations, both of them conducted by the very organizations—the War Department and the

U.S. Army—that had the most to lose should the charges be confirmed. The first, which took place in the Philippines between late April and mid-July 1902, was an inquiry by a board of officers into Major Gardener's controversial report. Since Gardener's charges related largely to conditions in Tayabas, the testimony heard by the board focused on that province, rather than Batangas. Still, the witnesses, who included Miguel Malvar and several other leaders of the Batangueño officer corps, discussed conditions in Batangas at some length and many of their statements about the U.S. Army's conduct of the war in Tayabas applied to the conflict in Batangas as well.[40]

The board, which was composed of three officers who had served under Bell, concentrated on Gardener's two principal accusations: that Tayabas had been pacified at least six months before Bell's arrival in the southern Tagalog region and that the U.S. troops had been guilty of atrocious behavior. The first charge was basically incorrect, and most of the witnesses who paraded before the board flatly contradicted Gardener, asserting that there was widespread support for the resistance in Tayabas up to the end of 1901. The other charge was much closer to the mark, and a large number of witnesses described in graphic detail the nasty conduct of the American troops. Such testimony notwithstanding, the board concluded on July 17, 1902, that Gardener's entire report was without foundation—that he had not accurately described conditions in Tayabas and had misrepresented the actions of the U.S. Army. Five months later, the judge advocate general, after reviewing the record of the proceedings, concurred with the board's judgment.[41]

The investigation into Caedo's allegations produced similar results. General Chaffee launched a probe into the matter on June 15, 1902, asking Bell to pose a number of specific questions to Caedo:

> It is desired to know if the Provincial Secretary wishes to be understood as meaning that the loss of one hundred thousand people in the province of Batangas from malaria and dysentery is due in any wise to the occupation of the Province by United States troops. . . . What date in the past does he fix as the starting point for the losses he refers to? How does he obtain data for the number—one hundred thousand?

Challenged, Caedo promptly backed down. The population loss, he explained, had begun long before the outbreak of the Philippine-American War, and his calculations had been based on data obtained from only two towns. "It was very far from the intention of the writer to attribute the loss of so many lives to any rigorous measures taken by the American troops of occupation, nor to give the impression that it had only occurred in the years 1900 and 1901." The provincial treasurer, an American named R. D. Blanchard, was then asked to comment on Caedo's report, and after a two-day investigation, he concluded that, while the death rate from disease had recently been high, the population of the province had "decreased but little."[42]

Finally, Bell looked into the question himself. At his request, the provincial authorities directed municipal officials to determine whether a population decline had occurred in their towns, and if so, what had caused it. Their reports came in, and after reading them, Bell filed his own report, dated September 10, 1902. The general's conclusion, not surprisingly, was that Caedo's assertions had been erroneous: that, while there had indeed been a population loss in Batangas, a number of developments—the revolution against Spain, emigration, diseases, as well as the war against the United States—had combined to produce that result.[43]

If Bell's conclusions were predictable, his report was intriguing all the same, because of a one-page attachment which summarized the municipalities' estimates of the population losses between 1896 and 1902. The municipal officials indicated that, over that six-year period, the province's population had fallen from 332,456 to 241,721—a decline of more than 90,000 people.[44] In fact, then, the loss estimated by the officials was not appreciably different from that suggested by Caedo's report. (Also, the population figure derived from the municipalities' estimates, 241,721, would turn out to be remarkably close to the 257,715 figure that census enumerators arrived at in March 1903.) Aware that the municipalities' totals raised troubling questions, Bell made an effort in the final paragraphs of his report to explain them away. He characterized the population figures and the estimated losses as "merely rough guesses," and then went on:

> Of course, I am unable to state what the losses may have been, as I have no data on which to base an accurate opinion, but *inasmuch as so many people could not have died or emmigrated [sic] without attracting considerable attention, and inasmuch as no report appears to have ever been made indicating such extraordinary losses,* it would seem to me reasonable to conclude that the estimates of losses made by the municipal councils are excessive, as well as that made in the report of the provincial [secretary] of last December. [Emphasis added.]

And there the investigation ended. Bell sent his report to General Chaffee, and Chaffee forwarded it to Washington with his endorsement. Conceding an "apparent heavy loss in population," he insisted that the U.S. occupation of the province and the operations of the American troops had not been responsible for it. "Probably fifty per cent of this is due to emigration to other provinces because of the disturbed conditions in Batangas due to insistent insurrection for nearly six years."[45]

The investigation of Caedo's allegations was nothing more than a charade. While it was true that Caedo, writing in December 1901, had overstated the population loss, it was just as true that Bell, writing in September 1902, was predisposed to understate it. In the intervening nine months, owing to the combined contributions of the concentration policy, malaria, and cholera, the province's population had fallen precipitously—in other words, the demographic catastrophe described by Caedo had actually come to pass. And while Bell was right in claiming that the revolution against Spain, migration, and other factors were in part responsible for the observed loss of population, he failed to acknowledge that throughout the American occupation of the province U.S. military operations, by forcing people to flee from the towns to the hills, had contributed to the high rate of mortality in the province.

These investigations as well as the criticism in the press that preceded them were extremely distressing to Bell. He believed, as he told Sen. Albert Beveridge in August 1902, "that what I was doing was the most humane thing I could do under the circumstances, and that my policy was inspired by sympathy and kindness and not by resentment or a desire to punish."[46] Even though the inquiries appeared to vindicate him, Bell remained uneasy, evidently wounded by the lingering implication that he had done something wrong. In December 1902, he published a compilation of the telegraphic circulars he had issued during the final campaign, and he passed it on to Secretary of War Elihu Root with a cover letter. "Everything I did during the campaign in Batangas, and nearly always the motive therefor, is indicated in the enclosed small pamphlet," he wrote. "I gave no verbal orders or authority for anything not authorized in this pamphlet. I should feel much gratified if you would find time to personally read it." Aware of Bell's discomfort, Root attempted to reassure the general: "I hope you will give yourself no uneasiness regarding the appreciation and approval which your course in the Batangas campaign receives from the War Department. An examination of the orders issued by you has developed no reason for changing the opinion expressed in a telegram [conveying President Roosevelt's congratulations] immediately after the surrender of Malvar."[47]

Bell need not have worried. By early 1903, the Philippine-American War was already becoming a dim memory to the U.S. public, and there was little residual interest in atrocities and demographic disasters in faraway Batangas. Bell moved on to another assignment, becoming head of the Infantry and Cavalry School at Fort Leavenworth, Kansas. In April 1906, President Roosevelt appointed him chief of staff of the U.S. Army, a post Bell retained until April 1910. When he died in 1919, he was lauded as one of the outstanding leaders of the U.S. Army in the post–Civil War era.[48]

Recovering the Philippine Past

THIS BOOK TAKES ISSUE with a widely held view about the Philippine past: the notion, stated in works of Teodoro Agoncillo and other scholars, that the Filipino resistance during the Philippine-American War was a mass-based phenomenon. The evidence I have assembled shows that, in the province of Batangas, the anticolonial struggle was both directed and assisted by members of local elites. It also suggests that, for much of the conflict, the indigenous lower classes were not necessarily dogged and enthusiastic supporters of the resistance.

How can it be that my findings differ so much from the standard version of the events? One possible answer, hinted at throughout this book, is that earlier writers may have overstated their case. Let us consider for a moment the writings of Agoncillo and Renato Constantino. Although both authors repeatedly assert that the Filipino "masses" were unabashedly patriotic and completely committed to fighting the Americans, they do not prove their assertions. True, throughout the Philippines, many lower-class Filipinos served in the Filipino Army and many others gave money and supplies to the soldiers in the field and otherwise contributed to the war effort. But the statements of both authors refer to attitudes as well as actions, and they provide no evidence to demonstrate why the lower classes acted as they did and what they felt about the war.[1] William Henry Scott's more recent study of the war in the Ilocos region displays similar characteristics. Although Scott proves that support for the resistance was widespread in the Ilocos, once he shifts from a description of behavior to an explanation of attitudes, he makes the same kind of undocumented assertions that can be found in Agoncillo and Constantino. "The simplest explanation for this support," Scott writes, "is the same patriotism that inspired the resistance itself—that is, the defense of native soil and the dream of independence."[2]

It should be noted, parenthetically, that Agoncillo, Constantino, and other writers on the Philippine-American War have thus far only scratched the surface on the issues of resistance and collaboration. Agoncillo's own research focuses almost exclusively on events at the center of the Philippine Republic—that is to say, on Manila, Malolos, and to a lesser extent, Cavite, and while he does make a case that a few "Haves" in those places collaborated with the Americans, we learn next to nothing about the actions and attitudes of Haves elsewhere in the archipelago. Constantino, on his part, has relied largely on Agoncillo's research. Scott and Orlino Ochosa deal exclusively with the Ilocano provinces. John Schumacher concentrates on the contributions of the indigenous clergy. Reynaldo Ileto, whose celebrated study of lower-class mentalities in the Tagalog provinces deals at length with the revolutionary period, is interested principally in *perceptions,* rather than in behavior or attitudes, and one wonders whether the perceptions he describes were widely shared by lowland peasants. Ma. Fe Hernaez Romero and Elias Ataviado, who write about Negros Occidental and the Bikol region, respectively, have not examined the extensive body of source materials on the war available in U.S. archives.[3] Despite the many merits of the aforementioned accounts, it is apparent that a great deal of basic spadework remains to be done.

A second possibility also merits consideration, and it is, I hasten to point out, suggested by some of the evidence in this book: that the differences between my own account of the resistance in Batangas and the Agoncillo/Constantino version of the entire anti-American struggle may be somewhat less pronounced than I appear to claim. To be sure, I disagree completely with what they have written about the role of upper-class Filipinos. On the other hand, it may be argued that I have merely called into question, but not undermined, the Agoncillo/Constantino position on lower-class attitudes during the resistance.

One point that emerges from my discussion of both the Philippine Revolution and the Philippine-American War is that the sources do not allow us to answer many key questions about the occupants of the lower rungs. Hence, while it is obvious that lower-class support for the resistance in Batangas was far from universal during the first year of the American occupation and also that Agoncillo and Constantino can be faulted for using words like "unshaken," "spontaneous," and "wholehearted" to characterize the attitudes of the lower classes, it is not at all obvious how faulty their characterization is. In *Battle for Batangas,* I demonstrate what lower-class attitudes were *not,* but, given the sources at my disposal, I cannot conclusively demonstrate what they were.

Furthermore, as my study strongly implies at several points, the occupants of the lower rungs had the *potential,* under the right circumstances, to rally enthusiastically to the anticolonial cause. In the struggle against Spain, Andres Bonifacio seemed to be capable of appealing effectively to them, and in the last year of the Batangueños' battle against the Americans, Malvar was able to do the same. One characteristic of both successful appeals was that they called not merely for political autonomy but also for freedom from upper-class oppression—which is to say, both Bonifacio and Malvar offered the lower rungs a very different vision of the future from someone like Aguinaldo, whose policies and pronouncements were designed to promote the interests of the upper classes. Their ability to mobilize popular support suggests that the lower classes (or, at least, a healthy percentage of them) may actually have felt a deep commitment to the ideal of Philippine independence, but that their notion of independence, one that fused both national and class aspirations, was at odds with that held by elite Filipinos. What they may have wanted was kalayaan, in the sense that Bonifacio had earlier used the word: freedom from both alien and upper-class oppression. Thus, so long as the anticolonial struggles were controlled by elites, lower-class participation had to be coerced. But, once Malvar signaled that the occupants of the lower rungs would be treated justly, they supported the resistance with genuine enthusiasm—the sort of enthusiasm that, according to Agoncillo and Constantino, they supposedly demonstrated throughout the Philippine-American War.

Having raised this second possibility, I feel compelled to add a few words of qualification. Although there may be a measure of truth in the Agoncillo/Constantino interpretation of lower-class attitudes, one should recognize that the questions I have raised about it are both fundamental and troubling. It surely makes a difference that some lower-class participants in the Batangueño resistance were either reluctant or unwilling, that some poor residents of Batangas collaborated with the enemy, and that patterns of support for the resistance changed over time. Such nuances are absent from the writings of Agoncillo and Constantino, and they are anything but insignificant.

One final possibility needs to be discussed: that the patterns of resistance and collaboration in the Philippines may have varied markedly from place to place. A few of the studies cited above provide evidence to that effect, and there are, in any event, other reasons for suspecting that such may have been the case. Anyone familiar with the Philippines is aware that there are striking social, economic, and ethnic differences among the many regions of the archipelago, and research conducted over the past two decades in the field of Philippine local history demonstrates that there was much variation in the historical evolution of those regions.[4] Under such circumstances, it seems logical, even likely, that Filipino attitudes and behavior during the war against the Americans would have been anything but monolithic—that, to elaborate on the point, there would have been comparatively more support for the Philippine Republic in Tagalog provinces like Batangas, in part at least because Aguinaldo's government was dominated by Tagalogs, and that, even within such provinces, the support would have been stronger among the political and economic elites than among the occupants of the lower rungs because Aguinaldo was committed to promoting elite interests.

As historians work their way through the mountains of documents in Philippine and American archives on the Philippine-American War, a clearer picture of the conflict will emerge, but it is doubtful, in my view, that it will bear much resemblance to the one painted by Agoncillo and his followers. Although such scholars would like us to believe that the masses struggled wholeheartedly against the colonial powers, and that elite Filipinos were relentlessly collaborationist, it seems almost certain that their characterizations are serious distortions of historical realities. Commitment to a cause was not a monopoly of the lower classes, nor was collaboration with the enemy a monopoly of the upper. I would guess, then, that as more research is done the picture that will emerge will be a variegated one (in contrast to the monochromatic one found in the books of Agoncillo and Constantino), with a host of local variables—ethnicity, social structure, economic conditions, the policies pursued by U.S. commanders in the region, and so on—determining the nature of the region's response to the Americans.[5] Rather than being a single national struggle, the Philippine-American War may actually have been a collection of distinctive local ones.

★ ★ ★

While this book focuses on a war, it is also, in some measure, a study of late nineteenth-century and early twentieth-century provincial society. One theme that runs through these pages is that, although the war was responsible for manifold disruptions, it did not alter—and, in some respects, merely reinforced—certain fundamental realities of provincial life. Indeed, what is most striking about the story I have told is how much continuity there was between peacetime Batangas and Batangas under siege.

First of all, as the preceding discussion about the nature of the resistance has already pointed out, there was a continuity in leadership in the province. The individuals who dominated political life in Batangas's municipalities in the last years of Spanish rule—men like Miguel Malvar, Santiago Rillo, and Martin Cabrera—were the same ones who emerged as the commanders of the provincial army during both the revolution against Spain and, later, the war against the United States. The leaders of the covert resistance to the U.S. forces were people of the same type. Yes, there were exceptions to the general rule—members of the economic elite like Manuel Arguelles who quickly made their peace with the Americans, ne'er-do-wells like Elias Mendoza and outlaws like Aniceto Oruga who became officers in Malvar's army—but, all in all, there were few of them.

There was a direct connection between this particular continuity and the course of the war in Batangas. For at least a year following the U.S. occupation of Batangas, members of the provincial economic and political elites constituted the backbone of the anticolonial struggle. But, as the pressure of U.S. military operations began to take their toll and more and more members of the political and economic elites decided to cast their lot with the enemy, the fragile nature of this resistance became obvious. It was far from surprising, therefore, that in the final year of the battle for Batangas Malvar made a determined effort to broaden the base of support by rallying the lower classes to his banner. A cause that offered only continuity had little appeal to those who were unhappy with their lot in the past.

Continuities of a different kind could also be observed in the provincial officer corps. In creating his command structure, Miguel Malvar relied primarily on individuals with whom he had close, and in most cases, long-standing, relationships—family members, compadres, trusted retainers,

friends from his secondary-school days. Such a method of institution formation may very well have had something to recommend it at the start, but over
the course of the war, its deficiencies became apparent, as conflict surfaced
between subordinates whose loyalty to Malvar could not overcome their
dislike for each other. Here, then, was an inherent fatal flaw in the Filipino
Army in Batangas: the very organizing principle of the officer corps was, at
the same time, a root cause of the ongoing tensions within the army.

Another type of continuity could be observed in the local disease regime.
Clearly, Batangas experienced a major demographic crisis during the years
of warfare against the United States, but that crisis can be understood only
in the context of long-term epidemiological trends in the province. Even
before the outbreak of the Philippine-American War, morbidity and mortality rates in Batangas were elevated as a result of several interrelated
developments: a persistent rinderpest epidemic, the disruptions caused by
the revolution against Spain, periodic food shortages, and epidemics of
smallpox and malaria. The epidemiological catastrophes that occurred in
Batangas between 1900 and 1902 were not, consequently, entirely of the
Americans' making. The malaria epidemic in eastern Batangas during the
first year of the American occupation was partly due to the effect of rinderpest on mosquito biting patterns. Even the high death rates during the
period of concentration and the subsequent cholera epidemic cannot be
blamed on the U.S. military alone. To point out all this is not to imply that we
should ignore the contributions of American policies and actions to Batangas's epidemiological woes; it is rather to assert that the war alone was not
responsible for all the wartime mortality.

★ ★ ★

In some scholarly circles, historical studies like this one—which is to say, in-
depth studies of small places over relatively short periods of time—are
decidedly out of favor. In favor are works of historical synthesis, efforts to
make sense out of the mountains of monographs that have been produced by
the members of the academy for the past few decades. For history to be
meaningful, we are told, it must go beyond arcane particularities to address
the needs and concerns of the widest possible audience of intelligent readers.
And what those readers need, above all, is an understanding of "significant
questions," "central themes," and long-term trends.[6]

Such a stance may make perfectly good sense to a certain number of
scholars writing about American or West European history, but for the
moment it makes no sense at all to those who focus on the Southeast Asian

past.[7] Underfunded and understudied, the field of Southeast Asian history is still in its early adolescence. Far from having too many monographs, it has too few, and until more of them are written, the sort of historical syntheses that can be produced are destined to be superficial at best. The subfield of Philippine history provides a graphic illustration of this last point. Despite the fact that the subject that has been explored in this monograph, the Philippine-American War, is considered to be a seminal event in the Philippine past, the simple truth—a truth that bears repetition—is that scholars have thus far examined only a tiny fraction of the available source materials on the conflict. Further, the observation just made about scholarship on the war applies with greater force to most other periods of Philippine history, since they have received even less attention. In light of such stark state-of-the-field realities, how can aspiring synthesizers be expected to write reliable syntheses?

So let me close with a plea, curious though it may seem: that readers of this book not be tempted to place inordinate weight on its findings. *Battle for Batangas* may raise important questions about the existing orthodoxy, but it is not a definitive account of the revolutionary period in the Philippines, or even perhaps of the revolutionary period in Batangas. What should be recognized, above all, is that no historian of the Philippines (myself included) has come close to exhausting the archival holdings on the period 1896–1902, and that much of the story remains to be told. I hope that other scholars will soon make an effort to tell it.

Appendix A

The Economic Elite of Batangas

Over the years, historians have written a good deal about the holdings, doings, comings, and goings of the economic elite of the provincial Philippines, and it is understandable why this should be so. The members of the economic elite often could write, often did write, sometimes even published their words, and were often written about by their contemporaries. A look through any of the 2,613 bundles of notarial records or any of the reports of provincial governors that are preserved in the stacks of the Philippine National Archives reveals that the Filipino names that figure most prominently are those of the economically powerful. At bottom, historians write so much about the wealthy because they are easy to write about.

Yet, if the literature dealing with provincial worthies is extensive, basic questions remain to be answered. One striking deficiency of the scholarship to date is that, with few exceptions, historians of the Philippines have made little effort to state precisely what criteria they use to determine elite status.

In a sense, this too is understandable. The task of providing an operational definition of a term like *economic elite* is fraught with difficulty; most difficult of all, it obliges the definer to draw lines between the presumed elite and the nonelite. Do we apply the term *economic elite* solely to an individual who has achieved a certain level of wealth or do we include members of that individual's family as well? And if the latter—which seems reasonable enough—do we restrict the application to members of the immediate family or extend it to all relatives living in the household of a rich man or woman? That last question is of no little statistical significance, since it was not uncommon for a man like Manuel Luz or Lorenzo Lopez to accommodate under his roof not only his own unmarried children but also the spouses and offspring of his married children (at least up to the point that the young couples accumulated enough money to purchase their own houses) as well as elderly parents, aunts, uncles, and cousins.

Once we have decided where to draw those lines, there are other decisions to be made. What geographical entity do we use as our unit of reference? If we decide to apply the term *economic elite* to individuals found at the apex of the economic hierarchy of every town, we would be obliged to include in that category the wealthiest family in the remote, economically backward community of Calatagan, even though its total wealth was perhaps only half as great as the one-hundredth leading family of Lipa. Or should we alternatively use the term only in referring to those who achieved a particular level of wealth—let us say, the possession of 2,500 pesos' worth of property—regardless of their rank order of wealth in the community? That decision would have the effect of eliminating every family in several towns and virtually every barrio-dweller in the province. Essentially, then, we must choose between a community-specific and provincewide standard for determining membership in the economic elite, and whichever one we use, we must make a determination about the exact point at which to draw our lines. If we choose the former, what percentage of the leading families do we include? If the latter, precisely how wealthy must the family be?

It should be obvious by now that, in the absence of agreed-upon criteria for determining elite status, the process of identifying the members of Batangas's economic elite becomes, to a certain extent, a tautological exercise: the size and composition of the elite will be determined, in large part, by the operational definition we adopt. But, as problematical as this procedure may seem, it is superior to the one that has been adopted to date—that of discussing the economic elite without even making the effort to define elite status.

Inseparable from the formidable problem of providing an operational definition is the problem of sources. Regardless of the operational definition we might prefer, the sources do not allow us the luxury of making a choice. Although a mountain of archival documents relating to late nineteenth-century Batangas has survived the ravages of climate, floods, fire, war, and white ants, there is only one collection with extensive data on economic status: several bundles of property assessment records for 1890 and 1891, which list residences and warehouses in the province with an annual rental value of more than 20 pesos. Since rental values in the province generally varied between 3 and 12 percent of the assessed value, those records provide us with a means of identifying the owners of many, if not most, of the residences in Batangas valued at more than 240 pesos.[1]

Even these records have lacunae. For three towns (Taal, Lian, and Tuy) out of twenty-two, no assessment documents could be located. Beyond that, the records that we do have must be used with caution. There was almost certainly some variation from one town to the next in estimating the value of buildings. In addition, while the assessment records probably identify for us the owners of most of the valuable residences in the province, they provide us with no information at all about landholdings, a significant omission in a society where land itself constituted the principal form of wealth. Most of those who owned expensive houses likely had estates of considerable size too, but there is no guarantee that all owners of large estates owned expensive residences; the world over, some people tend to consume more conspicuously than others. Hence, although the property assessment documents are useful *indicators* of wealth, they are not conclusive *proof* about a person's standing in the provincial economic hierarchy.

One last caveat about these sources should be noted. One may justifiably wonder whether the ownership of a dwelling valued at 240 pesos qualified a person for membership in the economic elite. A house of that value was, after all, a very different thing from one worth 1,000 or 2,000 pesos. It would have been made of *tabla y nipa* (boards and nipa), rather than of *materiales fuertes*—strong materials such as stone, hardwood, zinc, and galvanized iron. Furthermore, there was in all likelihood a world of difference between the total holdings of the owner of a 240-peso house and those of Lorenzo Lopez of Balayan, Manuel Luz of Lipa, and Manuel Arguelles of Batangas City—as great a gap, it might be argued, as that which separated the owner of a 240-peso house from the owner of a typical nipa house. A case might be made that, rather than identifying too few members of Batangas's economic elite, the assessment records have identified too many.

Whatever their deficiencies, these sources are the best we have, and while they perhaps identify as well-off some individuals who arguably were not and while they might occasionally fail to identify as well-off some who arguably were, they provide, all the same, a useful means of discovering the names of a large number of the province's economic elite. In this book, therefore, I have elected to restrict my use of the term *economic elite* to the members of Batangueño families—immediate families, that is—who lived above the 240-peso line.

What then was the approximate size of Batangas's economic elite? If we multiply the number of 240-peso houses listed in the sources (543) by 6—a justifiable procedure, based on the findings of the census of 1903 as well as my own research in house-by-house censuses—we find that the assessment documents have identified for us a grand total of 3,258 members of Batangas's economic elite, or 1.3 percent of the approximated population of the towns of Batangas for which we have records. But if we also take into the account the facts that (1) one of the omitted towns was Taal; (2) according to many sources, Taal was one of the most prosperous communities in the province; and (3) the assessment lists for the nineteen documented towns failed to include some properties that should have properly been included because of undervaluation by the owners, it seems reasonable to conclude that the figure of 3,258 should be adjusted upward. My own estimate is that, in the province as a whole, the 240-peso economic elite numbered somewhere between 4,500 and 6,000, or approximately 1.5 to 2 percent of the population.

Male Students from Batangas in Philippine Secondary Schools

School Year	Number of Batangueño Students
1866–1867	100
1871–1872	182
1876–1877	205
1881–1882	232
1886–1887	280
1891–1892	453

Source: Libros de Matrícula de Estudios Generales y de Aplicación de Segunda Enseñanza, 1866–1898, Archives of the University of Santo Tomas, Manila.

Appendix C

Mortality in Western Batangas, 1891–1898

	Burials in Time Period			
Town	1891–1895 (annual average)	1896	1897	1898
Balayan	744	848	1,848	1,404
Calaca	375	324	1,145	783
Lemery	446[a]	471	814	902
Lian	163	174	515	215

Source: Libros de Entierros, Parish Records of Balayan, Calaca, Lemery, and Lian.
[a]This average is for 1894 and 1895 only; Lemery's burial registers are incomplete or missing for earlier years.

Appendix D

Mortality in Eastern Batangas, 1891–1900

	Burials in Time Period		
Town	1891–1898 (annual average)	1899	1900
Batangas City	995[a]	965	1,986
Cuenca	190	303	454[b]
Ibaan	281	433	770
Lipa	1,421	1,277	2,476
Lobo	173	287	592[b]
San Jose	301	390	833
San Juan	450	580	1,373
Taysan	171	234	594

Source: Libros de Entierros, Parish Records of Batangas City, Cuenca, Ibaan, Lipa, Lobo, San Jose, San Juan, and Taysan; Estadística, Batangas, PNA.

[a]Excluding 1895, because data were incomplete for that year.

[b]Figures for Cuenca and Lobo are somewhat inflated for 1900 because, for some reason, a substantial number of nonresident deaths were recorded in both towns' parish books in that year.

Mortality in Selected Towns of Batangas, January–May 1902

Town	Number of Burials	Annualized Crude Death Rate[a]
Batangas City	1,921	139
Ibaan	297	99
Lipa	2,339	148
Lobo	501	208
San Juan	1,189	241
Taysan	212	150

Source: Libros de Entierros, Parish Records of Batangas City, Ibaan, Lipa, Lobo, San Juan, and Taysan.

[a]These figures are approximate. In estimating crude death rates, I used (albeit reluctantly) the population figures found in the 1903 census. It should be emphasized that the population was lower in 1903 than it would have been in January–May 1902 because (1) the census followed a cholera epidemic, and (2) the census-takers failed to count no fewer than 10,000 people in the province. But, while all that may suggest that the estimated crude death rates are high, it should also be noted that burials may have been underregistered during the months of concentration, since parish records often manifested that deficiency during times of disruption. On such matters, see May, "150,000 Missing Filipinos," 223–32, 237.

Abbreviations Used in the Notes

1C	First Cavalry
1D	First District
2D	Second District
3SB	Third Separate Brigade
8AC	Eighth Army Corps
28USV	Twenty-Eighth Infantry, U.S. Volunteers
38USV	Thirty-Eighth Infantry, U.S. Volunteers
39USV	Thirty-Ninth Infantry, U.S. Volunteers
AAG	Acting Adjutant General
Adj.	Adjutant
AG	Adjutant General
AGO	Adjutant General's Office
B	Battalion

BHQ	Batangas Headquarters Letterbook (found in PRP/Pr12–13/Batangas)
Brig.	Brigade
CI	*Contribuciones Industriales* (Industrial/Manufacturing Taxes), a record group in PNA
CO	Commanding Officer
Con.	Container
D/	Declaration by (declarations made by Filipinos about their involvement in the Philippine-American War; the declarations can be found in RG395)
Div.	Division
Div. Phil.	Division of the Philippines
DSL	Department of Southern Luzon
EC	Eliseo Claudio file (found in PRP/RL5)
EGB	*Elecciones de Gobernadorcillos* (Elections of Municipal Presidents), Province of Batangas, a record group in PNA
FMP	Frederick M. Presher Diary (found in SAW/1C, USAMHI)
FU	*Fincas Urbanas* (Urban Properties), a record group in PNA
GI	Gardener Inquiry (an inquiry into charges made by Maj. Cornelius Gardener, which can be found in two volumes in the records of the AGO: RG94/AGO421607-F, enclosures 2 and 3)
GO	General Order
HCC	Henry C. Corbin Papers, LCMD
HDP	Historical Data Papers, a collection of local histories, Philippine National Library
HSVR	Historical Sketches of Volunteer Regiments (in RG94)
JLJ	John Leland Jordan Papers, Tennessee State Library and Archives
LCMD	Library of Congress, Manuscripts Division
LSB	Letters Sent Book
PEF	*La Política de España en Filipinas,* a periodical published in Spain
PIR	Philippine Insurgent Records, microfilm, USNA (Citations take the form PIR/reel no./file.)
PNA	Philippine National Archives, Manila
PRP	Philippine Revolutionary Papers, Philippine National Library (Citations take the form PRP/box no./other identifying information.)

RG24	Records of the U.S. Navy, USNA
RG94	Records of the Adjutant General's Office, USNA (Citations take the form RG94/file number.)
RG112	Records of the Office of the Surgeon General, USNA
RG153	Records of the Judge Advocate General's Office, USNA Annex, Suitland, Maryland
RG391	Records of U.S. Army Mobile Units, USNA
RG395	Records of U.S. Army Overseas Operations and Commands, USNA (Citations take the form RG395/file number.)
RLB	Robert L. Bullard Papers, LCMD
RO	Regimental Orders
SAW	Spanish-American War Survey, a collection of manuscripts at the USAMHI (Citations take the form SAW/specific unit in which the soldier served.)
SD	Selected Documents (a file found in PIR and PRP)
Sec/War	Secretary of War
SR	*Sediciones y Rebeliones* (Acts of Sedition and Rebellion), a collection of bound volumes in PNA
THS	Thomas H. Selm Diary, Cornell University Library
USAMHI	U.S. Army Military History Institute, Carlisle Barracks, Pennsylvania
USMAL	U.S. Military Academy Library, West Point, N.Y.
USNA	U.S. National Archives, Washington, D.C.
USV	United States Volunteers
USWD	U.S. War Department, *Annual Reports of the War Department for the Fiscal Year Ended . . .* (year varies)
WHT	William Howard Taft Papers, LCMD

Notes

Introduction

1. Teodoro A. Agoncillo, *Malolos: The Crisis of the Republic* (Quezon City, 1960), viii–ix, 621–78.

2. Renato Constantino, *The Philippines: A Past Revisited* (Manila, 1979), 233–44.

3. For earlier formulations of these ideas, see Glenn A. May, "Filipino Revolutionaries in the Making: The Old School Tie in Late Nineteenth-Century Batangas," *Bulletin of the American Historical Collection* 9 (July–Sept. 1981): 53–64; id., "Resistance and Collaboration in the Philippine-American War: The Case of Batangas," *Journal of Southeast Asian Studies* 15 (March 1984): 69–90; and id., "Private Presher and Sergeant Vergara: The Underside of the Philippine-American War," in *Reappraising an Empire: New Perspectives on Philippine-American History,* ed. Peter W. Stanley (Cambridge, Mass., 1984), 35–57.

4. William Henry Scott, *Ilocano Responses to American Aggression, 1900–1901* (Quezon City, 1986).

5. Teodoro A. Agoncillo, *The Revolt of the Masses: The Story of Bonifacio and the Katipunan* (Quezon City, 1956).

6. For examples of critical treatments of the U.S. Army, see Leon Wolff, *Little Brown Brother: How the United States Purchased and Pacified the Philippine Islands at the Century's Turn* (New York, 1961), and Stuart Creighton Miller, *"Benevolent Assimilation": The American Conquest of the Philippines, 1899–1903* (New Haven, 1982). For more favorable assessments: John M. Gates, *Schoolbooks and Krags: The United States Army in the Philippines, 1898–1902* (Westport, Conn., 1973), and Brian McAllister Linn, *The U.S. Army and Counterinsurgency in the Philippines* (Chapel Hill, 1989).

7. See James C. Scott, *The Moral Economy of the Peasant: Rebellion and Subsistence in Southeast Asia* (New Haven, 1976); Benedict J. Kerkvliet, *The Huk Rebellion: A Study of Peasant Revolt in the Philippines* (Berkeley, 1977); Samuel Popkin, *The Rational Peasant: The Political Economy of Rural Society in Vietnam* (Berkeley, 1979).

Prologue

1. Decree of Emilio Aguinaldo, Nov. 13, 1899, reproduced in John R. M. Taylor, *The Philippine Insurrection against the United States: A Compilation of Documents with Notes and Introduction,* 5 vols. (Pasay City, 1971–73), 4:194–95. Aguinaldo's decree applied only to the troops in his immediate command in central and northern Luzon. Hence, Mariano Trias, Miguel Malvar, and other commanders in the southern Tagalog region were not bound to adopt guerrilla tactics, and they did not immediately do so.

2. On rumors: *Columnas Volantes,* June 25, July 2, Oct. 19, and Nov. 25, 1899, in PIR/92/D4. On U.S. ships: Entries, Nov. 4–5, 1899, Logbook of the U.S.S. *Princeton;* Entries, Dec. 29–31, 1899, Logbook of the U.S.S. *Mariveles,* RG24; D/Gregorio Aguila, Feb. 14, 1902, RG395/4229; D/Francisco Untalan, Feb. 15, 1902, RG395/2394.

3. Elias Mendoza to presidente local, Batangas City, Dec. 7, 1899; same to G. Farol, Dec. 16, 1899; same to Capitán de la 3a Compañía del Bn. Sungay no. 2, Dec. 31, 1899; same to Santiago Rillo, Dec. 31, 1899; same to Eliseo Claudio, Dec. 31, 1899; same to presidente local, Batangas City, Dec. 31, 1899; same to Vicente Agregado, Dec. 31, 1899, all in BHQ; Mariano Cabrera, "Plan de defensa de Batangas," Dec. 25, 1899, PIR/56/SD936.8.

Chapter 1. Late Nineteenth-Century Batangas

1. On the nature of the war, see Glenn A. May, *A Past Recovered: Essays on Philippine History and Historiography* (Quezon City, 1987), 18–19, 181; Linn, *U.S. Army and Counterinsurgency,* xi–xii, 19–20, 163–70.

2. See, e.g., the description of that same terrain by Charles J. Crane, a U.S. Army officer who marched to Tagaytay ridge in January 1900: Charles Jackson Crane, *The Experiences of a Colonel of Infantry* (New York, 1923), 327.

3. In my discussion of population, I have relied primarily on two censuses: Spain, Dirección general del instituto geográfico y estadístico, *Censo de la población de España según el empadronamiento hecho en 31 de diciembre de 1887,* 1:801; U.S. Bureau of the Census, *Census of the Philippine Islands: 1903,* 2:141–43. Such data must be used carefully, a point I make at length in my article "150,000 Missing Filipinos: A Demographic Crisis in Batangas," *Annales de démographie historique* (1985): 215–43. I have used them here only to provide a rough idea of the number of inhabitants in the province and in individual towns.

4. On the number and population of barrios, Bureau of the Census, *Census: 1903,* 2:141–43.

5. *FU,* Batangas, 1890 and 1891; *CI,* Batangas, 1894–96; Report of Manuel Moriano, May 14, 1892, in *EGB,* Balayan, 1892; U.S. Senate, Committee on the Philippines, *Hearings: Affairs in the Philippine Islands,* S. Doc. 331, 57th Cong., 1st sess., 1902, 3:2589–668. On workers' wages, see Manuel Sastrón, *Batangas y su provincia* (Malabong, 1895), 34, 124, 143, 182, 197.

6. *FU,* Batangas, 1890 and 1891; Inventory of property of Manuel Genato, Feb. 2 and Dec. 3, 1902, RG395/2354.

7. *FU,* Batangas, 1890 and 1891.

8. Sastrón, *Batangas,* 18–19, 169–73; Feodor Jagor, *Travels in the Philippines* (London, 1875), 100–01; John Foreman, *The Philippine Islands: A Historical, Geographical, Ethnographical, Social and Commercial Sketch of the Philippine Archipelago and Its Political Dependencies* (London, 1892), 339–43, 412–15; Bureau of the Census, *Census: 1903,* 4:76–84; *Gaceta de Manila,* Jan. 8 and Feb. 3, 1888; Teodoro M. Kalaw, *Aide-de-Camp to Freedom,* trans. Maria Kalaw Katigbak (Manila, 1965), 1–2; "Historical and Cultural Life of the City of Lipa," HDP.

9. Interview with Paz Luz Dimayuga, July 5, 1976. See also Maria Kalaw Katigbak, *Few There Were (Like My Father)* (Manila, 1974), 6–8, 20, 85–89; Foreman, *Philippine Islands,* 413; Sastrón, *Batangas,* 170–73; Wenceslao E. Retana, *El Indio Batangueño* (Manila, 1888), 94–100.

10. Bureau of the Census, *Census: 1903,* 4:77, 82–83, 325; *Gaceta de Manila,* July 15, 1893; Sastrón, *Batangas,* 18–19; Kalaw, *Aide-de-Camp,* 2; Interview with Paz Luz Dimayuga, July 5, 1976; Maria Kalaw Katigbak, "When Coffee Bloomed in Lipa," in *Filipino Heritage: The Making of a Nation,* ed. Alfredo Roces, 10 vols. (Manila, 1977–78), 7:1760–64; M. M. Alicante et al., *Soil Survey of Batangas Province* (Manila, n.d.), 5.

11. Kalaw, *Aide-de-Camp,* 1; Philippine Islands, *Guía oficial de Filipinas, 1891* (Manila, 1891), Appendix, 131; and *Guía oficial de Filipinas, 1892* (Manila, 1892), Appendix, 145–48; and especially, *CI,* Batangas, 11 bundles.

12. *FU,* Batangas, 1890 and 1891; *CI,* Batangas, bundles dated 1894–1898, 1894–1897, 1894–1896, and 1895–1897; Protocolos, Batangas, v. 1154, items numbered 3, 38, 97, and 98, and v. 1155, items numbered 4, 11, 12, 22, and 63, all in PNA.

13. Bureau of the Census, *Census: 1903,* 2:104–14; *CI,* Batangas; Retana,

Indio Batangueño, 58, 94–96; Sastrón, *Batangas,* passim. My earlier comments about census data (see note 3 above) should be kept in mind. In the case of the census of 1903, one should also realize that it was taken in a period of massive disruption—a situation that might also have contributed to the unreliability of the data. One might wonder too whether statistics compiled after 1900 can be used as trustworthy reflections of conditions before 1900. For all these reasons, I tend to view the statistics in the census of 1903 merely as suggestive *indicators* of the state of affairs in late nineteenth-century Batangas.

14. Retana, *Indio Batangueño,* 67–68; Sastrón, *Batangas,* 53, 80, 94–95, 106; Foreman, *Philippine Islands,* 343; Francisco Villacorta, *Administración espiritual de los padres agustinos calzados de la provincia del dulce nombre de las Islas Filipinas* (Valladolid, 1833), 62; Agustín de la Cavada y Mendez de Vigo, *Historia geográfica, geológica y estadística de Filipinas,* 2 vols. (Manila, 1876), 1:194; Bureau of the Census, *Census: 1903,* 2:112.

15. See Bureau of the Census, *Census: 1903,* 4:190, 254, 261, 269, 279, but also note that, as a number of scholars have argued, these particular data must be used very carefully. Information on tenancy was also derived from interviews, such as those cited in the next note.

16. Interviews with Emilio Vergara, Mataasnakahoy (note that here, in referring to the site of the interview, I have used a *k* rather than a *c* in the place name, to reflect the current-day spelling), July 27, 1976; Atanacio Ilagan, Nasugbu, July 28, 1976; and Jose Caubalejo, Calatagan, July 28, 1976. On Roxas, also see Sastrón, *Batangas,* 132, 148–49, where the Spanish landowner is depicted in a more favorable light by a fellow Spaniard; and G. Ruiz de la Bastida to Gobernador General, June 4, 1892, and Esteban Garcia (Guardia Civil) to Gobernador Civil, Batangas, Apr. 29, 1892 (both in *EGB,* Nasugbu, 1892), where his agents are accused of unsavory conduct.

17. For a sampling of some of the best literature on patron-client bonds in Southeast Asia, see Carl H. Landé, *Leaders, Factions and Parties: The Structure of Philippine Politics* (New Haven, 1964); Kerkvliet, *Huk Rebellion;* and James C. Scott, "The Erosion of Patron-Client Bonds and Social Change in Rural Southeast Asia," *Journal of Asian Studies* 32 (Nov. 1972): 5–37, and *Moral Economy,* 27, 41–52, 167–80.

18. Retana, *Indio Batangueño,* 92–93. For useful discussions of the exploitative side of landlord-tenant relations, see Scott, *Moral Economy,* 44–47, 167–73; Popkin, *Rational Peasant,* 74–78.

19. This is not to say that the response of lower-class Vietnamese would be uniform either. But it is clear that Ho Chi Minh had greater support among the Vietnamese peasantry than Aguinaldo had among rural Filipinos. I compare and contrast the two conflicts in "Why the United States Won the Philippine-American War, 1899–1902," *Pacific Historical Review* 52 (Nov. 1983): 353–77.

20. Retana, *Indio Batangueño,* 61; Sastrón, *Batangas,* 48–49. On the size of households, I consulted the documents entitled "Estado del número de habitantes" (1896) and "Estado urbano-agrícola-comercial" (1896) for San Juan, San

Luis, Santo Tomas, and Taal in Estadística, Batangas, PNA; and also the Parish Census, Lipa, 1894, Lipa Cathedral. In San Juan, the average number of inhabitants per household was 5.78; in San Luis, 5.03; in Santo Tomas, 6.02; and in Taal, 6.21. For Lipa, I calculated the average only for the barrio of Mataasnacahoy (now Mataasnakahoy): it worked out to be 5.74.

While the *average* house contained 6 occupants, there was a good deal of variation in household size. The aforementioned Lipa parish census revealed that in the barrio of Mataasnacahoy 30 of the 430 houses had more than 10 occupants, and one of them had as many as 19. There was also considerable variation in the composition of households. While 266 of the 430 houses—or 62 percent—were occupied by nuclear families alone, the other 38 percent were occupied by families with servants, families with relatives, several families living together, and several individuals who were apparently unrelated. Even in a discussion of the commonalities of the common people of Batangas, then, one is constantly reminded of their heterogeneity.

21. Retana, *Indio Batangueño*, 67–68; Sastrón, *Batangas*, 53.

22. Retana, *Indio Batangueño*, 49–51; Sastrón, *Batangas*, 52–53.

23. Retana, *Indio Batangueño*, 69–79; Sastrón, *Batangas*, 49–50, 53–54, 58–59; Kalaw, *Aide-de-Camp*, 8.

24. Cavada, *Historia*, 1:189; Sastrón, *Batangas*, 48; "Estado nominal del número de matrimonios," Batangas City, 1896, and "Estado nominal del número de defunciones," Batangas City, 1896, both in Estadística, Batangas, PNA. In that same year, there were 246 marriages in the town of Bauan, and in 229 (93 percent) of them, both parties were natives of the town. See "Estado nominal de número de matrimonios," Bauan, 1896, in Estadística, Batangas, PNA.

25. Retana, *Indio Batangueño*, 66.

26. On rice cultivation during that period, see Bureau of the Census, *Census: 1903*, 4:66–95.

27. Sastrón, *Batangas*, 61–63; Foreman, *Philippine Islands*, 409, 421; Retana, *Indio Batangueño*, 61–62.

28. "Estado del número de nacimientos," Province of Batangas, 1893, in Estadística, Batangas, PNA. No figures for the town of Bauan were included in the 1893 totals.

29. Philippine Islands, *Guía, 1891*, Appendix, 21–22; *Guía, 1892*, 481–82.

30. Joaquín Martínez de Zúñiga, *Status of the Philippines in 1800*, trans. Vicente del Carmen (Manila, 1973), 93–94; Foreman, *Philippine Islands*, 144; Sastrón, *Batangas*, 59–63, 102. Further information about the Caysasay Shrine was derived from Reynaldo Atienza, "History of Taal" (a typescript in the author's possession), and "Ang Mahal Na Birhen Ng Kaysasay" (a pamphlet printed by the Archdiocese of Manila and distributed at the shrine itself). In Rizal's famous novel *Noli Me Tangere*, Capitan Tiago and Doña Pía, who were childless, appealed to Our Lady of Caysasay. See Jose Rizal, *Noli Me Tangere*, trans. Leon Ma. Guerrero (London, 1961), 36.

31. Ken De Bevoise, "The Compromised Host: The Epidemiological Context of

the Philippine-American War" (Ph.D. diss., University of Oregon, 1986), 76–150; Sastrón, *Batangas,* 68–70, 94, 118.

32. Bureau of the Census, *Census: 1903,* 3:12–17; Carlo M. Cipolla, *The Economic History of World Population,* 7th ed. (Middlesex, Eng., 1978), 92–93. The figure for the Philippines as a whole was 36.12 per thousand. On the reliability of parish records and other sources of a demographic nature, see May "150,000 Missing Filipinos," 215–43.

33. On 1883, see Libros de Entierros, Parish Records of Calaca, Cuenca, Ibaan, San Jose, and Taysan. The number of burials was as follows for each parish: 855, 355, 720, 627, 534. Although we lack population figures for those towns for that year, I have estimated the population of each by calculating the average of the population figures found in the Spanish censuses of 1877 and 1887. The estimated population figures for those towns are: 10,486; 5,274; 8,810; 9,265; 6,513. The crude death rates for those towns work out to be 81.53, 67.31, 81.73, 67.68, 81.99. The population figures can be found in Spain, Instituto geográfico y estadístico, *Censo de la población de España según el empadronamiento hecho en 31 de diciembre de 1877,* 1:710–11; and *Censo . . . 1887,* 1:801. On 1889, see Bureau of the Census, *Census: 1903,* 3:13.

34. De Bevoise, "Compromised Host," 16–28, 45–56, 106–12; Sastrón, *Batangas,* 22–23.

35. Ken De Bevoise, "Until God Knows When: Smallpox in the Late-Colonial Philippines," *Pacific Historical Review* 52 (May 1990): 149–85; De Bevoise, "Compromised Host," 119–29; Sastrón, *Batangas,* 69–70; Libros de Entierros, Parish Records of Cuenca (for 1894), Nasugbu (Jan.–May 1894), San Juan (Mar. 1895).

36. May, "150,000 Missing Filipinos," 238–40; De Bevoise, "Compromised Host," 82–99; Sastrón, *Batangas,* 36, 68, 77–78, 94, 176, 227, 249.

37. Emma H. Blair and James A. Robertson, ed., *The Philippine Islands, 1493–1898,* 55 vols. (Cleveland, 1903–09), 46:76–112. Figures on enrollment and attendance were often unreliable. For some unbelievably high figures, see Cavada, *Historia,* 1:413, and Bureau of the Census, *Census: 1903,* 3:591–92. Figures which correspond more closely to those in the educational survey mentioned later in the text can be found in Philippine Islands, *Guía oficial de Filipinas, 1884* (Manila, 1884), 425; and *Guía oficial de Filipinas, 1889,* 2 vols. (Manila, 1889), 2:274.

38. Eliodoro G. Robles, *The Philippines in the Nineteenth Century* (Quezon City, 1969), 225–28.

39. Sastrón, *Batangas,* 103–04, 118, 139, 144, 159, 175, 192, 198–99, 211, 216, 224–25, 232.

40. The rest of the section on education, with the exception of the paragraph on girls' schools, is based on my article "Filipino Revolutionaries," 53–64. The principal sources used in the preparation of the article were documents located in the Archives of the University of Santo Tomas, Manila.

41. Evergisto Bazaco, *History of Education in the Philippines* (Manila, 1939), 354–64; Katigbak, *Few There Were,* 2.

42. Not all the members of the provincial intellectual elite were from wealthy households. Apolinario Mabini from Tanauan, for example, came from a family of moderate means, but was able, all the same, to attend secondary school and the University of Santo Tomas. There was no automatic correlation between wealth and education in nineteenth-century Batangas.

43. On the Propaganda Movement, see John N. Schumacher, S.J., *The Propaganda Movement: 1880–1895* (Manila, 1973); Cesar Adib Majul, *The Political and Constitutional Ideas of the Philippine Revolution,* rev. ed. (Quezon City, 1967); and León Ma. Guerrero, *The First Filipino* (Manila, 1963).

44. This section is based on my article "Civic Ritual and Political Reality: Municipal Elections in the Late-19th-Century Philippines," which appeared in May, *Past Recovered,* 30–52. The major sources used in the preparation of that piece were the records of municipal elections in Batangas, which can be found in *EGB.*

45. A few minor qualifications should be noted: if the incumbent gobernadorcillo were suspended, the acting gobernadorcillo would replace him as one of the thirteen voters. Furthermore, in that event, the voters would be required to make three choices instead of two for the post of gobernadorcillo, and the third name on the terna would be that of the third highest vote-getter rather than that of the incumbent gobernadorcillo.

Chapter 2. Revolution

1. On the revolution: Epifanio de los Santos, *The Revolutionists: Aguinaldo, Bonifacio, Jacinto* (Manila, 1973); Teodoro M. Kalaw, *The Philippine Revolution* (1925; reprint ed., Mandaluyong, 1969); Gregorio F. Zaide, *History of the Katipunan* (Manila, 1939), and *The Philippine Revolution,* rev. ed. (Manila, 1968); Agoncillo, *Revolt;* Majul, *Political and Constitutional Ideas;* Carlos Quirino, *The Young Aguinaldo: From Kawit to Biyak-na-Bato* (Manila, 1969); Nick Joaquin, *A Question of Heroes* (Makati, 1977); Constantino, *Past Revisited,* 164–255; Alfredo B. Saulo, *Emilio Aguinaldo* (Quezon City, 1983); Reynaldo C. Ileto, *Pasyon and Revolution: Popular Movements in the Philippines, 1840–1910* (Quezon City, 1979); John N. Schumacher, S.J., "The Religious Character of the Revolution in Cavite, 1896–1897," *Philippine Studies* 24 (Fourth Quarter 1976): 399–416, and *Revolutionary Clergy: The Filipino Clergy and the Nationalist Movement, 1850–1903* (Quezon City, 1981); Milagros C. Guerrero, "Luzon at War: Contradictions in Philippine Society, 1898–1902" (Ph.D. diss., University of Michigan, 1977); Jonathan Fast and Jim Richardson, *Roots of Dependency: Political and Economic Revolution in the Nineteenth-Century Philippines* (Quezon City, 1979). See also the fascinating debate on Ileto's book in *Philippine Studies:* Milagros Guerrero, "Understanding Philippine Revolutionary Mentality," *Philippine Studies* 29 (Second Quarter 1981): 240–56; Reynaldo Ileto, "Critical Issues in 'Understanding Philippine Revolutionary Mentality,'" *Philippine Studies* 30 (First Quarter 1982): 92–119; John N. Schumacher, S.J., "Recent Perspectives on the Revolution," *Philippine Studies* 30 (Fourth Quarter 1982): 445–92.

2. Agoncillo, *Revolt,* 293–312. See also Teodoro A. Agoncillo and Milagros C. Guerrero, *History of the Filipino People,* 5th ed. (Quezon City, 1977), 169–263; Constantino, *Past Revisited,* 164–255; David J. Steinberg et al., *In Search of Southeast Asia: A Modern History,* rev. ed. (Honolulu, 1987), 269–72. Reynaldo Ileto (*Pasyon,* 87–195) calls Agoncillo's account into question on many points, but essentially accepts his view of the revolution as a lower-class movement. Agoncillo's "revolt of the masses" thesis has been challenged most seriously by Schumacher ("Religious Character," 402; *Revolutionary Clergy,* 48–64, 268–71); and Fast and Richardson, *Roots of Dependency,* 67–84.

Historians have, of course, raised questions about other aspects of Agoncillo's account: his interpretation of the conflicts within the revolutionary camp, his view of Bonifacio, his understanding of what the revolution meant to its lower-class participants. Still, on the whole, his basic framework remains widely accepted.

3. Pio Valenzuela's memoirs can be found in *Minutes of the Katipunan* (Manila, 1978), 89–108. For Aguinaldo's memoirs, see Emilio Aguinaldo, *Mga Gunita ng Himagsikan* (Manila, 1964), and for Ricarte's, see Artemio Ricarte, *Memoirs of General Artemio Ricarte* (Manila, 1963). Santiago Alvarez's "Ang Katipunan at Ang Paghihimagsik" can be found in the Filipiniana Section of the Philippine National Library, Manila; a virtually identical version of the text, with the title "Si Andres Bonifacio, Ang Katipunan at Ang Himagsikan," can be found in the Filipiniana and Asia Division of the University of the Philippines Library, Diliman, Quezon City. Carlos Ronquillo's "Ilang Talata Tungkol sa Paghihimagsik nang 1896–97" can be consulted in the same division of the University of the Philippines Library. For the probably bogus "minutes" of the Katipunan, see *Minutes,* iii–v, 1–86.

4. Agoncillo, *Revolt,* 97; Fast and Richardson, *Roots,* 78; Ileto, *Pasyon,* 102. For the memoirs themselves: *Minutes of the Katipunan,* 89–108. On the date of composition of Valenzuela's memoirs, see Zaide, *History of the Katipunan,* 52–53.

5. That testimony can be found in *Minutes of the Katipunan,* 148, 152. See also W. E. Retana, *Archivo del bibliófilo filipino,* 5 vols. (Madrid, 1895–1905), 3:199ff.

6. See *Minutes of the Katipunan,* 93, 103–06.

7. Aguinaldo, *Mga Gunita,* 154. Santiago Alvarez ("Paghihimagsik," chap. 4) also provides figures (in this case, of Bonifacio's followers), but it is not clear if Alvarez is referring to actual members of the Katipunan or rather to those Filipinos who joined the revolutionary ranks once the uprising began.

8. Aguinaldo, *Mga Gunita,* 30–32; Schumacher, *Revolutionary Clergy,* 48–49; Soledad Borromeo-Buehler, "The *Inquilinos* of Cavite: A Social Class in the Nineteenth-Century Philippines," *Journal of Southeast Asian Studies* 16 (March 1985): 80, 98; Fast and Richardson, *Roots,* 68–74; Saulo, *Emilio Aguinaldo,* 87; Joaquin, *Question of Heroes,* 98–99; Orlino A. Ochosa, *The Tinio Brigade: Anti-American Resistance in the Ilocos Provinces, 1899–1901* (Quezon City, 1989), 15–16.

9. See Quirino, *Young Aguinaldo,* 40; and Zaide, *Philippine Revolution,* 352.

10. Agoncillo, *Revolt,* 97; Zaide, *Katipunan,* 53.

11. Juanito A. Marquez, "Lipa and the Philippine Revolution, 1896–1899" (M.A. thesis, Ateneo de Manila University, 1969), 31–32. Two other dubious sources refer to the existence of katipuneros in Batangas. According to Manuel Sastrón, the Katipunan had approximately fifteen thousand members in Batangas before the outbreak of the revolution. Sastrón, however, was a Spaniard, and he had no way of knowing the size of the society's membership. Another document—the "minutes" of the Katipunan—tells us that in January 1894 the secret society's leaders made a decision to establish a "government" in Batangas. But, the minutes are, as I state in the text, a most problematical source: they are filled with gross inaccuracies, and many historians—including myself—consider them to be a forgery. See Manuel Sastrón, *La insurrección en Filipinas y Guerra Hispano-Americana en el archipiélago* (Madrid, 1901), 53; and *Minutes of the Katipunan,* 37.

12. But, that point conceded, let us not be inclined to concede too much. For even if we grant the dubious authorities the benefit of the doubt, and if we consequently reach the debatable conclusion that the secret society had penetrated the province before the outbreak of the revolution, there is still no guarantee that its members would have come from humble backgrounds. More than a few of Cavite's katipuneros were both wealthy and politically influential. And according to Marquez, the possibly untrustworthy local historian of Lipa, several of the leading figures of that town's purported Katipunan chapter were members of the local economic elite. (Actually, Marquez says that the "rich elite" did not join the Katipunan in Lipa, but his list of leading katipuneros includes a number of men who were, based on the value of their homes, very well off. See Marquez, "Lipa," 32, 44.) Thus, even if there were indeed katipuneros in Batangas, it is not outside the realm of possibility that some of them would have come from the upper rungs of the provincial socioeconomic ladder.

13. "Expediente (reservado) Promovido por El Gobernador Civil de Batangas contra varios vecinos del pueblo de Taal denunciados como propagandistas de ideas anti-patrióticas y anti-religiosas," 1895, *SR,* v. 6; Manuelito M. Recto, "Prologue to a Revolution," *Bulletin of the American Historical Collection* 7 (Jan.– March 1979): 51–75.

14. Fr. Martin Hernandez to Gobernador Civil, Batangas, May 1, 1892, and Manuel Moriano to Gobernador General, May 14, 1892, *EGB,* Taal, 1892; "Expediente . . . contra varios vecinos del pueblo de Taal denunciados como propagandistas," 1895, *SR,* v. 6; Recto, "Prologue."

15. *EGB,* Tanauan, 1889.

16. Schumacher, *Propaganda Movement,* 94–114.

17. *EGB,* Tanauan, 1889.

18. Arsenio Manuel, *Dictionary of Philippine Biography* (Quezon City, 1955), 268–74; Luis Serrano, "Meet General Malvar," *Manila Times,* Sept. 27, 1962; Arturo Ma. Misa, "Historical Flashback on General Miguel Malvar: The Last

Insurrecto," *Sunday Times Magazine,* Oct. 13, 1963; Libros de Matrícula de Estudios Generales y de Aplicación de Segunda Enseñanza, 1881–89; Libros de Matrícula de Facultad, Real y Pontificia Universidad de Santo Tomás, 1889–1896, Archives of the University of Santo Tomas, Manila.

19. *EGB,* Santo Tomas, 1889; "Expediente de las elecciones verificadas en dicho pueblo," Santo Tomas, 1890, Malvar folder, PNA.

20. *EGB,* Santo Tomas, 1892; Miguel Malvar et al. to Gobernador General, June 4, 1892, with appended sworn testimony of various principales, Malvar Folder, PNA.

21. Miguel Malvar et al. to Gobernador General, June 4, 1892, with appended testimony, Malvar Folder, PNA; Fr. Félix Garcés to Gobernador Civil, Batangas, Apr. 8, 1892; G. Ruiz de la Bastida to Gobernador General, June 6, 1892, with endorsements; and Gregorio Viana to Gobernador Civil, Batangas, June 13, 1892, all in *EGB,* Santo Tomas, 1892.

22. "Yncidente relativo a las 2as elecciones de Gobernadorcillo y ministros de justicia del pueblo de Santo Tomas," [June 1892]; Julio Meer, Juan Villegas, et al., "Reclamación presentada por algunos vecinos en contra de las elecciones verificadas el 20 de Junio en el pueblo de Santo Tomas," June 21, 1892; and, G. Ruiz de la Bastida to Gobernador General, June 30, 1892, with endorsement, all in *EGB,* Santo Tomas, 1892.

23. See, for example, "Expediente . . . contra varios vecinos del pueblo de Taal denunciados como propagandistas," 1895, *SR,* v. 6.

24. Gregorio Catigbac to Gobernador General, Oct. 10, 1894, and Eduardo Rodriguez to Gobernador General, Oct. 23, 1894, *SR,* v. 7; "Expediente . . . contra varios vecinos del pueblo de Taal denunciados como propagandistas," 1895, *SR,* v. 6; Decree of Ramón Blanco, Feb. 17, 1896, *SR,* v. 41; Gobernador General to Gobernador Civil, Batangas, Feb. 17, 1896, *SR,* v. 42. The conflict in Taal was exacerbated by another problem, which surfaced at the same time. For many years, the Spanish government had encountered difficulty in collecting the *cédula* tax, a yearly levy that most adult Filipinos were required to pay. In September 1895, therefore, it issued a decree requiring the collection of all delinquent fees. The following month, a Spanish official arrived in Taal to supervise the collection of the town's deficit, which amounted to more than 28,000 pesos. What transpired next is not completely clear, but the official claimed that local authorities obstructed his tax-collection efforts and that the provincial governor sided with him. See "Expediente reservado promovido por el Gobernador Civil de Batangas contra varios vecinos del pueblo de Taal," 1895 (a different document from the one cited earlier in this footnote), *SR,* v. 8.

25. Agoncillo, *Revolt,* 38–78; Joaquin, *Question of Heroes,* 77–119; Quirino, *Young Aguinaldo,* 52–80.

26. The chronology of the Philippine Revolution can be established only by comparing the Filipino sources with the Spanish. When that is done, it becomes clear that Artemio Ricarte's memoir, often relied on by historians, cannot be trusted on certain matters of detail. On these early battles, see *PEF,* Sept. 30,

1896, pp. 320, 325; Oct. 31, 1896, pp. 395–96; Emilio Revertér Delmas, *La insurrección de Filipinas en 1896 y 1897,* 2 vols. (Barcelona, 1899), 1:449, 458–59, 557, 560, 564; Aguinaldo, *Mga Gunita,* 109–15; Alvarez, "Paghihimagsik," chap. 9; "Historical Data on the Municipality of Tuy," 1–3, 7, 69, 104, HDP; Ricarte, *Memoirs,* 17–19.

27. Alvarez, "Paghihimagsik," chaps. 9–11; *PEF,* Oct. 31, 1896, pp. 398–403; Nov. 30, 1896, pp. 454–56; Delmas, *Insurrección,* 1:587–90, 596–600, 636–38; Sastrón, *Insurrección,* 100, 116–20, 145; Ricarte, *Memoirs,* 17–19, 30; Pedro S. Achútegui and Miguel A. Bernad, *Aguinaldo and the Revolution of 1896: A Documentary History* (Quezon City, 1972), 28–33; "Historical Data of the Municipality of Nasugbu," 7, HDP.

28. Santiago Rillo to Emilio Aguinaldo, Apr. 28, 1897, and M. de la Rosa to Emilio Aguinaldo, Apr. 28, 1897, PRP/P9; Achútegui and Bernad, *Aguinaldo,* 210–16; Reynaldo C. Ileto, "Food Crisis During the Revolution: Western Batangas, 1897–98," *Kabar Seberang* 15 (1985): 106, 109–10. In addition to the references to massive migration in the correspondence of the revolutionaries, one can find indications of a sudden population decline in the parish records. Beginning in December 1896, the number of baptisms recorded in Lian and Balayan dropped by approximately 70 percent; and in Calaca by about 50 percent. But, of course, one must not take the parish data too literally. As I have suggested in my article "150,000 Missing Filipinos," under-registration of vital events was a recurrent problem, and some of the decline may have been due to that cause. See the Libros de Bautismos, Parish Records of Balayan, Calaca, and Lian.

29. Alvarez, "Paghihimagsik," chaps. 9–11; Aguinaldo, *Mga Gunita,* 113; Delmas, *Insurrección,* 587; Ricarte, *Memoirs,* 18; D/Miguel Malvar, n.d., RG395/4229; *PEF,* Oct. 31, 1896, p. 401.

30. D/Miguel Malvar, n.d., RG395/4229.

31. Alvarez, "Paghihimagsik," chaps. 12–13; Aguinaldo, *Mga Gunita,* 116; "Historical Data of the Municipality of Nasugbu," 7, HDP; Interrogation of Isabelo Padilla and Hilario Bautista, Oct. 27, 1896, *SR,* v. 3; Ricarte, *Memoirs,* 28–31. In addition, it might be noted that Eustacio Maloles (Malvar's brother-in-law), a university-educated native of the town of Santo Tomas, also held high rank in the local forces, as did Eleuterio Marasigan, a native of Calaca, and Anastasio Marasigan, who had been born in Taal but now lived in Calaca. Both Eleuterio and Anastasio Marasigan had attended secondary school, and both were relatively prosperous men—the owners of sugar mills and land, but not yet members of the 240-peso economic elite. On Maloles, see Miguel Malvar's Statement about Eustacio Maloles, Dec. 6, 1898, PRP/Pr10–11/Batangas; Malvar's letter of appointment to Maloles, Sept. 1, 1897, PRP/Pr12–13/Batangas; and Libros de Matrícula de Facultad, Real y Pontificia Universidad de Santo Tomás, 1889–96, Archives of the University of Santo Tomas, Manila. On Eleuterio and Anastasio Marasigan: Alvarez, "Paghihimagsik," chap. 9; Ricarte, *Memoirs,* 30; Statement by Anastasio Marasigan concerning Eustacio Maloles, June 19, 1898, PRP/Pr10–11/Batangas; Libros de Matrícula de Estudios Generales y de Aplica-

ción de Segunda Enseñanza, 1880–81, 1883–85, Archives of the University of Santo Tomas; *CI,* Batangas, bundles marked 1894–96, 1894–97, and 1894–98.

32. D/Miguel Malvar, n.d., RG395/4229.

33. Robles, *Philippines in the Nineteenth Century,* 64–70; Aguinaldo, *Mga Gunita,* 45–46, 48, 58–62; Isagani R. Medina, "La Madre de Los Ladrones (Mother of Bandits): Tulisanismo (Brigandage) in Cavite Province during the 19th Century," paper delivered at the Conference of the International Association of Historians of Asia, Singapore, Oct. 1986; *EGB,* Santo Tomas, 1892.

34. Interviews with Jose Caubalejo, Calatagan, July 28, 1976; Dionisio Laygo, Padre Garcia, July 27, 1976; Atanacio Ilagan, Nasugbu, July 28, 1976. I am, of course, aware of the dangers of relying on interviews with nonagenarians. On the other hand, despite the age of my interviewees, they might be as trustworthy as the memoirists upon whom most historians have relied to date. After all, they had considerably less reason to be duplicitous. On the validity of such interviews, see May, "Presher," 35–57.

35. Ileto, *Pasyon,* 107–34. Actually, Ileto is not himself concerned with what motivated peasants to join the ranks, but rather with how peasants perceived the events in which they participated. My argument here—that such perceptions may have led to certain behavior—is clearly speculative, as I try to make clear in the text.

36. Interview with Emilio Vergara, Mataasnakahoy, July 27, 1976.

37. Interviews with Calixto Silva, Lipa, July 27, 1976, and Jose Caubalejo, Calatagan, July 28, 1976. Patron pressure and inducement were not confined to Batangas. In his memoirs, Aguinaldo discussed how, in the months immediately preceding the outbreak of the revolution, he convinced the cuadrilleros (members of the rural constabulary) of his native town—technically, his subordinates, since he was capitán municipal—and a tenant to join the Katipunan. See Aguinaldo, *Mga Gunita,* 45–46.

38. Delmas, *Insurrección,* 1:423; Interrogation of Dionisio Cabrera, Oct. 27, 1896, *SR,* v. 3; Sastrón, *Insurrección,* 161.

39. Emilio Aguinaldo to Mga Pangulo, Gargano, Haligui, etc., Nov. 4, 1896, reel 52, Microfilms of the Records of the Archives of the Province of the Most Holy Rosary, University of Santo Tomas Library; Achútegui and Bernad, *Aguinaldo,* 210–11.

40. Sastrón, *Insurrección,* 303; Investigation of Florentino de Jesus, July–Aug. 1898, PRP/Pr10–11/B2.

41. Alvarez, "Paghihimagsik," chap. 9; Aguinaldo, *Mga Gunita,* 78.

42. On the early operations of the Caviteños: Alvarez, "Paghihimagsik," chap. 9; Aguinaldo, *Mga Gunita,* 63–108; Agoncillo, *Revolt,* 172–78; Quirino, *Young Aguinaldo,* 54–71.

43. Alvarez, "Paghihimagsik," chaps. 9–10; Ricarte, *Memoirs,* 18–19, 30; *PEF,* Oct. 31, 1896, pp. 398, 400; Nov. 30, 1896, pp. 454–56; Delmas, *Insurrección,* 1:587–90, 596, 637–38; Sastrón, *Insurrección,* 100, 116–17, 145.

44. *PEF,* Dec. 15, 1896, p. 489; Dec. 31, 1896, pp. 532–33; Quirino, *Young Aguinaldo,* 85–93.

45. D/Miguel Malvar, n.d., RG395/4229; *PEF,* Dec. 15, 1896, p. 493.

46. *PEF,* Dec. 31, 1896, pp. 528–29, 535; Delmas, *Insurrección,* 2:14, 61–62; Sastrón, *Insurrección,* 165, 167.

47. *PEF,* Feb. 15, 1897, pp. 75–76; Federico de Monteverde y Sedano, *Campaña de Filipinas: La división Lachambre, 1897* (Madrid, 1898), 97–104, 130–41, 379–80; Achútegui and Bernad, *Aguinaldo,* 234–35; Quirino, *Young Aguinaldo,* 100–01.

48. Aguinaldo, *Mga Gunita,* 160–245; Alvarez, "Paghihimagsik," chaps. 13–20; Achútegui and Bernad, *Aguinaldo,* 236, 248–49, 279–86; Quirino, *Young Aguinaldo,* 101–16, 129–44, 160–76; Agoncillo, *Revolt,* 196ff; Monteverde, *Campaña,* 145–321, 458–573.

49. Monteverde, *Campaña,* 401, 546–49; Sastrón, *Insurrección,* 232, 241, 275–76; *PEF,* Apr. 15, 1897, pp. 174–76; May 15, 1897, pp. 245–47; June 15, 1897, p. 296; Delmas, *Insurrección,* 2:453–54, 567–68; D/Miguel Malvar, n.d., RG395/4229; Ronquillo, "Ilang Talata," chap. 3.

50. See Constantino, *Past Revisited,* 186, 191; Agoncillo, *Revolt,* 292; Saulo, *Emilio Aguinaldo,* 128ff; Quirino, *Young Aguinaldo,* 126.

51. D/Miguel Malvar, n.d., RG395/4229; Aguinaldo, *Mga Gunita,* 179; Ronquillo, "Ilang Talata," chap. 4. The exact number of soldiers from Batangas can only be guessed at. In his memoirs, Aguinaldo referred to Rillo as "the representative of 2,000 rebels"; in Ronquillo's memoirs, Rillo is quoted as saying that there were 7,000 Batangueños in the territory administered by the Magdiwang council, in addition to the delegation that was attending the assembly at Tejeros (and Tanza).

52. Santiago Rillo to Emilio Aguinaldo, Oct. 12, 1898, PRP/P5; Libros de Matrícula de Estudios Generales y de Aplicación de Segunda Enseñanza, 1867–1873, Archives of the University of Santo Tomas; *EGB,* Tuy, 1892; Spain, *Guía oficial de las Islas Filipinas, 1897* (Manila, 1897), 554. Also see note 51 of this chapter.

53. For the background to the Tejeros assembly, see Agoncillo, *Revolt,* 200–09; Quirino, *Young Aguinaldo,* 117–18; Saulo, *Emilio Aguinaldo,* 116–26; Teodoro A. Agoncillo, *The Writings and Trial of Andres Bonifacio* (Manila, 1963), 17, 19, 86, 88; Ronquillo, "Ilang Talata," chap. 4; Alvarez, "Paghihimagsik," chap. 14. In this chapter, I refer to the meetings held on March 22 and 23 as the Tejeros assembly; in fact, however, most of the delegates transferred from Tejeros to Tanza (Santa Cruz de Malabon) midway through the proceedings.

54. Ronquillo, "Ilang Talata," chap. 4. Alvarez presents two different versions of the conference ("Paghihimagsik," chaps. 14 and 35); in the second, he suggests that Rillo played a major role. Most secondary accounts, which claim that De las Alas was the chief agent of change, are based on Ricarte, *Memoirs,* 36.

55. Ronquillo, "Ilang Talata," chap. 4; de los Santos, *Revolutionists,* 139.

56. Ronquillo, "Ilang Talata," chap. 4; Aguinaldo, *Mga Gunita,* 185.

57. D/Miguel Malvar, n.d., RG395/4229.

58. "Pepe" to Emilio Aguinaldo, Mar. 24, 1897, PRP/P9; Taylor, *Philippine Insurrection,* 1:297.

59. Agoncillo, *Writings and Trial,* 18, 86–87. Eight days later, Bonifacio indicated that he provided Malvar with twenty riflemen and *twenty-five* bolomen, plus some other riflemen commanded by "Luciano" (see Agoncillo, *Writings and Trial,* 21, 90). About the same time, Rillo informed Aguinaldo that he had heard reports to the effect that Malvar was loaning weapons to Bonifacio; that was unlikely, given Malvar's shortage of weapons (see Rillo to Emilio Aguinaldo, Apr. 14, 1897, PRP/P7; Taylor, *Philippine Insurrection,* 1:299).

60. Miguel Malvar to Secretary of Justice, Apr. 5, 1897, PRP/RL11/Malvar folder.

61. Juan Goco to Mga Cgg. na pinunong namanahala sa dalauang sanggunian, Apr. 13, 1897; Miguel Malvar to Emilio Aguinaldo, Apr. 17, 1897; and Juan Goco to Emilio Aguinaldo, Apr. 20, 1897, all in PRP/P9. See also Malvar to Emilio Aguinaldo, Apr. 14, 1897, and Santiago Rillo to Emilio Aguinaldo, Apr. 18, 1897, both in PRP/P9.

62. Achútegui and Bernad, *Aguinaldo,* 361, 370; Aguinaldo, *Mga Gunita,* 206, 235; Ronquillo, "Ilang Talata," chap. 5.

63. Juan Goco to Emilio Aguinaldo, Apr. 21, 1897; M. de la Rosa to Aguinaldo, Apr. 21, 22, 23, 24, and 25, May 1 and 2, 1897; and Hipolito Ruit to Aguinaldo, Apr. 26, 1897, all in PRP/P9; D/Miguel Malvar, n.d., RG395/4229; Ronquillo, "Ilang Talata," chap. 3; Ricarte, *Memoirs,* 46.

64. Achútegui and Bernad, *Aguinaldo,* 353–54.

65. Alvarez, "Paghihimagsik," chaps. 16–19; Ronquillo, "Ilang Talata," chap. 2; Aguinaldo, *Mga Gunita,* 206–27; Agoncillo, *Revolt,* 238–75; Saulo, *Emilio Aguinaldo,* 146–51; Quirino, *Young Aguinaldo,* 156–59, 163–71.

66. Libros de Entierros, Parish Records of Lian, Balayan, Calaca, and Lemery.

67. Libros de Bautismos, Parish Records of Lian, Balayan, and Calaca. In Lian, there were 348 baptisms in 1895, 299 in 1896, and 129 in 1897. In Balayan, the total in 1895 was 1121; in 1896, 935; and 1897, 412. Finally, in Calaca, the totals were 584 in 1895, 535 in 1896, and 315 in 1897.

68. Ileto, "Food Crisis," 109–10.

69. Ibid., 106, 111–13; also, on the matter of the requisitioning of carabaos by the Spanish troops, see Investigation of Florentino de Jesus, July–Aug. 1898, PRP/Pr10–11/B2.

70. Taylor, *Philippine Insurrection,* 1:299–300; Santiago Rillo to Baldomero Aguinaldo, Apr. 24, 1897, PRP/RL8/Rillo folder; Ileto, "Food Crisis," 107–09.

71. My comments about the prevalence of smallpox are based on the information on cause of death in the libros de entierros. Obviously, such information cannot be accepted at face value; the stated cause of death may have been incorrect in a substantial number of cases. Even so, those data provide useful hints about the diseases that prevailed at the time, and in the case of a disease

like smallpox, the chances of misdiagnosis were considerably reduced. See Libros de Entierros, Parish Records of Balayan, Calaca, Lemery, and Lian. Concerning both smallpox and malnutrition, see De Bevoise, "Compromised Host," 15–28, 119–29, and "Until God." Medical specialists are not uniformly convinced that malnourished people are more prone to contracting smallpox, although there is evidence that a higher death rate from smallpox prevails among the malnourished. De Bevoise discusses the medical literature on the subject in footnote 6 of "Until God."

72. On the incidence of malaria, see Libros de Entierros, Parish Records of Balayan, Calaca, and Lian. For further discussion of the transmission of malaria, see Glenn A. May, "150,000 Missing Filipinos," 238–40; and De Bevoise, "Compromised Host," 82–93, 221–27.

73. D/Miguel Malvar, n.d., RG395/4229; Baldomero Aguinaldo to Emilio Aguinaldo, Aug. 22, 1897, PRP/P9.

74. Felipe del Rio to Gobernador General, June 25, 1897, *SR,* v. 12.

75. *PEF,* Sept. 15, 1897, p. 420; Sastrón, *Insurrección,* 291.

76. Mariano Trias to Emilio Aguinaldo, July 31 and Aug. 3, 1897, PRP/P9; Alvarez, "Paghihimagsik," chap. 22; Ronquillo, "Ilang Talata," chap. 3; Sastrón, *Insurrección,* 300; Ricarte, *Memoirs,* 54; Luis Serrano, "The Man Who Saved His Captor," *Weekly Graphic,* Sept. 29, 1965.

77. On Caneo's participation, see Statement of Miguel Malvar about Sebastian Caneo, Dec. 7, 1898, PRP/Pr10–11/Batangas. On Caneo and the Colorum, see Ileto, *Pasyon,* 93–95; Alvarez, "Paghihimagsik," chap. 33; Ricarte, *Memoirs,* 82–84.

78. Ricarte, *Memoirs,* 54; Libros de Matrícula de Estudios Generales y de Aplicación de Segunda Enseñanza, 1873–74, 1877–82, Archives of the University of Santo Tomas, Manila; *United States v. Aniceto Oruga,* 1902, RG395/2398; "History and Cultural Life of Tanauan, Batangas," 109, HDP.

79. Medina, "Madre de Los Ladrones"; Alvarez, "Paghihimagsik," chaps. 6–7.

80. Medina, "Madre de Los Ladrones"; Enrique Escassi to Gobernador Civil, Batangas, June 21, 1892, and G. Ruiz de la Bastida to Gobernador General, June 30, 1892, both in *EGB,* Santo Tomas, 1892.

81. Eric Hobsbawm, *Bandits* (New York, 1969), 13.

82. Sastrón, *Insurrección,* 301, 303; D/Miguel Malvar, n.d., RG395/4229; Ricarte, *Memoirs,* 86; Kalaw, *Philippine Revolution,* 291.

83. Aguinaldo, *Mga Gunita,* 256–66; *PEF,* Jan. 31, 1898, pp. 21–22; Agoncillo, *Malolos,* 38–39.

84. Agoncillo, *Malolos,* 40–47; Quirino, *Young Aguinaldo,* 208–19.

85. Sastrón, *Insurrección,* 328; *PEF,* Feb. 15, 1898, p. 46.

86. Sastrón, *Insurrección,* 329; *PEF,* Jan. 15, 1898, p. 7; Feb. 15, 1898, p. 48; Compilation of dispatches relating to the surrender of Malvar's forces, Jan. 1898, *SR,* v. 31. It is apparent from a document in Taylor, *Philippine Insurrection* (1:456) that Malvar had reached Hong Kong by Feb. 14, 1898.

87. One should avoid the temptation of painting Malvar in too heroic colors.

As I have already hinted in the text, and as I will continue to suggest, there was an opportunistic streak in Malvar (and in Rillo as well). Like many other revolutionary leaders, Malvar and Rillo evidently kept for themselves several thousand pesos of the several hundred thousand pesos paid by Spain to end the fighting. In addition, there are indications that in April 1898, while Aguinaldo was busy talking to the U.S. consul in Singapore, Malvar was conducting negotiations with the Spanish consul in Hong Kong to secure autonomy (but not independence) for the Philippines. It is unclear whether Malvar was doing this on his own or with the knowledge of other members of the Filipino exile community in Hong Kong, and it is also unclear what his motives were. See Taylor, *Philippine Insurrection,* 1:462–63; D/Potenciano Hilario, Feb. 20, 1902, RG395/4229; *PEF,* Feb. 28, 1898, pp. 59, 64; Saulo, *Emilio Aguinaldo,* 216.

Chapter 3. Liberated Batangas

1. Agoncillo, *Malolos,* 133–38; Zaide, *Philippine Revolution,* 180–83; Saulo, *Emilio Aguinaldo,* 220–31.

2. Sastrón, *Insurrección,* 530–31; Kalaw, *Aide-de-Camp,* 13–15.

3. Kalaw, *Aide-de-camp,* 15; Marquez, "Lipa," 52–55; Report concerning G.N.N., c. June 1898; Report by unidentified person to Damaso Ybarra, c. June 1898; Entry for June 19, 1898, in "Vales pagados durante el mes de Junio de 1898," all in PRP/Pr10–11/B1; Statement by Anastasio Marasigan concerning Eustacio Maloles, June 19, 1898, PRP/Pr10–11/Batangas; Emilio Aguinaldo to Leon Apacible, June 12, 1898, xeroxed copy of letter in the possession of the Apacible family, Taal, Batangas. Also see note 31 of the previous chapter.

4. Taylor, *Philippine Insurrection,* 3:96; Sastrón, *Insurrección,* 530.

5. Sastrón, *Insurrección,* 534–36; Zaide, *Philippine Revolution,* 224; Eleuterio Marasigan, Plan of attack, July 16, 1898, PRP/Pr10–11/B1; Miguel Malvar to Leon Apacible, July 21, 1898, xeroxed copy of letter in the possession of the Apacible family, Taal, Batangas.

6. Emilio Aguinaldo, Decree, June 18, 1898; and "Instrucciones sobre el régimen de las provincias y pueblos," June 20, 1898, PRP/Katipunan Papers/folder 14; Agoncillo, *Malolos,* 227–29. The decrees are translated in Taylor, *Philippine Insurrection,* 3:113–25, but the translation contains numerous errors; among other things, it indicates that the minimum voting age was twenty, rather than twenty-one.

7. Guerrero, "Luzon at War," 47–70, 133–35, 140–49.

8. "Acta de elecciones populares," Balayan, July 3, 1898, PIR/74/SD1200.9; "Acta de elecciones populares," Batangas City, July 4, 1898, and the proceedings of the elections in Bauan, Calaca, Calatagan, Cuenca, and sixteen other towns in PRP/I15/Election Returns, Batangas, 1898.

9. "Acta de elecciones populares," Taal, Calatagan, San Luis, Ybaan, Lipa, Cuenca, and Lobo, all in July 1898, PRP/I15/Election Returns, Batangas, 1898.

10. "Acta de elecciones de Jefe provincial y 3 consejeros," Aug. 9, 1898, PRP/I15/Election Returns, Batangas, 1898.

11. Luis Luna to Emilio Aguinaldo, Aug. 7, 1898, in "Acta de elecciones populares," San Jose, 1898, PRP/I15/Election Returns Batangas, 1898; Felix Unzon to Miguel Malvar, July 8, 1898, PIR/56/SD936.5.

12. See the *expedientes* and letters appended to "Acta de eleciones populares," Bauan, 1898, in PRP/I15/Election Returns, Batangas, 1898 and 1899. My information about the composition of political factions in the Spanish period was derived from *EGB*, Bauan, 1889, 1890, and 1892. For other examples of problems with municipal officials: Manuel Genato to Emilio Aguinaldo, Nov. 15, 1898, PRP/P4; Genato to Sr. Secretario del Interior, Jan. 27, 1899, PRP/I3.

13. Entry of June 28, 1898 (signed by Santiago Rillo) in "Vales pagados durante el mes de Junio de 1898," PRP/Pr10–11/B1; V. Lukban to Emilio Aguinaldo, July 14, 1898, PRP/SD4.2; Santiago Rillo to Emilio Aguinaldo, Sept. 13, 1898, PRP/SD533.2; Mga guinoo sa bayan ng Tuy to Aguinaldo, Sept. 22, 1898, PRP/P2; Junta popular ng Liang to Emilio Aguinaldo, Oct. 22, 1898, PRP/P14; Ileto, "Food Crisis," 102–04.

14. Mga guinoo sa bayan ng Tuy to Aguinaldo, Sept. 22, 1898, PRP/P2; Ricardo Ramos to Presidente provincial, Batangas, Nov. 30, 1898, PRP/Pr10–11/B1; Ileto, "Food Crisis," 102–05.

15. Libros de Entierros and Libros de Bautismos, Parish Records of Lian, Balayan, and Calaca. We should not, of course, discount the possibility that the low baptismal totals were the result of defective registration, but we should also realize that, if baptisms were under-registered, so too were burials.

16. Aguinaldo, "Instrucciones," June 20, 1898, PRP/Katipunan Papers/folder 14; Guerrero, "Luzon at War," 101–04.

17. Mga guinoo sa bayan ng Tuy to Aguinaldo, Sept. 22, 1898, PRP/P2; M. del Rosario to Jefe Provincial, Batangas, Oct. 21, and Nov. 24, 1898; same to Presidente Local, Lian, Nov. 23, 1898, PRP/I14/Secretary of the Interior, Correspondence of the First Division, Letters Sent; Ciriaco Laurel to Jefe Provincial, Batangas, Nov. 30, 1898; Ricardo Ramos to Presidente Provincial, Nov. 30 and Dec. 14, 1898; and unidentified correspondent to Junta Popular, Lian, c. Dec. 1898, PRP/Pr10–11/B1; M. Genato to Secretario de Hacienda, Nov. 29, 1898, PRP/F14; Julian Ambalada to Secretario de Hacienda, Jan. 2, 1899, PRP/F16; Ileto, "Food Crisis," 104; Guerrero, "Luzon at War," 116.

18. See Judicial proceedings against Alejandro Plata (Balayan), Feb. 17, 1899, PRP/Pr10–11/Balayan; Judicial proceedings against Luciano Villanueva et al. (Nasugbu), c. Feb. 1899; and Judicial proceedings against Felipe Gonzales (Nasugbu), Oct. 31, 1898, PRP/Pr10–11/B1; Bibiano Ramos to Emilio Aguinaldo, Sept. 10, 1898, PIR/56/SD936.10; B. Ramos to Emilio Aguinaldo, Oct. 17, 1898, PRP/P7; M. Genato to Emilio Aguinaldo, Oct. 26, 1898, PRP/P3; M. Genato to Emilio Aguinaldo, Nov. 15 and Dec. 4, 1898, PRP/P4; Guerrero, "Luzon at War," 127; Ileto, "Food Crisis," 112.

19. These observations are based on an examination of Libros de Entierros and Libros de Bautismos for the towns of Batangas City, Cuenca, Lipa, Lobo, San Jose, San Juan, Taysan, and Ybaan.

20. Kalaw, *Aide-de-Camp,* 16–18; Marquez, "Lipa," 60–62.

21. John A. S. Grenville and George B. Young, *Politics, Strategy, and American Diplomacy: Studies in Foreign Policy, 1873–1917* (New Haven, 1966), 267–96; Thomas McCormick, "Insular Imperialism and the Open Door: The China Market and the Spanish-American War," *Pacific Historical Review* 32 (May 1963): 155–69; and *China Market: America's Quest for Informal Empire, 1893–1901* (Chicago, 1967), 107–25; Walter LaFeber, *The New Empire: An Interpretation of American Expansion, 1860–1898* (Ithaca, 1963), 361–62, 408–17.

22. McCormick, *China Market,* 107–25; H. Wayne Morgan, *William McKinley and His America* (Syracuse, 1963), 388–413; H. Wayne Morgan, *America's Road to Empire: The War with Spain and Overseas Expansion* (New York, 1965), 75–97; Lewis L. Gould, *The Spanish-American War and President McKinley* (Lawrence, Kan., 1982), 62–110; Ernest R. May, *Imperial Democracy: The Emergence of America as a Great Power* (New York, 1961), 243–62; David Trask, *The War with Spain in 1898* (New York, 1981), 382–85, 439–56. Also consult Paolo E. Coletta, "McKinley, the Peace Negotiations, and the Acquisition of the Philippines," *Pacific Historical Review* 30 (Nov. 1961): 341–50; and Ephraim K. Smith, "A Question from Which We Could Not Escape: William McKinley and the Decision to Acquire the Philippine Islands," *Diplomatic History* 9 (Fall 1985): 363–75.

23. Gould, *Spanish-American War,* 63–67; Trask, *War with Spain,* 382–88; Russell A. Alger, *The Spanish-American War* (New York, 1901), 326; U.S. Adjutant General's Office, *Correspondence Relating to the War with Spain,* 2 vols. (Washington, D.C., 1902), 2:635, 676–78.

24. Trask, *War with Spain,* 391, 409–22; Agoncillo, *Malolos,* 175–214; Zaide, *Philippine Revolution,* 205–20; Miller, "*Benevolent Assimilation,*" 42–46.

25. May, *Imperial Democracy,* 252–62; Trask, *War with Spain,* 435–72; Gould, *Spanish-American War,* 97–110; Morgan, *America's Road,* 91–98.

26. Gould, *Spanish-American War,* 110–18; Miller, "*Benevolent Assimilation,*" 46–66; Agoncillo, *Malolos,* 409–52.

27. Malvar's whereabouts can be determined from Malvar to Eliseo Claudio, Jan. 28, 1899, EC; Malvar to Elias Mendoza et al., Feb. 8, 1899, PIR/72/SD1162.7; D/Vicente Agregado, Feb. 12, 1902, and D/Manuel Macatangay, Mar. 27, 1902, RG395/4229. In his own declaration (D/Miguel Malvar, n.d., RG395/4229), Malvar indicated that he was ordered to the front in March 1899, but, as we shall see, the order did not come until the end of April.

28. Taylor, *Philippine Insurrection,* 3:125–27, 229–34. (The central government, however, also had the power to make appointments above the rank of captain: see Taylor, *Philippine Insurrection,* 3:44–45, 129.)

29. Since no complete muster roll of the Filipino Army in Batangas exists, it is necessary to piece together a picture of the officer corps from correspondence, newspaper accounts, and other surviving sources. On Rillo, see Pass issued by Santiago Rillo to Venancio Conde, Mar. 20, 1899, PRP/Pr10–11/B1; and D/Manuel Scarella, May 19, 1902, RG395/4229. On Laurel, see Taylor, *Philippine Insurrection,* 4:52, and Leon Novenario to Eliseo Claudio, Nov. 21, 1899, EC. On

Gonzales, see the Promissory Note signed by Santiago Malihan, July 12, 1899, EC. On Catigbac and Bolaños: *Columnas Volantes,* June 25, 1899, p. 2; and July 9, 1899, p. 3, in PIR/92/D4. On Lopez: Joaquin Mendoza to Eliseo Claudio, Feb. 2, 1899, EC. On various others: Santiago Rillo to Sr. Secretario de Guerra, Aug. 30, 1899, PRP/AN8. Some leading military figures of the revolution of 1896—Ananias Diocno of Taal and Eleuterio Marasigan of Calaca, for example—were sent on an expedition to Panay in late 1898, and they fought in the Visayas during the Philippine-American War. See Agoncillo, *Malolos,* 420–29; Taylor, *Philippine Insurrection,* 2:375–416; Eleuterio Marasigan to Emilio Aguinaldo, Mar. 17, 1899, PRP/P3.

30. May, "Filipino Revolutionaries," 53–64. There were 88 students enrolled in the Malabanan school in the school year 1881–82; and 95 in 1882–83. Of the latter, 37 had been enrolled during the previous year; 58 had not. Hence, during those two school years, a total of 146 students (88 + 58), including Miguel Malvar, were enrolled at the Malabanan school. See Libros de Matrícula de Estudios Generales y de Aplicación de Segunda Enseñanza, 1881–83, Archives of the University of Santo Tomas, Manila.

31. Statement of Manuel Scarella about Elias Mendoza, Mar. 17, 1902, RG395/2394; Miguel Malvar to Elias Mendoza et al., Feb. 8, 1899, PIR/72/SD1162.7.

32. Crisanto Borruel to Eliseo Claudio, Feb. 1, 1899, EC. See also Geronimo Hormilla to Jefe Militar, Batangas, c. Feb. 1900, PRP/Pr10–11/B1; Segundo Danis y Natividad to Sr. Secretario de Guerra, c. July 1899, PRP/AN8.

33. As we shall see, there was more than a little insubordination in the U.S. Army, too. But, unlike their Filipino counterparts, American commanders could deal with insubordinate behavior summarily and effectively. Officers who failed to follow orders could be relieved or otherwise punished. If a Filipino commander attempted to adopt a similar approach with an insubordinate warlord, the warlord might decide to leave the field and take his followers with him.

34. Taylor, *Philippine Insurrection,* 4:587–91. For earlier regulations relating to conscription, see Taylor, *Philippine Insurrection,* 3:231–32.

35. "Relación . . . de los quintos . . . de los pueblos expresados," c. Nov. 1899, PRP/Pr12–13/Miscellaneous; Headquarters, Batangas City to Capitán encargado del depósito de quintos, Lipa, Sept. 29, 1899; same to Sr. capitán comandante de la 5a Compañía de Batallón Sungay, Oct. 31, 1899; same to Sr. capitán de la 2a compañía del Bn Sungay, no. 2, Oct. 31, 1899; same to Sr. presidente local de Bauan, Nov. 27, 1899; Elias Mendoza to Sr. Capitán de la 3a Compañía del Bn S. no. 2, Dec. 14, 1899, BHQ. On desertion, see note 49 in this chapter.

36. Emilio Aguinaldo and Vicente Albano Pacis, *A Second Look at America* (New York, 1957), 98–99.

37. Vivencio R. Jose, "The Rise and Fall of Antonio Luna," *Philippine Social Sciences and Humanities Review* 36 (Mar.–Dec. 1971): 172–441; Agoncillo, *Malolos,* 453–539; Taylor, *Philippine Insurrection,* 2:194–258.

38. USWD, 1899, 1, pt.5:30–74, 364–66.

39. Emilio Aguinaldo to Mariano Trias, Apr. 30, 1899, PIR/36/SD638.2; Taylor, *Philippine Insurrection,* 2:232.

40. Miguel Malvar to Sebastian Caneo et al., May 5, 1899; Malvar to Caneo, May 7, 1899; R. Banaad to Caneo, May 9, 1899, PRP/Pr10–11/Batangas.

41. USWD, 1899, 1, pt.4:134–36; Malvar to Sebastian Caneo et al., May 11, 12, and 18, 1899, PRP/Pr10–11/Batangas; Malvar to Col. Solis, June 9, 1899, PRP/RL11/Malvar.

42. USWD, 1899, 1, pt.4:136–41; 1, pt.5:366–71; USWD, 1900, 1, pt.5:272–385; Taylor, *Philippine Insurrection,* 2:232–33, 4:664–68; *Historical Sketch of the operations, etc. of the Twenty-First Regiment of U.S. Infantry* (St. Paul, 1903), 4–6, found in RG391/21st Infantry, Regimental Histories and Historical Notes.

43. Taylor, *Philippine Insurrection,* 4:669–70; *Columnas Volantes,* July 25, 1899, pp. 3–4; D/Crisanto Borruel, Feb. 15, 1902, RG395/2398; Eustacio Maloles, "Diario de Operaciones realizadas por las fuerzas del Batallón Banajaw," PIR/56/SD942.3. I am grateful to Rey Ileto for providing me with a copy of the last document.

44. Robert Hall to AG, 1Div., 8AC, Aug. 3, 1899, Box 2, Robert Hall Papers, USMAL; *Twenty-First Regiment,* 7–9; D/Crisanto Borruel, Feb. 15, 1902, RG395/2398; Maloles, "Batallón Banajaw," PIR/56/SD942.3.

45. Maloles, "Batallón Banajaw," PIR/56/SD942.3; *Columnas Volantes,* Aug. 9, 1899, p. 6; Juan Buenafe to Eliseo Claudio, Aug. 16, 1899; Briccio Casala to Claudio, Oct. 17, 1899; and Miguel Malvar to Claudio and Felix Reyes, Oct. 19, 1899, EC.

46. *Twenty-First Regiment,* 9–10; "Historical Sketch of the Foreign Service of the 10th Battery Field Artillery," Con. 2, Charles P. Summerall Papers, LCMD; James Parker to Henry Lawton, Sept. 21 and Oct. 2, 1899, James Parker Papers, USMAL; Juan Buenafe to Eliseo Claudio, Aug. 16, 1899, EC.

47. "10th Battery Field Artillery"; James Parker, *The Old Army: Memories, 1872–1918* (Philadelphia, 1929), 241–42; USWD, 1900, 1, pt.7:166–69; Reme (pen name), "Notas de la Guerra," article in incomplete issue of *Columnas Volantes* (probably Oct. 11, 1899), found in PIR/92/D4; Maloles, "Batallón Banajaw," PIR/56/SD942.3.

48. Maloles, "Batallón Banajaw," PIR/56/SD942.3; Malvar to Eliseo Claudio and Felix Reyes, Oct. 19, 1899, EC; *Twenty-First Regiment,* 11–13; USWD, 1900, 1, pt.4:347–57; Parker, *Old Army,* 243–44; "10th Battery Field Artillery."

49. On desertion: Headquarters, Batangas City to unidentified, Oct. 11, 1899; same to Pedro Punsalan, Oct. 12, 1899; same to Presidentes locales de los pueblos de San Jose, Bauan, Rosario, Lipa y Batangas, Oct. 14, 1899; same to presidente local, Calaca, Oct. 16, 1899; same to presidentes de los pueblos de Rosario, San Juan y Lobo, Oct. 23, 1899; same to presidente local, Talisay, Oct. 24, 1899; same to presidente local, Tanauan, Oct. 24, 1899; same to presidente local, Lipa, Nov. 25, 1899, BHQ. On shortage of supplies: Juan Buenafe to Eliseo Claudio, Aug. 16, 1899, EC. On pay: Roman Abril to Eliseo Claudio, Oct. 23, 1899, EC. On

illness: Pass issued by Juan Buenafe, Dec. 1, 1899; Director, Hospital Militar to Eliseo Claudio, Dec. 4, 1899, EC.

50. On contributions: *Columnas Volantes,* June 25, 1899, p. 6; July 2, 1899, p. 4; Aug. 9, 1899, p. 6; Donations of town of Taysan to the soldiers, Aug. 24, 1899, PRP/Pr10–11/B1; D/Francisco Untalan, Feb. 15, 1902, RG395/2394; D/Potenciano Hilario, Feb. 20, 1902, RG395/4229. On the hospital: *Columnas Volantes,* July 2, 1899, p. 3; Aug. 9, 1899, p. 6. On celebrations: *Columnas Volantes,* Aug. 9, 1899, p. 6; Aug. 30, 1899, pp. 2–4.

51. *Columnas Volantes,* June 25, 1899, p. 2; July 9, 1899, p. 3.

52. Miguel Malvar to Elias Mendoza et al., Feb. 8, 1899, PIR/72/SD1162.7.

53. For the decrees and regulations relating to militia organizations, see Taylor, *Philippine Insurrection,* 3:125–27; 4:9–13, 511. On appointments: D/ Vicente Agregado, Feb. 12, 1902 (Agregado was, in fact, Miguel Malvar's classmate at the Malabanan school); D/Feliciano Cantos, Feb. 18, 1902; D/Fernando Garcia, June 7, 1902; D/Gabino Abaya, Feb. 21, 1902; and D/Jose Castillo, Feb. 21, 1902, all in RG395/4229.

54. Malvar to Elias Mendoza et al., Feb. 8, 1899, PIR/72/SD1162.7; Headquarters, Batangas City to Capn Comdte del destac. de Bauan, Oct. 1 or 2, 1899, BHQ; Mariano Cabrera, "Plan de defensa de Batangas," Dec. 25, 1899, PIR/56/ SD936.8.

55. U.S. Navy Department, *Annual Reports of the Navy Department for the Year 1899* (Washington, D.C., 1899), 419, 436; *Annual Reports of the Navy Department for the Year 1900* (Washington, D.C., 1900), 507–08; Entries, Mar. 28–29, 1899, Logbook of the U.S.S. *Charleston;* Entries, May 2–4, 6–7, 1899, Logbook of the U.S.S. *Petrel;* and Entries, May 2–7, Oct. 29, Nov. 4–5, 1899, Logbook of the U.S.S. *Princeton,* RG24; D/Feliciano Cantos, Feb. 18, 1902; D/Gabino Abaya, Feb. 21, 1902, RG395/4229; D/Francisco Untalan, Feb. 15, 1902, RG395/2394. Also see note 59 of this chapter.

56. Guerrero, "Luzon at War," 71–84; Taylor, *Philippine Insurrection,* 4:157– 59, 625–26; Manuel Genato to Eliseo Claudio, June 14, 1899, EC.

57. D/Apolonio Belmonte, Feb. 15, 1902, RG395/2398.

58. D/Jose Villanueva, Feb. 12, 1902, RG395/2380; Headquarters, Batangas City to Santiago Rillo, Sept. 23, 1899, BHQ.

59. Statement of Manuel Scarella about Elias Mendoza, Mar. 17, 1902, RG395/2394; D/Manuel Scarella, May 19, 1902, RG395/4229; Entries, Mar. 28– 29, 1899, Logbook of the U.S.S. *Charleston,* RG24; Navy Department, *Annual Reports . . . 1899,* 419; Santiago Rillo to Eliseo Claudio, Mar. 29, 1899, EC.

60. Statement of Manuel Scarella about Elias Mendoza, Mar. 17, 1902, RG395/2394.

61. Spy report from the southern Tagalog region, c. June or July 1899, v. 17, Worcester's Philippine Collection (a collection of documents and papers of Dean C. Worcester), Department of Rare Books and Special Collections, University of Michigan.

62. Headquarters, Batangas City to Capn Comdte del destac. de Bauan, Oct. 1 or 2, 1899; same to capitán comandante Bn Maquiling no. 1, Bauan, Oct. 2, 1899; same to Comandante del pueblo de Lobo, Oct. 2, 1899, BHQ.

63. Elias Mendoza to presidente local, Batangas City, Dec. 7, 1899; same to G. Farol, Dec. 16, 1899; same to Capitán de la 3a Compañía del Bn. Sungay no. 2, Dec. 31, 1899; same to Santiago Rillo, Dec. 31, 1899; same to Eliseo Claudio, Dec. 31, 1899; same to presidente local, Batangas City, Dec. 31, 1899; same to Vicente Agregado, Dec. 31, 1899, all in BHQ; Mariano Cabrera, "Plan de defensa de Batangas," Dec. 25, 1899, PIR/56/SD936.8.

64. D/Crisanto Javier, Feb. 17, 1899, RG395/4229; D/Francisco Untalan, Feb. 15, 1902, RG395/2394; *Columnas Volantes,* Oct. 19, 1899, p. 5; Nov. 25, 1899, p. 5.

Chapter 4. The Invasion, January 1900

1. Biographical sketch of John Leland Jordan, JLJ; Military Service Record of John L. Jordan, RG94; John L. Jordan to Adj., 38USV, Oct. 5, 1899, and John L. Jordan to AG, U.S. Army, July 1, 1900, RG94/LSB, 38USV, Co. D.

2. Jordan to Adj., 38USV, Oct. 1 and 3, 1899, RG94/LSB, 38USV, Co. D; George Anderson to AG, Washington, Sept. 16 and 23, Oct. 15, 1899, Jan. 4, 1900, RG94/LSB, 38USV; "History of the 38th Infantry, U.S. Vols.," RG94/HSVR.

3. John L. Jordan to Elizabeth King Jordan, Dec. 28, 1899, JLJ.

4. Albert N. Marquis, ed., *Who's Who in America, 1908–1909* (Chicago, 1908), 1675, 2026; Karl I. Faust, *Campaigning in the Philippines* (San Francisco, 1899), 147–51, 156–58, 169–77, 184–86, 192–93, 233–40; James A. LeRoy, *The Americans in the Philippines,* 2 vols. (Boston, 1914), 2:30–36, 45–48, 138–39; Theodore Schwan to Henry Corbin, Oct. 25, 1899, Con. 1, HCC. In his biography of Robert Bullard, Allan Millett writes that Schwan assisted Otis in making the plans for the invasion; that is likely, since Schwan was Otis's chief of staff, but I have found no evidence to prove it. See Allan R. Millett, *The General: Robert Lee Bullard and Officership in the United States Army* (Westport, Conn., 1975), 124.

5. USWD, 1900, 1, pt.4:369; pt.5:388, 416; pt.6:641, 645.

6. USWD, 1900, 1, pt.4:369; pt.5:388–89; pt.6:641–42.

7. On the quality of the weapons: W. H. B. Smith and Joseph E. Smith, *The Book of Rifles,* 4th ed. (Harrisburg, Pa., 1972), 156–62, 357–62. On Filipino marksmanship: Interview with Crisostomo Cuasay, San Luis, July 26, 1976.

8. On those weapons: USWD, 1900, 1 pt.5:542–46; Graham A. Cosmas, *An Army for Empire: The United States Army in the Spanish-American War* (Columbia, Mo., 1971), 5, 158, 201; W. H. B. Smith and Joseph E. Smith, *Small Arms of the World,* 10th ed. (Harrisburg, Pa., 1973), 100–02, 116, 129–30.

9. Interviews with Severino Magsombol, San Luis, July 22, 1976; Emilio Vergara, Mataasnakahoy, July 27, 1976; and Calixto Silva, Lipa, July 27, 1976.

10. Artemio Ricarte to Mariano Barruga, Dec. 21, 1899, PIR/70/SD1140.1; USWD, 1900, 1, pt.4:365; John L. Jordan to Elizabeth King Jordan, Jan. 10, 1900, JLJ; Artemio Ricarte, *Memoirs of Artemio Ricarte* (Manila, 1963), 100–01.

11. My estimate of the size of Trias's force in Cavite and northwestern Laguna is a rough one based on D/Mariano Noriel, Apr. 28, 1902, RG395/2394; USWD, 1900, 1, pt.4:370; pt.5:434; pt.6:643.

12. USWD, 1900, 1, pt.6:642.

13. USWD, 1900, 1, pt.5:389, 417, 425–27, 509, 510, 512, 550. On the uniforms and gear: Robert H. Rankin, *Uniforms of the Army* (New York, 1967), 52–53; GO no. 75, Dec. 2, 1899, RG94/RO, 28USV. On the use of the Chinese by the U.S. Army: Beaumont B. Buck, *Memories of Peace and War* (San Antonio, 1935), 68–69, 72; Robert L. Bullard to Q.M., 39USV, Dec. 20, 1899, and same to CO, Co. A, 39USV, Dec. 29, 1899, RG94/LSB, 39USV.

14. USWD, 1900, 1, pt.5:389–90, 419, 427–28; D/Mariano Noriel, Apr. 28, 1902, RG395/2394.

15. USWD, 1900, 1, pt.5:428; George Gelbach, "A Trip to the Philippine Islands with the U.S. Army," SAW/46USV.

16. USWD, 1900, 1, pt.5:391–92, 419–21, 428–30, 551–52, 561; D/Mariano Noriel, Apr. 28, 1902, RG395/2394.

17. USWD, 1900, 1, pt.5:431–32; pt.6:626, 628–39, 635–39; William E. Birkhimer, "28th Infantry, United States Volunteers," RG94/HSVR.

18. USWD, 1900, 1, pt.4:378–79; pt.5:394, 439; Mariano Trias to Ambrosio Mojica, Apr. 18, 1900, PIR/77/1271.1.

19. USWD, 1900, 1, pt.5:393–94, 429–30, 435, 553–54.

20. USWD, 1900, 1, pt.5:394, 439; pt.6:633, 646.

21. Diary Entry, Nov. 26, 1899, Diary 1, Con. 1, RLB; Millett, *General,* 32–119.

22. Diary Entries, Dec. 7, 19, 23, and 24, 1899, Jan. 3, 1900, Diary 1, Con. 1, RLB; John Henry Parker, "Memories of the Service," John Henry Parker Papers, USMAL; Robert Bullard to Theodore Schwan, Jan. 2, 1900, RG94/LSB, 39USV; "History of the Thirty-Ninth Infantry, U.S. Volunteers," RG94/HSVR; USWD, 1900, 1, pt.7:393–94; Millett, *General,* 125–26; Maloles, "Batallón Banajaw," PIR/56/SD942.3.

23. USWD, 1900, 1, pt.4:377; Parker, "Memories."

24. Diary Entry, Jan. 24, 1900, Diary 1, Con. 1, RLB; Bullard to Chief of Staff, the Palace, Jan. 10, 1900, RG94/LSB, 39USV.

25. Maloles, "Batallón Banajaw," PIR/56/SD942.3.

26. Ibid.; "Thirty-Ninth Infantry"; Bullard to Chief of Staff, the Palace, Jan. 10, 1900, RG94/LSB, 39USV; "Historical Sketch of the Foreign Service of the 10th Battery Field Artillery," Con. 2, Charles P. Summerall Papers, LCMD.

27. Mariano Cabrera, "Plan de defensa de Batangas," Dec. 25, 1899, PIR/56/SD936.8; Entries, Dec. 29, 1899–Jan. 7, 1900, Logbook of U.S.S. *Mariveles,* RG24.

28. Bullard to Chief of Staff, the Palace, Jan. 10, 1900, RG94/LSB, 39USV; "Thirty-Ninth Infantry"; Diary Entry, Jan. 24, 1900, Diary 1, Con. 1, RLB.

29. Ibid.; USWD, 1900, 1, pt.5:516, 539; "10th Battery Field Artillery"; Maloles, "Batallón Banajaw," PIR/56/SD942.3.

30. Bullard to Chief of Staff, the Palace, Jan. 10, 1900, RG94/LSB, 39USV; Diary Entry, Jan. 24, 1900, Diary 1, Con. 1, RLB; Maloles, "Batallón Banajaw," PIR/56/SD942.3.

31. George Anderson to AG, Bacoor, Jan. 4, 1900, RG94/LSB, 38USV; John L. Jordan to Thomas Wards, Apr. 29, 1900, RG94/LSB, 38USV, Co. D.

32. USWD, 1900, 1, pt.4:379; pt.6:646–47.

33. George Anderson to AG, Schwan's Brig., Jan. 21, 1900, RG94/LSB, 38USV; Crane, *Experiences,* 326–27.

34. Anderson to AG, Schwan's Brig., Jan. 21, 1900, RG94/LSB, 38USV; Crane, *Experiences,* 327–28; Diary Entry, Jan. 11, 1900, THS; "History of the 38th Infantry."

35. Anderson to AG, Schwan's Brig., Jan. 21, 1900, RG94/LSB, 38USV; Diary Entry, Jan. 12, 1900, THS.

36. Diary Entry, Jan. 24, 1900, Diary 1, Con. 1, RLB; Anderson to AG, Schwan's Brig., Jan. 21, 1900, RG94/LSB, 38USV; Millett, *General,* 128.

37. USWD, 1900, 1, pt.4:380–82; pt.5:395–96, 420, 441–47; pt.6:647–48.

38. Kalaw, *Aide-de-Camp,* 18–19; Interviews with Dionisio Laygo, Lipa, July 27, 1976, and Calixto Silva, Lipa, July 27, 1976.

39. Melecio Bolaños to Sr. Presidente Local de Taysan, Jan. 13, 1900 (transmitting Malvar's order of Jan. 9, 1900), PRP/Pr8, Taysan; Ventura Amparo to Sr. Presidente Local de Rosario, Jan. 12, 1900, PRP/Pr8, Rosario; Mariano Cabrera to Eliseo Claudio, Jan. 9, 1900, EC; George Anderson to AG, Schwan's Brig., Jan. 21, 1900, RG94/LSB, 38USV.

40. Ileto, *Pasyon,* 94–96, 176–77.

41. "History of the 38th Infantry"; "10th Battery Field Artillery"; John L. Jordan to Elizabeth King Jordan, Jan. 23, 1900, JLJ; George Anderson to AG, Schwan's Brig., Jan. 14 and 21, 1900, RG94/LSB, 38USV.

42. George Anderson to AG, Schwan's Brig., Jan. 14 and 21, 1900, RG94/LSB, 38USV; Crane, *Experiences,* 329–30.

43. Diary Entry, Jan. 24, 1900, Diary 1, Con. 1, RLB; Bullard to AG, Dep. Pac., Jan. 16, 1900, RG94/LSB, 39USV; Anderson to AG, Schwan's Brig., Jan. 14 and 21, 1900, RG94/LSB, 38USV; Crane, *Experiences,* 330–31.

44. Diary Entry, Mar. 6, 1900, Supplement to Diary 1, Con. 1, RLB; Crane, *Experiences,* 331–32.

45. Diary Entry, Jan. 24, 1900, Diary 1, Con. 1, RLB; Crane, *Experiences,* 332–33; Anderson to AG, Schwan's Brig., Jan. 14 and 21, 1900, RG94/LSB, 38USV; John L. Jordan to Adj., 1B, 38USV, Feb. 15, 1900, RG94/LSB, 38USV, Co. D; Robert M. Nolan to W. A. Holbrook, Feb. 16, 1900, RG94/LSB, 38USV, Co. G; USWD, 1900, 1, pt.5:453.

46. USWD, 1900, 1, pt.5:446; Crane, *Experiences,* 333–34; Diary Entry, Jan. 24, 1900, Diary 1, Con. 1, RLB; Millett, *General,* 129–30.

47. USWD, 1900, 1, pt.5:448–49, 451–52, 534; Diary Entry, Jan. 24, 1900, Diary 1, Con. 1, RLB.

48. Santiago Rillo to Mariano Cabrera, Jan. 13, 1900, EC.

49. Mariano Cabrera, "Plan de defensa de Batangas," Dec. 25, 1899, PIR/56/SD936.8; Mariano Cabrera to Eliseo Claudio, Jan. 14, 1900, PIR/56/SD936.7; D/Manuel Scarella, May 19, 1902, RG395/4229; Charles H. Muir, Enclosure to 13th Endorsement, Dec. 15, 1905, RG94/AGO1078175.

50. D/Pablo Yturralde, Feb. 20, 1902; D/Feliciano Cantos, Feb. 18, 1902; and D/Francisco Abas, Feb. 18, 1902, RG395/4229; Celestino Gutierrez to Jefe Local de Taysan, Jan. 15, 1900, PRP/Pr8, Taysan; USWD, 1900, 1, pt.4:384; pt.5:457.

51. USWD, 1900, 1, pt.4:384; pt.5:457; Entry, Jan. 15, 1900, Logbook of U.S.S. *Mariveles,* RG24; Charles H. Muir, Enclosure to 13th Endorsement, Dec. 18, 1905, RG94/AGO1078175.

52. USWD, 1900, 1, pt.5:397, 452, 455.

53. "History of the 38th Infantry"; Charles H. Muir, Enclosure to 13th Endorsement, Dec. 18, 1905, RG94/AGO1078175; USWD, 1900, 1, pt.5:530–31; John L. Jordan to Elizabeth King Jordan, Jan. 23 and Feb. 18, 1900, JLJ; Diary Entry, Jan. 16, 1900, THS. Published reports by Schwan and Bates suggested—incorrectly, it appears—that Gardener's column did most of the fighting and occupied the town (USWD, 1900, 1, pt.4:383–84; pt.5:455; pt.6:650). Gardener's role was challenged by Muir and others, and Gardener was grilled about his actions in an official inquiry. (See the first two sources cited in this note as well as Gardener's testimony in GI, pp. 822–27.)

54. USWD, 1900, 1, pt.5:399, 457–61; Diary Entry, Jan. 17, 1900, THS.

55. USWD, 1900, 1, pt.5:399, 459, 465.

56. Loyd Wheaton to AG, Manila, Jan. 16, 1900, RG395/2403; W. H. Johnston to AG, Wheaton's Brig., Jan. 17 and 18, 1900, RG395/2411; Walter Schuyler, "History of the 46th Infantry, U.S.V.," RG94/HSVR.

57. Johnston to AG, Wheaton's Brig., Jan. 18, 1900, RG395/2411.

58. The only hint about the identity of the Filipino commander is provided by Captain Jordan, who in a letter to his mother indicated that the enemy was led by "General San Miguel" (see Jordan to Elizabeth King Jordan, Jan. 23, 1900, JLJ). Probably, he was referring to Malvar, since Malvar's troops sometimes referred to him as San Miguel. There was, in fact, a general named Luciano San Miguel in the Filipino Army, but at the time he was in the Zambales Mountains in northwestern Luzon.

59. C. H. Muir to Adj., 38USV, Jan. 20, 1900, RG94/LSB, 38USV; George Anderson to Theodore Schwan, Mar. 20, 1900, RG94/LSB, 38USV.

60. W. H. Johnston to AG, Wheaton's Brig., Jan. 20, 1900, RG395/2411; George Anderson to Adj., Schwan's Brig., Jan. 20, 1900, RG94/LSB, 38USV; Entry, Jan. 19, 1900, Logbook of U.S.S. *Marietta,* RG24.

61. C. H. Muir to Adj., 38USV, Jan. 20, 1900, RG94/LSB, 38USV; John L. Jordan to Adj., 1B, 38USV, Jan. 20, 1900, RG94/LSB, 38USV, Co. D; Jordan to Elizabeth King Jordan, Jan. 23, 1900; JLJ; "History of the 38th Infantry."

62. Muir to Adj., 38USV, Jan. 20, 1900, RG94/LSB, 38USV; "History of the 38th Infantry."

63. W. H. Johnston to AG, Wheaton's Brig., Jan. 20, 1900, RG395/2411;

Schuyler, "History of the 46th Infantry"; Entry, Jan. 19, 1900, Logbook of U.S.S. *Marietta,* RG24.

Chapter 5. With the Americans

1. George Anderson to AG, Los Baños, Jan. 26, 1900; Anderson to Barry, AG, Manila, Jan. 28, 1900; B. A. Read to CO, Lipa, Feb. 2, 1900, RG94/LSB, 38USV; C. J. Crane to AG, 8AC, Jan. 26, 1900, RG94/LSB, 38USV, 2B; USWD, 1900, 1, pt.5:473; Loyd Wheaton to AG, 1Div., Jan. 29, 1900, RG395/2403; Diary Entries, Feb. 1–4, 1900, THS.

2. Mariano Trias to Sr. Jefe Militar del distrito de Infanta, Feb. 23, 1900, PIR/77/SD1271.3; Trias to Ambrosio Mojica, Apr. 18, 1900, PIR/77/SD1271.1.

3. Santiago Rillo to Eliseo Claudio, Jan. 20 and 29, 1900; Felix Farol to Eliseo Claudio, Jan. 22, 1900; Nicolas Ramos to Claudio, Jan. 25, 1900; Juan Buenafe to Claudio, Jan. 30, 1900, EC; D/Crisanto Borruel, Feb. 15, 1902, RG395/2398.

4. See for example Eliseo Claudio to Santiago Rillo, Jan. 21, 1900; Felix Farol to Claudio, Jan. 22 and 24, 1900; Nicolas Ramos to Claudio, Jan. 25, 1900, EC.

5. USWD, 1900, 1, pt.5:411–12, 526–27, 529–35; "Historical Sketch of the 45th Infantry, U.S.V.," Joseph H. Dorst Papers, USMAL. Detailed reports of most of these encounters can be found in RG94/LSB, 38USV and 39USV.

6. George Morgan to AG, 1Div., 8AC, Feb. 7, 1900, RG94/LSB, 28USV; George Anderson to AG, Wheaton's Brig., Feb. 9, 1900, RG94/LSB, 38USV; Theodore Schwan to Henry C. Corbin, Feb. 16, 1900, Con. 1, HCC.

7. John L. Jordan to Elizabeth King Jordan, Feb. 5, 1900, JLJ.

8. Endorsement of W. Healey (by order of Wheaton) to L.R. no. 203, Mar. 8, 1900, RG395/2403.

9. USWD, 1900, 1, pt.4:442–43; pt.5:207–10; John C. Bates to Birkhimer, Apr. 15, 1900, RG395/2411. In late November 1900, the western part of Batangas was temporarily included in the First District. (See GO no. 127, HQ, Div. Phil., Nov. 26, 1900, Box 2, Robert Hall Papers, USMAL.) Then, in April 1901, the Second District was abolished, and all of Batangas was included in the First. That reorganization is discussed in chapter 8.

10. Marquis, ed., *Who's Who, 1908–1909,* 155–56; Faust, *Campaigning,* 222, 224; LeRoy, *Americans,* 2:43, 70.

11. Matthew Steele to Stella Steele, Apr. 29, 1900, Matthew F. Steele Papers, USAMHI; Diary Entry, May 2, 1900, Diary 1, Con. 1, RLB; Dan Campbell, "A Brief Sketch of the Life of William Edward Birkhimer" (including quotations from Campbell's diary), William E. Birkhimer Papers, USAMHI; C. Van Ness Radcliffe, "William E. Birkhimer, A Personal Appraisal," SAW/28USV.

12. W. Healey (by order of Birkhimer) to COs, 28USV, 30USV, 37USV, 38USV, and 39USV, Apr. 22, 1900; Endorsement of William Birkhimer to L.R. no. 505, Apr. 24, 1900; William Birkhimer to CO, 37USV, May 3, 1900, RG395/2403. On Birkhimer's ambition, see Diary Entry, May 2, 1900, Diary 1, Con. 1, RLB.

13. According to the War Department's official published report, Hall took

over on June 26, 1900 (USWD, 1900, 1, pt.5:210). But the Army's unpublished records reveal that Birkhimer was still running the district until July 2 (see Birkhimer to AG, DSL, July 2, 1900, RG395/2403). For about three weeks in October 1900, when Hall led an expedition to the island of Polillo, Birkhimer again assumed command of the Second District.

14. Military Scrapbook of Robert Hall; Hall to AG, 1Div., 8AC, June 8 and Aug. 3, 1899, Boxes 1 and 2, Robert Hall Papers, USMAL; John W. Leonard, ed., *Who's Who in America, 1906–1907* (Chicago, 1906), 755; Faust, *Campaigning,* 156; LeRoy, *Americans,* 2:119.

15. W. Healey (by order of Hall) to CO, Tanauan, July 3, 1900, RG395/2403; McKenna (by order of Hall) to COs, 28USV, 30USV, etc., Sept. 2, 1900, RG395/2405.

16. The Army's monthly reports document my point about decreased scouting under Hall. See, for example, Report of Operations for the Garrison of Lipa, Nov. 1900–Feb. 1901, RG395/4147.

17. Hall to AG, Div. Phil., Mar. 27, 1901, and Hall to AG, DSL, Apr. 7, 1901, RG395/2403.

18. USWD, 1900, 1, pt.5:51–57, 207–09; USWD, 1901, pt.7:391–94. Units assigned to neighboring provinces—the Thirtieth Infantry, U.S. Volunteers, for example—occasionally took part in operations in Batangas.

19. On the pay of steelworkers and teachers: John W. Chambers, *The Tyranny of Change: America in the Progressive Era* (New York, 1980), 3; and R. Freeman Butts and Lawrence A. Cremin, *A History of Education in American Culture* (New York, 1953), 454. On quarters: Diary Entry, Jan. 24, 1900, Diary 1, Con. 1, RLB; G. Morgan to AG, 1Div., 8AC, Feb. 19, 1900, RG94/LSB, 28USV; John L. Jordan to Elizabeth King Jordan, Feb. 22, 1900, JLJ; Diary Entry, Mar. 3, 1900, THS; W. Holbrook to AG, 2D, DSL, July 14, 1900, RG395/5052; Diary Entry, Sept. 21, 1900, FMP. On the food, see the report of the Commissary General in USWD, 1901, 1, pt.2:445–51, 456–63; Questionnaire of Homer V. Cook, SAW/1C; Millett, *General,* 124; G. Morgan to Adj., 28USV, Dec. 10, 1900, RG94/LSB, 28USV; George Anderson to Chief Commissary, Manila, June 24, 1900, RG94/LSB, 38USV; Ira Morison to Chief Commissary, Apr. 3, May 12 and 28, June 14, and July 9, 1900; and Morison to Commissary, 38USV, Sept. 2, 1900, RG94/LSB, 38USV, Commissary.

20. My description of the enlisted men is based largely on the hundreds of questionnaires and other material in the SAW. See also Millett, *General,* 113–19. The Army's records indicate that almost all the men were at least twenty-one (see RG94/Descriptive and Clothing Books, 28USV), but a large number of teenage enlistees evidently lied about their age (see George Anderson to AG, Washington, Oct. 15, 1899, RG94/LSB, 38USV). The Army did not want married men in the Federal Volunteer regiments, unless they had special skills (see, for example, George Anderson to H. V. Stevens, Sept. 7, 1899, RG94/LSB, 38USV). On the limited training: Diary Entries, May 1–July 7, 1900, FMP; "Outline of Book: The

Life of Homer V. Cook," SAW/1C; "Records and Events of Company H, 28th Infantry, USV," SAW/28USV; William Weber, *With the Thirtieth Infantry United States Volunteers,* 2d ed. (Carthagena, Ohio, 1945).

21. Questionnaires of Frank Rose and Myron Murgittroyd, SAW/30USV; William Weintz, SAW/28USV; James Franklin Edwards and Robert McNair, SAW/30USV; and Royal W. Bigelow, SAW/6C.

22. Diary Entries, May 1–Sept. 21, 1900, FMP; Questionnaires of Frederick M. Presher, SAW/1C; Allen Mummery, SAW/30USV; Georges Le Vallée, SAW/6C; Solomon Kenyon, SAW/38USV; Lacy Waddell Trapp and Claude F. Line, SAW/2Inf.

23. For a good discussion of the officers, see Millett, *General,* 116–17. My account is based as well on the SAW, the Bullard Papers (RLB), the John Leland Jordan Papers (JLJ), and other manuscript collections.

24. On inferiority, see Questionnaire of Bernard Lichtig, SAW/30USV; and Theodore Schwan to Henry C. Corbin, Oct. 25, 1899, Con. 1, HCC. On "niggers": Diary Entry, Oct. 31, 1900, Charles E. Portenier Diary, SAW/28USV; Diary Entries, July 31, Aug. 13, Sept. 7, 1900, John D. Brenton Diary, SAW/28USV (Olympia-Cooling Collection); Diary Entry, Feb. 3, 1900, Diary 1, Con. 1, RLB. On "gugus": Questionnaire of William Weintz, SAW/28USV; Diary Entry, Jan. 21, 1901, FMP. For one possible explanation of the origin of the word "gugu," see Stanley Karnow, *In Our Image: America's Empire in the Philippines* (New York, 1989), 131.

25. Although Americans of that day were optimistic, American society had fundamental problems. For insight into the two sides of turn-of-the-century America, see Eric F. Goldman, *Rendezvous with Destiny: A History of Modern American Reform,* rev. ed. (New York, 1955), 54–65, and Robert H. Wiebe, *The Search for Order, 1877–1920* (New York, 1967). On the enthusiasm of soldiers, see, for example, Diary Entry, Aug. 7, 1900, FMP.

26. On the cutting of wires, see George Anderson to AG, Schwan's Brig., Feb. 4, 1900, RG94/LSB, 38USV; M. Richardson to AG, 2D, June 30, 1900, RG94/LSB, 39USV; George Anderson to AG, 2D, July 16, 1900, RG94/LSB, 38USV; C. J. Crane to AG, 2D, DSL, Sept. 23, 1900, RG94/LSB, 38USV, 2B. For a discussion of wire-cutting in another theater, see Scott, *Ilocano Responses,* 30–31.

27. John L. Jordan to Elizabeth King Jordan, Feb. 18, 1900, JLJ; Diary Entry, Dec. 7, 1900, FMP; Diary Entry, Mar. 8, 1900, Supplement to Diary 1, Con. 1, RLB.

28. John L. Jordan to Elizabeth King Jordan, Mar. 24, 1900, JLJ; see also "Record and Events of Company H, 28th Infantry, USV," SAW/28USV.

29. William Birkhimer to John Parker, June 17, 1900, RG395/2403.

30. During June 1900, the U.S. troops stationed at Batangas City set off on twelve separate expeditions. All in all, the men marched approximately four hundred miles. They had no battles with Malvar's forces and captured only one

enemy soldier. See George S. Anderson to AG, 2D, DSL, July 5, 1900, RG395/2408. The following account of Nichols's expedition is based on Ross A. Nichols to Adj., 38USV, June 23, 1900, RG395/2408.

31. The account of Troop K's frustrations is based on Diary Entry, Jan. 21, 1901, FMP.

32. John L. Jordan to Elizabeth King Jordan, Apr. 15, 1900, JLJ; George S. Anderson to Eliza (sister), Dec. 4, 1900, George Anderson Papers, USMAL; Diary Entry, Feb. 3, 1900, Diary 1, Con. 1, RLB.

33. Questionnaire of Bernard Lichtig, SAW/30USV; Homer V. Cook to Don Rickey, Feb. 10, 1969, Homer V. Cook Papers, SAW/1C.

34. The song can be found in the Notebook of Albert E. Gardner (Troop B, First Cavalry), Albert E. Gardner Papers, SAW/1C.

35. William Birkhimer to Maj. Carson and Col. Bullard, June 19, 1900, RG395/2403; Millett, *General*, 147–48; Crane, *Experiences*, 340; "History and Cultural Life of the Barrio of San Marcelino" (Taysan), 2–3; "History and Cultural Life of the Barrio of Mahabang Parang" (San Luis), 1; "History and Cultural Life of the Barrio of Taliba" (San Luis), 2, all in HDP; Diary Entries, Apr. 15 and Aug. 21, 1900, THS.

36. John H. Parker to AG, DSL, June 21, 1900, RG395/2408.

37. John L. Jordan to Elizabeth King Jordan, Apr. 3, 1900, JLJ; George Anderson to AG, Wheaton's Brig., Mar. 27, 1900, RG94/LSB, 38USV; Proclamation of Miguel Malvar, Feb. 9, 1901, PIR/39/SD692.1.

38. The figure provided on the number of hostile actions is only an estimate. The official published reports of the War Department listed only forty-seven hostile actions for the *eleven*-month period June 1, 1900–April 30, 1901 (see USWD, 1900, 1, pt.5:214–20; USWD, 1901, 1, pt.5:243–49, 267–78), but I came across reports of scores of others in RG94 and RG395. My research has convinced me that any effort to be precise about the number of actions in Batangas during the unconventional phase of the war is probably futile, if not misguided. The contacts in Batangas and other provinces varied considerably in duration, in the number of soldiers involved, etc., and a mere total provides no sense of that variation. It is more useful, I think, simply to restate my general points: contacts were frequent, they occurred almost anywhere, and most were brief.

39. For examples of such actions see Robert Hall to AG, DSL, July 7 and Aug. 19, 1900, RG395/2405; G. Bickham to Adj., 28USV, Oct. 9, 1900, RG94/LSB, 28USV; C. J. Crane to Adj., 38USV, July 22, 1900, RG94/LSB, 38USV, 2B.

40. A. L. Parmeter (by order of John Bates) to Commanding General, 1D, DSL, Oct. 13, 1900, RG395/2353; Arthur Wagner (by order of John Bates) to COs, 1D, 2D, 3D, 4D, Oct. 27, 1900, RG395/2334.

41. For an example of an American-initiated action, see Robert Hall to AG, DSL, Aug. 4, 1900, RG395/2405. Several officers attributed successful operations to information provided by Filipino informants (e.g., T. Lebo to AG, DSL, Jan. 7, 1901, RG395/4208), but these were relatively rare occurrences at this stage of the

war. For an example of a guide misleading U.S. troops: R. W. Leonard to AG, 2D, DSL, July 1, 1900, RG94/LSB, 28USV. The question of informants is discussed at greater length in chapters 6 and 7.

42. My narrative of the battle is based on R. W. Leonard to AG, 2D, DSL, July 6, 1900; Birkhimer to AG, Calamba, July 7, 1900; Birkhimer to AG, 2D, DSL, July 15 and 19, 1900, RG94/LSB, 28USV; Robert Hall to AG, DSL, July 18, 1900, RG395/2405; Diary Entry, July 31, 1900, John D. Brenton Diary, SAW/28USV (Olympia-Cooling Collection); Entries of July 16 and 17, 1900, Logbook of U.S.S. *Villalobos*, RG24; Frank W. Carpenter to Clarence R. Edwards, July 31, 1900, Box 1, Clarence R. Edwards Papers, Massachusetts Historical Society; Robert Hall to AG, Div. Phil., Sept. 5, 1900, RG395/2403.

43. USWD, 1901, 1, pt.5:236–37, 307–09; John Bates to AG, Div. Phil., Oct. 23, 1900, RG395/2334.

44. The casualty figures are only rough estimates, based on my research in USWD, 1900 and 1901, RG94, RG395, PIR, and PRP. After engagements, U.S. officers often provided firm figures, but on occasion they wrote only that "many" or "several" enemy soldiers had been wounded or killed. It should again be stated that the published reports of the War Department listed only a fraction of the engagements—and, consequently, a fraction of the Filipino casualties.

45. R. L. Bullard to AG, DSL, Oct. 3, 1900, RG94/LSB, 39USV; Millett, *General,* 143, 147; Linn, *U.S. Army and Counterinsurgency,* 128–29. On the high rate of illness in other regiments operating in Batangas: D. H. Genity to Chief Surgeon, DSL, July 31, Aug. 7, and Sept. 11, 1900, RG94/LSB, 28USV; George Anderson to Chief Surgeon, DSL, Aug. 12, 1900, RG94/LSB, 38USV.

46. GO no. 25, Mar. 8, 1900; Special Order no. 42, Mar. 30, 1900, RG94/RO, 28USV; Diary Entries, Jan. 7–Feb. 22, 1900, Charles E. Portenier Diary, SAW/ 28USV; Memorandum of F. W. Ward, Dec. 22, 1900, RG395/3089; Weber, *Thirtieth Infantry;* Diary Entry, Aug. 7, 1900, FMP.

47. On bull sessions: Diary Entries, Sept. 29, Oct. 7, 8, 17, 26, and Nov. 7, 1900, THS. On games of chance: Questionnaires of Allen Mummery and Bernard Lichtig, SAW/30USV; John Spurlock, SAW/38USV; and Claude Line, SAW/2Inf.; Diary Entries, Oct. 1 and 7, Nov. 7 and 15, 1900, THS. On baseball: Transcript of Interview with Matthew Cook, n.d., SAW/30USV; Diary Entries, Oct. 14 and Nov. 18, 1900, THS. On drinking: Records of Summary Courts Martial, San Jose, RG395/5014; Records of Summary Courts Martial, Bauan, RG395/3089; Records of Summary Courts Martial, Lipa, RG395/4144.

48. On brawls and altercations, see the records of courts martial cited in the previous note; Charges and specifications preferred against Julius Netterberg, Apr. 24, 1900, RG94/LSB, 39USV, Co. M; Records of Courts Martial of John Ryan, Alfred Brown, August Schrader, and Edward Sheffrich, RG94/Records of Courts Martial, 28USV.

49. On relationships with women: Questionnaire of Frank Rose, SAW/ 30USV; and Homer V. Cook, SAW/1C; L. B. Gandy to Provost Marshal, Lipa,

Dec. 3, 1901, RG395/4138; Circular no. 3, May 31, 1900, RG94/Orders, Cos. A–F, 28USV; W. G. Doane to T. Dewey, June 2, 1900, and C. J. Crane to V. Calao, June 17, 1900, RG94/LSB, 38USV, 2B. On other contacts, see Company Orders no. 2 and 3, Company B, Feb. 12 and 20, 1900, RG94/Orders, Cos. A–F, 28USV; W. Holbrook to Adj., 38USV, Apr. 2, 1900, RG94/LSB, 38USV, 2B; Diary Entry, Sept. 21, 1900, THS; and, in particular, the excellent discussion of white-brown relations in De Bevoise, *Compromised Host,* 179–88.

50. D/Francisco Yturralde, Feb. 18, 1902, RG395/4229; Crane, *Experiences,* 358–59; De Bevoise, *Compromised Host,* 187.

51. See De Bevoise, *Compromised Host,* 181–84.

52. Ibid., 183–84. In Lipa, after a number of shopkeepers were forced by U.S. soldiers to give credit, the post commander instructed his men not to make such demands in the future. "The above mentioned inhabitants," he asserted, "are noncombatants whom it is our duty to protect." Battalion Order no. 21, Mar. 2, 1900, RG94/Battalion Orders, 38USV, 2B.

53. Records of Summary Courts Martial, Lipa, RG395/4144. See also Trial of Edward Coy, Mar. 14, 1900, RG153/16477; and Trial of Walter Shearer, June 7, 1900, RG153/18223.

54. Trial of Walter Wilburn, Mar. 30, 1900, RG153/16588; Trial of Fay Grubb, Mar. 19–29, RG153/16679.

55. Trial of Frank E. Detterman, Apr. 12–15, 1900, RG153/17681; and Trial of Robert W. Phillips, Apr. 19–May 5, 1900, RG153/17574.

56. Homer V. Cook to Don Rickey, Feb. 10, 1969, Homer V. Cook Papers, SAW/1C.

57. Diary Entries, Dec. 1–4, 1900, Nelson E. Bishop Diary, SAW/39USV.

58. Diary Entries, Mar. 30–Apr. 4, 1900, THS. The U.S. Army subsequently investigated the fires, but concluded incorrectly (as Thomas Selm's diary, cited above, makes clear) that Filipinos had probably set the fires. See the records of the investigation in RG94/AGO1078175.

59. John M. Gates, *Schoolbooks and Krags: The United States Army in the Philippines, 1898–1902* (Westport, Conn., 1973), 86–87, 136–39; Glenn A. May, *Social Engineering in the Philippines: The Aims, Execution, and Impact of American Colonial Policy, 1900–1913* (Westport, Conn., 1980), 78–79.

60. Gates, *Schoolbooks,* 88–89; May, *Social Engineering,* 44.

61. May, *Social Engineering,* 44–45.

62. Gates, *Schoolbooks,* 277, 290.

63. USWD, 1900, 1, pt.5:422.

64. William Birkhimer to COs, 28USV, 30USV, 37USV, etc., May 1, 1900; Birkhimer to AG, DSL, Oct. 21, 1900, RG395/2403.

65. For testimony on the value of schools, see Gates, *Schoolbooks,* 138–39.

66. Frank Bruckemma to Albert Todd, Aug. 26, 1900, RG395/2403; F. Ward to AG, DSL, Jan. 14, 1901, RG395/3089; R. L. Bullard to AG, 2D, Aug. 15, 1900, RG94/LSB, 39USV; May, *Social Engineering,* 79.

67. Diary Entry, Mar. 10, 1900, Diary 1, Con. 1, RLB.

68. Birkhimer to AG, DSL, Oct. 22, 1900, RG395/2403. For another example of this sort of thinking see Diary Entry, Aug. 17, 1900, Diary 1, Con. 1, RLB.

Chapter 6. With the Batangueño Guerrillas

1. Interview with Emilio Vergara, Mataasnakahoy, July 27, 1976. In the documentary evidence, I have found several reports of attempted ambushes near San Jose that bear some resemblance to the one described by Vergara: J. W. Moore to Adj., 2B, Lipa, Apr. 28, 1900, RG94/LSB, 38USV, Co. H; Robert Nolan to Adj., Lipa, Aug. 12, 1900, RG94/LSB, 38USV, Co. G; and Robert Hall to AG, DSL, Aug. 23, 1900, RG395/2405.

2. On Aguinaldo's hopes about the U.S. presidential election, see Aguinaldo to Mariano Trias, July 7, 1900, PIR/34/SD612.2.

3. On Trias: Taylor, *Insurrection*, 2:358; Trias to Ambrosio Mojica, Apr. 18, and May 23, 1900, PIR/77/SD1271.1, 2; Trias to Artemio Ricarte, Mar. 29, 1900, PIR/19/SD226.7; Trias to Licerio Geronimo, Sept. 4, 1900, PIR/70/SD1140.4.

4. GI, pp. 278, 664–65; Testimony of Candido Gonzales, Feb. 19, 1902, and Roman de Jesus, Feb. 24–27, 1902, RG395/5486; D/Pedro Cantos, Feb. 25, 1902, RG395/5495.

5. This description first appeared in a circular written by Lt. Stuart Heintzelman, Aug. 11, 1901, PIR/39/SD692.5. Heintzelman's words were repeated in later intelligence reports and circulars—for example, J. F. Bell to Station Commanders, Dec. 24, 1901, J. Franklin Bell Papers, USAMHI.

6. M. Bolaños to Eliseo Claudio, May 21, 1900, EC; D/Manuel Scarella, May 19, 1902, RG395/4229; D/Crisanto Borruel, Feb. 15, 1902, RG395/2398.

7. D/Manuel Scarella, May 19, 1902, RG395/4229; D/Crisanto Borruel, Feb. 15, 1902, RG395/2398; J. S. Powell to Adj., 38USV, June 1, 1900, RG395/2408; GI, p. 689.

8. Interviews with Damian Decipeda, San Luis, July 26, 1976; Emilio Vergara, Mataasnakahoy, July 27, 1976; and Calixto Silva, Lipa, July 27, 1976; Librado T. Austria, "Gen. Miguel Malvar: The Last Insurrecto," *Sunday Times Magazine,* Sept. 26, 1965, pp. 22–23.

9. Taylor, *Philippine Insurrection,* 4:159–60; GI, pp. 106, 148–49, 652.

10. D/Fernando Garcia, June 7, 1902, RG395/4229; D/Crisanto Borruel, Feb. 15, 1902, RG395/2398; Orders of Miguel Malvar, Oct. 27, 1900, PIR/39/SD692.4.

11. On taxation: D/Graciano Babao, Mar. 8, 1902; D/Jose Babasa, Feb. 18, 1902; D/Silvestre Borbon, Feb. 18, 1902, RG395/2398; D/Jose Villanueva, Feb. 12, 1902, RG395/2380; D/Ventura Tolentino, Feb. 15, 1902; D/Fernando Garcia, June 7, 1902, RG395/4229; Circular from M. Bolaños, [Feb. or Mar. 1900], PRP/Pr12–13/Rosario.

12. Orders of Miguel Malvar, Oct. 27, 1900, PIR/39/SD692.4; Linn, *U.S. Army and Counterinsurgency,* 130–31.

13. Orders of Miguel Malvar, Sept. 13, 1900, PRP/RL11/Malvar; Orders of Miguel Malvar, Oct. 27, 1900, PIR/39/SD692.4; GI, pp. 647, 654, 681.

14. See Linn, *U.S. Army and Counterinsurgency*, 16–20, 72–74; Scott, *Ilocano Responses*, 52–53, 69.

15. GI, pp. 650–51.

16. On the difficulty of communicating with subordinates: Crisanto Borruel to Eliseo Claudio, Apr. 30, 1900; M. Bolaños to Claudio, May 21, 1900; Santiago Rillo to Claudio, July 17, 1900; and Placido Gamboa to Claudio, July 25, 1900, EC.

17. Memorandum of a conference in Taysan, Mar. 14, 1900, PIR/56/SD936.9; D/Fernando Garcia, June 7, 1902, RG395/4229.

18. D/Fernando Garcia, June 7, 1902, RG395/4229; L. Goodier to Adj., 38USV, Mar. 16, 1900, RG395/5007.

19. Eulalio Buenafe to Eliseo Claudio, Apr. 8, 1900; Briccio Casala to Claudio, Apr. 8, 1900, EC.

20. For information about another attack (near Talisay in March 1901), see Diary Entries, Mar. 28–Apr. 2, 1901, Warren Dean Diary, USMAL; USWD, 1901, 1, pt.5:246.

21. Damaso Ybarra to Eliseo Claudio, Oct. 27, 1900, EC; Claudio to Ybarra, Oct. 29, 1900, BHQ. Earlier in the war Claudio had been in charge of a military unit that was also known as the San Miguel Column; unfortunately, the records of that unit are fragmentary. See Damaso Ybarra to Eliseo Claudio, Feb. 6, 1900, EC.

22. Interviews with Natividad Aguila, Batangas City, Sept. 15, 1984, and Antonio Claudio, Quezon City, Nov. 4, 1986; Libros de Entierros, 1900, Parish Records of Batangas City; *FU*, Batangas, 1890 and 1891; Philippine Islands, *Guía, 1892,* 624; *Guía, 1893,* 380; *Guía, 1895,* 557; *Guía, 1897,* 550; *Guía, 1898,* 794; Arturo H. Soriano to Eliseo Claudio, Jan. 2, 1899, and Enrique Claudio to Eliseo Claudio, Dec. 15, 1899, EC.

23. On Ramirez: *EGB*, Taysan, 1889; Charles Leonard to Adj., Batangas, Nov. 6, 1901, RG395/2354. On Scarella: D/Manuel Scarella, May 19, 1902, RG395/4229. On Farol: Libros de Matrícula de Estudios Generales y de Aplicación de Segunda Enseñanza, 1890–92, Archives of the University of Santo Tomas, Manila. On Ybarra: Ybarra to Claudio, Oct. 27, 1900, EC.

24. Sastrón, *Batangas*, 249.

25. The census of 1887 indicated that the town's population was 5,125; according to that of 1903, taken after a cholera epidemic, it was 5,781. On U.S. garrisons: T. Lebo to AG, 2D, DSL, Sept. 18, Oct. 19, and Dec. 16, 1900, RG391/LSB, 1C.

26. Regarding informants, see Claudio to Felix Farol, Nov. 3, 1900; Claudio to Damaso Ybarra, Nov. 19, 1900, BHQ; Celestino Gutierrez to Claudio, Nov. 27, 1900; and Felix Farol to Claudio, Dec. 7 and 8, 1900, EC. On the replacement of the friars, see Schumacher, *Revolutionary Clergy*, 50–52, 66–68.

27. On the money payments: George Anderson to AG, 2 Brig., 1Div., Apr. 1, 1900, RG94/LSB, 38USV; Military Governor to Commanding General, DSL, May 24, 1900, RG395/2353. My interviewees indicated that many soldiers surrendered weapons because of it (interviews with Severino Magsombol, San Luis, July 22, 1976; Damian Decipeda, San Luis, July 26, 1976; and Dionisio Laygo, Padre Garcia, July 27, 1976).

28. On the attempts to increase the number of weapons: Damaso Ybarra to Claudio, Oct. 27, Nov. 4, Dec. 17, 1900, EC; Proclamation of Mariano Trias, Nov. 24, 1900, PIR/19/SD226.13. On shifting of weapons: Ybarra to Claudio, Nov. 30, 1900; Tomas Ramirez to Claudio, Dec. 3, 1900, EC.

29. Ybarra to Claudio, Nov. 23, 1900, EC; Claudio to Ybarra, Nov. 26, 1900, BHQ; George Morgan to AAG, Wheaton's Brig., Mar. 3, 1900, RG94/LSB, 28USV; J. W. Craig to AG, 2D, DSL, Jan. 29, 1901, RG395/5052; D/Manuel Reyes, Feb. 10, 1902, RG395/4153; Linn, *U.S. Army and Counterinsurgency,* 132.

30. Mariano Trias to Damaso Ybarra, Sept. 7, 1899, and Damaso Ybarra to Emilio Aguinaldo, Sept. 30, 1899, PIR/38/SD676.4; Philippine Islands, *Guía, 1892,* 687; *Guía, 1895,* 483.

31. Ybarra to Claudio, Oct. 27 and Nov. 9, 1900, EC; Claudio to Ybarra, Oct. 29, 1900, BHQ.

32. D/Manuel Scarella, May 19, 1902, RG395/4229; Celestino Gutierrez to Claudio, Nov. 28, 1900, EC.

33. Scarella to Claudio, Nov. 3 and 25, 1900, EC.

34. Celestino Gutierrez to Claudio, Nov. 27, 1900; Scarella to Claudio, Nov. 30, 1900, EC; Claudio to Scarella, Nov. 28, 1900, BHQ. Ybarra's order must be understood in light of the American practice of burning the barrio closest to the scene of any ambush. If the Filipino troops mounted an ambush near a barrio that had not turned over rice, and the Americans burned the barrio, Malvar's men would lose valuable food supplies.

35. Scarella to Ybarra, Jan. 2, 1901; Claudio to Ybarra, Jan. 11, 1901, EC.

36. Scarella to Ybarra, Jan. 2 and 3, 1901; Scarella to Claudio, Jan. 2, 1901, EC; Claudio to Ybarra, Jan. 4 and 6, 1901, BHQ.

37. Ybarra to Claudio, Jan. 8, 1901; Claudio to Ybarra, Jan. 11, 1901, EC.

38. Ybarra to Claudio, Jan. 25 and 27, 1901, EC; Claudio to Scarella, Jan. 27, 1901, BHQ; D/Manuel Scarella, May 19, 1902, RG395/4229; S. B. Arnold to AG, DSL, Mar. 23, 1901, RG395/4208. My interpretation of the outcome of the affair is perhaps debatable; there is no direct evidence that Malvar intervened to settle the matter, although there is evidence that Claudio sought his compadre's intervention and that Ybarra subsequently backed down and agreed to a compromise.

39. On the Casala-Ybarra conflict: Ybarra to Claudio, Nov. 28, 1900; Casala to Claudio, Dec. 16, 1900, EC. On Yrineo: Ybarra to Claudio, Nov. 9 and Dec. 16, 1900, EC; Claudio to Ybarra, Dec. 30, 1900, BHQ; Julio Ynfante to Juan Cailles, Nov. 7, 1900, PIR/37/SD653.9. On the Malvar-Noriel conflict: Emilio Aguinaldo to Mariano Trias, July 7, 1900, PIR/34/SD612.2.

40. Interview with Emilio Vergara, Mataasnakahoy, July 27, 1976. On forced

service, also see L. E. Goodier to AG, 2D, DSL, Sept. 30, 1900, RG395/2412; and G. Langhorne to AG, 1D, DSL, Feb. 9, 1901, RG94/LSB, 39USV. The second document is particularly enlightening; it discusses Cipriano Lopez, a wealthy resident of Balayan as well as a lieutenant colonel in the Filipino Army, who had required sixty of his laborers to serve with him.

41. Felix Farol to Claudio, Dec. 15 and 16, 1900, EC; Claudio to Ybarra, Dec. 17, 1900, BHQ; D/Fernando Garcia, June 7, 1902, RG395/4229.

42. Claudio to Ybarra, Nov. 30, 1900; Claudio to Ramirez, Nov. 30, 1900, BHQ; T. C. Lebo to AG, 2D, DSL, Dec. 5, 1900, RG391/LSB, 1C; Robert Hall to AG, DSL, Dec. 6, 1900, RG395/2405.

43. Ramirez to Claudio, Dec. 13, 1900; Ybarra to Claudio, Dec. 14, 1900; Casala to Claudio, Jan. 17, 1901; Ybarra to Claudio, Jan. 18, 1901; Ramirez to Claudio, Jan. 24 and 26, 1901, EC.

44. Farol to Claudio, Nov. 22, Dec. 5, 12, and 16, 1900, EC.

45. Enrique Claudio to Eliseo Claudio, Nov. 15, 1900, EC; William Birkhimer to AG, Calamba, July 17, 1900, RG395/2411; Testimony of Segundo Simonte, Feb. 28, 1902, RG395/5486.

46. On Farol's company: Farol to Claudio, Nov. 8, Dec. 8, and Dec. 15, 1900, EC. On Ramirez's: Tomas Ramirez, Report of company strength, Dec. 1, 1900, EC. On Claudio: Malvar to Claudio, Apr. 20, 1901; Ybarra to Claudio, Apr. 27, 1900, EC.

47. Ybarra to Claudio, Nov. 30 and Dec. 27, 1900; Juan Cantos to Ybarra, Jan. 20, 1901, EC; Claudio to Ybarra, Dec. 30, 1900, BHQ.

48. GI, p. 657; D/Jose Villanueva, Feb. 12, 1902, RG395/2380; D/Fermin Arceo, Feb. 17, 1902, RG395/4229; D/Crisanto Borruel, Feb. 15, 1902, RG395/2398; Claudio to Ramirez, Dec. 17, 1900, BHQ; Ramirez to Claudio, Dec. 23, 1900, EC.

49. D/Crisanto Borruel, Feb. 15, 1902, RG395/2398; D/Manuel Scarella, May 19, 1902, RG395/4229.

50. On visits to families: Felix Farol to Claudio, Dec. 18 and 26, 1900, EC; D/Remigio Luna, Feb. 17, 1902, RG395/4229. On Malvar: GI, p. 665; Stuart Heintzelman, circular to post commanders, Aug. 11, 1901, PIR/39/SD692.5. On girlfriends: D/Manuel Scarella, May 19, 1902, RG395/4229; William Murphy to Adj., 3B, 39USV, RG94/LSB, 39USV, Co. I. On assistance of women: Frank S. Long to Robert Hall, Feb. 23, 1901, RG395/2414; D/Francisco Abas, Feb. 18, 1902; D/Alejo Acosta, Feb. 12, 1902; D/Fermin Arceo, Feb. 17, 1902; D/Manuel Lira, Feb. 14, 1902, RG395/4229.

51. Enrique Claudio to Eliseo Claudio, Nov. 15, 1900; Celestino Gutierrez to Claudio, Nov. 23 and 27, 1900; Pedro Sarmiento to Claudio, Dec. 10, 1900, EC.

52. Libros de Casamientos, v. 13, Parish Records of Lipa.

53. Ibid.

54. On the relationship between McKinley's election and the establishment of the Federal party, see Glenn Anthony May, "America in the Philippines: The Shaping of Colonial Policy" (Ph.D. diss., Yale University, 1975), 78–79. On the

organization of the Lipa chapter: Report of Operations of the Garrison of Lipa, Jan. 1901, RG395/4147.

55. USWD, 1901, 1, pt.4:128; pt.5:237; Taylor, *Insurrection,* 2:358; 5:315–18; Mariano Trias to his countrymen, [March 1901], PIR/52/SD896.1.

56. Notes of an interview between Panopio and Malvar, March 1901, PIR/56/SD936.3.

57. Ibid.; Jacob Kline to AG, 2D, DSL, Mar. 21 and 26, 1901, RG395/4134; Hall (AG) to CO, Lipa, Mar. 23, 1901, RG395/2405; USWD, 1901, 1, pt.4:128.

58. Felix Farol to Claudio, Dec. 20, 25, and 28, 1900; Tomas Ramirez to Claudio, Feb. 8, 1901; Celestino Gutierrez to Claudio, Feb. 11, 1901; Claudio to Ybarra, Feb. 15, 1901, EC.

Chapter 7. In the Towns: Batangas City

1. D/Diego Gloria, Feb. 14, 1902, and D/Florencio Caedo, Feb. 14, 1902, RG395/4229; Philippine Islands, *Guía, 1889,* 2:129; *Guía, 1893,* 381.

2. John L. Jordan to Elizabeth King Jordan, Feb. 18 and 22, 1900, JLJ; D/Mariano Dinglasan, Feb. 19, 1902, RG395/4233; D/Graciano Babao, Mar. 8, 1902, RG395/2398.

3. Information about the agricultural activities of the residents of Batangas City can be found in many documents in RG395/2380, 2398, 4229, and 4233. See, for instance, D/Jose Villanueva, Feb. 12, 1902, RG395/2380, and D/Crisanto Bagsit, Feb. 19, 1902, RG395/2398.

4. D/Ynocencio Aguilera, Feb. 18, 1902; D/Pedro Sarmiento, Feb. 18, 1902, RG395/4229.

5. On such activities: Kalaw, *Aide-de-Camp,* 8; Sastrón, *Batangas,* 80.

6. D/Pedro Sarmiento, Feb. 18, 1902; D/Anacleto Magtibay, Feb. 17, 1902, RG395/4229; D/Jose Babasa, Feb. 18, 1902, RG395/2398; D/Mariano Yturralde, Feb. 14, 1902; D/Remigio Luna, Feb. 17, 1902, RG395/4229.

7. D/Fermin Arceo, Feb. 17, 1902, RG395/2398.

8. Philippine Islands, *Guía, 1893,* 380; *FU,* Batangas, 1891; D/Potenciano Hilario, Feb. 20, 1902, RG395/4229.

9. D/Potenciano Hilario, Feb. 20, 1902, RG395/4229; Arthur Wagner to George Anderson, Apr. 6, 1900, RG395/4212; George Anderson to Felipe Calderon, Apr. 25, 1900, RG94/LSB, 38USV.

10. D/Potenciano Hilario, Feb. 20, 1902, RG395/4229.

11. Case of Potenciano Hilario, c. 1902, RG395/2398.

12. On Babasa: D/Manuel Scarella, May 19, 1902; D/Fernando Garcia, June 7, 1902, RG395/4229; USWD, 1900, 1, pt.6:656; John L. Jordan to Elizabeth King Jordan, Feb. 5, 1900, JLJ. On the assistance of others, see Scarella's declaration and D/Ventura Tolentino, Feb. 15, 1902; D/Leoncio Arceo, Feb. 17, 1902; D/Ramon Canin, Feb. 13, 1902, RG395/4229; D/Silvestre Borbon, Feb. 18, 1902, RG395/2398; D/Domingo de los Santos, Feb. 21, 1902, RG395/2398; D/Jose Villanueva, Feb. 12, 1902, RG395/2380; and D/Vicente Soriano, Feb. 19, 1902, RG395/4229. Babasa, Rea, and Olmos had, like Fermin Arceo and Eliseo Claudio,

served on the ayuntamiento of Batangas City. See Philippine Islands, *Guía, 1893,* 380; and *Guía, 1897,* 550.

13. D/Graciano Babao, Mar. 8, 1902; D/Jose Babasa, Feb. 18, 1902; D/Silvestre Borbon, Feb. 18, 1902, RG395/2398; D/Jose Villanueva, Feb. 12, 1902, RG395/2380; D/Fernando Garcia, June 7, 1902, RG395/4229.

14. On tax collection, see D/Vicente Soriano, Feb. 19, 1902; D/Ynocencio Aguilera, Feb. 18, 1902; D/Dalmacio Serrano, Feb. 13, 1902; D/Emilio Mercado, Feb. 18, 1902; D/Macario Gutierrez, Feb. 28, 1902; D/Ventura Atienza, Feb. 21, 1902; D/Juan Gutierrez, Feb. 14, 1902; and D/Ventura Tolentino, Feb. 15, 1902, all in RG395/4229.

15. On Lipa: D/Juan Calao, Dec. 24, 1901; D/Benito Reyes, Dec. 24, 1901; D/Jose Templo, n.d.; D/Alfonso Barretto, Feb. 14, 1902; D/Sixto Roxas, Feb. 13, 1902; D/Catalino Dimayuga, D/Catalino Reyes, and D/Antonio Briones, Feb. 10, 1902, all in RG395/4153; W. T. Johnston to AG, 3SB, July 23, 1902 (2 letters), RG395/2354. On Father Castillo: G. Morgan to Adj., 28USV, Sept. 30, 1900, RG395/5351; Diary Entry, Jan. 13, 1902, FMP; Schumacher, *Revolutionary Clergy,* 128–29; Linn, *U.S. Army and Counterinsurgency,* 137.

16. See, for example, George Anderson, Report for Companies A, B, and C, 1st Batt., 38USV, for May 1900 (actually written June 5, 1900), RG395/2408.

17. On abuses in collection: D/Vicente Soriano, Feb. 19, 1902, RG395/4229, and Damaso Ybarra to Eliseo Claudio, Oct. 27, 1900, EC. On Rillo: D/Domingo de los Santos, Feb. 21, 1902, and D/Potenciano Hilario, Feb. 20, 1902, RG395/4229. On Ybarra: D/Alejo Acosta, Feb. 12, 1902; D/Vicente Yturralde, Feb. 10, 1902, RG395/4229; and D/Pablo Berba, Feb. 17, 1902, RG395/2398. On forced conscription: D/Francisco Abas, Feb. 18, 1902, and D/Francisco Mendoza, Feb. 18, 1902, RG395/4229; and D/Tomas de Rivera, Feb. 17, 1902, RG395/4233.

18. D/Vicente Agregado, Feb. 12, 1902; D/Anacleto Magtibay, Feb. 17, 1902; and D/Crisanto Javier, Feb. 17, 1902, all in RG395/4229.

19. D/Mariano Arce, Feb. 18, 1902, RG395/4229.

20. On fear of the soldiers to whom the declarations were made, see GI, pp. 451, 455–58, 603, which refers to declarations that were made in Tiaong, Tayabas. On lying about involvement, see the previous document as well as D/Alejo Acosta, Feb. 12, 1902, RG395/4229 (and the note appended to it by the U.S. authorities commenting on Acosta's failure to tell the truth). Acosta's account is also contradicted by D/Ysidoro Dinglasan, Feb. 18, 1902, RG395/4233. For a lengthier discussion of the evidential value of the declarations, see May, "Resistance and Collaboration," 73–75.

21. D/Dalmacio Serrano, Feb. 13, 1902, RG395/4229. See also D/Juan Lira, Feb. 15, 1902; D/Brigido Cepillo, Feb. 25, 1902; and D/Manuel Aranas, Feb. 18, 1902, all in RG395/4229, and several other declarations.

22. See D/Potenciano Hilario, Feb. 20, 1902; D/Mariano Macatangay, Feb. 18, 1902, RG395/4229; and D/Jose Villanueva, Feb. 12, 1902, RG395/2380.

23. D/Silvestre Borbon, Feb. 18, 1902, RG395/2398; D/Ramon Canin, Feb. 13, 1902; D/Potenciano Hilario, Feb. 20, 1902 (on Hilario, also see D/Marcelo Llana,

Feb. 17, 1902); D/Alejo Acosta, Feb. 12, 1902 (a note appended to the declaration by the U.S. authorities discusses the Rillo-Acosta connection); and D/Leoncio Arceo, Feb. 17, 1902, RG395/4229. The two classmates were Mariano Maca-tangay and Vicente Agregado; the latter was an enthusiastic supporter at first, but as this chapter has already shown, he had second thoughts about the resistance after the ransacking of his mother-in-law's house (see Libros de Matrícula de Estudios Generales y de Aplicación de Segunda Enseñanza, 1881–83, Archives of the University of Santo Tomas, Manila).

24. Agoncillo, *Malolos,* viii; Constantino, *Past Revisited,* 233, 236.

25. Malvar had a long-standing relationship with Sebastian Caneo, the head of the Colorum, the religious organization whose peasant members expected that independence would bring the millennium, and with it, a new social order. But the Colorum's members do not appear to have played a significant role in supporting Malvar before 1901. On that connection, see the next chapter and Ileto, *Pasyon,* 205.

26. Interview with Damian Decipeda, San Luis, July 26, 1976. Also interviews with Emilio Vergara, Lipa, July 27, 1976; Dionisio Laygo, Padre Garcia, July 27, 1976; and Jose Caubalejo, Calatagan, July 28, 1976.

27. D/Feliciano Cantos, Feb. 18, 1902, RG395/4229; D/Domingo Borbon, Feb. 17, 1902, RG395/2398.

28. A few words are in order about the term *collaboration.* The 1933 version of the *Oxford English Dictionary* listed only one definition for the word *collaborate:* "To work in conjunction with another or others, to co-operate; esp. in a literary or artistic production, or the like." In those days, when one thought of collaboration, what came to mind was Gilbert and Sullivan or Marx and Engels. In the 1972 supplement of that dictionary, a second definition appeared—"To co-operate traitorously with the enemy"—and, in fact, the word had commonly been used in that way since World War II. *Webster's Third International Dictionary* (1961) adds the following: "collaborate: . . . 2: to cooperate with or to assist usu. willingly an enemy of one's country (as an invading force)." See *The Oxford English Dictionary,* 12 vols. (Oxford, 1933), 2:613; R. W. Burchfield, ed., *A Supplement to the Oxford English Dictionary,* 3 vols. (Oxford, 1972–82), 1:573; and Philip Babcock Gove, ed., *Webster's Third International Dictionary* (Springfield, Mass., 1961), 443.

For a discussion of the war in the Philippines, the first-mentioned definition is obviously inappropriate. The other two are superficially similar, but, on examination, somewhat different. The *OED* definition uses the word *traitorously,* and because of that its connotation is a bit more pejorative. For the same reason, the *OED* definition is rather restrictive: it refers only to those whose cooperation is traitorous; hence, it does not apply to those whose cooperation falls short of traitorous behavior. Finally, one should recognize that this definition is ambiguous. What is meant by the word *traitorously?* What standard does one apply? But there are problems, too, with the definition in *Webster's.* It is restrictive in a different way. By using the words *usu. willingly, Webster's* is making a judgment about attitude—a judgment that the *OED* does not appear to make. One can, after all, act traitorously but feel otherwise.

The definition I have used here—simply, to cooperate with the enemy—is somewhat broader than both above-cited definitions. In fact, I use the word in the same way that most contemporary scholars of British imperialism use it. No pejorative connotation is implied and no attitude is assumed.

29. My account of Arguelles's activities is based on *FU,* Batangas, 1891; Sketch of the life of Manuel Arguelles, typescript, City Library, Batangas City; Agoncillo, *Malolos,* 240–41, 398–99, 435–39, 515–17; Guerrero, "Luzon at War," 50–51, 57–60, 74, 76; Jane S. Ragsdale, "Coping With the Yankees: The Filipino Elite, 1898–1903" (Ph.D. diss., University of Wisconsin, 1974), 249–51, 317; and Jose Alejandrino, *The Price of Freedom,* trans. Jose M. Alejandrino (Manila, 1949), 145–49.

30. Another elite resident of the town, Marcelo Llana, also collaborated in 1900, and he too went to Manila when he decided to do so. See D/Marcelo Llana, Feb. 17, 1902, RG395/4229.

31. Padrón general de chinos, Batangas, 1895, PNA; L. E. Goodier to Adj., 38USV, Mar. 7, 1900, RG395/5007; L. Wheaton to Adj., 1Div., Mar. 8, 1900 (and enclosure, G. Anderson to AG, Wheaton's Brig., Mar. 8, 1900), RG395/2403; L. E. Goodier to AAG, 2D, DSL, June 9, 1900, RG395/2408; Charles Muir to AG, DSL, July 11 and 12, 1900, RG94/LSB, 38USV; Arthur Wagner to CO, Batangas, Nov. 4, 1900 (and the enclosed record of the trials of Marcelo de Castro and Gregorio de Castro, July 16, 1900), RG395/4212; John L. Jordan to Elizabeth King Jordan, Mar. 10, 1900, JLJ.

32. Arthur Wagner to CO, Batangas, Nov. 4, 1900 (and the enclosed record of the trials of Marcelo de Castro and Gregorio de Castro, July 16, 1900), RG395/4212. Regarding another killing of a collaborator: C. J. Crane to Valerio Calao, July 17, 1900, RG94/LSB, 38USV.

33. D/Jose Villanueva, Feb. 12, 1902, RG395/2380, and D/Fermin Arceo, Feb. 17, 1902, RG395/4229.

34. Nicomedes Yrineo to heads of barrios of Pinamucan, Tabangao, etc., June 1, 1900 (an enclosure in E. Abbott to Adj., 38USV, June 11, 1900, RG395/2408); Proclamation of Mariano Trias, Nov. 24, 1900, PIR/19/SD226.13; Proclamation of Martin Cabrera, Jan. 2, 1901, RG395/2353; D/Florencio Caedo, Feb. 14, 1902, and D/Marcelo Llana, Feb. 17, 1902, RG395/4229.

35. On elections: D/Jose Villanueva, Feb. 12, 1902, RG395/2380; Arthur Wagner to George Anderson, Apr. 6, 1900, RG395/4212; George Anderson to Military Secretary, Governor General, Apr. 8, 1900, and George Anderson to AG, 2D, DSL, May 11, 1900, RG94/LSB, 38USV; Case of Potenciano Hilario, c. 1902, RG395/2398. On schools: Frank Bruckemma to Albert Todd, Aug. 26, 1900, RG395/2403.

36. George Anderson, Report for Companies A, B, and C, 1st Batt., 38USV, for May 1900 (actually written June 5, 1900); L. E. Goodier to AAG, 2D, DSL, June 9, 1900, RG395/2408; T. Lebo to AG, DSL, Jan. 7, 1901, RG395/4208.

37. D/Juan Gutierrez, Feb. 14, 1902, RG395/4229. See also D/Jose Seria, Mar. 11, 1902, and D/Maximino Abacan, Feb. 19, 1902, RG395/4229.

38. A. L. Parmeter to CO, Batangas, Feb. 5, 1901, RG395/2408; D/Vicente Agregado, Feb. 12, 1902; D/Fermin Arceo, Feb. 17, 1902; D/Mariano Arguelles, Feb. 17, 1902; D/Florencio Caedo, Feb. 14, 1902, RG395/4229; D/Graciano Babao, Mar. 8, 1902, RG395/2398; D/Jose Villanueva, Feb. 12, 1902, RG395/2380.

39. D/Vicente Agregado, Feb. 12, 1902; D/Anacleto Magtibay, Feb. 17, 1902; D/Calixto Macatangay, Feb. 19, 1902, RG395/4229.

40. George Anderson to AG, 2D, DSL, June 5, 1900, RG94/LSB, 38USV; De Bevoise, "Compromised Host," 221–27; May, "150,000 Missing Filipinos," 238–39.

41. May, *Social Engineering,* 12–19, 41–50, 81–84. Anacleto Magtibay, among others, indicated that his change in attitude toward the resistance was due in part to the work of the Philippine Commission. See D/Anacleto Magtibay, Feb. 17, 1902, RG395/4229.

42. D/Graciano Babao, Mar. 8, 1902, RG395/2398. See also D/Mariano Arguelles, Feb. 17, 1902, RG395/4229.

43. D/Ramon Canin, Feb. 13, 1902, RG395/4229.

44. Agoncillo and Guerrero, *History of the Filipino People,* 295–98; Constantino, *Past Revisited,* 238–45.

45. D/Diego Gloria, Feb. 14, 1902; D/Florencio Caedo, Feb. 14, 1902; D/Ramon Canin, Feb. 13, 1902, RG395/4229; D/Crisanto Borruel, Feb. 15, 1902, RG395/2398. On the membership of the municipal council: Council Minutes, Municipal Council of Batangas City, May 24, 1901, Records Section, Office of the City Mayor, Batangas City.

46. This account of Jose Villanueva's actions and motives is based on D/Jose Villanueva, Feb. 12, 1902, RG395/2380.

47. On Lipa, see the declarations in RG395/4153.

48. Libros de Entierros, Parish Records of Batangas City, Ibaan, Lipa, San Jose, San Juan, and Taysan. Crude death rates can be roughly estimated by using the population figures in the census of 1903, keeping in mind, however, that the census had certain defects and that it followed a cholera epidemic. See Bureau of the Census, *Census: 1903,* 2:141–43. A considerable increase in recorded burials could be observed in Cuenca and Lobo as well (both are in eastern Batangas), but a substantial percentage of the increase was due to the fact that, for some reason, a large number of nonresident deaths were recorded in both towns' parish books in 1900.

49. Libros de Bautismos, Parish Records of Batangas City, San Jose, and Taysan. The figures for Lipa were 2,253 in 1899, 1,959 in 1900, and 1,515 in 1901 (Libros de Bautismos, Parish Records of Lipa).

50. In Balayan, the number of burials fell from 581 in 1899 to 363 in 1900; in Calaca, from 287 to 211; and in Lian, from 65 to 64. In Nasugbu, the number of burials increased from 112 to 137, and in Lemery, from 492 to 517. Libros de Entierros, Parish Records of Balayan, Calaca, Lemery, Lian, and Nasugbu.

51. My conclusion that malaria was the principal killer is somewhat specula-tive. The libros de entierros, which included statements concerning cause of death, are not informative on the matter. They suggest that the principal cause of death in 1900 was *calentura,* or simple fever. Indeed, 121 of the 127 people who were buried in San Juan in the month of July 1900 were said to have succumbed to calentura, and 250 of the 319 people buried in Lipa in December 1900 were said to have died from the same cause. Unfortunately, however, such data tell us little, since as we all know from experience fever is but a symptom of disease, not a disease itself. Still, there are strong indications that malaria was prevalent throughout the archipelago at the time, and also that a majority of the deaths attributed to calentura were actually caused by malaria. See De Bevoise, "Com-promised Host," 82, 221–27; May, "150,000 Missing Filipinos," 235, 238–39; Libros de Entierros, Parish Records of San Juan and Lipa.

Chapter 8. A Second Wind

1. Miguel Malvar to Juan Cailles, Apr. 4, 1901, PIR/39/SD692.3; same to Pedro Caballes, Apr. 10, 1901, PIR/42/SD752.62.

2. Miguel Malvar, "Mga Capatid at Casamasama sa Paquiquihamoc," Apr. 12, 1901, PIR/39/SD692.7. My own translation of parts of this proclamation differs slightly from that in Ileto, *Pasyon.* See pp. 200–03 of that book.

3. Miguel Malvar to Arcadio Maxilom, May 14, 1901, PIR/39/SD692.8; Mi-guel Malvar, "Al Pueblo Filipino y su Ejército," PIR/53/SD902.2.

4. Ileto, *Pasyon,* 200. Also see 62–72, 106–07, 143–44.

5. On upper-class dissatisfaction with Caneo, see Guerrero, "Luzon at War," 215–16, 229; Ileto, *Pasyon,* 148–49, 205. In 1899, Caneo had served under Malvar in military operations in Laguna (see chap. 3), and in December of that year, he had been commissioned by Malvar to organize a group of spies who were to be planted in towns occupied by the Americans. By January 1901, he had been promoted to lieutenant colonel. See Miguel Malvar to Sebastian Caneo, Dec. 10, 1899, PRP/Pr10–11/Batangas; GI, pp. 43–45; Ileto, *Pasyon,* 205.

6. Miguel Malvar to Eliseo Claudio, Apr. 20, 1901, EC.

7. "Noticias adquiridas de la Jefatura Superior F.M. del Gobierno Departa-mental del Sur," c. Apr. 1901, PIR/44/SD772.6.

8. Miguel Malvar, "Disposiciones e Instrucciones generales," Apr. 28, 1901, PIR/44/SD772.10; Taylor, *Philippine Insurrection,* 5:329–33.

9. "Ympresiones," June 28, 1901; "Noticias e impresiones de esta Jefatura Superior," c. July 1901; "Mga balita ayon sa mga sulat galing sa estranjero at sa Maynila," c. July 1901, PIR/43/SD755.19, 22, and 26; Malvar, "Resumen de las disposiciones e instrucciones generales . . . ," June 25, 1901, PIR/69/SD1132.1; Malvar, "Disposiciones e Instrucciones generales," Aug. 28, 1901, PIR/45/SD792.3.

10. U.S. Philippine Commission, *Report: 1901,* 2:93–96.

11. U.S. Senate, Committee on the Philippines, *Hearings: Affairs in the Phil-*

ippine Islands, S. Doc. 331, 57th Cong., 1st sess., 1902, 1:36; Taft to Elihu Root, Apr. 27, 1901, WHT; Diary entry of May 2, 1901, Diary, v. 3, Bernard Moses Papers, University of California Archives, Berkeley, Calif.

12. USWD, 1901, 1, pt.7:13, 17–18.

13. D/Manuel Macatangay, Mar. 27, 1902 (and additional statements of Apr. 5 and Apr. 9, 1902), RG395/4229; Statement of Potenciano Villegas, Apr. 5, 1902, RG395/2398; D. Ybarra to Sr. Comte de la Columna San Miguel et al., May 1, 1901, PRP/Pr10–11/B1.

14. D/Marciano Malpica, Mar. 18, 1902; D/Silverio Rivera, Mar. 19 and 21, 1902; D/Lazaro Villegas, Mar. 19, 1902; and D/Epifanio Ramos, c. Mar. 1902, all in RG395/5238.

15. See files 2380, 2398, 4229, and 4233 in RG395.

16. D/Catalino Reyes, Feb. 10, 1902; D/Antonio Briones, Feb. 10, 1902; and D/Manuel Reyes, Feb. 10, 1902, all in RG395/4153; D/Nicolas Catigbac, n.d., and files of Francisco Jesus, Teodoro Paula, Domingo Vergara, and many others in RG395/2397.

17. D/Jose Villanueva, Feb. 12, 1902, RG395/2380. On the date of Chaffee's trip to Batangas, see Wade to CO, Lipa, July 7, 1901, RG395/4138.

18. Ileto, *Pasyon,* 205–06; S. R. Gleaves to CO, San Pablo, Nov. 2, 1901, RG395/5101; J. Kline to AG, 3SB, Dec. 20, 1901, RG395/4134; F. West to AAG, 3SB, Nov. 17, 1901, RG395/2354.

19. D/Florencio Caedo, Feb. 14, 1902, RG395/4229.

20. On Bauan, see LBM to Malvar, c. June–July 1901, PIR/43/SD755.28.

21. On Ylagan: Report of Council of War, Calapan, Mindoro, May 8, 1901, PIR/43/SD755.25; F. West to AAG, 1D, DSL, May 5, 1901, RG395/5351.

22. J. A. Cole to AG, 3SB, Nov. 22, 1901, RG395/3010; Senate, *Affairs,* 3:2609–12.

23. USWD, 1901, 1, pt.7:388, 416.

24. On the efforts to arrange surrenders: USWD, 1901, 1, pt.5:247–51; Mariano Trias to Malvar, Apr. 13, 1901, and Malvar to Trias, Apr. 19, 1901, both in PIR/52/SD896.7; Hall (AAG) to AG, DSL, Apr. 14, 1901, and same to CO, Bay (Laguna), Apr. 18, 1901, RG395/2405; N. Gonzales to Malvar, Apr. 28, 1901, PIR/43/SD755.20; J. Kline to AG, 1D, May 13, 1901, RG395/4134; Sumner to AG, DSL, May 10, 1901; same to Traub, May 14, 1901; and same to J. Wade, May 19, 1901, all in RG395/2346.

25. Bruce Catton, *Glory Road* (Garden City, N.Y., 1952), 35–37, 174–75; id., *Terrible Swift Sword* (New York, 1963), 296–98, 431–32; id., *Never Call Retreat* (New York, 1965), 18–22, 105.

26. Career Summary of Samuel S. Sumner, an enclosure in H. C. Corbin to Albert J. Beveridge, May 6, 1902, Con. 136, Albert Beveridge Papers, LCMD; Marquis, ed., *Who's Who in America, 1908–1909,* 1842; Margaret Leech, *In the Days of McKinley* (New York, 1959), 248–50; Richard Harding Davis, *The Cuban and Porto Rican Campaigns* (New York, 1898), 173–223; Samuel Sumner to Theodore Roosevelt, Apr. 17 and May 14, 1900, series 1, reel 5, Theodore Roose-

velt Papers, LCMD; same to same, Mar. 5, 1901, series 1, reel 9, Theodore Roosevelt Papers; USWD, 1901, 1, pt.5:245.

27. Sumner to AG, DSL, May 23, 1901, RG395/2349.

28. USWD, 1901, 1, pt.5:251–52; 1, pt.7:411–12; Diary Entries, May 26–July 3, 1901, Charles Dudley Rhodes Diary, LCMD.

29. T. Lebo to AG, 1D, DSL, May 26, 1901, RG395/4208.

30. J. W. Craig to AG, 1D, DSL, June 7, 1901, and same to Capt. Blocksom, June 7, 1901, both in RG395/5052.

31. J. W. Craig to AG, 1D, DSL, June 14, 1901, RG395/5052.

32. Diary Entries, June 7–9, 1901, Charles Dudley Rhodes Diary, LCMD.

33. USWD, 1901, 1, pt.7:412; J. Kline to AG, DSL, June 10, 1901, RG395/4134; Miguel Malvar to Sr. Presidente del Comité Central Filipino en el Extranjero, July 4, 1901, PIR/69/SD1132.8; *Twenty-First Regiment,* 21–22.

34. Sumner to AG, DSL, June 18, 1901, RG395/2349.

35. Linn, *U.S. Army and Counterinsurgency,* 139–40.

36. Sumner to AG, DSL, June 18, 1901, RG395/2349.

37. Linn, *U.S. Army and Counterinsurgency,* 138–39.

38. On the probability that Wade was responsible, see Senate, *Affairs,* 3:2854–55, and Linn, *U.S. Army and Counterinsurgency,* 230.

39. USWD, 1, pt.7:417, 423.

40. F. S. West (by command of Sumner) to W. S. McCaskey, July 19, 1901, RG395/2349. For further indications of Sumner being overruled by Wade on the question of property destruction, see S. Sumner's endorsement (apparently to a report written by Lieut. McNair), July 16, 1901, RG395/2348.

41. Sumner to AG, DSL, Aug. 2, 1901, RG395/5101.

42. Tomas Ramirez to Claudio, May 28, 1901; Severino Ylagan to Claudio, May 28 and June 9, 1901, EC.

43. A. B. Wells to AG, 1D, DSL, June 18, 20, and 21, 1901, RG395/4208; USWD, 1901, 1, pt.7:412; USWD, 1902, 9:137; Briccio Casala to C. Gutierrez, June 21, 1901; Isidoro Quinio to E. Claudio, June 21, 1901; Casala to Claudio, June 24, 1901, EC.

44. Tomas Ramirez to Claudio, July 13, 1901; Felix Farol to Claudio, July 13, 24, and 26, 1901; C. Gutierrez to Claudio, July 31, 1901; J. Ramirez to Claudio, July 31, 1901, EC; S. B. Arnold to CO, Lobo, July 28, 1901, RG395/4208.

45. Tomas Ramirez to Claudio, July 13, 1901; Felix Farol to Claudio, July 13, 24, and 26, 1901; C. Gutierrez to Claudio, July 31, 1901; J. Ramirez to Claudio, July 31, 1901, EC; S. B. Arnold to CO, Lobo, July 28, 1901, RG395/4208.

46. USWD, 1902, 9:141, 292–93; A. B. Wells to AG, 1D, Aug. 8, 1901, RG391/1C, Letters Sent; Felix Farol to Claudio, Aug. 8, 1901, EC; Claudio to Malvar, Aug. 19, 1901, BHQ.

47. Sumner to AG, DSL, Aug. 13, 1901, RG395/2349.

48. B. Casala to Claudio, Aug. 26 and 27, 1901; Tranquilino Zara to Claudio, Aug. 29, 1901; Claudio to Fernando Garcia, Sept. 8, 1901; C. Gutierrez to Claudio, Sept. 15, 1901, all in EC; D/Fernando Garcia, June 7, 1902, RG395/ 4229.

49. Mariano Cabrera to Martin Cabrera, Aug. 8, 1901, PIR/43/SD763.1.

50. On refusal to obey: LBM to Malvar, c. June–July 1901, PIR/43/SD755.28; Valentin Burgos to Martin Cabrera, PIR/45/SD793. On lack of coordination: Mariano Cabrera to Martin Cabrera, Aug. 8, 1901, PIR/43/SD763.1; Aguedo Cabrera to Martin Cabrera, May 17, 1901, PIR/43/SD793. On abuses: Mauro Encarnacion to Martin Cabrera, May 29, 1901, PIR/43/SD793.

51. Diary Entry, July 28, 1901, FMP; J. Hartman to AG, DSL, July 27, 1901; Felipe Patricio to Martin Cabrera, July 27, 1901, PIR/43/SD755.21; USWD, 1902, 9:142.

52. On Buenafe: J. F. Morison to Adj., Batangas, July 30, 1901, RG395/4212; and A. B. Wells to AG, DSL, Aug. 18, 1901, RG395/4208. (The captured man was, at first, incorrectly identified as Lucio Buenafe, Juan's brother.) On Panganiban: USWD, 1901, 1, pt.7:412. On Laurel: USWD, 1902, 9:143.

53. USWD, 1902, 9:190.

54. Adna Chaffee to Henry C. Corbin, Sept. 2, 1901, Con. 1, HCC.

55. Sumner to AG, DSL, Sept. 4, 1901, RG395/2349.

56. On concentration, see Linn, *U.S. Army and Counterinsurgency,* 112, 291, 335; and Scott, *Ilocano Responses,* 143–44.

57. E. S. West (by command of Sumner) to COs, Batangas and Laguna, Sept. 23, 1901; Herman Hall (by Sumner's order) to CO, 20th U.S. Infantry, Sept. 24, 1901; and same to CO, Tanauan and Lipa, Sept. 24, 1901, all in RG395/2349.

58. Sumner to AG, DSL, Sept. 28, 1901, RG395/2349.

59. A. B. Wells to AG, DSL, Aug. 29, 1901, RG395/4208.

60. F. West to AAG, 1D, DSL, Sept. 21, 1901, and Oct. 25, 1901, RG395/5351.

61. P. A. Connolly to E. S. West, Sept. 27, 1901, RG395/5007.

62. See, for example, May, "Presher," 42–43; Antonio Gozos to S. Sumner, Nov. 7, 1901, RG395/2354.

63. USWD, 1902, 9:146–47; Diary Entries, Sept. 28 and 29, 1901, FMP; F. Ward to AG, Batangas, Sept. 29, 1901, and J. Hartman to AG, 3SB, Jan. 4, 1902, RG395/3089; Senate, *Affairs,* 3:2328.

64. Joseph L. Schott, *The Ordeal of Samar* (Indianapolis, 1964), 27–55.

65. Adna Chaffee to Henry C. Corbin, Sept. 30, 1901, Con. 1, HCC.

66. William H. Taft to Elihu Root, Oct. 14, 1901, WHT.

67. Adna Chaffee to Henry C. Corbin, Oct. 25, 1901, HCC.

68. Chaffee to Corbin, Nov. 5, 1901, and Nov. 18, 1901, Con. 1, HCC; USWD, 1902, 9:264; S. Sumner to T. J. Wint, Nov. 10, 1901, RG395/2348; USWD, 1902, 9:151–54; J. Guthrie to Adj., Batangas, Nov. 17, 1901, RG395/2354; H. Hall to AG, Batangas, Nov. 22, 1901, RG395/5052; May, "Presher," 44.

69. On impressment, see, for example, J. Hartman to Adj., 1C, Oct. 31, 1901, RG395/4212. On the recovery of Claudio's column, see Tomas Ramirez to E. Claudio, Oct. 14 and 15, 1901, EC.

70. C. Gutierrez to Claudio, Sept. 15, 1901; Severino Ylagan to Claudio,

Sept. 21, 1901; unknown writer to Claudio, Sept. 28, 1901; Claudio to Pangulo, San Agapito, Nov. 1, 1901, all in EC; Schumacher, *Revolutionary Clergy,* 129.

71. Tomas Ramirez to E. Claudio, Nov. 15, 1901, EC; USWD, 1902, 9:152.

72. Miguel Malvar, "Resumen de las disposiones e instrucciones generales . . . desde el 29 de Agosto hasta la fecha," Sept. 9, 1901, PIR/53/SD902.8; Malvar, "Resumen de las disposiciones e instrucciones generales . . . desde el 10 de Septiembre hasta la fecha," Oct. 27, 1901, PIR/53/SD902.8; Malvar, "Resumen de las disposiciones e instrucciones generales . . . desde el 28 de Octubre hasta la fecha," Nov. 11, 1901, PIR/53/SD902.10; Taylor, *Philippine Insurrection,* 5:355–57.

73. On Diocampo, see note 63 of this chapter. On Nazareth: J. I. Morison to AG, 3SB, Nov. 27, 1901; *U.S. v. Andres Paz,* June 1902; *U.S. v. Gabriel Macahia,* June 1902, all in RG395/2354. On Cabatay: B. Casala to E. Claudio, Oct. 25, 1901, EC; and "In re Murder of Maximo Cabatay," Mar.–June, 1902, RG395/ 2398.

74. As I noted in chapter 7, it was common for noncombatants to claim, after the events, that they cooperated with the guerrillas out of fear. For additional testimony, see *U.S. v. Gregorio Cueto,* Jan. 1902; *U.S. v. Gregorio Balmes,* Jan. 1902, and other cases in RG395/2398.

75. GI, pp. 650–51.

76. Miguel Malvar, Order, Nov. 11, 1901, PRP/RL11/Malvar; Briccio Casala to E. Claudio, Nov. 23, 1901, PIR/56/SD936.6; same to same, Nov. 30, 1901, EC.

Chapter 9. Concentration and Conquest

1. James H. Blount, *The American Occupation of the Philippines, 1898–1912* (New York, 1913), 393; Daniel B. Schirmer, *Republic or Empire: American Resistance to the Philippine War* (Cambridge, Mass., 1972), 237–39; Richard E. Welch, Jr., *Response to Imperialism: The United States and the Philippine-American War* (Chapel Hill, 1979), 138–39.

2. Kalaw, *Philippine Revolution,* 300.

3. Zaide, *Philippine Revolution,* 354; Constantino, *Past Revisited,* 250–51.

4. Wolff, *Little Brown Brother,* 358; Miller, *"Benevolent Assimilation,"* 260. See also Stuart Creighton Miller, Response to Brian Linn, *Pilipinas* 7 (Fall 1986): 57.

5. Taylor, *Philippine Insurrection,* 2:295.

6. Gates, *Schoolbooks,* 260–63; Linn, *U.S. Army and Counterinsurgency,* 159–60. Although Linn defends Bell against his harshest critics, he does acknowledge major flaws in Bell's campaign.

7. Harris Starr, ed., *Dictionary of American Biography, Supplement One* (New York, 1944), 67–68; Marquis, ed., *Who's Who in America, 1908–1909,* 130; *New York Times,* Feb. 7, 1901, p. 3; Arthur MacArthur, "Report of the Field Operations of the Second Division, Eighth Army Corps, for the Months of March, April and May, 1899," enclosures 55–58, RG94/AGO312821; Diary Entry, Feb.

10, 1899, William A. Kobbé Diary, USAMHI; William H. Taft to Elihu Root, Feb. 8, 1901, WHT.

8. Linn, *U.S. Army and Counterinsurgency,* 59–60; Scott, *Ilocano Responses,* 143–44, 161–78, 198–200. (The long quotation can be found on p. 143 of Scott's book.)

9. Adna Chaffee to Henry C. Corbin, Nov. 18, 1901, Con. 1, HCC; William H. Taft to Elihu Root, Aug. 25, 1901, and Oct. 14, 1901; J. Franklin Bell to Taft, May 26, 1901, and Sept. 25, 1901, WHT.

10. George F. Becker to Henry C. Lodge, Dec. 17, 1900 (containing an extract of a letter written by Bell to an unidentified correspondent on Oct. 30, 1900), RG94/AGO354897; J. Franklin Bell to Henry C. Corbin, May 17, 1901, Con. 1-A, HCC.

11. Diary Entry, Nov. 29, 1901, Diary, v. 6, Bernard Moses Papers, University of California Archives, Berkeley, Calif.

12. USWD, 1902, 9:231–32, 264, 268.

13. Ibid., 9:155–56, 278, 312–14; A. B. Wells to AG, 3SB, Dec. 9, 1901, RG395/4208; J. Kline to AG, 3SB, Dec. 8, 1901, RG395/4134; Report of Operations of the Garrison of Ambulong (Tanauan), Batangas, Dec. 1901, RG395/2379; *U.S. v. Cipriano Villanueva,* RG395/2394.

14. Felix Farol to Eliseo Claudio, Dec. 8, 9, and 10, 1901, EC; D/Fernando Garcia, June 7, 1902, RG395/4229; USWD, 1902, 9:312–14.

15. Proclamation of Briccio Casala, Dec. 13, 1901; Casala to Eliseo Claudio, Dec. 15, 1901, EC; Edgar Conley to COs, Ibaan and San Jose, Dec. 11, 1901, and A. B. Wells to AG, 3SB, Dec. 17, 20, and 21, 1901, RG395/4208; USWD, 1902, 9:156–59; D/Fernando Garcia, June 7, 1902, RG395/4229.

16. M. F. Davis, comp., *Telegraphic Circulars and General Orders . . . Issued by Brigadier General J. Franklin Bell* (a pamphlet filed in RG94/AGO415839), 1–2. On Bell's decision not to require people to enter the zones, see USWD, 1902, 9:232.

17. GO no. 372 (by command of General Chaffee), Dec. 3, 1901, RG395/5101; Inspector of Customs, Batangas, to Adj., Batangas, Dec. 6, 1901, RG395/2349; USWD, 1902, 9:270–71; Davis, comp., *Telegraphic Circulars,* 13–14, 16.

18. Davis, comp., *Telegraphic Circulars,* 4–5.

19. Ibid., 4, 16–17, 21; J. F. Bell to COs, All Stations, Batangas and Laguna, Dec. 18, 1901, J. Franklin Bell Papers, USAMHI.

20. Davis, comp., *Telegraphic Circulars,* iii.

21. Senate, *Affairs,* 2:1691; Davis, comp., *Telegraphic Circulars,* 3.

22. Davis, comp., *Telegraphic Circulars,* 3. The text of GO 100 can be found in U.S. Senate, Committee on the Philippines, *Issuance of Certain Military Orders in the Philippines,* S. Doc. 347, 57th Cong., 1st sess., 1902, pp. 10–22.

23. On the application of GO 100 before Bell's arrival, see Gates, *Schoolbooks,* 190–92, 206–08; Millett, *General,* 145–48. Bell's directives are in Davis, comp., *Telegraphic Circulars,* 3, 8–9. On Bell's intention to retain the power to authorize executions, see Davis, comp., *Telegraphic Circulars,* viii. The ambiguity of Bell's

prose appears to be, in part, responsible for the disagreement between Stuart Miller and Brian Linn on the subject of Bell's policy of retaliation. See Brian M. Linn, "Stuart C. Miller and the American Soldier: Review Article," *Pilipinas* 7 (Fall 1986): 47; Miller, Response to Brian Linn, *Pilipinas* 7 (Fall 1986): 57–58. See also USWD, 1902, 9:270.

24. Adna Chaffee to Henry C. Corbin, Dec. 18, 1901, Con. 1, HCC.

25. May, "Presher," 45; Report of Operations for the Garrison of Bauan for the Month of December 1901, RG395/2379; Senate, *Affairs,* 2:1684–94; A. B. Wells to AG, 3SB, Dec. 17, 1901, RG395/4208; J. Kline to AG, 3SB, Dec. 12 and 13, 1901, RG395/4134; H. Hall to AG, Batangas, Dec. 23, 1901, RG395/5052; M. Kobbé to AG, 3SB, Jan. 1, 1902, RG395/2354.

26. USWD, 1902, 9:268, 271, 276; Senate, *Affairs,* 2:1691.

27. Senate *Affairs,* 2:1690–92, 1698–99; M. F. Davis to CO, Batangas, Dec. 26, 1901, RG395/4212; A. B. Wells to AG, 3SB, Jan. 8, 1902, RG395/4208; T. J. Wint to AG, 3SB, Feb. 8, 1902, with enclosures, RG395/2379.

28. Davis, comp., *Telegraphic Circulars,* 10, 12, 25; M. F. Davis to CO, Batangas, Dec. 26, 1901, RG395/4212.

29. Attempts at justification can be found in W. B. Burtt to Adj., San Pablo Expeditionary Column, Jan. 18, 1902, and H. R. Richmond to Herman Hall, Jan. 12, 1902, both enclosures in T. J. Wint to AG, 3SB, Feb. 8, 1902, RG395/2379.

30. H. Hall to AG, Batangas, Jan. 13, 14, and 28, 1902, RG395/5052; T. J. Wint to Adj., San Pablo Expeditionary Column, Jan. 18, 1902, with enclosures, RG395/2379; S. Price to Adj., Batangas, Feb. 7, 1902, and George V. H. Moseley to Adj., Batangas, Feb. 7, 1902, RG395/2354.

31. T. J. Wint to Adj., San Pablo Expeditionary Column, Jan. 18, 1902, with enclosures, RG395/2379; E. S. West to Post Adj., Taal, Feb. 7, 1902, RG395/2354; Diary Entries, Feb. 19–22, 1902, Charles Dudley Rhodes Diary, LCMD; Boss Reese to Adj., Batangas, Feb. 19, 1902, RG395/2354.

32. May, "Presher," 45–47.

33. For the testimony about Hennessy as well as various assessments of his character by Bell and others, see Morris C. Foote to AG, Div. Phil., Dec. 1902, with enclosures, RG94/AGO476653; George B. Davis to Sec/War, Apr. 10, 1903, RG94/AGO389439 (filed with AGO489591); M. F. Davis to F. B. Hennessy, June 30, 1902, RG395/2354.

34. See testimony of witnesses about U.S. outrages, Dec. 1902, in Foote to AG, Div. Phil., Dec. 1902, op. cit.

35. See, for example, Senate, *Affairs,* 3:2610, 2644–45, 2651; Charges and Specifications Preferred Against Pvt. Fred M. Ashton, Mar. 1902, RG395/2354; Homer V. Cook to Don Rickey, Feb. 10, 1969, Homer V. Cook Papers, SAW/1C.

36. Charges made by Maria Marasigan, Jan. 25, 1902, RG395/2394; *U.S. v. Juan de Guzman and Julio Gutierrez,* c. Feb. 1902, RG395/2354; G. S. Anderson to CO, Tanauan, Feb. 15, 1902, RG395/4134; "History and Cultural Life of Taysan" and "History and Cultural Life of the Town of San Luis," HDP.

37. Endorsement of Loyd Wheaton, Feb. 21, 1900, RG395/2403.

38. Davis, comp., *Telegraphic Circulars,* 20. Also see Endorsement of Roger Fitch (by command of A. B. Wells), Feb. 10, 1902, RG395/4208.

39. P. A. Connolly to Provost Marshal, 3SB, Mar. 1, 1902, RG395/2354; Statement of Nicolas Gonzales, Apr. 23, 1902, RG395/2354; Bonifacio Ramirez to Sr. Juez Preboste gral., Batangas, May 10, 1902, RG395/4287.

40. May, "Presher," 47–48.

41. Adna Chaffee to AG, Washington, Jan. 14, 1902, RG94/AGO416094 (filed with AGO352161); G. S. Anderson to Bell, Jan. 16, Feb. 1, 6, and 8, 1902, RG395/4134; Senate, *Affairs,* 2:1706, 1710.

42. Adna Chaffee to Henry C. Corbin, Jan. 31, 1902, Con. 1, HCC.

43. Briccio Casala to E. Claudio, Dec. 15, 1901, EC; D/Fernando Garcia, June 7, 1902, RG395/4229; USWD, 1902, 9:279, 315.

44. D/Paulino Dueñas, Apr. 22, 1902, RG395/4233; B. Casala to E. Claudio, Dec. 15, 1901, EC.

45. Senate, *Affairs,* 2:1725; W. Fassett to Adj., Batangas, Feb. 25, 1902, RG395/4212; J. S. Galbraith to AG, 3SB, Feb. 26, 1902, RG395/4208; USWD, 1902, 9:169.

46. Edgar Conley to CO, Military Prison, Grand Island, Dec. 20, 1901, RG395/4287; Senate, *Affairs* 3:2638, 2656; P. A. Connolly, Report of Native Prisoners, San Jose, Jan. 1902; W. B. Burtt, Report of Native Prisoners, Santo Tomas, Jan. 31, 1902; Herman Hall, List of Native Prisoners, San Juan, Jan. 1902, RG395/2398; Morris C. Foote to AG, Div. Phil., Dec. 1902, with enclosures, RG94/AGO476653.

47. D/Fermin Arceo, Feb. 17, 1902; D/Leoncio Arceo, Feb. 17, 1902; D/Vicente Yturralde, Feb. 10, 1902; D/Felix Aguirre, Feb. 10, 1902; and D/Juan Gutierrez, Feb. 14, 1902, all in RG395/4229.

48. See RG395, files 2380, 2398, 4153, 4229, 4233, and 5238.

49. For the Wagner report, see Senate, *Certain Military Orders,* 22–24. See also Bureau of the Census, *Census: 1903,* 3:289–90, and, on the question of Batangas's population at the time, May, "150,000 Missing Filipinos," 236–43.

50. Bureau of the Census, *Census: 1903,* 3:289–90.

51. Libros de Entierros, Parish Records of Balayan, Batangas City, Calaca, Ibaan, Lipa, Lobo, and Taysan. On the question of under-registration in the parish books and on the problems of calculating crude death rates for 1902, see May, "150,000 Missing Filipinos," 228–32, 237.

52. See May, "150,000 Missing Filipinos," 237–39.

53. Davis, comp., *Telegraphic Circulars,* 25–29.

54. On the amount of rice supplied by the army: "Statement Showing Quantities of Rice No. 2 Shipped . . . ," in Bell, Annual Report of the Third Sep. Brig. to July 1, 1902, RG395/2354. (I am grateful to Reynaldo Ileto for providing me with copies of this document and of the letter cited in the next note.) On shortages: Endorsement of E. F. Willcox, Feb. 20, 1902, RG395/5351; and G. S. Anderson to Bell, June 1 and 8, 1902, RG395/4134.

55. USWD, 1902, 9:273; Simeon Luz to Civil Governor, Manila, Sept. 8, 1902, file 3047/10, Records of the Bureau of Insular Affairs, U.S. National Archives.

56. De Bevoise, "Compromised Host," 40–41, 87–88.

57. See Glenn A. May, "The 'Zones' of Batangas," *Philippine Studies* 29 (First Quarter 1981): 98.

58. Monthly Sanitary Report, Lipa, May 1, 1902; A. G. Hennissee to AG, Batangas, May 5, 1902; and G. S. Anderson to Bell, June 8, 1902, all in RG395/4134; De Bevoise, "Compromised Host," 214.

59. Miguel Malvar, "The Reason for My Change in Attitude," n.d., PIR/53/SD902.3; Malvar, "Memorandum of the motives of my change of attitude," May 7, 1902, enclosure in Adna Chaffee to Henry C. Corbin, May 27, 1902, Con. 1, HCC; George Anderson to Bell, Jan. 5, 10, and 18, 1902, RG395/4134; Senate, *Affairs,* 2:1717–18, 1720.

60. Senate, *Affairs,* 2:1712–13.

61. Ibid., 2:1720.

62. Herman Hall to Bell, Feb. 24 and Mar. 1, 1902, RG395/5052; Roger Fitch to CO, Ibaan, Mar. 17, 1902, RG395/4208; J. F. Bell to Chaffee, Mar. 15, 1902, enclosure in Adna Chaffee to Henry Corbin, Mar. 17, 1902, Con. 1, HCC; M. F. Davis to CO, Batangas, Mar. 21, 1902, Box 38, George Van Horn Moseley Papers, LCMD.

63. USWD, 1902, 9:325–28; Oscar Brown to AG, Batangas, Apr. 9, 1902, RG395/4134; M. Davis to L. Van Schaick, Apr. 11, 1902, RG395/2349.

64. Miguel Malvar, "The Reason for My Change in Attitude," n.d., PIR/53/SD902.3; GI, pp. 651, 682–83; Malvar, "Memorandum of the motives of my change of attitude," May 7, 1902, enclosure in Chaffee to Corbin, May 27, 1902, Con. 1, HCC; Oscar Brown to Col. Wint, Apr. 14 and 16, 1902; Oscar Brown to Bell, Apr. 14 and 15, 1902, RG395/4134.

65. Statement of Nicolas Gonzales, Apr. 23, 1902, RG395/2354; USWD, 1902, 9:175–76.

66. M. Davis to CO, Lipa, Apr. 13, 1902; and Davis to All Station Commanders, Apr. 26, 1902, RG395/4142; Adna Chaffee to AG, Washington, May 5, 1902, RG94/AGO415839; W. Bowen, Report of the Garrison of Tanauan, Apr. 1902, RG395/2379.

Epilogue

1. On the arrival of cholera in the province, see Henry D. Thomson and James Phalen to Chief Surgeon, 3SB, July 28, 1902, RG112/Series 26/90497.

2. Reynaldo C. Ileto, "Cholera and the Origins of the American Sanitary Regime in the Philippines," in *Imperial Medicine and Indigenous Societies,* ed., David Arnold (Manchester, 1988), 125–48; De Bevoise, "Compromised Host," 237–45; J. R. McAndrews to AG, 3SB, June 15, 1902, RG395/2377; Henry D. Thomson and James Phalen to Chief Surgeon, 3SB, July 28, 1902, and E. C. Chichester to Chief Surgeon, Div. Phil., July 30, 1902, RG112/Series 26/90497.

3. J. G. Galbraith to Surgeon, Batangas, Mar. 28, 1902, and A. B. Wells to AG, 3SB, Apr. 17, 1902, RG395/4208.

4. Anderson to J. F. Bell, June 8, 1902, RG395/4134; G. C. Saffarrans to AG, Batangas, June 15, 1902, RG395/5052. On shortages in Tanauan: F. K. Ward to AG, 3SB, May 13, 1902, RG395/2354.

5. On cattle: Gasser to AG, 3SB, July 28, Aug. 1 and Aug. 5, 1902, RG395/2354; on human labor: Gasser to AG, 3SB, July 28, 1902, RG395/2354. I am grateful to Reynaldo Ileto for providing me with copies of these documents, as well as several cited in the next two notes.

6. On locusts: G. C. Saffarrans to AG, Batangas, June 23, 1902, RG395/5052; L. Gasser to AG, 3SB, July 28, Aug. 1 and 5, and Sept. 30, 1902, RG395/2354.

7. Gasser to AG, 3SB, July 28, and Aug. 1, 1902; J. A. Baer to AG, 3SB, Aug. 7, 1902, all in RG395/2354; G. C. Saffarrans to Lt. Bell, Commissary, Aug. 8, 1902, and Saffarrans to Capt. Galbraith, Brig. Commissary, Aug. 13, 1902, RG395/5052.

8. U.S., Philippine Commission, *Report of the U.S. Philippine Commission, 1902,* 1:394; *Report of the U.S. Philippine Commission, 1903,* 2:123; Headquarters, Third Separate Brigade, "List of Cases and Deaths from Cholera," c. Sept. 1902, RG395/2377; Bureau of the Census, *Census: 1903,* 3:141. Burials were seriously under-registered in the parish records during the cholera epidemic for reasons that will become clear later in this chapter.

9. G. C. Saffarrans to AG, Batangas, July 22, 1902, RG395/5052; USWD, 1902, 1:613.

10. Bureau of the Census, *Census: 1903,* 3:239.

11. R. Pollitzer, *Cholera* (Geneva, 1959), 873–74; O. Felsenfeld, "A Review of Recent Trends in Cholera Research and Control," *Bulletin of the World Health Organization* 34 (1966): 161–95; Chun Hui Yen, "A Recent Study of Cholera with Reference to an Outbreak in Taiwan in 1962," *Bulletin of the World Health Organization* 30 (1964): 811–25; J. F. Tamayo et al., "Studies of Cholera El Tor in the Philippines," *Bulletin of the World Health Organization* 33 (1965): 645–49; Bireswa Banerjee and Jayati Hazra, *Geoecology of Cholera in West Bengal* (Calcutta, 1974), 57–58.

12. Libros de Entierros, San Juan; G. C. Saffarrans to Chief Surgeon, 3SB, Aug. 28, 1902, RG395/5052; J. R. McAndrews to AG, Batangas, July 14, 1902, RG395/2377.

13. J. F. Bell to AG, Div. Phil., Sept. 10, 1902, RG94/AGO453824-A (filed with AGO415389).

14. Franklin M. Kemp to Surgeon General, USA, June 24, 1902, RG112/Series 26/90497.

15. For the census figures, see Bureau of the Census, *Census: 1903,* 2:123. For a discussion of the undercount in the 1903 census, see May, "150,000 Missing Filipinos," 223–28.

16. As Calixto Silva, a resident of Lipa and veteran of the war, remarked to

me, "When the people realized they were overpowered, they were forced to accept the Americans." Interview with Calixto Silva, Lipa, July 27, 1976.

17. Monthly Report of Native Prisoners, Malagi Island, May and June 1902, RG395/4287; Allen Smith to Provost Marshal, 3SB, July 1, 1902, RG395/2394.

18. On Claudio: In re Murder of Maximo Cabatay, c. June 1902, RG395/2398. On Ramirez: Brigade Provost Marshal to Sheriff, Batangas, June 3, 1902, RG395/4287.

19. On U.S. colonial policy, see May, *Social Engineering,* chaps. 3–9. In the barrio and municipal histories found in HDP there are repeated references to the appreciation of Batangueños for American reforms, especially the introduction of primary schools in the barrios; further evidence on the popularity of the American primary schools was derived from interviews, particularly one with Paz Luz Dimayuga, Lipa, July 5, 1976.

20. On the political elite of Lipa: George S. Anderson to D. H. Boughton, May 19, 1902, RG395/4134; Marquez, "Lipa and the Philippine Revolution," 71; Bayani Sarmiento, compiler, "Batangas Provincial Governors and Board Members," typescript, Records Section, Office of the City Mayor, Batangas City; Anthony Tuohy, *Album histórico de la primera asamblea filipina* (Manila, 1908), 29. On Batangas City: Council Minutes, Municipal Council of Batangas City, 1901–10, Records Section, Office of the City Mayor, Batangas City; biographical sketch of Juan Buenafe, typescript provided by Bayani Sarmiento, Office of the City Mayor, Batangas City. On Cabrera and Luna: Sarmiento, comp., "Provincial Governors." On Aguila: "History and Cultural Life of the Town of San Jose," 3, HDP. On Gonzales: "History and Cultural Life of Tanauan, Batangas," 1, HDP; Sarmiento, comp., "Provincial Governors."

21. J. F. Bell to Adna Chaffee, May 14, 1902, enclosure in Chaffee to H. C. Corbin, May 27, 1902, Con. 1, HCC; Receipts signed by Miguel Malvar, July 4, 1902, and J. A. Baer to J. F. Bell, Sept. 9, 1902, RG395/2354; Serrano, "Man Who Saved His Captor"; Miguel Malvar, Jr., "General Malvar: The Soldier as Farmer," *The Barangay Forum* 1 (Sept. 1966): 42–45.

22. Interview with Dr. Isabel Malvar Villegas and Dr. Jose Villegas, Santo Tomas, Sept. 1984; Journal Entries of Sept. 20, 1910, and Oct. 14, 1911, W. Cameron Forbes Papers, Houghton Library, Harvard University; Act. no. 3015, March 1922, file 2618/163, Records of the Bureau of Insular Affairs (RG350), U.S. National Archives.

23. On the independence issue and Philippine political parties, see Peter W. Stanley, *A Nation in the Making: The Philippines and the United States, 1899–1921* (Cambridge, Mass., 1974), 123–37.

24. W. P. Duvall to AG, Washington, Nov. 30, 1909, with enclosures, RG94/AGO1562452-H; Confidential Report, Feb. 11, 1910, enclosure 6 in RG94/AGO1562452-W; H. H. Bandholtz to Sec/War, Mar. 6, 1910, RG94/AGO1562452-Y; Confidential Report, May 12, 1910, enclosure 13 in RG94/AGO1562452-A3;

W. P. Duvall to AG, Washington, Aug. 6, 1910, RG94/AGO1562452-A5. See also Ricarte, *Memoirs,* 201.

25. Kit G. Machado, "From Traditional Faction to Machine: Changing Patterns of Political Leadership and Organization in the Rural Philippines," *Journal of Asian Studies* 33 (Aug. 1974): 523–47.

26. J. F. Bell to All Station Commanders, Batangas, Dec. 19, 1901, RG395/4138; Daniel Cornman to AG, 3SB, Jan. 2, 1902, RG395/3284; Report of Native Prisoners in Confinement at Santo Tomas, Jan. 31, 1902, RG395/2398; Report of Native Prisoners at Tanauan, Feb. 1902, RG395/2394; Roger S. Fitch to AG, 3SB, Apr. 2, 1902, RG395/2354; GI, pp. 43–45.

27. Ileto, *Pasyon,* 255–56, 298–99; H. H. Bandholtz to Sec/War, Mar. 6, 1910, RG94/AGO1562452-Y; Confidential Report, Mar. 15, 1910, enclosure 25 in RG94/AGO1562452-A1; Philippine Islands, Bureau of Constabulary, *Annual Report: 1910,* 6.

28. For discussions of the use (and misuse) of the term *ladrones,* see Ileto, *Pasyon,* 211–12, 214; Constantino, *Past Revisited,* 252, 355.

29. W. Cameron Forbes to Henry L. Higginson, Sept. 2, 1902, W. Cameron Forbes Papers, Houghton Library, Harvard University.

30. *U.S. v. Aniceto Oruga,* 1902, RG395/2398; W. Bowen to Commissary General of Prisoners, May 24, 1902, RG395/2394; Philippine Islands, Bureau of Constabulary, *Annual Report: 1905,* 129; Ricarte, *Memoirs,* 196.

31. Constabulary, *Annual Report: 1905,* 54, 131.

32. Ileto, *Pasyon,* 213–29, 237–44; Constabulary, *Annual Report: 1905,* 129–32.

33. Constabulary, *Annual Report: 1905,* 132; Excerpts from the Minutes of the Philippine Commission, Jan. 31, Mar. 24, and Apr. 25, 1905, v. 11, Worcester's Philippine Collection, Department of Rare Books and Special Collections, University of Michigan.

34. Guy V. Henry, Autobiography (manuscript), p. 31, Box 2, Guy V. Henry Papers, USAMHI: Constabulary, *Annual Report: 1905,* 36–37, 54, 66–69, 131–33; *Annual Report: 1906,* 3–4; *Annual Report: 1907,* 4.

35. H. H. Bandholtz to Director of Constabulary, Mar. 27, 1907, W. Cameron Forbes Papers, Houghton Library, Harvard University; Philippine Islands, Bureau of Constabulary, *Annual Report: 1909,* 6; *Annual Report: 1910,* 6; Ileto, *Pasyon,* 255–56, 298–99.

36. For Roosevelt's praise, see Davis, comp., *Telegraphic Circulars,* 46–47.

37. Welch, *Response to Imperialism,* 138–39; Miller, *"Benevolent Assimilation,"* 208–11.

38. Senate, *Affairs,* 2:849–50, 860, 881–88.

39. Ibid., 3:2327, 2656.

40. The Gardener Inquiry (GI), which included more than a thousand pages of testimony, can be found in two volumes in the records of the Adjutant General's Office: RG94/AGO421607-F, enclosures 2 and 3.

41. The report of the investigating board is filed with the above-cited two

volumes of testimony. The final report of the Judge Advocate General, dated Dec. 22, 1902, is the first document in the same file: RG94/AGO421607.

42. Endorsements of J. S. Kerr (by command of Gen. Chaffee), June 15, 1902; Florencio R. Caedo, June 28, 1902; M. F. Davis (by command of J. F. Bell), June 28, 1902; and R. D. Blanchard, June 30, 1902, all in RG94/AGO453824-A (filed with AGO415839).

43. J. F. Bell to Adna Chaffee, July 1, 1902, and J. F. Bell to AG, Div. Phil., Sept. 10, 1902, enclosures 2 and 3 in RG94/AGO453824-A (filed with AGO415839).

44. The attachment actually contained a computational error. It indicated that the loss in population was 87,812; the figure should have been 90,735.

45. Endorsement by Adna Chaffee, Sept. 12, 1902, in RG94/AGO453824-A (filed with AGO415839).

46. J. F. Bell to Albert Beveridge, Aug. 16, 1902, Con. 136, Albert Beveridge Papers, LCMD.

47. J. F. Bell to Elihu Root, Dec. 6, 1902, and Root to Bell, Feb. 3, 1903, RG94/AGO415839-I.

48. Harris Starr, ed., *Dictionary of American Biography, Supplement One* (New York, 1944), 67–68; *Who Was Who in America, 1897–1942* (Chicago, 1968), 80; *New York Times,* Jan. 9, 1919, p. 11; Jan. 10, 1919, p. 12; and Jan. 12, 1919, p. 22.

Conclusion

1. Agoncillo, *Malolos,* viii–ix, 621–78; Constantino, *Past Revisited,* 233–44.

2. Scott, *Ilocano Responses,* 68.

3. Ochosa, *Tinio Brigade;* Schumacher, *Revolutionary Clergy;* Ileto, *Pasyon;* Ma. Fe Hernaez Romero, *Negros Occidental between Two Foreign Powers, 1888–1909* (Bacolod, 1974); Elias M. Ataviado, *Lucha y Libertad,* 2 vols. (Manila, 1941). See also the treatments of the war in John A. Larkin, *The Pampangans: Colonial Society in a Philippine Province* (Berkeley, 1972), 119–28; Norman G. Owen, "Winding Down the War in Albay, 1900–1903," *Pacific Historical Review* 48 (Nov. 1979): 557–89; Alfred W. McCoy, "'Muy Noble y Muy Leal': Revolution and Counterrevolution in the Western Visayas, Philippines, 1896–1907," research paper, Research School of Pacific Studies, Australian National University, 1978; David R. Sturtevant, *Popular Uprisings in the Philippines, 1840–1940* (Ithaca, 1976), 96–138; Peter Schreurs, *Angry Days in Mindanao* (Cebu City, 1987); Lewis E. Gleeck, Jr., *Nueva Ecija in American Times: Homesteaders, Hacenderos, and Politicos* (Manila, 1981), 1–12; id., *Laguna in American Times: Coconuts and Revolucionarios* (Manila, 1981), 1–12; and id., "Pangasinan in American Times (1899–1946): Diversified Agriculture, Rebellion, and Collaboration (I)," *Bulletin of the American Historical Collection* 11 (Jan.–Mar. 1983): 12–19.

4. For a sampling of the literature, see Alfred W. McCoy and Ed. C. de Jesus, eds., *Philippine Social History: Global Trade and Local Transformations* (Que-

zon City, 1982). McCoy emphasizes commonalities in his introduction, but the following chapters provide a good deal of evidence about regional differences.

5. In *U.S. Army and Counterinsurgency* Brian Linn emphasizes the different approaches adopted by U.S. commanders on the island of Luzon.

6. See, for example, Carl N. Degler, "In Pursuit of an American History," *American Historical Review* 92 (Feb. 1987): 1–12; Gertrude Himmelfarb, "Some Reflections on the New History," *American Historical Review* 94 (June 1989): 662–65.

7. These calls for less "splintering" and more "coherence" have been severely criticized by some historians of the United States and Western Europe as well. For a compelling critique, see Joan Wallach Scott, "History in Crisis? The Others' Side of the Story," *American Historical Review* 94 (June 1989): 689–92.

Appendix A

1. The assessment records are found in *FU,* Batangas, 1890 and 1891. For the royal decrees relating to the property tax, consult Miguel Rodríguez Berriz, *Diccionario de la administración de Filipinas: Anuario de 1888,* 2 vols. (Manila, 1888), 2:502–06; and *Diccionario de la administración de Filipinas: Anuario de 1889* (Manila, 1889), 312–26. My statement about the relationship between the rental and assessed values is based on the assessment records themselves.

Glossary

Alcalde   Mayor; the second leading official, next to the civil governor, in the *ayuntamiento* (municipal corporation).

Altarcito   Small altar (found in many Filipino homes).

Ayuntamiento   Municipal corporation; governing body in a small number of Philippine towns during the Spanish period.

Barangay   Administrative subdivision of a town, consisting of a designated number of families.

Barrio   Village; a territorial subdivision of a town.

Basi   Wine made from the juice of sugar cane.

Cabeza de barangay   Headman of a *barangay,* an administrative subdivision of a Philippine town.

Capitán municipal   Municipal mayor.

Carabao   Water buffalo.

Carromato   Two-wheeled, horse-drawn cart.

Cavan   Unit of dry measure equivalent to seventy-five liters.

Cazadores   Light infantry; Spanish troops in the Philippines.

Chico (tsiko)   Fruit of the sapodilla tree.

Colorum Society   Religious brotherhood based on the slopes of Mount San Cristobal.

Compadre (kumpadre)   Godfather or male sponsor of one's child in baptism, confirmation, or marriage.

Consejero   Councillor; member of a municipal or provincial council.

Cortes   Spanish national legislature.

Cuadrilleros   Rural guards in the Philippines.

Gobernadorcillo   Municipal mayor.

Guardia Civil   Civil guard in the Philippines.

Indio   Spanish term for native Filipino.

Jefe del pueblo   Municipal mayor (during period of the Philippine Republic).

Jefe provincial   Provincial governor (during period of the Philippine Republic).

Kalayaan   Liberty or independence; to late nineteenth-century Tagalogs, the term also meant a condition of bliss, equality, brotherhood, and justice.

Katipunan   Gathering, assembly, or society; the secret society that launched the revolution against Spain in 1896.

Ladrón   Robber, highwayman, or bandit.

Lanzones (lansones)   Fruit cultivated extensively in the southern Tagalog region.

Macabebe Scouts   Mercenaries from the town of Macabebe in the province of Pampanga.

Magdalo   Council of the Katipunan led by Baldomero and Emilio Aguinaldo.

Magdiwang   Council of the Katipunan led by Mariano Alvarez.

Monte   Card game.

Pacto de retro   Business transaction similar to a land mortgage.

Palay   Unhusked rice.

Panguingui (pangginggi)   Card game.

Pangulo   Leader.

Pico (piko)   Game in which a player hops on one foot and attempts to kick a stone across lines.

Población   Town center, where the church, public buildings, and principal market are located.

Principalía   Individuals in a Philippine municipality who were qualified to participate in municipal elections during the Spanish period.

Regidor   Alderman (a member of the *ayuntamiento,* or municipal corporation).

Sari-sari store   Variety store.

Sitio   Hamlet; a portion of a barrio.

Sorteo   Selection by lot of twelve individuals who would be permitted to vote in a Philippine municipal election.

Supremo   Supreme or highest ruler or officer.

Tangga   Game of coins.

Teniente   Lieutenant or deputy; a barrio official.

Terna   List of three names (of the leading candidates for the post of *gobernadorcillo*) that municipalities passed on to the central government.

Tuba   Alcoholic drink made from the juice of nipa or buri palms.

Tubigan   Game in which members of one team attempt to cross lines guarded by members of the opposing team.

Voluntario   Volunteer.

Yaya   Female caretaker of children.

A Note about Sources

In writing this book, I have relied largely on unpublished primary sources. Since most of these materials are either unknown or little-known to most readers, I have decided to provide a brief description of them. For references to relevant secondary literature, readers are urged to consult the notes.

Six archival collections have provided the bulk of my source material: the Philippine National Archives (Manila), the University of Santo Tomas Archives (Manila), the Philippine National Library (Manila), the U.S. National Archives (Washington, D.C., and Suitland, Maryland), the U.S. Army Military History Institute (Carlisle Barracks, Pennsylvania), and the Genealogical Library of the Church of Jesus Christ of Latter-Day Saints (Salt Lake City, Utah).

The mammoth collections of the Philippine National Archives (PNA) consist primarily of bureaucratic documents generated by the Spanish colonial administration in the Philippines. Although holdings cover the entire

Spanish colonial period, most documents relate to the nineteenth century. The PNA collections contain a wealth of data about life in Batangas in the decades immediately preceding the Philippine-American War. They enabled me to place the particularities of the battle for Batangas into a larger developmental context—for example, to observe the continuities between local political leadership in the final years of Spanish rule and military command in the subsequent struggles for self-rule—and provided me with mountains of information about the residents of the province—e.g., data on landholding, home ownership, commercial activities, and the like. Since little has been written about turn-of-the-century Batangas (there are, for example, no book-length scholarly studies, no biographical dictionaries), and since few of the Filipino actors in the battle for Batangas left personal papers that tell us about their lives, such data proved to be essential in enabling me to situate those actors in the context of Batangueño society.

A number of record groups in the PNA were useful. The many bound volumes of *Sediciones y Rebeliones* touched on subversive activities in the province in the 1880s and 1890s, and the bundles of *Elecciones de Gobernadorcillos* were revealing about the nature of political power in the province. There were abundant data on socioeconomic status in the record groups entitled *Fincas Urbanas, Contribuciones Industriales,* and *Protocolos.* Other record groups of value were *Chinos, Estadísticas, Cabezas de Barangay,* and *Varias Personas.*

Like the PNA, the University of Santo Tomas Archives yielded information about prerevolutionary Batangas—specifically, about higher education in the province in the second half of the nineteenth century. The principal sources that I examined were two sets of huge bound volumes entitled "Libros de Matrícula de Estudios Generales y de Aplicación de Segunda Enseñanza" (covering the years 1866–98) and "Libros de Matrícula de Facultad, Real y Pontificia Universidad de Santo Tomás" (covering 1889–98); the first-mentioned volumes list secondary students enrolled in Philippine secondary schools, and the second, university students. These books not only document the rapid expansion of post–primary education in late nineteenth-century Batangas; they provide additional biographical information about prominent residents of the province, including many individuals who played key roles in the Philippine Revolution and Philippine-American War.

The Filipiniana section of the Philippine National Library (PNL) houses the principal collection of Philippine-language sources on the Philippine Revolution and the Philippine-American War—the Philippine Revolutionary Papers (PRP). Amounting to several hundred boxes of documentary material, the PRP consists of the official records of Aguinaldo's central government, letters and correspondence of local governments and regional commands, and a mass of other documents, all of which were confiscated by U.S. military units during the Philippine-American War. Immediately after the war, these documents were shipped to Washington, D.C., where they were deposited with the Bureau of Insular Affairs and were called the Philippine Insurgent Records (PIR). The records were transferred to the Adjutant General's Office in 1938, to the U.S. National Archives in 1948, and then, in the late 1950s, a microfilm copy was made of the entire collection (U.S. National Archives Microcopy 254; 643 reels), and the originals (subsequently renamed the PRP) were returned to the Philippines.

Since the return of the collection to the Philippines, it has been reorganized on several occasions, and in its present form, it bears relatively little resemblance to the microfilmed version, with the exception of one part of the collection known as the Selected Documents series. In the course of my own research, I consulted both the PRP and the PIR, and in general, I found it much easier to use the former. Hence, as my notes indicate, with the exception of references to the Selected Documents series, I have generally cited the PRP. (One peculiarity of those citations should be noted. On a number of occasions, I have not been able to specify the exact box where a particular document can be found; typically, at those times, I list two boxes—e.g., Pr10–11—rather than one. I found it necessary to adopt that procedure when I discovered on a recent trip to Manila that the PRP had been reorganized once again; that the box numbers listed on my notecards no longer corresponded exactly to the boxes in the reorganized PRP; that, in some cases, the documentary material formerly included in a single box was now lodged in two; and that, short of rechecking every affected citation, I could not determine the precise box in which some documents were located.)

As a scrutiny of my notes should make clear, the PRP furnished me with much information about Batangas's role in both the Philippine Revolution of 1896 and the subsequent struggle against the United States. Particularly useful was the captured correspondence file of Eliseo Claudio, one of the leaders of the Filipino guerrilla units in the Lobo-Batangas City area. (I cite it in the notes as EC.)

In the Filipiniana section of the PNL, there are two other intriguing sources: the Historical Data Papers (HDP), a collection of local histories, with data on various aspects of Batangas's past; and Santiago Alvarez's unpublished memoir, "Ang Katipunan at Ang Paghihimagsik," a lengthy document that provided vital information about the Philippine Revolution in Batangas.

The U.S. National Archives (USNA) houses a number of record groups that I used extensively in my research. The most important is Record Group 395 (RG395), the Records of U.S. Army Overseas Operations and Commands, which includes hundreds of files relating to American military activities in Batangas. These files also tell us a good deal about the Filipino resistance. As I explain in chapter 7, during the final stages of the battle for Batangas, many Batangueños were obliged by the U.S. command to provide accounts of their actions during the conflict, and more than one hundred of these statements, some of them running to a dozen or more manuscript pages, can be found in RG395. Such records made it possible for me to describe conditions in the occupied towns of Batangas in considerable detail.

Also of value are the documents in Record Group 94 (RG94), the Records of the Adjutant General's Office. The general correspondence files of the Adjutant General's Office contain many relevant sources, but because the indexes and finding aids are inadequate, those files are somewhat difficult to use. RG94 also includes the records of the Federal Volunteer regiments, which served in the Philippines through early 1901; since the majority of U.S. soldiers who served in Batangas in 1900 came from those units, those sources enabled me to document the activities of the U.S. Army in Batangas during the first phase of the province's occupation.

Six other collections in the National Archives yielded data: Record Group 24, the Records of the U.S. Navy; Record Group 112, the Records of the Office of the Surgeon General; Record Group 153, the Records of the Judge Advocate General's Office (available at the National Archives annex, Suitland, Maryland); Record Group 350, the Records of the Bureau of Insular Affairs; Record Group 391, the Records of U.S. Army Mobile Units; and the aforementioned Microcopy 254 (the microfilmed copy of the PIR, now the PRP). I also benefited enormously from assistance provided by the archives' Cartographic Branch.

The U.S. Army Military History Institute (USAMHI), located at Carlisle Barracks, Pennsylvania, has superb documentary holdings relating to the Philippine-American War. Especially useful is a large body of source material known collectively as the Spanish-American War Survey (SAW). Approximately two decades ago, the USAMHI began a systematic attempt to collect letters, diaries, memoirs, photographs, and other sources concerning the Spanish-American War and related conflicts—including, of course, the

Philippine-American War. As part of its record-gathering effort, it also contacted as many U.S. veterans of those wars as it could locate and sent them
questionnaires about their involvement. The impressive result of the
USAMHI's labors is the SAW. Included in the SAW are dozens of questionnaires, memoirs, diaries, and other documents relating to the battle for
Batangas, and I have relied on these materials heavily in writing about the
actions, attitudes, and worldviews of the U.S. fighting men in Batangas.

In addition to (and physically separated from) the SAW, the USAMHI
houses the personal papers of a large number of U.S. Army officers, some of
whom served in the Philippine-American War. Several of these collections
shed light on conditions in the southern Tagalog region, among them the
papers of J. Franklin Bell, William E. Birkhimer, Beverly C. Daly, Guy V.
Henry, Jr., William A. Kobbé, Clenard McLaughlin, and Matthew F. Steele.

For detailed information about morbidity and mortality in Batangas at
the turn of the century—subjects that I discuss at length in this book—I
have found it necessary to examine parish records. In most towns of the
Philippines, and in sixteen of twenty-two in Batangas, there are substantial
collections of ecclesiastical records relating to baptisms, burials, marriages,
and confirmations. In my own research, I focused on baptismal and burial
registers. A few of these records were examined at the parish repositories,
but the majority were consulted on microfilm—loaned to me by the Genealogical Department of the Church of Jesus Christ of Latter-Day Saints (Salt
Lake City, Utah), which has copied the surviving parish books in the Philippines.

Several other unpublished sources should be mentioned. Vital information about the Philippine Revolution in Batangas was derived from Carlos
Ronquillo's fascinating memoir, "Ilang Talata Tungkol sa Paghihimagsik
nang 1896–97," located in the Filipiniana and Asia Division of the University of the Philippines Library. A few letters relating to the liberation of
Batangas in 1898 are in the possession of the Apacible family, Taal, Batangas. In the City Library of Batangas City, there are several unpublished
sketches of leading Batangueños. The Records Section of the Office of the
City Mayor in Batangas City has two key items: the Council Minutes of the
Municipal Council of Batangas City (which I examined for the years 1901–
10), and an unpublished typescript entitled "Batangas Provincial Governors
and Board Members," written by Bayani Sarmiento, a municipal official.

A number of manuscript repositories in the United States hold the personal papers of U.S. soldiers and government officials who were involved in
one way or another with the Batangas campaigns. At the Manuscripts Divi-

sion of the Library of Congress (Washington, D.C.), I found items of interest in the papers of Albert Beveridge, Robert Lee Bullard, Henry C. Corbin, George Van Horn Moseley, Charles Dudley Rhodes, Theodore Roosevelt, Charles P. Summerall, and William H. Taft. Also useful were the collections of the U.S. Military Academy Library (West Point, N.Y.), particularly the manuscripts of George S. Anderson, Warren Dean, Joseph H. Dorst, Robert H. Hall, James Parker, and John H. Parker. Two valuable collections were the papers of Thomas H. Selm (a private in the Thirty-Eighth Infantry, U.S. Volunteers), which can be examined at Cornell University Library, Ithaca, N.Y., and those of John Leland Jordan (a captain in that same regiment), located at the Tennessee State Library and Archives, Nashville, Tennessee. (I am grateful to Professor Allan R. Millett, who provided me with a xeroxed copy of the Jordan papers.) Additional relevant documents were discovered in the Clarence R. Edward papers (Massachusetts Historical Society, Boston, Massachusetts), the W. Cameron Forbes papers (Houghton Library, Harvard University, Cambridge, Massachusetts), the Bernard Moses papers (University of California Archives, Berkeley, California), and Worcester's Philippine Collection (a collection of documents and papers of Dean C. Worcester, Department of Rare Books and Special Collections, University of Michigan, Ann Arbor, Michigan).

As my notes suggest, my understanding of the Filipino side of the Philippine-American War was enhanced by interviews. In June and July 1976, I had the opportunity to speak to more than a dozen Batangueños who lived through the battle for Batangas, including a number of former soldiers in Malvar's forces. Of particular importance were my interviews with Jose Caubalejo, Damian Decipeda, Paz Luz Dimayuga, Atanacio Ilagan, Dionisio Laygo, Severino Magsombol, Calixto Silva, and Emilio Vergara. Information about Miguel Malvar was supplied by Dr. Isabel Malvar Villegas and Dr. Jose Villegas of Santo Tomas. Natividad Aguila of Batangas City and Antonio Claudio of Quezon City furnished me with essential biographical data about Eliseo Claudio.

A variety of published primary sources were indispensable as well. In producing my description of late nineteenth-century Batangas, I relied heavily on two contemporary accounts: Manuel Sastrón, *Batangas y su provincia* (Malabong, 1895), and Wenceslao E. Retana, *El Indio Batangueño* (Manila, 1888). Additional information came from U.S. Bureau of the Census, *Census of the Philippine Islands: 1903;* Philippine Islands, *Guía oficial de Filipinas* (Manila, 1884–98); Teodoro M. Kalaw, *Aide-de-Camp to Freedom,* trans.

Maria Kalaw Katigbak (Manila, 1965); and an assortment of travelers' accounts which are listed in my notes.

On the Philippine Revolution in Batangas, a number of published memoirs should be consulted: Emilio Aguinaldo, *Mga Gunita ng Himagsikan* (Manila, 1964); Artemio Ricarte, *Memoirs of General Artemio Ricarte* (Manila, 1963); and the translated memoirs of Pio Valenzuela, which can be found in *Minutes of the Katipunan* (Manila, 1978). Further documentation on the Filipino side of the struggle against the Spaniards is available in John R. M. Taylor, *The Philippine Insurrection against the United States: A Compilation of Documents with Notes and Introduction,* 5 vols. (Pasay City, 1971–73); Pedro S. Achútegui and Miguel A. Bernad, *Aguinaldo and the Revolution of 1896: A Documentary History* (Quezon City, 1972); and Teodoro A. Agoncillo, *The Writings and Trial of Andres Bonifacio* (Manila, 1963). For the Spanish perspective on the revolution in Batangas, see Manuel Sastrón, *La insurrección en Filipinas y Guerra Hispano-Americana en el archipiélago* (Madrid, 1901); Emilio Revertér Delmas, *La insurrección de Filipinas en 1896 y 1897,* 2 vols. (Barcelona, 1899); Federico de Monteverde y Sedano, *Campaña de Filipinas: La División Lachambre, 1897* (Madrid, 1898); and the bimonthly periodical *La Política de España en Filipinas.* One key source concerning the province of Batangas during the period immediately following the expulsion of the Spaniards is the newspaper *Columnas Volantes,* published in Lipa. (An incomplete file of that newspaper's issues can be found in the PIR, microfilm reel 92, package D4.)

On the Philippine-American War in Batangas, the following published primary sources were useful: Taylor, *Philippine Insurrection;* Kalaw, *Aide-de-Camp;* U.S. War Department, *Annual Reports of the War Department* (1898–1902); U.S. Navy Department, *Annual Reports of the Navy Department* (1898–1902); U.S. Senate, Committee on the Philippines, *Hearings: Affairs in the Philippine Islands,* S. Doc. 331, 57th Cong., 1st sess., 1902; Charles J. Crane, *The Experiences of a Colonel of Infantry* (New York, 1923); Arthur W. Orton, *An Up-to-Date History of the 39th U.S. Vol. Inf.* (n.p., 1949); James Parker, *The Old Army: Memories, 1872–1918* (Philadelphia, 1929); *Historical Sketch of the operations, etc. of the Twenty-First Regiment of U.S. Infantry* (St. Paul, 1903). On postwar Batangas, two essential published sources are U.S., Philippine Commission, *Report of the U.S. Philippine Commission* (1902–10), and Philippine Islands, Bureau of Constabulary, *Annual Reports* (1905–10).

Index

Abas, Francisco, 122
Acosta, Alejo, 196
Advincula, Lucas, 73
Africa family, 9, 192
Agoncillo, Felipe, 40, 47, 277
Agoncillo, Flaviano, 40
Agoncillo, Teodoro: and Philippine-
American War, xvii–xviii, 196, 197,
286–90; and Philippine Revolution,
xix, 37, 39, 52, 312
Agregado, Vicente, 193, 342
Agriculture, 23–24, 61, 186, 201–02.
See also Coffee; Rice; Sugar
Aguila, Fernando, 276
Aguila family, 33
Aguilera, Doña Ramona, 193
Aguilera, Ynocencio, 186
Aguilera Solis, Gregorio, 9, 29, 71, 73–
74, 219, 276
Aguinaldo, Baldomero, 38, 54
Aguinaldo, Emilio, 37, 39, 53, 75, 199,
213, 214; military operations of, 1, 48,
53, 67, 79–80; and guerrilla warfare,
1, 88, 99–100, 116–17, 179, 306; and
Tejeros assembly, 54–57; and Boni-
facio, 56–59, 65; retreat of, 62; gov-
ernment of, 67–70, 73, 213; decrees
of, 76, 79; and 1900 election, 164–65,
183; capture of, 165, 183, 211, 247
Aguirre, Felix, 263
Aguirre, Gregorio, 263
Alas, Severino de las, 57
Alfonso, 73

Alvarez, Mariano, 39, 54, 57, 64
Alvarez, Santiago, 37, 50, 53, 64
Ammunition. See Army, Filipino
Anderson, George S., 94, 190, 191, 271;
and invasion, 112, 118, 120, 122, 124,
125; opinions of, 133, 147
Anglo-Boer War, 100, 242
Anopheles minimus var. flavirostris, 26,
61, 205, 265, 266, 267
Anti-imperialists, 164–65, 216, 224,
234, 243
Anting-anting, 167–68
Apacible, Galicano, 29
Aranas, Eugenio, 71–72
Arce, Mariano, 193
Arceo, Fermin, 187, 188–89, 201, 263
Arceo, Leoncio, 191, 196, 263
Arellano, Cayetano, xviii, 183
Arguelles, Manuel, 12, 19, 23, 199, 290,
295
Army, Filipino, xvii, 75; officer corps of,
xix, 50–51, 76–79, 80, 174–78, 218,
290–91, 322–23; rank-and-file of, xix,
51; weapon shortages of, 2, 52, 100,
124–25, 168, 173, 225, 232, 233–34,
239; ammunition shortages of, 2, 96,
152, 164, 168, 173–74, 218, 231, 233,
239; conventional operations of, 48,
52–56, 68–69, 79–84, 101–27, 170–
72; and reasons for fighting, 51–52,
78, 197; conscription into, 51–52, 79,
176, 178, 180, 193, 197, 216, 232, 239;
military inexperience of, 52; conflicts

371